1 MONTH OF
FREE
READING

at

www.ForgottenBooks.com

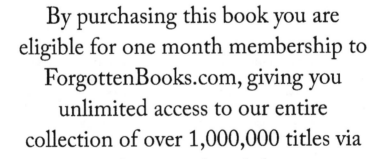

By purchasing this book you are eligible for one month membership to ForgottenBooks.com, giving you unlimited access to our entire collection of over 1,000,000 titles via our web site and mobile apps.

To claim your free month visit:

www.forgottenbooks.com/free67177

ISBN 978-0-656-04199-2
PIBN 10067177

COMMUNISM
IN THE UNITED STATES

Communism
in the United States

BY EARL BROWDER

General Secretary, Communist Party of the United States

International Publishers · New York

CONTENTS

CONTENTS

Introduction

EARL BROWDER's book offers the key to an understanding of Communism in the United States. This work was hammered out in the very heat of the struggle of the American masses for a better life in a most momentous period of their history. It was produced in the fight for the great historic liberation struggle of the American workers, toiling farmers, Negroes, middle classes, and all oppressed and exploited. It was produced by one who is guided by the scientific theory of Marxism-Leninism and by its great masters—Marx, Engels, Lenin, Stalin.

Very appropriately, Browder's book opens with the famous Manifesto of the Communist Party of the United States adopted at its 8th National Convention, held in April, 1934. In a concrete and convincing way, this historic document shows that there is only one way out of the present state of insecurity, unemployment, mass misery and untold suffering, oppression, capitalist reaction, fascism and war. It is the revolutionary way, the Bolshevik way, the way of the Socialist Revolution and Soviet Power in the United States.

Millions of American toilers—workers, farmers, Negroes, intellectuals and other middle class groups—are still wondering in daze and confusion at the "sudden" change to the worse that has taken place in their lives. They ask: Where has this disaster come from? What was it that has knocked the bottom out from under our feet? What shall we do to help ourselves? What can we do to ward off the coming of even greater disasters—fascism and a new war?

Earl Browder's book helps us to find an answer to these questions. In chapters 2, 3, 4, 6, 7 and 9, we are led to an examination of the nature of the economic crisis and its passage into a "depression of a special kind," the capitalist way out and the revolutionary way out, the role of reformism and how it perpetuates capitalism and paves the way for fascism, the impossibility of planning under capitalism, etc. Having gained a correct understanding of these fundamental questions, we are then in a position to see clearly the class content of the policies of the American bourgeoisie.

But the book does much more than that. Its pivot is the struggle of the Communist Party of the United States to win and lead the toiling masses of this country—in the first instance, the industrial proletariat—to the fight for the revolutionary way out of the crisis. It is from this central angle that Browder deals with all the questions of the present epoch. It is a scientific examination and analysis of existing conditions with the aim of determining the road to the abolition of these conditions and the way of organizing the masses to struggle for it. In other words, this book undertakes to answer not only the question of why things are as they are but also what changes are necessary and how they can be brought about.

As is well known, the author of this work occupies an outstanding position of leadership in the Communist Party of the United States. This fact has a direct and intimate bearing upon the nature and character of the book which is made up of articles and speeches by the author produced during the last three years. This makes the contents of the book a presentation of Communist Party principles and policies, of its theory and practice, of its day-to-day struggles to win the American masses for the revolutionary way out and for a Soviet America. It is a presentation of Communism in America.

Earl Browder analyzed the New Deal, at its very inception, as a new way of carrying through in life the same class policies of the monopolies as those championed by the Old Deal. In making this analysis, the author pointed out the contradictions inherent in the New Deal, contradictions which were bound to sharpen, in the first instance, the relations between the capitalist class and the working class (and all toilers), and also the relations between the conflicting and competing groups within the capitalist class itself. This was the Communist Party's answer to the position of the President of the American Federation of Labor, William Green, that the New Deal constituted a "partnership between Labor and Capital" leading to even closer class collaboration than heretofore. This was also the answer of the Communist Party to the position of the leaders of the Socialist Party, among them at the time, Norman Thomas, that the New Deal constituted a "step to Socialism."

The Supreme Court decision has brought to a head all the contradictions of the New Deal. It signalizes first of all, as already pointed out, a new offensive upon the toiling masses by the capitalist class. Precisely because the New Deal, in the two years of its operation, has done its best to weaken the position of the working class and all toilers, the most reactionary circles of the monopolies and their spokesmen, Roosevelt's Right opponents, feel now that the time has arrived for a fresh and more widespread attack upon the standards of living of the masses and upon their democratic rights. At the same time, Roosevelt continues his special New Deal maneuvers, resorting even to more "Left" phrases and methods, whose effect is to assist rather than hamper the offensive of the reactionaries and fascists. Thus the Supreme Court decision also shows a sharpening of the contradictions within the capitalist class itself. In brief, this whole development demonstrates fully the correctness of the position of the Communist

Party, as expounded by Browder in this work, that the general crisis of the capitalist system is deepening, that the revolutionary crisis is maturing also in the United States, and that fascisation and war preparations are becoming evermore the major line of policy of the American bourgeoisie.

This brings us to the central task of the present period—the struggle against war and fascism. The author devotes a considerable part of the book to this question, notably the six chapters from 10 to 16 inclusive. From a study of these chapters, and of the book as a whole, the reader will gain a thorough understanding of the whole question of the United Front. It will become clear why the Communist Party takes the position that, in the present period, the United Front of the workers and all toilers against the capitalist offensive, fascisation and war preparations, is the only way to defend effectively the interests of the masses, to ward off the outbreak of a new war and the coming of a fascist dictatorship. It will also become clear why the Communist Party considers the United Front, in this period, the major road along which the masses will become prepared, on the basis of their own experiences, to struggle for the revolutionary way out of the crisis and for a Soviet government in the United States under the leadership of the Communist Party.

In the struggle for the United Front against the capitalist offensive, the strike movements of the workers in the industries and the fight for unemployment relief and insurance (H. R. 2827) occupy a foremost position. It is on this sector of the class struggle that the most decisive battles have occurred during the past three years, and will continue to occur, in the unfolding of the epochal fight between the capitalist way out of the crisis and the revolutionary way out. Just recall the San Francisco general strike and the Pacific Coast marine strike of which it was an outgrowth, the national textile strike, the great unemployed movements and the growing mass support for H. R. 2827, etc. These cannot, of course, be isolated from the whole course of events with which Browder's book is concerned. However, for a special study of these particular developments, chapters 10, 11, and 12, are of special value.

.It will become clear, from a study of this work, why the Communist Party considers the organization and unfolding of strike struggles a basic phase of the fight against the capitalist offensive, fascisation and war preparations. This has to do first with the Communist conception of the role of the working class as the leader of the fight against capitalism, the leader of its allies, the toiling farmers, the Negroes and the oppressed middle groups of the cities. And it also has to do with the particular significance of strike struggles in the present period in the United States which is characterized especially by the growth and importance of strike movements.

Bearing this in mind, the reader will follow more profitably Browder's discussions of the role of the Communists in trade unions. The reader will then be able to grasp more fully the significance of one of the most fundamental strategic principles of 'the Communist Party, namely, the fight for the organization of trade unions (and against company union-ism), the fight for trade union unity, and the entrenchment of the Com-munist Party itself in the large shops of the basic industries. In this connection, the reader will find of special value chapter 5 of this work which discusses the Open Letter to the Party issued by its Extraordinary Conference held in the summer of 1933.

Closely connected with this is the position of the Communist Party on the question of the formation of a Labor Party. Chapters 9 and 16 are devoted more particularly to this question. The reader will find here an exposition of the whole political situation out of which the ques-tion arose and the solution of it proposed by the Communist Party—the struggle for a mass anti-capitalist Labor Party based primarily upon the trade unions—as against bourgeois third party movements including those which carry the label (but not the essence) of "Labor" Party. In the coming period the struggle for a Labor Party will develop into a major feature of the class struggle in the United States, organically con-nected with all the other phases of the class struggle especially with the fight for militant mass industrial unions in the basic industries and for the extension of the United Front.

The book deals throughout with the vital question of the allies of the American proletariat—the toiling farmers, the Negroes, the exploited middle classes of the cities, and the revolutionary movements of the colonial and dependent countries, especially those oppressed by Ameri-can imperialism (China, Cuba, the Caribbean and South America gen-erally). Chapters 17 and 18 go into a special discussion of the liberation struggles of the Negro people, the meaning and special char-acteristics of these struggles, and their basic value as allies of the socialist revolution in the United States. The reader will gain a clear understanding of the vital importance of such struggles as the fight for freedom of the Scottsboro boys, for the freedom of Angelo Herndon, and for equal rights for the Negroes generally.

A major feature of this work, one that underlies and crowns the whole structure, is the treatment of the question of how to build the Com-munist Party into the mass party of the American proletariat and the leader of all oppressed. Strictly speaking, the entire book deals with this question, and for this reason: that the existence of a strong mass Communist Party is the chief prerequisite for the United Front and for the overthrow of capitalist rule. This flows from the Marxist-Leninist conception of the leading role of the proletarian party, the new and special type of party that is embodied in the Communist Party, and of the role of the non-Party mass organizations of the workers and other toilers as "transmission belts" (Stalin) from the Party to the class. More specifically and concretely this question is dealt with in chapters

2, 5, 7, 8, 9 and 11. These show how the Communist Party of the United States continually works to improve itself, day by day, eliminating weaknesses of methods of work and forms of organization, developing more effective ways of reaching the masses and organizing them for the struggle against their enemies.

Inseparably connected with the above, and with the entire contents of this work, is the relation between the Communist Party of the United States and the Communist International of which it is a section. In every phase of this book the reader will see how the Communist Party of this country functions as an organic part of the world party of Communism. It will become evident to the reader how the experiences and struggles of the various national sections of the Communist International give rise to the general line of the world party formulated by its world Congresses and by the plenary sessions of its Executive Committee. It will also become evident from this work how this general line of the world party, the Communist International, serves as the starting point and daily guide for the national sections, such as the Communist Party of the United States, in the formulation of their special policies and methods directed to the realization of the international line and discipline. This world party of Communism, which the Second (Socialist) International was never able to achieve, a world party with such a leading component part as the Communist Party of the Soviet Union and such a leader as Stalin, is the source of the greatest strength and inspiration to the revolutionary movement in each capitalist country.

We are now brought to a question which is of decisive importance in the present epoch. It is the question of the struggle for the defense of the Soviet Union. Browder's book demonstrates its full significance. It shows concretely and in a living manner how the Soviet Union, by its historical successes in the building of socialism and by the tremendous growth of its economic, political and military strength, has come to be the center of a new world system, the system of socialism, undermining the decaying capitalist system and revolutionizing by its very existence the whole world situation. Browder shows throughout the book how the socialist successes of the Soviet Union, the abolition of unemployment and establishment of social security, and the great cultural upswing, the steady improvement in the conditions and well-being of the masses in contrast to the nearly 17 million unemployed in the United States, the growing ruination of the toiling farmers and the emergence of an American peasantry, the steady deterioration of the standard of life of the American masses, the degeneration of American bourgeois culture, the growth of reaction and fascisation, the preparations for new imperialist wars of the American bourgeoisie in contrast to the consistent and truly international peace policy of the Soviet Union—how these contrasts revolutionize, inspire and strengthen the American proletariat and all fighters against capitalist reaction. Browder further shows how, in virtue of the above developments, the Soviet Union stands out as the chief fortress of international working class strength, the chief bulwark against capitalist reaction, national hatred and chauvinism, fascism and war. In brief, Browder shows how the Soviet Union is the only fatherland of the workers and all toilers the world over, whose major international task is to seek the defeat of the enemies of the Soviet Union,. chief among them being German fascism, and to engage daily in the defense of the Soviet Union. Browder does that by showing how the accomplishment of this chief international task is vitally dependent upon and inseparably connected with the daily revolutionary struggles of the American masses against their main enemy at home, the American bourgeoisie.

And lastly some basic questions connected with the philosophy of Communism, its world outlook, its methods of studying the world in order to change it. The reader will find an introduction to this subject in chapter 19 dealing with theory as a guide to action. It will impress the reader as an eye-opener and key to the solution of many difficult problems which remain hopelessly insoluble on the basis of bourgeois philosophy. Chapter 21, dealing with the revisionism of Sidney Hook, a shining light in the camp of counter-revolutionary Trotskyism, carries the discussion of this subject further, throwing a critical light upon the methods and nature of Pragmatism, a variety of idealism. And chapters 20 and 22, on literature and religion, discuss other angles of the same subject, besides offering a method of United Front approach to certain important non-proletarian sections of the toiling population of the United States.

This work of Earl Browder offers the reader an invaluable source of knowledge on Communism in the United States. And by virtue of this fact, it also points the way to what to do and how to promote the revolutionary struggle for an America of happiness, plenty and security.

ALEX BITTELMAN.

Manifesto of the Communist Party of the United States *

To All Workers of the U.S.A.:

We speak to you in the name of 25,000 members of the Communist Party who elected the delegates of this Eighth National Convention; in the name of several hundred thousand workers who elected fraternal delegates from trade unions, unemployment councils, workers' clubs, fraternal societies; in the name of the miners, steel workers, metal workers, auto workers, textile workers, marine workers, railroad workers, whose delegates constitute a majority of this convention.

To you, the working class and toiling farmers of the United States, this Convention of workers addresses itself, to speak a few plain words about the crisis, and about the possibility of finding a way out.

The crisis of the capitalist system is becoming more and more a catastrophe for the workers and toiling masses. Growing millions of the exploited population are faced with increased difficulties in finding the barest means of livelihood. Unemployment relief is being drastically cut and in many cases abolished altogether. Real wages are being reduced further every month, and labor is being speeded up to an inhuman degree.

The vast majority of the poor farmers are slowly but surely being squeezed off the land and thrown on the "free" labor market to compete with the workers. The oppressed Negro people are loaded down with the heaviest economic burdens, especially of unemployment, denied even the crumbs of relief given to the starving white masses, and further subjected to bestial lynch law and Jim-Crowism. Women workers and housewives are especially sufferers from the crisis, and from the fascist movements to drive them out of industry. Millions of young workers are thrown upon the streets by the closing of schools and simultaneously are denied any chance to earn their living in the industries.

WHAT THE NEW DEAL HAS GIVEN THE WORKERS

The suffering masses have been told to look to Washington for their salvation. Mr. Roosevelt and his New Deal have been decked out with the rainbow promises of returning prosperity. But the bitter

* Manifesto of the Eighth Convention of the Communist Party of the U.S.A., April, 1934.—*Ed.*

13

truth is rapidly being learned that Roosevelt and his New Deal represent the Wall Street bankers and big corporations—finance capital—just the same as Hoover before him, but carrying out even fiercer attacks against the living standards of the masses of the people. Under Roosevelt and the New Deal policies, the public treasury has been turned into a huge trough where the big capitalists eat their fill. Over ten billion dollars have been handed out to the banks and corporations, billions have been squeezed out of the workers and farmers by inflation and by all sorts of new taxes upon the masses. Under the Roosevelt regime, the main burden of taxation has been shifted away from the big capitalists onto the impoverished masses.

The N.R.A. and the industrial codes have served further to enrich the capitalists by establishing fixed monopoly prices, speeding up trustification, and squeezing out the smaller capitalists and independent producers.

The labor provisions of the N.R.A., which were hailed by the A. F. of L. and Socialist leaders as "a new charter for labor," have turned out in reality to be new chains for labor. The fixing of the so-called minimum wage, at below starvation levels, has turned out in reality to be a big effort to drive the maximum wage down to this point. The so-called guarantee of the right to organize and collective bargaining has turned out in reality to be the establishment of company unions. The last remaining rights of the workers they now propose to take away by establishing compulsory arbitration under the Wagner Bill, camouflaged as an attempt to guarantee workers' rights. Roosevelt has given official governmental status to the company unions, in the infamous "settlement" in the auto industry. This new step toward fascism is announced as a "new course" to apply to all industries.

All these domestic policies are openly recognized as identical in their content with the measures of professed fascist governments. This rapid movement toward fascism in the United States goes hand in hand with the sharpening of international antagonisms and the most gigantic preparations for war ever before witnessed in a pre-war period. More than a billion dollars have been appropriated for war purposes during this year. A large proportion of this has been taken directly out of the funds ostensibly appropriated for public works. Hundreds of millions are being spent on military training in the so-called Civil Conservation Camps, run by the War Department.

The policies of the government in Washington have one purpose, to make the workers and farmers and middle classes pay the costs of the crisis, to preserve the profits of the big capitalists at all costs, to establish fascism at home and to wage imperialist war abroad.

A. F. OF L. AND SOCIALIST PARTY LEADERS SUPPORT ROOSEVELT

How can the workers and farmers fight against these policies which are driving them into starvation? The leaders of the A. F. of L. have openly identified themselves with the policies of the Roosevelt administration. To the extent that these leaders control the trade unions, they prevent or demoralize the struggle of the workers and deliver them helpless into the hands of the capitalists. The Socialist Party supports the A. F. of L. leaders and endorses and actively supports every particular policy of the New Deal: inflation, N.R.A., A.A.A., P.W.A., C.W.A., C.C.C., the Wagner Bill, etc., hailing these fascist and war measures as "steps toward socialism."

It is clear that the workers and farmers cannot fight back the capitalist attacks unless they break away from the policies of the A. F. of L. and Socialist Party leaders. As against the united front which these leaders have set up with the capitalist government, the toiling masses must establish their own working-class united front from below, against the capitalist class and the Roosevelt administration.

ONLY THE COMMUNIST PARTY FIGHTS FOR THE WORKERS

Only the Communist Party has consistently organized and led the resistance to the capitalist attacks. The enemies of the Communist Party try to scare away the workers and farmers from this struggle by shouting that the Communist Party is interested only in revolution, that it is not sincerely trying to protect the living standards of the masses. They do this in order to hide the fact that they, one and all, pursue the single policy of saving the profits of the capitalists, no matter what it may cost in degrading the living standards of the masses.

The Communist Party declares that wages must be maintained no matter what is the consequence to capitalist profits.

The Communist Party declares that unemployment insurance must be provided at the expense of capitalist profits.

The Communist Party declares that the masses of workers and farmers must not only fight against reduction in their living standards, but must win constantly increasing living standards at the expense of capitalist profits.

The Communist Party declares, if the continuation of capitalism requires that profits be protected at the price of starvation, fascism and war for the masses of the people, then the quicker capitalism is destroyed, the better.

It is no accident that the only serious project for unemployment insurance that has come before the Congress of the United States is the Workers' Social and Unemployment Insurance Bill H. R. 7598,* which

* Later introduced as H. R. 2827.—*Ed.*

was worked out and popularized among the masses by the Communist Party. Only the Communist Party has made a real fight for unemployment insurance and by this fight finally forced before Congress the first and only bill to provide real unemployment insurance.

It is no accident that the Workers' Social and Unemployment Insurance Bill is being bitterly fought, not only by the Republican and Democratic Parties, but also by the American Federation of Labor and the Socialist Party leaders, as well as by little groups of their satellites, Musteites, Trotskyites, and Lovestoneites.

It is no accident that whenever a big strike movement breaks out, the capitalist press shrieks that it is due to Communist influence, and the A. F. of L. and Socialist Party leaders wail that the masses have got beyond their control.

It is true that all struggles for daily bread, for milk for children, against evictions, for unemployment relief and insurance, for wage increases, for the right to organize and strike, etc., are directly connected up with the question of revolution. Those who are against the revolution, who want to maintain the capitalist system, are prepared to sacrifice these struggles of the workers in order to help the capitalists preserve their profits.

Only those can courageously lead and stubbornly organize the fight for the immediate interests of the toiling masses, who know that these things must be won even though it means the destruction of capitalist profits, and who draw the necessary conclusion that the workers and farmers must consciously prepare to overthrow capitalism.

The crisis cannot be solved for the toiling masses until the rule of Wall Street has been broken and the rule of the working class has been established. The only way out of the crisis for the toiling masses is the revolutionary way out—the abolition of capitalist rule and capitalism, the establishment of the socialist society through the power of a revolutionary workers' government, a Soviet government.

EXAMPLE OF THE REVOLUTIONARY WAY OUT

The program of the revolutionary solution of the crisis is no blind experiment. The working class is already in power in the biggest country in the world, and it has already proved the great superiority of the socialist system. While the crisis has engulfed the capitalist countries—at the same time in the Soviet Union, where the workers rule through their Soviet power, a new socialist society is being victoriously built.

The Russian working class, from its own resources and its socialist system, restored the national economy which had been shattered by six years of imperialist war and intervention. It overcame the age-long backwardness of Russia and brought its industrial production to the first place in Europe, to more than three times the pre-war figure. It rooted out the last breeding ground of capitalism by the successful inclusion of agriculture in the socialist system. It completely abolished unemployment and tremendously raised the material well-being and cultural standards of the toiling masses. Upon the basis of its socialist system, the Soviet Union has become the most powerful influence for peace in an otherwise war-mad world.

Its victories are an unending source of inspiration and encouragement to the toiling masses of every country. They are the living example of the possibility of finding a way out of the crisis in the interests of the toilers. The experience of the victorious workers of the Soviet Union before, during and after the seizure of power, throw a brilliant light showing the path which must be followed in every land, the path of Bolshevism, of Marx, Engels, Lenin and Stalin.

In the same period of successful testing of the Bolshevik road in the Soviet Union, we have also the example of the results of the policies of the Socialist Parties of the Second International. The Socialist Parties stood at the head of the majority of the working class in Germany and Austria. The revolutionary upheavals of 1918 in these countries placed power in the hands of the Socialist Parties. Their leaders repudiated the Bolshevik road, and boasted of their contrasting "civilized," "peaceful," "democratic," "gradual transition to Socialism" through a coalition government together with the bourgeoisie on the basis of restoring the shattered capitalist system. To this end they crushed the revolution in 1918.

They followed the policy of "the lesser evil," supported the government of Bruening with its emergency decrees against the workers, disarmed the working class, led the workers to vote for Field Marshal von Hindenburg, and finally crowned their infamy by voting in the Reichstag for Hitler after having paved the way for fascism since 1918. In Austria they supported the Dollfuss fascist government as the "lesser evil," enabling Dollfuss to turn his cannon against the homes of the Austrian workers.

Their "civilized" methods opened wide the gates for the most barbarous regime in the modern history of Europe. Their "peaceful" methods gave birth to the most bloody and violent reaction. Their "democracy" brought forth the most brutal and open capitalist dictatorship. Their "gradual transition to socialism" helped to restore the uncontrolled rule of finance-capital, the master of fascism. The German and Austrian working class, after 16 years of bitter and bloody lessons of the true meaning of the policies of the Socialist Parties, of the Second International, have now finally begun to turn away from them and at last to take the Bolshevik path.

U.S.A. IS RIPE FOR SOCIALISM

In every material respect, the United States is fully ripe for socialism. Its accumulated wealth and productive forces, together with an inexhaustible supply of almost all of the raw materials, provide a complete material basis for socialism. All material conditions exist for a society which could at once provide every necessity of life and even a degree of luxury for the entire population, with an expenditure of labor of three or four hours a day.

This tremendous wealth, these gigantic productive forces, are locked away from the masses who could use them. They are the private property of the small parasitic capitalist class, which locks up the warehouses and closes the factories in order to compel a growing tribute of profit. This paralysis of economy in the interest of profit, at the cost of starvation and degradation to millions, is enforced by the capitalist government with all its police, courts, jails and military.

There is no possible way out of the crisis in the interest of the masses except by breaking the control of the state power now in the hands of this small monopolist capitalist class. There is no way out except by establishing a new government of the workers in alliance with the poor farmers, the Negro people, and the impoverished middle class.

There is no way out except by the creation of a revolutionary democracy of the toilers, which is at the same time a stern dictatorship against the capitalists and their agents. There is no way out except by seizing from the capitalists the industries, the banks and all of the economic institutions, and transforming them into the common property of all under the direction of the revolutionary government. There is no way out, in short, except by the abolition of the capitalist system and the establishment of a socialist society.

WHAT IS "AMERICANISM"?

The necessary first step for the establishment of socialism is the setting up of a revolutionary workers' government. The capitalists and their agents shriek out that this revolutionary program is un-American. But this expresses, not the truth, but only their own greedy interests. Today, the only Party that carries forward the revolutionary traditions of 1776 and 1861, under the present-day conditions and relationship of classes, is the Communist Party. Today, only the Communist Party finds it politically expedient and necessary to remind the American working masses of how, in a previous crisis, the way out was found by the path of revolution. Today, only the Communist Party brings sharply forward and applies to the problems of today that old basic document of "Americanism," the Declaration of Independence.

Applying the Declaration of Independence to present-day conditions, the Communist Party points out that never was there such a mass of people so completely deprived of all semblance of "the right to life, liberty and pursuit of happiness." Never were there such "destructive" effects upon these rights by "any form of government," as those exerted today by the existing form of government in the United States. Never have the exploited masses suffered such a "long train of abuses" or been so "reduced under absolute despotism" as today under capitalist rule. The "principle" which must provide the foundation of the "new government" mentioned in the Declaration of Independence is, in 1934, the principle of the dictatorship of the proletariat; the new form is the form of the workers' and farmers' councils—the Soviet power. The "new guards for their future security," which the workers must establish, are the installing of the working class in every position of power, and the dissolution of every institution of capitalist class rule.

WHAT A WORKERS' GOVERNMENT WOULD DO

The first acts of such a revolutionary workers' government would be to open up the warehouses and distribute among all the working people the enormous unused surplus stores of food and clothing.

It would open up the tremendous accumulation of unused buildings —now withheld for private profit—for the benefit of tens of millions who now wander homeless in the streets or crouch in cellars or slums.

Such a government would immediately provide an endless flow of commodities to replace the stores thus used up by opening all the factories, mills and mines, and giving every person a job at constantly increasing wages.

All former claims to ownership of the means of production, including stocks, bonds, etc., would be relegated to the museum, with special provisions to protect small savings. No public funds would be paid out to anyone except for services rendered to the community.

Unemployment and social insurance would immediately be provided for all, to cover all loss of work due to cause outside the control of the workers, whether by closing of factories, by sickness, old age, maternity, or otherwise, at full wages without special costs to the workers.

Such a government would immediately begin to reorganize the present anarchic system of production along socialist lines. It would eliminate the untold waste of capitalism; it would bring to full use the tremendous achievements of science, which have been pushed aside by the capitalist rulers from consideration of private profit. Such a socialist reorganization of industry would almost immediately double the existing productive forces of the country. Such a revolutionary government would secure to the farmers the possession of their land and provide them with the necessary means for a comfortable living; it would make it possible for the farming population to unite their forces in a co-operative socialist agriculture, and thus bring to the farming population all the advantages of modern civilization, and would multiply manifold the productive capacities of American agriculture. It would proceed at once to the complete liberation of the Negro people from all oppression, secure the right of self-determination of the Black Belt, and would secure unconditional economic, political and social equality.

With the establishment of a socialist system in America, there will be such a flood of wealth available for the country as can hardly be imagined. Productive labor, instead of being a burden, will become a desirable privilege for every citizen of the new society. The wealth of such a society will immediately become so great that, without any special burdens, tremendous surpluses will be available for use as free gifts to the economically backward nations, in the first place, to those which have suffered from the imperialist exploitation of American capitalism—Cuba, Latin America, the Philippines, China—to enable these peoples also to build a socialist society in the shortest possible time.

FIGHT FOR BREAD IS A FIGHT AGAINST CAPITALISM

The capitalist way out of the crisis lies along the way of wage-cuts, speed-up, denial of unemployment insurance, fascism and war. The revolutionary way out of the crisis begins with the fight for unemployment insurance, against wage-cuts, for wage increases, for relief to the farmers—through demonstrations, strikes, general strikes, leading up to the seizure of power, to the destruction of capitalism by a revolutionary workers' government.

The Communist Party calls upon the workers, farmers and impoverished middle classes to unite their forces to struggle uncompromisingly against every reduction of their living standards, against every backward step now being forced upon them by the capitalist crisis, against the growing menace of fascism and war. The Communist Party leads and organizes this struggle, leading toward the only final solution—the establishment of a workers' government.

The establishment of a socialist society in the United States will be at the same time a death blow to the whole world system of imperialist oppression and exploitation. It will mark the end of world capitalism. It will be the decisive step towards a classless society throughout the world, towards World Communism!

II

The Revolutionary Way Out *

INTRODUCTION

OUR Eighth Convention meets at a time when the capitalist world is approaching a new explosion. Any day, any month, we may receive the first news of Japanese imperialism beginning its long-prepared invasion of the Soviet Union. At any time the madman who holds power in Germany may launch the wild adventure of anti-Soviet intervention which is the keystone of his policy, or may set fire to the fuses of the whole system of explosive European relations. Who can say on what day the powers now engaged in a gigantic naval race may have their present navies thrown into action by one power's fear of being left behind in the race? Who can foretell when the tightening lines of class struggle in any one of a dozen countries may not, by some "small" incident like the exposé of Stavitsky corruption, be ignited with the flames of a revolutionary civil war?

The world stands on the brink of revolutions and wars. This is the fruits of more than four years of unprecedented capitalist crisis. This crisis period is approximately the period between our Seventh and Eighth National Conventions. Through this period capitalist society has continuously disintegrated. The crisis has penetrated into and undermined the industry and agriculture of every capitalist and colonial country; it has upset the currency and credit relationships of the entire world. Even the United States, still the strongest fortress of world capitalism, has been stripped of its last shred of "exceptionalism," stands fully exposed to the fury of the storms of crisis, and, relatively speaking, is registering its deepest effects. The economic losses due to the crisis, in the United States alone begin to approach the figures of the total losses of the World War.

A great upsurge of class struggles is sweeping the capitalist world. A wave of liberation struggles sweeps the colonies and oppressed nations. In Spain the fascist dictatorship has been overthrown and the forces of a Soviet revolution are gathering. In Cuba a revolutionary upheaval drove out the bloody tyrant, Machado. A general strike sweeps France, embracing the main body of the working class. In

* Report of the Central Committee to the Eighth Convention of the Communist Party, held in Cleveland, Ohio, April 2-8, 1934.—*Ed.*

Germany the rising wave of proletarian revolution is checked, but only temporarily, by loosening the fascist mad dogs, the foul refuse of the insane asylums and criminal underworld, against the German masses. In Austria, the lightning flash of the heroic barricade fighting of the betrayed Austrian workers, revealed for an instant the doom that is being prepared for capitalism beneath the blanket of fascism with which the bourgeoisie seeks to smother the flames of revolution. Also in the United States the upsurge of mass resistance to the capitalist policy of driving the masses into starvation, a policy intensified behind the demagogic cloak of Roosevelt's "New Deal," has already been answered by the capitalists with machine-guns at Ambridge; by increasing appropriations for police and military; by fascist preparations of War Department occupation of the strategic points in the economic system; by incorporating the A. F. L. leadership into the government machinery; by the "new course" of compulsory arbitration and legalization of company unions "charted" by Roosevelt in the automobile settlement and the Wagner "labor" bill. A wave of chauvinism is being roused by capitalist press and statesmen, without precedent in time of peace. Fascism is rearing its ugly head more boldly every day in the U. S. A.

The rape of China by Japanese imperialism, the wars in Latin-America in which American and British imperialisms begin to settle accounts— these were but the first links in the chain of imperialist wars being forged by the blows of the crisis. The rise of fascism in Germany and Austria further shattered the post-war system of international relationships. The imperialist powers are arming to the teeth. They are desperately striving to come to an arrangement that the next decisive step in the armed redivision of the world shall be a counter-revolutionary invasion of the Soviet Union. War budgets are shooting upward at a speed matched only by the speed of deterioration of the living standards of the masses.

Meanwhile, the Soviet Union, the land where the victorious working class is building socialism, moves in a direction exactly opposite to that of the capitalist world. While the capitalist world suffered economic paralysis, in the Soviet Union a historically backward land has leaped forward to the first place in Europe, and in the whole world second only to the United States. While living standards in the capitalist world took a catastrophic drop of 40 to 60 per cent, in the Soviet Union they leaped upward by more than 100 per cent. While capitalist policy is directed with all energy to cut down production in the face of growing millions of starving and poverty-stricken workers and farmers, in the Soviet Union the productive forces have been multiplied manifold, a half continent of 52 nations, of 165,000,000 population is being lifted out of poverty into material well-being and a rich cultural life. While the capitalist world drives feverishly toward war, the Soviet Union emerges more and more as the great bulwark of world peace. Clearly the world is divided into two systems, moving in opposite directions.

This is the world situation, described by the general staff of our World Party, the Executive Committee of the Communist International, as a situation "closely approaching a new round of revolutions and wars," in which the Communists of the United States meet in our Eighth National Convention to chart our course for the next period, to prepare our forces for the next great task, to win the majority of the American workers and their allies for the revolutionary way out of the crisis, for the uncompromising fight for immediate economic and political needs, for the overthrow of capitalism, for the building of a new, socialist system by a revolutionary Workers' Government.

I. THE GROWTH OF HUNGER, FASCISM, AND THE DANGER OF IMPERIALIST WAR

The economic crisis is in its fifth year. It has lasted far longer than any previous crisis. It has been more far-reaching and destructive. That is because it occurs in the midst of the general crisis of the whole capitalist system. Characteristic of this fact are:

(a) The crisis affected every capitalist and colonial country.

(b) It penetrated every phase of economy, industry, agriculture, trade, credit, currency, state finances.

(c) The crisis itself resulted in intensifying the concentration and centralization of capital, with consequent intensification of labor, which was a basic cause for the unexampled depth of the crisis.

(d) It has at the same time sharply degraded the technical level of agriculture, causing it to abandon machine labor for hand labor, mechanical power for horse and man power, further sharpening the contradiction between city and country.

(e) The chief feature of overproduction is that it is sharpest in the field of means of production, far exceeding the capacity of capitalistically-limited society to use them to the full, thus closing the doors to a revival by vast new capital investments.

(f) Existence of giant monopolies, further strengthened during the crisis (as by the N.R.A. codes, etc.) results in sustaining monopoly profits at the cost of the rest of economy, reducing mass purchasing power, and hindering the absorption of accumulated stocks.

(g) The crisis comes in a period when the imperialist powers have already divided the world among themselves, when there are no further fields of expansion, except at the expense of one another (or of the Soviet Union), and when the uneven development of the imperialist powers makes imperative a redivision of the world which is only possible through the arbitrament of war.

(h) Finally, this crisis comes after world capitalism has already suffered the fatal shattering blows of the last World War, as a result of which its world-system was broken at its weakest link, out of which emerged a new, a rival world economic system, the system of socialism in the Soviet Union.

The influence of the general crisis of capitalism upon the course of the economic crisis can be seen in volume of industrial production during the past five years in the principal industrial countries. I quote the figures given by Comrade Stalin in his report to the 17th Congress of the Communist Party of the Soviet Union:

VOLUME OF INDUSTRIAL PRODUCTION
(Per Cent of 1929)

	1929	1930	1931	1932	1933
U. S. S. R.	100.0	129.7	161.9	184.7	201.6
U. S. A.	100.0	80.7	68.1	53.8	64.9
England	100.0	92.4	83.8	83.8	86.1
Germany	100.0	88.3	71.7	59.8	66.8
France	100.0	100.7	89.2	69.1	77.4

These figures clearly reveal the division of the world into two systems which are travelling in opposite directions. While in the capitalist countries production declined between 1929 and 1933 by from 15 to 35 per cent, the socialist industry of the Soviet Union increased by more than 100 per cent.

These figures also show that from 1932 to 1933, the capitalist world increased its production in all countries, whereas previously the course had been downward from year to year. This fact has been joyously hailed by capitalist spokesmen as heralding the end of the crisis, the beginning of recovery, the promise of returning prosperity. This conclusion is also supported by the Socialist Party leaders and the reformist trade union bureaucrats. What is the true significance of this fact?

A clear answer was already given to this question by Comrade Stalin at the 17th Congress, supplementing and further developing the Thesis of the 13th Plenum of the Executive Committee of the Communist International. Comrade Stalin said:

It means that, apparently, industry in the principal capitalist countries had already passed the lowest point of decline and did not return to it in the course of 1933.

Some people are inclined to ascribe the phenomenon to the influence of exclusively artificial factors, such as a war-inflation boom. There cannot be any doubt that the war-inflation boom plays not an unimportant role here. It is particularly true in regard to Japan, where this artificial factor is the principal and decisive force in some revival, principally in the munition branches of industry. But it would be a crude mistake to attempt to explain everything by the war-inflation boom. Such an explanation would be wrong, if only for the reason that the changes in industry which I have described are observed, not in separate and chance districts, but in all, or nearly all, industrial countries, including those countries which have a stable currency. Apparently,' side by side with the war-inflation boom, the operation of the internal economic forces of capitalism also has effect here.

Capitalism has succeeded in somewhat easing the position of industry *at the expense of the workers*—increasing their exploitation by increasing the intensity of their labor; *at the expense of the farmers*—by pursuing a policy of paying the lowest prices for the products of their labor, for foodstuffs and partly for raw materials; *at the expense of the peasants in the colonies and in the economically weak countries*—by still further forcing down the prices of the products of their labor, principally raw materials, and also of foodstuffs.

Does this mean that we are witnessing a transition from a crisis to an ordinary depression which brings in its train a new boom and flourishing industry? No, it does not mean that. At all events at the present time there are no data, direct or indirect, that indicate the approach of an industrial boom in capitalist countries. More than that, judging by all things, there cannot be such data, at least in the near future. There cannot be, because all the unfavorable conditions which prevent industry in the capitalist countries from rising to any serious extent still continue to operate. I have in mind the continuing general crisis of capitalism in the midst of which the economic crisis is proceeding, the chronic working of the enterprises under capacity, the chronic mass unemployment, the interweaving of the industrial crisis with the agricultural crisis, the absence of tendencies towards any serious renewal of basic capital which usually heralds the approach of a boom, etc., etc.

Apparently, what we are witnessing is the transition from the lowest point of decline of industry, from the lowest depth of the industrial crisis to a depression, not an ordinary depression, but to a depression of a special kind which does not lead to a new boom and flourishing industry, but which, on the other hand, does not force it back to the lowest point of decline. (Joseph Stalin, *The State of the Soviet Union*, pp. 13-15.)

It would be a vulgar fatalism to think that no matter what measures the capitalist class undertakes, they have no effect upon capitalist economy. It would equally be wrong to think such effects are exclusively negative, to fail to see how capitalist industry has eased its position (even if only temporarily) at the great expense of the workers and toiling masses. We must avoid such mistakes, to be able to unmask the crude illusions propagated by the labor agents of capitalism, and prevent them from sowing confusion in the working-class ranks.

Many facts lead to the conclusion that the economic crisis in the United States has already passed its lowest point. Furthermore, the various measures undertaken by the capitalist class itself, and the operation of the internal economic forces of capitalism, facilitated the passing of the economic crisis into the stage of depression.

In the course of the crisis, American capitalism lowered production costs and increased its profits mainly through a more intensive exploitation of the employed workers. In this process, the productivity of labor was increased mainly through more intensive exploitation and speed-up. American capitalism has utilized the great standing army of the unemployed for this purpose where it could select the best, most physically-fit, workers whom starvation forced to work under the worst conditions at lowest wages.

The improved situation for capitalist industry came as a result of the sharp reduction of the living standards of the workers and the further ruination of the poor and middle farmers. But this is not all.

It is a fact that through the long duration of the crisis the index of overproduced commodity reserves declined. This decline in great degree proceeded through actual physical destruction of commodities. It is very likely, also, that especially in the light industries where production sharply declined, there consumption at the existing low prices served to greatly diminish the overproduction. Increasing profits also serve, even in small degree, to encourage new capital investments in production goods and building. Further, a large part of debts were wiped out through bankruptcy, further mergers; while confiscation of a huge portion of middle-class savings through the closing of banks, made a serious contribution to capitalist profits.

This is the road travelled by American capitalism in the crisis. It is not the road to a new prosperity. At the same time, however, it would be absolutely stupid to refuse to see those improvements in its economic situation that American capitalism did make. But whatever improvements took place, as a result of war-spending and inflation, and also from the further impoverishment of workers and farmers and the operation of the internal economic forces of capitalism, they all facilitated the passing of the crisis into the stage of depression.

The economic crisis in the United States, as in the rest of the capitalist world, is interwoven with the general crisis of capitalism. The depth of the general crisis, the blows delivered by the world crisis to United States economy, are the first factors which make it impossible for American capitalism to return to boom and prosperity. The very measures employed to improve the immediate situation, even though they helped in passing over from crisis to depression, had the effect of deepening the general crisis of capitalism.

Even the capitalists, in their confidential discussions, are adopting the view that the depression will be a prolonged one, that a quick recovery is impossible. Thus the Kiplinger Agency, in its weekly letter of March 17, speaks on this point as follows:

Washington feeling about the course of recovery: Most private discussions by the authorities here reflect a resignation to the idea of slow and irregular recovery, not rapid recovery. Some progress, then a set-back. Further progress, then a breathing spell. Talk of spring boom has disappeared. Talk of fall boom, under belated inflationary influences, has lessened.

Yes, there is an improvement in business and industrial activity in the United States. There are also changes in the movement of the economic crisis. It is apparent that the crisis has passed its lowest point and entered the stage of depression. This has been accomplished by measures which deepen the general crisis (war preparations, inflation, ruination of farmers and small business, impoverishment of the masses, etc.). That means that the depression is not the prelude to new boom and prosperity, as the minstrels of the "New Deal" are singing. It will be prolonged. It will be a period of increased misery for the toilers.

Against this background of the perspective of continued and prolonged depression, given us so clearly in the analysis of Comrade Stalin, it is more than ever clear that the policies being followed by the capitalists, in their frantic efforts to find a way out of the crisis, "in the near future cannot but lead," as the 13th Plenum of the Executive Committee of the Communist International pointed out, "to the still greater disturbance of state finances and to a still further intensification of the general crisis of capitalism." Thus the economic and political factors at work determine that "the capitalist world is now passing from the end of capitalist stabilization to a revolutionary crisis." This it is that determines the "perspectives of development of fascism and the world revolutionary movement of the toilers." (13th Plenum of the E. C. C. I., *Theses and Decisions*.)

What is fascism? It is "the open, terrorist dictatorship of the most reactionary, most chauvinist and most imperialist elements of finance capital." (*Ibid.*)

What is its purpose? It is to enforce the policy of finance capital, which is to bolster up its profits at the cost of degrading the living standards of the toiling population, to violently smash the resistance of the working class, to behead the working class by the physical extermination of its leading cadres, the Communists.

Where does it find its mass basis? Among the petty-bourgeoisie, by demagogic promises to the desperate, impoverished farmers, shopkeepers, artisans, office workers and civil servants, and particularly the declassed and criminal elements in the big cities. It also tries to penetrate the more backward strata of the workers.

How is it possible for fascism to develop sufficient power to defeat the workers? This is only possible by obtaining help within the working class, thus disrupting its unity and disarming it before fascism.

But fascism cannot win mass support directly in the working class ranks. It must find indirect support. This it finds in the Socialist Party leadership and the reformist trade union officialdom. These leaders, influencing the majority of the working class, hold back the workers from revolutionary struggle which alone can defeat and destroy fascism, and under the slogan of defense of democracy, and "choosing the lesser evil," lead the workers to submit to and support the intermediate steps to the introduction of fascism. That is why we call these leaders "social-fascists," and their theories "social-fascism."

In the United States, fascism is being prepared along essentially the same lines that it was prepared in Germany and Austria.

The Socialist and A. F. of L. leaders are taking essentially the same course taken by their brothers in Europe. But the workers in the United States have the tremendous advantage of having before their eyes the living example of the events in Europe, of being able to judge by results the true meaning of policies which they are asked to follow here. That is the supreme importance of every worker in America studying and thoroughly understanding the experiences of our brothers across the waters.

What are the ideas, the misconceptions, with which the social-fascists confuse and disarm the workers?

First, is the idea that fascism is the opposite of capitalist democracy, and this democracy is therefore the means of combating and defeating fascism. This false idea serves a double purpose. By means of counterposing "democracy against dictatorship," it tries to hide the fact that the capitalist "democracy" is only a form of the capitalist dictatorship; it tries to identify in the worker's mind the fascist dictatorship with the proletarian dictatorship in the Soviet Union, and thus cause the worker to reject the road of revolution. At the same time, this slogan is used to hide the fact that capitalist democracy is not the enemy, but the mother of fascism; that it is not the destroyer, but the creator of fascism. It uses the truth that fascism destroys democracy, to propagate the falsehood that democracy will also destroy fascism. Thus does the Socialist Party and trade union officialdom, to the extent that the workers follow them, tie the working class to the chariot wheels of a capitalist democracy which is being transformed into fascism, paralyze their resistance, deliver them over to fascism bound and helpless.

In Germany this meant support to Hindenburg, Bruening, Von Papen, Schleicher; and their "emergency decrees" directed against the workers. In the United States, it is support·to Roosevelt, LaGuardia, the N.R.A., and the "emergency decrees" of the strike-breaking labor boards, arbitration boards, "code authorities," etc. In each case, the slogan is "choose the lesser evil"; in each case, the workers are asked to "fight against fascism" by supporting the men and measures that are introducing fascism.

Second, is the idea that fascism represents, not finance capital, but rather a "revolutionary movement" directed against both finance capital and against the working class by the impoverished middle classes. This idea helps finance capital to get and keep control over these middle classes, strengthens their illusions, divides the workers from them and prevents the workers from setting themselves the task of winning over the middle classes to support of the proletarian revolution, causes the workers to support their misleaders in their alliance with finance capital "against fascism." In Germany, this idea was, concretely, alliance with Hindenburg against Hitler; in Austria, with Dollfuss against the Nazis; in the United States with Roosevelt "against Wall Street."

Third, with the victory of fascism in Germany and Austria, the Socialist and trade union leaders bring forth the idea that this event is the crushing defeat of the revolution, the restabilization of capitalism, the beginning of a new and long era of fascist reaction. This helps fascism by spreading panic, defeatism, and passivity among the workers. It serves to create a fatalistic acceptance of fascism as inescapable and undefeatable. The true significance of the rise of fascism is quite different. True, fascism is a heavy blow against the working class. True, fascism turns loose every black reactionary force against the working class, and tries to physically exterminate its vanguard, the Communist Party. But at the same time it is a sign of deepening crisis of capitalism; it solves not one of the basic problems of the crisis, but intensifies them all; it further disrupts the capitalist world system; it destroys the moral base for capitalist rule, discrediting bourgeois law in the eyes of the masses; it hastens the exposure of all demagogic supporters of capitalism, especially its main support among the workers—the Socialist and trade union leaders. It hastens the revolutionization of the workers, destroys their democratic illusions, and thereby prepares the masses for the revolutionary struggle for power.

Through fascism, the capitalist class hopes to destroy the threat of revolution at home. Through imperialist war, it hopes to destroy the successful revolution in the Soviet Union, and by armed redivision of the world to find the way out of the crisis.

What are the prospects for success of this capitalist program?

Such prospects are very bad indeed. The revolutionary movement of the working class and poor farmer allies cannot be destroyed. This was proved by the fall of the bloody tsarist autocracy in old Russia. It was proved again by the failure of the ferocious terror of Chiang Kai-Shek in China to halt the rise of the victorious Chinese Soviet Republic. It was proved on our own doorstep last August, by the revolutionary overthrow of the Butcher Machado and his fascist dictatorship in Cuba. It is being proved every day by the heroic work of the Communist Party of Germany. It is proved by the crisis in the Second International, and the mass turning of European workers toward the Bolshevik path. It was proved by the destruction of the fascist dictatorship in Spain. Terror cannot destroy the proletarian revolution.

Neither is there hope for world capitalism that it can solve its problems through war. It tried this way in 1914-1918. But instead of solving problems, this only reproduced them on a larger scale and in sharper form. That effort lost for capitalism the largest country, one-sixth of the world, to the victorious working class of the Soviet Union. Now they speculate on recovering this lost territory for capitalism, through another war. But this time they will face a working class infinitely better prepared than in 1914-1918. The working class in the Soviet Union is now fully armed with the weapons of modern warfare, based upon a modernized industry and a solid socialist economy. The working class in the capitalist countries is no longer under the undisputed sway of the Socialist and trade union leaders. In every country there is a growing mass which has already begun to learn the lessons of the victory in the Soviet Union, which has already grouped itself around the Communist Party, which is arming them with the weapons of revolution—the theory and practice of Marx, Engels, Lenin and Stalin—of Bolshevism.

If the imperialists venture upon another war, they will receive a crushing defeat worse than the last war. On the borders of the Soviet Union they will meet military defeat at the hands of an invincible Red Army. At the rear, the working class will be transforming the imperialist war into a civil war of the oppressed masses for the overthrow of capitalism. Such a war will surely end in the birth of a few more Soviet Republics.

II. THE UPSURGE OF THE MASS STRUGGLES AND THE WORK OF THE COMMUNIST PARTY

The United States, stronghold of world capitalism, exhibits at the same time its deepest contradictions. The blows of the economic crisis struck heaviest, relatively, here. The contrast between mass hopes and illusions in 1929, and bitter reality in 1934, is greater than almost anywhere else. The greatest accumulated wealth and productive forces, side by side with the largest mass unemployment and starvation of any industrial country, stares every observer in the face. Revolutionary forces in the United States, developing more slowly than elsewhere, are yet of enormously greater potentiality and depth.

All capitalist contradictions are embodied in Roosevelt's "New Deal" policies. Roosevelt promises to feed the hungry, by reducing the production of food. He promises to redistribute wealth, by billions of subsidies to the banks and corporations. He gives help to the "forgotten" man, by speeding up the process of monopoly and trustification. He would increase the purchasing power of the masses, through inflation which gives them a dollar worth only 60 cents. He drives the Wall Street money changers out of the temple of government, by giving them complete power in the administration of the governmental machinery of the industrial codes. He gives the workers the right of organization, by legalizing the company unions. He inaugurates a regime of economy, by shifting the tax burden to the consuming masses, by cutting appropriations for wages, veterans, and social services, while increasing the war budget a billion dollars, and giving ten billions to those who already own everything. He restores the faith of the masses in democracy, by beginning the introduction of fascism. He works for international peace, by launching the sharpest trade and currency war in history.

Roosevelt's program is the same as that of finance capital the world over. It is a program of hunger, fascization and imperialist war. It differs chiefly in the forms of its unprecedented ballyhoo, of demagogic promises, for the creation of mass illusions of a saviour who has found the way out. The New Deal is not developed fascism. But in political essence and direction it is the same as Hitler's program.

Under cover of these mass illusions, Roosevelt launched the sharpest, most deep-going attack against the living standards of the masses. Even though the workers were still under the influence of illusions about Roosevelt (these illusions continue to stand up under repeated blows!) they could not but recognize what was happening to them. They answered with a wave of strikes. More than a million workers struck in 1933 in resistance to the New Deal policies. Over 750,000 joined the trade unions.

During this period the unemployed movement also deepened and consolidated itself, in spite of a serious lag. Especially important, it reacted to the new forms of governmental relief, the C. W. A. and forced labor camps, and began a movement on those jobs to protect living standards. The movement for the Workers' Unemployment Insurance Bill began to take on a broad mass character.

Struggles involving the masses of impoverished farmers, veterans, students, professionals, stimulated by the strike wave, gathered about the rising working class movement, and to a greater degree than ever before came in political contact with the workers.

This first wave of struggle against the Roosevelt "New Deal" was stimulated and clarified by the fact that the Communist Party, from the beginning, gave a bold and correct analysis of the "New Deal," and a clear directive for struggle against it. Events since last July confirmed entirely the analysis then given. Every serious effort to apply that program to struggle has brought gains for the workers.

There is no need to revise our analysis. Now we can sum up the results of nine months' experience.

What has happened to the "New Deal"? Has it failed? Many workers, in the first stages of disillusionment, come to that conclusion. They are disillusioned with the result, but still believe in the intention. The S. P. and A. F. of L. leaders try to keep them in this stage. But this conclusion is entirely too simple. The "New Deal" has not improved conditions for the workers and exploited masses. But that was never its real aim; that was only ballyhoo; that was only bait with which to catch suckers. In its first and chief aim, the "New Deal" succeeded; that aim was to bridge over the most difficult situation for the capitalists, and to launch a new attack upon the workers with the help of their leaders, to keep the workers from general resistance, to begin to restore the profits of finance capital.

At the recent code hearing in Washington, this purpose was stated frankly by General Hugh Johnson, in an effort to overcome the resistance of the more backward capitalists to some features of the N. R. A. program. General Johnson, speaking of the difficult position of capital at the time of the birth of the "New Deal" and what was its aim, declared:

I want to tell you, if you have not yourselves observed, that throughout that whole difficult and trying period, when in panic and under the urge of extremists, the wreck of our system was threatened, the strong, sane, moderate mind that upheld you was that of the President. I ask you to remember that at that time both industrial and banking leadership had fallen, in the public mind, to complete and utter disrepute. Humanity always seeks a scapegoat. A British Government, unable to sustain itself on any other issue, was elected on the slogan "Hang the Kaiser." Don't forget that, at that time, these gentlemen and the bankers were almost (to an inflamed public mind) the Kaiser.

That is clear enough. No Communist could have put it more clearly!

Without the collaboration of the A. F. of L. leadership, it must be emphasized, this program could never have been carried out over the resistance of the workers. This truth, which we pointed out in advance, is now the boast of Green, Lewis & Co., in their conferences with Roosevelt, Johnson and the employers. Whenever a strike has been broken, the main "credit" belongs to Green and his associates. Every vicious code provision against the workers, for company unions, has borne the signature of Green & Co. Section 7a, the new "charter for labor," turned out in reality to be the legalization of company unionism and compulsory arbitration. Even the A. F. of L. leaders are allowed to organize only where and when this is required to block the formation of revolutionary or independent trade unions. The Wagner Bill to interpret Section 7a, now before Congress, which received such vigorous support and high praise from Socialist and A. F. of L. leaders, is already, even before passage, openly admitted to be legal confirmation of the company unions, the enforcement of compulsory arbitration.

Again we turn to the outspoken General Johnson for a colorful description of the role of the A. F. of L. leaders. In his March 7th speech to the capitalists, Johnson poured out his soul in eloquent tribute to Green & Co. He said:

We know something about what is toward in this country—the worst epidemic of strikes in our history. Why suffer it? Here is a way out. Play the game. Submit to the law and get it over quickly. I want to tell you this for your comfort. I know your problems. I would rather deal with Bill Green, John Lewis, Ed McGrady, Mike MacDonough, George Berry and a host of others I could name, than with any Frankenstein that you may build up under the guise of a company union. In fact—take it from me and a wealth of experience—their interests are your interests.

Again the worthy General leaves nothing to add!

Now, for a brief glance at the results of the "New Deal" as registered in governmental statistics.

First, the Reconstruction Finance Corporation: Payments authorized by the R. F. C. up to the end of 1933, amounted to $5,233,800,000. More than 80 per cent of this enormous sum went directly to banks, insurance companies, railroads, mortgage loan companies, credit unions, etc., in loans or purchase of preferred stock; and for what is called "agricultural credit" which means advances to financial institutions holding uncollectable farm mortgages. About 12 per cent went for "relief," payment for forced labor on municipal and state work. These enormous subsidies, the size of which staggers the imagination, are the source of a large part of the renewed profits of the big corporations.

Second, inflation and price-fixing: These measures have resulted in such rise in living costs that even the A. F. of L. leaders, close partners of Roosevelt and Johnson, have to admit a decided drop in the purchasing power of employed workers. An indication is the drop of nine per cent, from September to December, in the volume of consumers' goods actually purchased.

Third, the Government budget: Here we find the realization of Roosevelt's promise to remember the "forgotten man." The shift of the burden of taxes, the basis of the budget, comparing the current year with 1928-1929, is as follows:

Government income from taxation on corporations, rich individuals, and wealthy middle-class, declined from $2,231,000,000 to $864,-000,000—a saving to the rich of $1,467,000,000. At the same time, taxation of workers and consuming masses increased from $1,571,-000,000 to $2,395,000,000—an increase of the tax burden amounting to almost the total taxes now paid by the rich.

On the expenditure side of the budget, changes took the following direction: To banks, corporations, wealthy individuals and property owners, increased payments of 413 per cent. Expenditures for war purposes, increased by 82 per cent. Against these increases, economy was practiced by reducing wages of government employees, and veteran allowances, by 38 per cent and 27 per cent.

Fourth, distribution of National Income: Roosevelt promised that he would begin to remedy the maldistribution of the national income, whereby the rich get too much and the poor get too little. How this has been carried out is disclosed in a report submitted to the U. S. Senate by the Bureau of Foreign and Domestic Commerce on Jan. 1, 1934. Summarizing its findings, the report says:

Wages have suffered the most severely in the general decline since 1929, with a falling off of sixty (60) per cent in those industries in which it was possible to segregate this item. Salaries dropped forty (40) per cent, much less rapidly than wages, with the most severe curtailment occurring in 1932. A significant divergence in declining trends is apparent as between labor income and property income; by 1932 the former had fallen off by forty (40) per cent, while property income distributed receded but thirty (30) per cent. This situation was brought about by the maintenance of interest payments rather uniformly up to 1932, with only a small decline then.

This pictures the development under the Hoover regime. Roosevelt's "New Deal" promised to reverse this trend. Actually, what happened in 1933 was that the purchasing power of the workers went backward (a fact testified by the A. F. of L. and the Bureau of Labor Statistics) while property income took a sharp rise. A recent report of a group of large selected corporations which in 1932 showed a loss of about 45 millions, showed that in 1933 they had been restored to the profit side of the ledger by about a half-billion dollars.

Fifth, the workers' housing: In estimating the social effects of the shift of national income away from the workers and to property owners, it must be remembered that even in 1932 the majority of workers lived just at or even below the subsistence level. Every loss of income has been a direct deduction from daily necessities of life. This is sharply expressed in the catastrophic worsening of housing conditions. The epidemic of tenement house fires, burning to death hundreds of men, women and children, is but a dramatic revelation of one corner of the inhuman conditions under which growing millions are reduced.

Sixth, breaking up the home: A barometer of the degeneration of living standards is the growing army of wandering, homeless people, especially children. The "New Deal" proposed to turn the army of unattached boys into a military reserve through the Civilian Conservation Corps. Some 380,000 boys were so recruited in 1933; but in spite of this mass militarization, all reports agree that a larger number than before of homeless youth wandered the country.

Seventh, collapse of the school system: Conditions in the school system in rich America reflect the catastrophic situation of the masses. No improvement is to be seen under the "New Deal," but on the contrary, a sharp worsening takes place. Just a few details, presented not by Communist agitators but by the U. S. Commissioner of Education, George F. Zook, and the National Education Association, describing the current school year, after Mr. Roosevelt's "New Deal" was at work. Over 2,290,000 children of school age cannot find a place. Over 2,000 schools in rural communities failed to open this year in 24 states (the other 24 states, probably, being ashamed to report because their conditions are worse!). Some 1,500 commercial schools and 16 institutions of higher learning have been completely liquidated. School terms in nearly every large city are from one to two months shorter than they were 70 to 100 years ago. The average term in the United States, 170 school days per year, is less than that for France, Germany, England, Sweden, Denmark. School teachers' wages are generally from four to twenty-four months in arrears, although interest on bonds is paid promptly. In Chicago, where teachers are behind in their wages by $25,000,000, the committee enforcing the economy program contains, among its 29 members, all affiliated with big business, five directors of the largest banks, and 14 residents of exclusive Lake Shore Drive ("the Gold Coast"). Unemployed teachers are estimated at a quarter million. Teachers' wage rates have been cut by 27 per cent. In 14 states even this reduced salary is far behind in payment.

It is impossible to go into all the ramifications of the result of a "successful" New Deal program. We have shown enough to fully expose that the "success" was in giving more to the rich, and taking away from the poor even that which they had.

The New Strike Wave and New Steps in Fascization

Our Central Committee, at the moment of the ebb of the 1933 strike wave (our 17th Plenum), was able already to foresee the rise of a new strike wave in the early spring of 1934. It is now being realized all around us on a large scale. In this movement an even larger role is being played by the revolutionary forces than in 1933. This also results in a larger proportion of victorious strikes.

This new wave of struggles has already brought the Roosevelt administration to a new stage in the development of its labor policy. This was announced by Mr. Roosevelt himself, when he declared that "we have charted a new course," in his announcement of the "settlement" in the automobile industry.

What is this "new course"?

The auto manufacturers themselves gave a correct estimate of it, when they declared to the correspondent of the N. Y. *Herald Tribune* their "delight" with the outcome. *"The manufacturers were particu-*

larly pleased that the clarification of section 7a seems to uphold their contention in behalf of the company union."

This "new course," like the previous "new courses," is launched with the signature of William Green and the officialdom of the A. F. of L., with the blessings of Norman Thomas and the Socialist Party.

What is new in this course, is the public adoption of the company union as an integral part of the "corporate state" scheme, where previously, in the official plans, the A. F. of L. had been granted (on paper) a monopoly. This means more open coming forward of the government to prevent or smash the strike movements. For months a debate raged behind the scenes among the capitalists, on which horse to place their money, the A. F. of L. or the company union. Two camps had existed, which sharply divided the highest councils. Upon the basis of experience in the first strike wave and the beginnings of the second, both camps had modified their views and came together in one united judgment, embodied in Roosevelt's "new course." On the one hand, the company union advocates had been convinced of the complete docility and reliability for their purposes of Green, Lewis, and the whole official A. F. of L. family; they have been converted to the view of Johnson in this respect. On the other hand, the proponents of the A. F. of L. have been convinced that, in spite of Green & Co.'s absolute "reliability" in purpose, their *ability* to control their membership is growing less and less each day. Already last fall, Roosevelt had a sharp intimation of this, when John L. Lewis had to admit his failure to drive the strikers of the captive mines back to work, and Roosevelt had to do the job personally. Another major example of the same sort was the auto situation, where the A. F. of L. leaders frankly told the President that they were helpless to stop the strike movement unless Roosevelt himself intervened. The whole strike wave, rising against the Canute-like commandments of Green & Co. drove the lesson home. *Conclusion:* Neither one nor the other, neither A. F. of L. nor company union, alone, but both together, in a constantly closer association, and in preparation for merging the two under Government auspices. That is the essence of the "new course." Of course, differences continue—we must not be confused by them.

This "new course" is now in process of being incorporated into the Wagner Bill, which in its original form provided for a sort of Watson-Parker Law (compulsory arbitration on the railroads) for all industries. The original purpose to bind the unions with the strong chains of arbitration machinery, to choke down the strike wave, is now to be supplemented by guarantees of effectiveness through binding the trade unions with the company unions.

LaGuardia, in the midst of "handling" the taxi drivers' strike in New York City, knew how to "take a hint." He promptly abandoned the settlement which he had prepared, to which the workers had agreed but which the companies had rejected, and called a representative of the A. F. of L. from Washington to negotiate the incorporation of the taxi company union into the A. F. of L. He was "correct in principle" in this question, but too hasty and crude in action, so the execution of his proposal has been postponed for a more favorable stage setting.

An organic part of the whole "new course" toward labor is the sharp turn in the question of unemployed relief. Roosevelt has in his hands unexpended billions, which he demanded from Congress for relief purposes. But suddenly, so suddenly as to shock a host of loyal "new dealers" and bring bitter protests from them (including such a close friend of Roosevelt as Governor Lehman of New York), the C. W. A. is closed down, and millions of unemployed are thrown back upon the bankrupt local governments. Why this "new course" toward the unemployed? The answer is given in the cynical words published on the front page of the Cleveland *Plain Dealer* (Sunday, April 1st):

Those not so pleased with the new relief standards think the administration, finding perhaps that its grants of power to the labor unions were greater than the administration would now like to have them, may have thought of an abrupt ending of C. W. A. and a lowering of direct relief expenditures as an effective way of glutting the labor market and taking some of the spirit out of the unions.

What are the main strategic tasks of the Communist Party, that flow from this analysis of the situation?

First, to help the masses of workers, who are coming to realize that they must halt their mutually destructive competition and begin to act unitedly against a hostile ruling system, to find the road to independent class organization and class struggle in the fight for their daily bread.

Second, to organize every possible form of resistance and counter-struggle against the attacks of reaction, against every reduction of living standards, for wage increases, for more relief, for jobs, for unemployment insurance, against cultural reaction, against Negro oppression, for civil rights, for the right to organize and strike.

Third, to find the broadest possible forms of organization of the struggle, to apply, with Bolshevist flexibility, the tactic of the united front from below.

Fourth, to expose the true role of every hidden agent of capitalist reaction in the ranks of the working class—the leaders of the A. F. of L., of the Socialist Party, the Muste group, the renegades, by concrete analysis of their actions and policies.

Fifth, to raise the political consciousness of the struggling workers, to bring to them an understanding of the class structure of society, of the fact that two main classes are fighting for control, that Roosevelt, leading the present ruling class, finance capital, stands for degradation, hunger, misery, oppression, fascism, war—that only the working class exercising state power, can open up a new era of peace, progress, and prosperity for the entire human race.

Sixth, to imbue the broadest masses with the fundamentals of Marxism-Leninism, to arm them with the lessons of successful revolution, against the treacherous slogans and ideas of social-fascism.

Seventh, to create strongholds of revolutionary mass organizations in the most important industries, localities, and factories.

Eighth, to consolidate everything that is most active, intelligent, fearless and loyal in the working class into a compact, monolithic leadership of the mass struggle, into the Communist Party, organically united with the revolutionary workers and oppressed peoples of the world in our Communist International.

RESULTS OF THE FIRST WAVE OF STRUGGLE AND ORGANIZATION UNDER THE NEW DEAL

The year 1933 and beginning of 1934, with its wave of strikes and organizations, left its mark upon the working class. All forms of labor organizations increased. We can divide these into four main groups: (1) company unions, embracing workers estimated variously from one to three millions; (2) A. F. of L. (and allied organizations such as Railroad Brotherhoods), 500,000 new members with a total membership of two and a half to three million; (3) independent unions—150,000 new members, with a total membership around 250,000; (4) Trade Union Unity League, and allied organizations,—100,000 new members; total membership 125,000.

The first conclusion that must be drawn from these figures is the tremendously increased importance of the struggle against company unionism. The company union is the first line of defense in the factories for the capitalists against the rising strike wave. The line of struggle against company unionism requires simultaneous development of revolutionary work inside the company union, utilizing every opportunity for raising the demands of the workers, fighting for these demands, and putting forward militant candidates for all elective posts, thus disrupting the employer-controlled organizations from within. It has been proved possible, at times, to transform them into real trade unions, but only by open struggle. At the same time we must mobilize all independent trade union forces for the open smashing of the company unions.

The second conclusion is the greatly increased importance of revolutionary work inside the American Federation of Labor. The largest section of newly organized workers in trade unions is in the A. F. of L. The bulk of these, in turn, are in some of the most important industries —such as mining and textile, with important groups also in auto, steel and metal. Precisely these new strata in the A. F. of L. are the least consolidated under the reactionary leadership, the most active in pressing forward their demands, and therefore the most ripe for revolutionary leadership. In connection with the struggle against company unionism, a struggle for the rights of the A. F. of L. workers to fight for their immediate demands, large numbers of them can be immediately brought under revolutionary leadership by correct work. These new recruits to the A. F. of L. are not contentedly witnessing the A. F. of L. leaders signing away their rights as was done in the steel and auto codes; they are not content when they see their unions smashed through the mediation of the National Labor Board (Weirton, Budd, Edgewater, etc.). They are in open revolt when, as in the auto settlement last week, their leaders commit them to the legalization of the company union, and the outlawing of their strike movement. Now, more than ever before, correct and energetic work among the members of the A. F. of L., giving them independent leadership through the crystallization of revolutionary opposition groups, bringing them into action against their leaders and in open strikes and other forms of struggle for their immediate demands, is a first line task of the Communist Party.

How supremely important is this work, is shown by the serious results flowing from every smallest effort that is made. The broadest circle of this work is the movement for the Workers' Unemployment Insurance Bill (H. R. 7598). This bill has secured the direct support of over 2,000 A. F. of L. local unions, many city central bodies and even a few State Federations of Labor. In 23 cities, we have functioning general leading committees for work in the A. F. of L. The revolutionary elements, directly under our guidance, are established leaders of around 150 local unions, with 50,000 to 60,000 members. Minority opposition groups function in about 500 more local unions. This considerable beginning is of significance because it emphasizes the enormous possibilities that exist when we get a full mobilization of all available forces in this field. These results, which change the course of development for hundreds of thousands more, come from only the first steps with very fragmentary mobilization, and in the face of still existing underestimation of and even opposition to systematic development of this work.

The independent unions have emerged as a major factor in more than a few light industries only during the past year. In the main, they are the result of the mass revolt against the A. F. of L. betrayals, and could not yet be brought into the revolutionary unions for various reasons, chief among them being the weaknesses in the work of the T. U. U. L. Systematic building of revolutionary groups inside them, with careful formulation of policies and leadership of their struggles, is an essential feature of our trade union strategy. In the independent unions we must have the most careful distinction between the honest but confused leadership which has been thrown up from the

rank and file, on the one hand; and the conscious opportunist, reformist, social-fascist elements in the leadership on the other hand, who head
the independent movements only in order to bring them back under the
domination of the A. F. of L. leadership. In this latter group, an
important role is played by the Musteites, Lovestoneites, and Trotskyites. The sharpest political struggle must be made against the "left"
reformists and the renegades, while every effort must be made to win
over to our class struggle policies the honest elements in the independent
trade union leadership.

The revolutionary unions of the T. U. U. L. with their 125,000
members, while numerically the smallest of these main groups of the
trade union movement, are by no means least important. The T. U.
U. L. unions in developing the whole mass movement of resistance to
the N. R. A. and the whole capitalist offensive, in the development of
the strike movements, have played a decisive role. This is brought
out by an examination of the statistics of the strike movement in 1933,
as shown in the following table:

	Membership	Led in Strikes	New Members
A. F. of L.	2,500,000	450,000	500,000
Indep. Unions	250,000	250,000	150,000
T. U. U. L.	125,000	200,000	100,000
Unorganized		100,000	
	2,875,000	1,000,000	750,000

From these figures we see that the T. U. U. L. although not quite 5
per cent of the total trade union membership, directly led 20 per cent
of all strikes and gained 20 per cent of all new members. The independent unions, a little under 10 per cent of the total membership, led
25 per cent of the strikes. The A. F. of L. unions, comprising over 85
per cent of the membership, led 45 per cent of the strikes. This illus-
trates the role of the leadership of these three groups in relation to the
strike movement. The A. F. of L. leadership is the center of resistance
to strikes, and center of strikebreaking activities within the ranks of
the workers. The T. U. U. L. unions were the driving force in the
leadership and development of the strikes against all the strikebreakers.
The independent unions represented those masses breaking away from
the A. F. of L. leadership, but still carrying with them part of the old
burden of unclear and even openly reformist leadership which continued
trying to carry through the A. F. of L. policies within the unions.

The growing importance of the independent and T. U. U. L. unions
is emphasized by the fact that they comprised fully one-third of all
the increased trade union membership that resulted from the strike
movement, and that together they led 45 per cent of the strikes, an

equal number with the A. F. of L. In addition to this, it is clear that the 450,000 strikers under A. F. of L. leadership were not led into struggle by that leadership but in spite of and against it. Our opposition work in the A. F. of L. played in this a significant part in some industries. It would have been impossible for a strike movement of such volume to rise from the A. F. of L. ranks without the influence of the strike movement of equal volume outside the A. F. of L. developed and led by the T. U. U. L. and independent unions.

Our Draft Resolution places before the Convention, as a central point in our present trade union strategy, the task of unifying the independent unions with the revolutionary unions, beginning separately in each industry, and, upon the basis of successful work there, moving towards the consolidation of all class trade union forces into a single Independent Federation of Labor.

We must avoid, if possible, the crystallization of a third trade union center, intermediate between the A. F. of L. and the T. U. U. L. We must be prepared to go a long way to secure organizational unity of all genuine class trade union forces. The possibility of success in this direction is already indicated in the partially successful merger of the T. U. U. L. and the independent Shoe Workers' Unions. This experience gives a clear indication of our general line in practice.

Of great importance to us in this period was the rise of mass revolutionary unions on the Pacific Coast area, among agricultural and cannery workers, fishermen and lumber workers. These organizations and the historic struggles conducted by them have definitely established the fact that our movement has fully taken over and absorbed the specifically American revolutionary traditions and forces in that territory, which before the rise of the Communist Party was organized in and around the I. W. W.

The rise of the revolutionary Agricultural Workers' Unions, especially in the California area, has a further special significance for our Party. This is the first beginning of mass organization among a category of workers which, in spite of the scattered and decentralized character of its labor in most areas, constitutes numerically the largest single category of the working class. Agricultural workers in the United States comprise two and a half to three million workers. Large numbers of them are favorably situated for organization, especially in the sections of the industry organized on the lines of mass production for the city markets—fruit, vegetable and dairy farming. Large numbers of these workers are massed around the industrial centers, in the East and Middle West also, within easy reach of the organized labor movement in the cities. Serious trade union organization of these workers provides a most important extension of the working class base of the revolutionary movement. At the same time, they furnish the necessary class base for revolutionary organization among the poor and middle

farmers, who are more and more revolting against the capitalist attacks. It is the organized agricultural workers which in the first place
will provide a firm basis for working class hegemony in the alliance
between the working class as a whole with the movement of the revolting farmers. The necessity of the general leadership of the working
class over the movements of all other sections of the exploited population if all of their forces are to be unified for the common struggle
against capitalism, should make it clear to every district of the Party
that their work in reaching and organizing the agricultural workers
acquires an extraordinary importance at the present time.

Struggles of the Farmers and Movements of Mixed Class Character

The movement for organization of rising strike struggles among the
employed workers, together with the growing organization and struggles
of the unemployed, has served as a powerful stimulus to the activities
of other sections of the exploited population, and attracts these other
groups around the working class as the leader and organizing center.
We have seen the serious beginnings of this process in relation to the
farmers' movement. This movement is beginning to take on a different
character from that seen in previous farmers' movements. The new
characteristics have been brought forward most clearly in those struggles and organizations of the farmers which have found their organizing
center in the Farmers' Committee of Action, and the two national
Farm Conferences held by it in 1932 in Washington, and in 1933 in
Chicago, and especially its left wing, the United Farmers League.
What is new in this farmers' movement is first, the political clarity
with which it has attacked the traditional nostrums with which the
farmers have been fooled so many times in the past (Currency Reform,
etc.), and its resolute combating of the anti-farmer policies of the
Roosevelt "New Deal" (crop reduction, etc.). It is distinguished by
its ability to rise above sectional and race divisions, by its proclamation
of the unity of Negro and white farmer, by its formulation of a national outlook and program, as against the narrow, regional, provincial
approach. It has struck at the heart of the farmers' problems in its
demand for the cancellation of mortgages, debts and back taxes, raising
sharply the most vital issues which determine class alignments. Above
all, it has been able not only to proclaim the abstract principle of the
worker-farmer alliance, but actually to begin to realize it in daily life
and struggles.

A mass movement of a mixed class nature that has begun to take on
a revolutionary trend in the United States in the past period, is that
of the war veterans. The veterans' movement comprises workers,
farmers and a larger proportion of middle class elements. It is unified
not by its class composition but by its common demands for payment

of the adjusted compensation certificates (bonus), for disability allowances and hospitalization, all of which have been under heavy attack by the Roosevelt administration. The tremendous revolutionary potentialities in this movement were startlingly revealed by the great Bonus March in 1932, which was a tremendous outburst of mass indignation against the Hoover regime. That these forces are again gathering, that they are exerting tremendous pressure, that they are threatening to burst forth again into mass action, was dramatically shown by the panicky action of Congress in over-riding Roosevelt's veto of the Congressional replacement of a small portion of what the Roosevelt regime had stolen from the veterans. An indispensible role has been played in this veterans' movement by the still small, but very active Workers' Ex-Servicemen's League. If this organization would receive more co-operation and assistance, more systematic help in recruiting all the potential forces of veterans, who are as yet inactive in this work, the results in bringing into active expression the mass forces of the veterans' revolt would mature much faster. The veterans' movement is a most valuable ally to the revolutionary working class movement. It stands as one of the important tasks of the entire Party in mobilizing the auxiliary forces for the working class movement in the United States.

Another auxiliary movement of growing importance that has appeared as a serious factor only in the last two years, is the revolutionary movement among the students. In the student movement we are also dealing with a mixed class composition. The movement began principally in the higher institutions of learning with predominantly middle class composition. It has rapidly spread to the secondary schools and involved a large number of proletarian students in its activities. Led and organized by the National Student League, this movement has established a base in hundreds of high schools, colleges and universities; it has become national in scope; it has exerted a great and growing influence upon all intellectual circles. From the beginning it has been clearly revolutionary in its program and activities. One of the strongest points has been its clear recognition that the leading role belongs to the workers and not to the students in the general revolutionary movement. Especially the students' movement has made a valuable contribution in extending the organized mass movement against war and fascism among the masses of youth. The students' movement, in fact, is a pioneer in the development of the general anti-war movement through its Students' Anti-War Congress in Chicago in December, 1932, which first united, on a national scale, anti-war forces of various political and class origins. Its participation in the youth section of the American League Against War and Fascism has constituted one of the most active and valuable phases of that organization's work. By organized participation in helping strike actions, defense movements, the Scottsboro case, etc., the students have been brought to participation in the general class struggles and learned the practical meaning of working class leadership. The weakness of this movement still remains that its leading cadres are still largely drawn from the middle class elements of the colleges and universities, that it does not yet sufficiently base itself upon the larger bodies of proletarian students in the secondary schools, nor sufficiently draw them into active leadership of the movement.

The broadest movement of mixed-class composition has been the American League Against War and Fascism, formed at the great U. S. Congress Against War, held in New York last October. The Congress itself, while predominately working class in composition, embraced the widest variety of organizations that have ever been united upon a single platform in this country. It gathered the most significant strata of the intellectuals. The breadth of the movement was not secured by sacrificing clarity of program. On the contrary, while its program is distinctly not that of the Communist Party, it is so clear and definite in facing the basic issues, that to carry it out in practice entails clearly revolutionary consequences. It is a real united front program of immediate struggle against war and fascism. That is the reason for the frantic efforts to break up and scatter the American League Against War and Fascism that have been and are being made by the Socialist Party leaders, Musteites, and the renegades from Communism. The unbridled ferocity of the attacks made against the League by these elements, and by their comrades-in-arms of the National Civic Federation, Ralph Easley, Matthew Woll & Co., should be an indication to us of the revolutionary value of this broad united front organization. In serious self-criticism, we must say that although our movement responded excellently (in most places) to the call to the National Congress, it did not follow up this congress everywhere with serious local organizational work to consolidate the potential movement that had been brought together. Only in a few places has this work been seriously begun. In every locality the non-Party and mixed-class character of the movement must be carried forward, but not at the expense of dropping the working class and Communist participation as has too often been the case. The American League in its program proclaims that the working class is the basic force for the struggle against war; from the beginning it has never tried to avoid the issue of Communist Party participation in this broad united front. It is our task to see that the American League, organizationally, gets that working class foundation and active participation of the Communists for which its program provides.

THE STRUGGLE FOR NEGRO RIGHTS

One of the chief tasks of the Communist Party, which has come sharply to the front of our practical work, is the liberation of the Negro people from the special oppression under which they suffer. In organizing and leading the struggle for Negro rights, the Communist Party is carrying out the slogan first enunciated by Karl Marx when he was organizing international support by the European workers to the emancipation of the Negro chattel slaves in America. Marx said: "Labor in a white skin cannot be free while labor in a black skin is branded." The cause of the emancipation of the Negroes from their special oppression is inextricably bound up with the cause of the emancipation of the working class from the oppression of capitalism. Because our Party, as a whole, has not yet firmly mastered the theoretical basis for our Negro program, it is necessary again at this convention to continue to discuss it.

From its inception, the Communist Party of the United States placed the demands for Negro rights in its program. In the first period of our work, up to 1929, we cannot claim any important results. This was because the Party, in spite of its correct general orientation, did not have a clear Bolshevik understanding of the Negro question as the problem of liberation of an oppressed nation. The Party had not yet entirely emancipated itself from the limitation of the bourgeois-liberal approach to Negro rights, nor from the social-democratic denial of the Negro question with its formula that the Negroes can find their emancipation only with the establishment of Socialism, and as a part of the working class. The Party, however, was continually struggling with this question and constantly raising it again for discussion. As a result of this, the problem was brought to the consideration of our World Party at the Sixth Congress of the Communist International. The resolution there worked out, subsequently elaborated by a special resolution in October, 1930, finally armed our Party politically for a decisive step forward in rousing and organizing the liberation movement of the Negroes, in uniting Negro and white workers in a firm and unbreakable solidarity.

The characteristic of the position of the Negroes in America as an oppressed nation is expressed in: (1) the fact that the basic Negro population, engaged in cultivating the land, is systematically excluded from independent possession of the land which it cultivates; (2) that it is thereby reduced to a position of semi-serfdom in the form of specially exploited tenants and sharecroppers; (3) that this special exploitation is enforced by a system of legal and illegal discrimination, segregation, denial of political rights, personal subjection to individual exploiters, and all forms of violent oppression culminating in the most brutal and barbarous system of murder, that it has become notorious all over the world as lynch-law. It is difficult to find anywhere in the world such examples of barbarous tortures as are used in America to enforce the special oppression of the Negro people.

The historical origin and development of the Negro population of America as chattel slaves imported from Africa, together with their ready identification due to their special racial characteristics, have facilitated the efforts of the white ruling class in the creation of the institutions and customs of special national oppression that were set up following the smashing of the system of chattel slavery in the Civil War.

These things give the Negro question its character as that of an oppressed nation. The Negroes have never yet been emancipated. The form of their oppression was only changed from that of chattel slavery, which constituted an obstacle to the further development of capitalism, to the more "modern" forms of so-called free labor (which means that the employer is freed from all obligation when he has paid the hourly or daily starvation wage), and half-feudal forms of share-cropping, etc., whereby an imperialist nation oppresses and exploits a weak nation. The position of the masses of the Negroes, as farmers denied the possession of the land, is the foundation for the special oppression of the Negro people as a whole. All phases of struggle for Negro rights must take as their foundation and starting place, therefore, the struggle for possession of the land by the landless Negro farmers. This can only be achieved by breaking through the rule of the white landlord ruling class, the carrying through of the agrarian revolution, such as was carried through in Europe in the first half of the nineteenth century when the foundations were laid for modern capitalism. The agrarian revolution, that is, the distribution of land among those who work the land, is historically part of the bourgeois-democratic revolution. But this revolution was never carried through entirely in any country, and hardly at all in the weak nations; the pre-capitalist social and economic forms of oppression and exploitation of the weak nations has been carried over to modern times and incorporated into the system of finance capital and modern imperialism.

The struggle for the completion of the bourgeois-democratic revolution for the Negroes, as for other oppressed nations, thus becomes today objectively a revolutionary struggle to overthrow imperialism. As such it is an ally of the revolutionary proletariat against the common enemy—finance capital. Such agrarian revolution can be realized only through winning national self-determination for the Negroes in that territory in which they constitute the majority of the population and the basic productive force upon the land, or as a by-product of a victorious proletarian revolution in the country as a whole. The basic slogan of Negro liberation is therefore the slogan of self-determination; the basic demand of the Negroes is the demand for the land. Throughout the United States the struggle for Negro liberation is expressed in the struggle for complete equality, for the abolition of all segregation laws and practices (Jim-Crowism), the struggle against the ideas, propagated by the white ruling class, of Negro inferiority (a form of national chauvinism which we call white chauvinism), which is used to justify the oppression of the Negroes and to keep the Negro and white toilers divided.

These basic political considerations have been, by experience, proved to be absolutely necessary weapons to make effectual even the smallest struggle for Negro rights. Let us consider, for example, the world famous Scottsboro case, which has represented one of the major political achievements of the Communist Party in the last period. How impossible it would have been to rouse the Negro masses in the United States in millions to the support of the Scottsboro boys; how impossible to have joined with them millions of white toilers and middle classes; how impossible to have stirred the entire world, as was done—if the Scottsboro case had been taken up from the liberal-humanitarian point of view, or if it had been approached from the narrow social-democratic viewpoint! The Scottsboro case stirred America to its depths, not merely because nine friendless Negro boys were threatened with an unjust death, but because their cause was brought forward clearly as a symbol of the national oppression of twelve million Negroes in America, because the fight for their freedom was made the symbol for the fight of the Negro farmers for their land, of the fight for the self-determination in the Black Belt, of the fight against lynchings, against Jim-Crowism, against the smallest discriminations, for unconditional social and political equality for the Negroes.

Only the Bolshevik understanding of the Negro question makes possible such an effective fight for the smallest advance for the Negroes to realize their smallest demands; that is why historically it was left for the Communist Party to be the first to raise effectively, on a national scale, the slogan of Negro liberation, since the almost-forgotten days of the Abolitionists.

The Communists unconditionally reject the social-democratic approach of the Second International to the Negro question and to the national question generally, which under the guise of a strictly "working class" evaluation of the Negro question, in actuality carries through the capitalist class program of national oppression. That does not mean, however, that the Communist Party ignores the class divisions among the Negroes, or that it is indifferent to what class influences and leads the Negro masses.

The Communist Party points out that the Negroes also are divided into classes; that in addition to the class of Negro farmers, there is a considerable and growing proletariat, a Negro middle class and a Negro bourgeoisie. The Negro bourgeoisie, also subjected to the special oppression of the Negro people as a whole, has been corrupted into accepting this position of inferiority, and even capitalizing upon this inferior position for its own class gain. This Negro bourgeoisie has become the thorough-going agent of the white ruling class. It maintains a pitiful "superiority" to the Negro masses by means of the condescending support offered to it by the white ruling class. It capitalizes a share of the double rents extracted from the Negro masses by the white landlords through the system of Jim-Crow segregation; it earns these concessions from the white ruling class by energetically exhorting the Negro masses to be patient and long-suffering, to realize their own inferiority, to understand the position of white capitalists and landlords as their rulers as an inescapable visitation inflicted upon them by an all-wise God.

As the Negro masses begin to revolt against this position of inferiority, the Negro bourgeoisie begins to develop special means of heading off and controlling this revolt. They speculate upon the distrust and suspicions created among the Negro masses against white workers generally through generations of oppression. They appeal to the Negroes to make a virtue out of their segregation, to voluntarily isolate themselves, not to trust any white man, to rely upon themselves alone; they bring forth all sorts of utopian schemes, such as the *Back-to-Africa* movement, the *Support-Negro-Business* movement, the so-called Pacific (pro-Japanese movement), and so forth, to create the illusions of some possible way out of their misery without direct conflict with the white ruling class. All of these ideas, tendencies, and moods are what we identify collectively as bourgeois-nationalism, or national-reformism. Such a nationalism contributes nothing to the national liberation of the Negro people; on the contrary, it is an instrument of the white ruling class, just as is white chauvinism, to keep the white and Negro masses separated and antagonistic to one another, and thereby to keep both enslaved.

We have had a thousand practical examples of how this Negro bourgeois-nationalism works out in practice. We saw it in the Scottsboro case, when all the bourgeois Negro leaders held up their hands in horror because white and Negro Communists joined hands together to rouse the masses to save the Scottsboro boys. They declared that the Scottsboro boys were in danger, not from the white ruling class whose hearts could, they said, be touched by quiet humanitarian pleading, but that they were in danger rather from the prejudices raised against them by the fact that masses were demanding their release as a part of the demand for national liberation. It was clearly revealed that the bourgeois proposal that the Negroes "stand on their own feet" was not merely a proposal to keep them separate from the white workers, but to throw themselves on the mercy of the white ruling class.

From all these facts flow the Communist position on the Negro question. The Communists fight everywhere against white chauvinism, against all ideas of Negro inferiority, against all practical discrimination against the Negroes; the Communists fight especially against white chauvinist ideas in the ranks of the workers, and above all against any white chauvinist influence penetrating the ranks of the Communist Party. The Communists declare that the white workers must stand in the forefront of the struggle for Negro rights and against white chauvinism. At the same time, the Communists fight against Negro bourgeois-nationalism which is only the other side of white chauvinism. In this fight against Negro nationalism, it is especially the Negro Communists who have to be the most active and alert.

The danger of Negro nationalism is at the moment especially sharp, precisely because of the fact that the successes of the Communist leadership in the fight for the Scottsboro boys has aroused the Negro bourgeoisie under the proddings of their white masters to a most active and bitter counter-offensive against us.

The main organizational channels of the struggle for Negro rights are, first of all, the trade unions and unemployment councils. Here we draw in the Negro working class forces, we secure the only reliable leading forces to organize the struggle of the Negro masses as a whole. Further basic forms of organization of the Negroes are the unions of sharecroppers and tenant farmers. It is one of our most proud achievements that we have been able through our political influence to bring into existence the Share Croppers' Union in the South, which is already approaching 6,000 members.

A more broad and all-inclusive organizational form for the Negro liberation struggles is the League of Struggle for Negro Rights. This should embrace in its activities all of the basic economic organizations of Negro and white workers standing on the program of Negro liberation, and further unite with them all other sections of the Negro population drawn towards this struggle, especially those large sections of the petty-bourgeoisie, intellectuals, professionals, who can and must be won to the national liberation cause. The L. S. N. R. must, in the first place, be an active federation of existing mass organizations; and secondly, it must directly organize its own membership branches composed of its most active forces and all supporters otherwise unorganized. The present beginnings of the L. S. N. R. and its paper, *The Liberator*, which with only a little attention have already shown mass vitality, must be energetically taken up, and spread throughout the country.

THE PARTY MUST WIN THE YOUTH

A few words are necessary here about the special problems of the youth, although this will be the subject of a special report and discussion. The winning of the working class youth is the problem not of our youth organizations alone, but the problem of the entire Party. In the past this has not only been forgotten, but there has even been allowed to develop a sort of organizational rivalry between the youth and adult organizations, a rivalry not in the nature of socialist competition, but of the adult organizations trying to grab away as quickly as possible from the youth organizations every rising young leader who shows special organizational or political capacity. The idea has been that as soon as the youth movement produces a leader who is "good enough for Party work" that this means he is wasting his time if he remains any longer in what is looked upon as a sort of probationary kindergarten. This frivolous attitude toward youth work must be eliminated from our movement. Certainly, our enemies are more serious about winning the youth, and especially the rising fascist groups. Who shall blame the unprepared, politically unarmed, and desperate masses of young workers who fall victim to the demagogy of fascism, if we drift along without any serious, large-scale efforts to reach these youth, to organize them, to politically educate them, to fight for their daily needs, to raise their class consciousness, and to give them a recognized place in the whole revolutionary movement? Every Party unit, and every Party committee, must take as a part of its daily concrete tasks, the work among the youth, the establishment of their organizations, the solution of their political problems, and material help to their movement. The Young Communist League, instead of being less than a fourth the size of the Party, must be expanded in the next period to become larger than the Party; that means, that the youth must find a serious place in the trade unions and other mass organizations; that it must be helped to politically enrich the life of its organizations, to concretize its struggles for the young workers' needs, to broaden out the scope of its activities, to include everything that interests, attracts and holds the masses of young workers, also including their social, sport and cultural needs.

Special attention is also necessary to the tasks of winning and organizing women industrial workers and housewives in the revolutionary movement. The capitalist class has drawn women into industry on a much larger scale than we have drawn them into revolutionary activities and organizations. We will continue to lag behind the capitalists in this respect only at the price of continued weakness in the revolutionary movement. This question becomes all the more pressing because we are faced with a perspective of imperialist war in the near future. Under war conditions, everybody knows vast additional masses of women will be drawn into industry and especially into munitions manufacturing. Furthermore, large-scale mobilization of men workers into the armies will create gaps in our ranks which can only be filled by the bold promotion of women workers. That means we should long ago have been seriously and systematically preparing the women forces, and boldly promoting them to leading responsible posts. The mobilization of masses of women workers requires special attention to their particular needs, formulation of special demands, the creation of special opportunities to consider their problems in connection with the problems of the whole working class, through conferences, etc. Especially, it requires more systematic recruitment of women into the trade unions, and above all, into the Communist Party.

PROBLEMS OF THE STRUGGLE FOR THE UNITED FRONT

The increasingly sharp attacks against the workers raise more insistently than ever the necessity of establishment of the working class fighting front to resist these attacks and to win the demands of the workers. The working class in the United States is still largely unorganized. That part which is organized is largely under the influence of the A. F. of L. bureaucracy, which keeps it split up in innumerable ways by craft divisions, by discriminations against the Negroes and foreign-born, by divisions between the skilled and unskilled, etc. That smaller section which has begun to question the capitalist system is further divided between the leadership of the Socialist Party and the Communist Party, while a considerable section stands aside, still bewildered by these divisions and the problems it does not yet understand, and further confused by the shouts of those small but active groups, the renegades from Communism, the Musteites, etc.

What is the road to working class unity in the midst of all this disorganization and confusion? The A. F. of L. and Socialist leaders shout that the Communists are splitters and disrupters. This charge is repeated by the renegades and the Musteites. The capitalist press is especially active in spreading this explanation of the divisions among the workers. According to them, if the Communist Party could only suddenly be abolished, the working class would find itself miraculously united and happily on the road to the solution of its problems.

These gentlemen will excuse us if we cannot accept their version of the problem of working class unity. We cannot achieve the united front of the auto workers under the leadership of William Green and the A. F. of L., for example, in the fight against the recent sell-out and legalization of company unions, because it was precisely William Green who signed his name to that sell-out, and who is using all his efforts to prevent the workers' struggle against it. We cannot get the united front of the steel workers to fight against the monstrous steel code under the leadership of William Green and the other A. F. of L. bureaucrats, because Green is one of the sponsors of this code. We can't build the united front under the A. F. of L. and S. P. leaders in the fight for unemployment insurance, the Workers' Bill (H. R. 7598— later in the 74th Congress, H. R. 2827), because they give their support to the Wagner Bill, which is a refusal of unemployment insurance. We can't have the united front led by these gentlemen and the Negro reformists for Negro rights, because it is precisely they who deny these rights to the Negroes in the trade unions, who declare the Negroes themselves provoke lynching by the demands for equal rights. A united front with Norman Thomas and S. P. leaders, to develop strike struggles of the workers would be immediately wrecked by the statement of Norman Thomas, "Now is not the time to strike." No, it is clear, unity behind these gentlemen means a united surrender to the capitalist attacks. That is not the kind of unity the workers need. We need a united fighting front of the workers against the capitalists and all their agents. But that means that unity must be built up, not *with* these leaders on their present policies, but *against* them. That means not a united front from the top, but a united front built up by the workers from below in the organization and struggle for their immediate needs.

The Communists set no conditions to the united front except that the unity shall be one of struggle for the particular demands agreed upon. But on this condition we must be sternly insistent. Sometimes we find people who want to make a united front with us in words, but who seriously hesitate to carry it out in action. When we insist upon action, they tell us we have bad manners, that we are disrupters; that we are breaking up the united front. For example, only last August, here in the city of Cleveland, we participated in a conference together with delegates from hundreds of workers' organizations, including Muste and his associated leading group. We worked out a program of struggle against the N. R. A., for unemployment insurance and relief, and the unification of the unemployed mass organizations. From that conference we went out to fight, to carry out the program adopted. Mr. Muste and his associates left the conference only to forget all about the decisions taken there, to which they had signed their names. They never turned a hand to realize the decisions they had agreed to. They had pledged themselves to support the Workers' Unemployment Insurance Bill, but they have maintained ever since the silence of death on this question. Instead, they support the Wagner Bill along with the Socialist and A. F. of L. leaders. They pledged themselves to help merge the unemployed mass organizations; instead, they have done everything possible to prevent any unification from below, and have themselves refused to even answer any letters on the question so far as the top leadership is concerned. They pledged an uncompromising fight against the N. R. A.; but instead of this, they carry on an agitation copied from the Socialist Party, asking the workers to use the "good sides" of the N. R. A. to achieve the "benefits" that it grants them. United front with such leaders on such terms is no united front at all. The Communist Party will continue in the future, as it has in the past, to denounce all such "unity" in words which is violated in deeds.

In spite of all of these enemies of the real united front, the Communist Party moves steadily forward in building a broad united front movement. Let us examine just a few of these successful united front efforts. First of all, the movement for unemployment insurance: It was the Communist Party that popularized the issue of unemployment insurance, formulated the Workers Unemployment Insurance Bill; it took the lead in bringing into existence the broad mass unemployment council movement, which popularized the bill; it helped to initiate the A. F. L. Rank and File Committee for Unemployment Insurance, which has held two national conferences in support of the Workers' Bill and has secured the endorsement of 2,000 unions, over a dozen central bodies, and several state federations; it was the work of the Communist Party which resulted in the endorsement of the Bill by dozens of city governments, including that of the city of Minneapolis which, joined with the pressure of the whole mass movement, caused Ernest Lundeen, Farmer Labor congressman, to introduce the Bill in Congress although his Party refuses to support the Bill. It was the Communist Party which took the political lead and did most of the practical work which gave organized expression to the support of this Bill by a million to a million-and-a-half organized workers.* *Truly, this is a united front in struggle for unemployment insurance.* The A. F. L. leaders, Socialist Party, the Muste group, the Lovestoneites, the Trotskyites, one and all, they sneered at the Workers' Unemployment Insurance Bill, they sabotaged the fight for it or openly opposed it; they threw their support to the Wagner Bill which is the Roosevelt government's attempt to head off unemployment insurance; they did everything possible to prevent the unity of the workers in support of the only real unemployment insurance bill that is before the country. *But we Communists have built up the united front of the workers over the heads of these leaders, and against all of their disruptive efforts.* In this united front we have lined up all the awakened, honest and intelligent elements in the labor movement and the sympathizing middle classes. We have welcomed them, one and all, into the united front. We have made possible and easy their participation in it; we have been the main force that brought this united front into existence and we have jealously guarded its unity.**

Another illuminating experience was our relations with the Socialist Party leaders in the U. S. Congress Against War, and in the American League Against War and Fascism that was set up there. The National Executive Committee of the Socialist Party voted to join this united front. Eleven of their nominees were added to the Arrangement Committee; their first act was to propose to exclude from the Congress the revolutionary unions of the T. U. U. L., a proposal which was, of course, refused. Their second act was to demonstratively withdraw

* In January, 1935, this had increased to approximately five million.
** At the hearings of the Labor Committee of United States Congress in February, the S. P. and the unemployed organizations led by its members and by the Musteites, finally endorsed the Workers' Bill.

from the Congress Committee in an attempt to disrupt the Congress before it was held. Surely the workers will not gain unity through following such leadership.

Some of the "left" socialist leaders remained with the Congress, and the League for a time, such as J. B. Matthews and Mary Fox. It is interesting to re-read today, the words of J. B. Matthews, spoken only a few months ago. He said: "This Congress proves beyond any dispute that the United Front of working class elements, of pacifists, of middle-class war-resisters, is a possibility . . . This program presented to you is the basis for continuing this Union—for strengthening it step by step. We must stand together. We dare not fail."

But the Socialist Party leaders put heavy pressure on them and threatened them with expulsion (and incidentally the loss of their jobs). Then these valiant "left" leaders quickly found an excuse to withdraw and make another attempt to disrupt the united front against war and fascism. They abandoned this program to which they had already pledged themselves. Already their names are signed to a new program issued by S. P. and liberal leaders which sees the war danger in the movements of the Red Army in Siberia.

In this latest effort to break up the united front, the Socialists have found their most energetic helpers in Reverend Muste, Mr. Cannon, and Mr. Lovestone, who have attacked us with a bitterness of vituperation that is surely the envy of Ralph Easley and Matthew Woll. The renegades furnish most of the ideas for the struggle against Communism. This is especially true of the counter-revolutionary Trotsky and his agents. They lead the shouts for smashing the Communist Party. All this is done in the name of "unity." Each and all proclaim that they are the unifiers, and that the Communists are the disrupters.

From the beginning of this movement, the Communist Party safeguarded itself against all the lying accusations of its enemies by having a large majority of non-Communist individuals in every controlling committee of the movement. The Communists threw all their forces into support of the U. S. Congress Against War. We welcomed every person and every organization that came into the movement, and agreed to support its declared objectives. The political and organizational platform of the American League was adopted unanimously at a Congress of 2,616 delegates, from 35 states, embracing a variety of organizations, ranging from churches and peace societies, Socialist Party branches, religious organizations, workers' cultural clubs, fraternal societies, revolutionary trade unions, A. F. of L. unions, independent unions, farmers' organizations, Negro organizations, youth organizations, the Muste groups (including even the Lovestoneites), and 130 delegates from various branches of the Communist Party. Was there ever a more promising beginning of the establishment of a united front movement against war and fascism in the United

States? Since the Congress, a serious start has been made in spreading this united front throughout the country and among all strata of the population who were sincerely interested in fighting war and fascism. It is true there was some lagging in this work because we Communists mistakenly refrained from pressing ourselves forward, hoping that our initiative would be taken up by the non-Communists. That was a weakness and mistake on our part. It only encouraged every enemy of unity, every jackal of a renegade, to rally their forces for their latest attempt to disrupt the League. Again we have defeated the disrupters. The place of the deserting leaders is being taken by new recruits to this united front, non-Communists, whose influence reaches wider than that of the deserters. Into the front ranks must be drawn trade unionists, especially from the A. F. of L. We are calling upon all Communists and sympathizing organizations to boldly step forward in comradely co-operation with all other elements, to build the League in every locality to circulate its excellent monthly journal, *Fight,* and to prepare for the great second U. S. Congress Against War, which is being called for next October.*

We could recite a thousand local examples of the successful application of the united front tactic, initiated by the Communist Party. The Communists are the only organized political group in America that is always, day in and day out, consistently, earnestly and loyally striving to build up the united front of the workers and their allies in the fight for their immediate political and economic needs.

IMMEDIATE DEMANDS AND REVOLUTION

Our enemies accuse us that we are not really interested in winning these immediate demands. They say that we only use them as a means to an ulterior purpose, which has no relation to these demands, i.e., the revolution. They say we only use the united front in order to manipulate our associates as cats' paws to pull our own revolutionary chestnuts out of the fire.

For example, I have a recent issue of the *Haverhill* (Mass.) *Evening Gazette,* which contains a vicious editorial attack against the Communists. The occasion is a shoe workers' strike that has been going on for more than three weeks. The Haverhill shoe employers want to defeat the workers' demands by forcing them to submit to arbitration.

Some of the leaders, among them the Lovestoneite, I. Zimmerman, wanted to submit to the bosses' demands. The Communists showed the workers how defeat has come to all workers who have submitted their cause to so-called impartial boards. They called upon the workers to strike until the bosses grant them their very reasonable demands. The Communists have been the most active and devoted organizers

* See p. 198.—*Ed.*

and leaders of this fight. This enrages the *Haverhill Evening Gazette*.
Let me quote a few paragraphs from its editorial:

Today Haverhill's shoe industry with its scores of factories and thousands
of workers is in grave danger of destruction.

The industry cannot survive under the terms laid down by the strike
leadership. To yield to those terms is to submit to industrial death. To
compromise with this leadership is to make a fatal dicker with an evil force.

This leadership does not care what becomes of Haverhill. Let Haverhill
become an industrial leper. Let the homes of the Haverhill workers be lost
because Haverhill jobs have been destroyed. Let the hopes of Haverhill
workers be doomed because their means of livelihood have been taken from
them. What does this leadership care? It doesn't care.

This leadership's motive is political; its purpose, revolutionary. Haverhill
has been deliberately selected as the site for a demonstration of Communist
Power. The demonstration is now taking place. It is part of the grandiose
Communist scheme for an American revolution.

Then the *Gazette* draws the conclusion that the workers must "forget
for the moment negotiations to end the strike, forget compromises or
an agreement, forget everything but the urgent necessity of ridding
the Haverhill industry of this evil, dangerous, strike leadership."
This attack is a typical concrete example of the general charge
against the Communists that we are not really interested in winning
immediate demands, but only in an abstract "revolution." Keeping
this in mind, let us analyze this concrete charge a little more closely.
What is the substance of it? It is, that if the bosses grant the
demands of the workers (to recognize the union and give a small wage
increase) that "the industry cannot survive." The bosses cannot afford
to grant the workers what they demand. The leadership of the workers
is "evil" and "dangerous," because this leadership refuses to abandon
the demands of the workers, refuses to hand them over to a supposedly
impartial tribunal to decide. The complaint is that this leadership is
fighting, too uncompromisingly, to achieve now the immediate demands
of these workers. That's why the *Haverhill Gazette* proposes to drive
this leadership out of town and tries to rouse mob violence against it.
They are interested in preserving the profits of the bosses at the expense
of lower wages to workers. They don't give a rap about the hypothetical revolution that they talk about. That's why they speak very
kindly about other leaders and Mr. I. Zimmerman, who also claims to
be a Communist and for the revolution, but who is ready to abandon
the workers' demands in Haverhill at this moment. They will allow
Zimmerman to talk all he wants to about some future revolution as
long as he doesn't fight too hard for the immediate demands of the
Haverhill workers.
  This is the reality behind every concrete example of the charge

against the Communists that we sacrifice the immediate interests of the workers to the future revolution.

Is it true that there is a determining relationship between the fight for immediate demands and the revolutionary goal of the working class? Yes, there is such a determining relationship. But it is not that put forward by the *Haverhill Gazette* and all the other enemies of the Communist Party. The relationship is quite different. Let us take the case of a group of leaders heading a fight for immediate demands of a particular body of workers. They unitedly formulate these demands with the participation and approval of all the workers; they present demands to the boss; the boss says: "No, it is impossible for me to grant such demands without going out of business." The workers in other shops and industries are putting forward their demands. All the bosses get together and say: "It is impossible to grant such demands without sacrificing profits. Profits are the mainspring of the capitalist system. To sacrifice profits means to destroy capitalism. This means to destroy the jobs of the workers. Therefore, in the interests of the workers, we must fight for lower wages as the only way to preserve capitalism." Among the workers' leaders there takes place a division into two groups—one group says: "Of course, we're not trying to overthrow capitalism; we're not trying to put our boss out of business; we're not revolutionists; if our demands endanger the boss or the capitalist system, we're ready to compromise them or abandon them altogether, and even submit to worsening of conditions; we're willing to do whatever is necessary to save our boss and the capitalist system." The other group says: "The workers' demands are just and necessary; they must be granted; the productive forces of this industry and the entire country are sufficient to provide this and many times more; the capitalist is only anxious to protect his own profits; he can easily afford to pay; but even if he can't, then so much the worse for him and his system. We understand that the workers sooner or later must do away with capitalism and establish a Socialist system. If our fight for higher wages, now, hastens the coming of socialism, hastens the coming of the working class revolution, then so much the better. We will fight all the harder for higher wages."

This gives an example of the true relation between immediate demands and revolutionary aims. The A. F. of L. leaders and many Socialist Party leaders set as their guiding rule to do everything to avoid revolution, to save capitalism; that is why they join Roosevelt in putting across the New Deal and the N. R. A., that's why they say "now is not the time to strike"; that's why if the workers strike in spite of them, they try to break the strike and send the workers back without gaining their demands, to tie up the workers' organizations in arbitration courts, etc. That is also why those who are revolutionists, those who are preparing the working class to establish socialism, to overthrow capitalism, they are the only ones who can at all times and in all places be depended upon to fight to the last ounce of energy for the winning of the immediate demands of the workers, without consideration of what result this has in decreasing the profits of the bosses. We revolutionists know that in America we have productive capacity sufficient, if properly used, to give every man, woman and child, a comfortable and happy life. We're going to organize and fight for the realization of a constantly improving standard of living; we're going to resist with all our power the capitalist efforts to reduce the standard of living, no matter how much Roosevelt may tell us of the necessities of "economy" and "sacrifice." The workers have sacrificed too much already, and we're going to prepare the working class to stop sacrificing. We help them to understand that to realize a full and happy life, they will finally have to take power, overthrow the capitalists, and take possession of the industries themselves through their own Workers' Government.

Thus we see that it is only the revolutionists who will fight to the end for the immediate demands of the workers, and for better food, clothing and shelter for the toilers. Anyone who is against revolution or afraid of it, inevitably comes to the point where he betrays the workers' interests, surrenders them to the interest of capitalist profits.

The tactic of the United Front must be applied in all mass activities. In each case a special form suitable for the occasion must be found concretely. That means the whole Party must be trained to alertness against distortions of the united front and against deviations. These are of two general types: the right deviation which consists of hiding the face of the Party, sacrificing the main political line, emphasizing the formal aspects of the united front at the expense of the real struggle. The "left" deviation, which is opportunism covered with deft phrases, is characterized by contempt for the patient, systematic, daily work necessary to win the workers who are under reformist leadership; by rigid and mechanical approach to united front problems; by fear to plunge boldly into the broadest mass struggles.

In all of our election campaigns, we have the problem of giving them a united front character. The coming Congressional elections must everywhere be made a real united front drive, with the objective of electing at least a few Communist Congressmen from a few concentration points.

We must pay a good deal of attention to two important local united front efforts, namely, the Cleveland and Dearborn elections last year. In Cleveland, the comrades correctly set themselves the task of involving the mass movement of small homeowners in the Communist election campaign. But they made many serious errors in doing this. They encouraged or tolerated the tendency of the Homeowners' Federation to go into politics on its own hook and to transform itself into a political party. The Homeowners' Federation took the initiative in nominating aldermanic candidates, and only as an afterthought, were other working-class organizations drawn in, while the Communist Party, as such, was pushed entirely into the background. Let nobody understand our criticism of this as trying to protect narrow Party interests as against the interests of the Homeowners' Federation. No, we are insisting equally upon the interests of the Homeowners' Federation, when we demand that such an organization shall not be transformed into a political party. To attempt to make a political party out of such mass organizations is to seriously threaten their future work and growth, and turn them aside from their proper function. At the same time this has a liquidating effect upon the Communist Party. It does not consolidate the unity of the masses of workers, but rather threatens to break up that unity.

Similarly in the Dearborn election campaign: Dearborn is the city of the Ford Motor factories; it is a company town. There was a mass revolt against the Ford domination in the city government. We correctly decided to unite this revolt around a workers' ticket, participated in by the Communist Party and with Communists as the central candidates. But in practically carrying through this correct line, the comrades retreated before the "red scare," hid the face of the Party in this united front, evaded some of the most crucial political issues. Thus, our comrades contributed to the creation of such an atmosphere of timidity and evasion, that under sharp attacks from Ford's agents, some of the weaker elements on the workers' ticket fell into panic entirely, and the candidate for Mayor, at one point, signed a resignation from the struggle.

We must again emphasize that, while workers' tickets are permissible under certain special circumstances, and especially in company towns, this under no circumstances means the abandonment of the independent role of the Communist Party. To push the Communist Party into the background, to allow it to be forgotten, is fatal to the success of a particular campaign, as well as endangering our future development. The tendency to bring forward workers' tickets in large industrial cities as a substitute for the Communist Party is generally wrong; it is a tendency to surrender to Farmer-Laborism.

Recently, in South Dakota, our comrades seized the opportunity of a broad State conference of farmers and the Unemployed Council movement to launch a campaign of a leading Communist for Governor of that State. This was correct *under the circumstances,* even though the Communist Party, as such, had not yet named publicly its candidates. But there is a danger that the further development of this campaign in South Dakota may have a tendency to develop under the flag of non-partisanism. If this is permitted, the movement is in danger of sliding off into the old traditional path of Farmer-Laborism with disastrous results to the workers and farmers in South Dakota. To prevent this, the Communist Party there must come to the front most energetically. The candidate for Governor must make his campaign openly and frankly as the nominee not only of the broad united front, but also of the Communist Party. He must speak as a Communist. The Party must not dissolve its own activities into the broad movement and lose itself there. On the contrary, the Communist Party must be tremendously strengthened in the course of this campaign and must prove in practice its right to the title of leader of the exploited masses of South Dakota.

There are still some tendencies in our movement to look upon the united front as purely a matter of addressing letters to the top committees of various organizations and conducting negotiations with these committees. But this is not the essence of a united front at all. Letters and negotiations with top committees of reformist organizations have their place at certain moments: they can be used to dramatize issues before the broadest masses and arouse these masses to action and to a movement toward unity. But if such letters and negotiations become an end in themselves, if they are constantly repeated without any results, then they serve not to build the movement for unity, but on the contrary, to demoralize and dissipate it, to discredit the whole slogan of the united front.

The united front tactic plays a growingly important role in the trade union field and strike movements. This is especially true in the struggle against company unions, and in those industries where two or more trade unions are already being built among the workers. In every case, revolutionary forces must come forward as the practical fighters for uniting all workers against the company unions, for finding the forms to unify the struggles of the workers in the A. F. of L., T.U.U.L. and independent unions. An excellent example of correct effort in this direction was the proposal for united action submitted by the delegates of the Steel and Metal Workers' Industrial Union to the Conference of the Republic Steel Mill locals of the Amalgamated Association of Iron, Steel & Tin Workers held recently in Ohio. Another example of the correct united front tactics in the trade union struggles was the work in the Western Pennsylvania mine fields during the big strikes there, in which the National Miners' Union declared its support for the demand for the recognition of the United Mine Workers, and in which the S.M.W.I.U. successfully began the establishment of united action of the striking miners with the steel workers. Another example of the correct application of the united front was the Automobile Workers' Conference held last week in Detroit on the joint call of the Auto Workers' Union and the Mechanics Educational Society, participated in also by rank and file delegates from the A. F. of L. auto unions, with the slogan of joint struggle against company unions, and for the auto workers' demands. Many other examples could be brought forward and should be analyzed. Comrade Stachel in his special report on the trade union question is going to go more into detail in analyzing the whole of our trade union problems now.

In all united front activities, the Communists must always grant the right to all other groups, and reserve the right for themselves, of mutual criticism. It is permissible and correct to make specific agreements of non-criticism during the actual carrying through of joint actions agreed upon, within the scope of the specific agreement, so long as these agreements are loyally adhered to by all sides. But the Communists can never agree to be silent, to refrain from criticism, on any breaking of agreements for struggle, on any betrayal or desertion of the fight. Any such agreements would not be contributions to unity, but rather to disunity.

"LEFT" SOCIAL-FASCISM AND ITS ROLE

The relationship between immediate demands and revolution has become closer than ever with the deepening of the capitalist crisis. The capitalists are driving more and more to reduce the standards of living. The Socialist leaders and the A. F. of L. are more and more driven by their subordination to the Roosevelt program to openly betray the struggle of the workers for the means of living. Where formerly they had time and room to maneuver in and fool the workers, they now more and more have come out quickly and openly with their strike-breaking role. As a result, the masses are becoming quickly disillusioned. There is a real crisis among the social-fascists; their followers are turning away from them.

A little example of the speed of this development has been seen in the two taxi drivers' strikes in New York City. Two months ago the taxi workers went out demanding the recognition of their union and increased pay. When they first struck, who were their leaders? Mayor LaGuardia, himself, appeared as a sort of godfather to them; Socialist Judge Panken was their principal spokesman; liberal Socialist Morris Ernst was the arbitrator; the Socialist Party spoke of it patronizingly as "our" union. Quickly the scene changed. The arbitrators got to work. When the men hesitated to compromise their demands, La-Guardia quickly changed from the kindly godfather to the threatening policeman. The liberal Socialist councillors and arbitrators pressed the taxi men to accept the settlement dictated by LaGuardia; the men finally accepted under the impression that they had gotten part of their economic demands, plus the recognition of their union. The Communists told the taxi strikers they had been betrayed. The taxi strikers were still loyal to these "leaders" and they tore up the *Daily Worker* that told them the truth, and beat up the Communists. Disappointed though they were, they would have nothing to do with the "Communist disrupters" and "reds." But when they got back to work, they found that they had been not only cheated out of their supposed victories, but were completely denied the right of their own organization. The companies began installing company unions; the men threatened to strike against them; they returned to their old leaders for advice and were told not to make any more trouble, to submit to the N.R.A. code of $13.00 per week; that the company had a right to organize company unions if they wished. In desperation, the men went on strike again to enforce the recognition of their union. Already they had arrayed against them all their former friends; every newspaper in the city vilified them; LaGuardia threatened them; the police arrested them and beat them up; the Socialists washed their hands of them; the A. F. of L. threatened to come in and take over. sponsorship of the company union. Only the Communist Party, the revolutionary trade unions and the *Daily Worker* came to the assistance of the taxi strikers. Result: the same taxi drivers who a few weeks ago were tearing up the *Daily Worker,* and beating up Communists, today cheer the *Daily Worker,* send delegations to the Communist Party Convention, and are no longer afraid or ashamed that their union is being called a red union. In a few brief weeks the social-fascists lost their influence over them; these men, who in overwhelming majority a few weeks ago were actively antagonistic, became Communist sympathizers.

The same thing is happening on a larger and smaller scale everywhere. The class lines are tightening; the class struggle is sharpening; the masses can learn quicker now than ever before on which side the leaders stand—with the capitalists or with the workers. The social-fascist leaders are being exposed before the masses as capitalist agents.

In this crisis the social-fascist leadership finds it necessary to invent new means to keep the workers fooled and under their control. For this purpose, they are beginning, wherever the situation gets too hot for them, to establish a division of labor—one part of them becomes the "right wing," which carries through the dirty work of the direct sell-out; the other part becomes a "left-wing" which mildly deplores the necessity of submitting to the sell-out, and which consoles the workers with an ineffective opposition and a sugar-coating of radical and even revolutionary and Communist phrases. This left-reformism, left social-fascism, is springing up everywhere today, and is especially dangerous. One form of it is the self-styled "American Workers Party," headed by the Rev. Muste. Another is the Lovestone group, with its I. Zimmerman in the shoe industry and its S. Zimmerman in the needle trades. Another is the Trotzky group in the food industry. They are characterized by the multiplicity of their banners, their hatred of the Communists, their radical hot-air, and their practical service to the A. F. of L. and Socialist Party officialdom.

A classical example of this left social-fascism is given by the "Communist Oppositionist," S. Zimmerman in Local 22 of the International Ladies' Garment Workers' Union. Zimmerman's "Communist" revolutionary phrases have become invaluable instruments in the hands of the I.L.G.W.U. officials and the Socialist Party. The workers in Local 22 are becoming disillusioned with the officialdom. They can't be fooled any more by the old means. They are prepared to give a large vote for revolutionary policy. So the S. P. and A. F. of L. officials decide that here is an occasion to apply the good old American saying "if you can't lick 'em, join 'em." They find ready at hand in the person of S. Zimmerman their own "Communist" to lead Local 22, and safely preserve these workers under their control. They assure the workers: "Your choice is no longer between reformist and revolutionary leadership. Now you choose between two kinds of revolutionists—the practical, the realistic Zimmerman, or the impractical, utopian, disruptive Communists. You're not even choosing between non-Communists and Communists, because we're even prepared to give you a Communist to lead you." Thus in the recent elections in Local 22, the A. F. of L. officials, Socialist Party, the Socialist press, created a firm fighting united front in support of the "Communist" Zimmerman. Thus, these little groups of renegades, trading on the name of Communism, hire themselves out to the blackest reaction in the labor movement, and become "mass leaders" in the service of social-fascism.

The example of the Zimmermans gives the type of the whole tribe of left social-fascists that is being born out of the crisis of social-fascist leadership. They are the most dangerous enemies of the workers' struggles today. We can move forward only to the extent that we expose their true character, and thus drive them out of the workers' movement.

In this respect we must say that too often we still see remnants of a certain liberal, tolerant attitude towards the renegades. To some extent this is born out of the fact that we have such a new membership in our movement—because we are growing so rapidly. Many of our members are not familiar with the direct facts of the history and functions of these people who call themselves "Communists." Too many of our members still do not understand that Trotskyism and the Trotskyists are not a "branch" of the Communist movement but rather a police agency of the capitalist class.

There is also a real leftward movement among Socialist workers which tries, often confusedly, to give expression to a revolutionary policy. A symptom of such a movement is the platform recently issued by the Revolutionary Policy Committee in preparation for the S. P. Convention in June. Some of its proposals have been included for action in the official agenda adopted for the Convention. It must be said that the Revolutionary Policy Committee comes much closer to revolutionary formulations on central issues than does the Muste

"A.W.P."; and further that it is much less vicious in its attacks upon Communism than is Muste or the renegades. The composition of this "left-wing," however, gives little ground for expecting it to lead the real leftward development of the S. P. members toward the united front with the Communists and eventually toward unification. It is not homogeneous; many of its members are known for their vacillating, compromising character. In all probability this effort also will collapse into another contribution to that "left" social-fascism whose object is to disrupt and disperse the left-ward movement of the workers.

All Socialist Parties, in their division of labor, are producing not only "left" wings, but also open fascist groupings. Thus in Japan, the Socialist Party split with its general secretary going over with a section of the Socialist Party to "national socialism," a crude imitation of Hitler adapted to Japanese war policy. Thus in France, the "neo-socialists" have split from the Socialist Party, in order to pass over openly to a national chauvinist platform, open fascism. The American Socialist Party also has its open fascist grouping, which centers here in Ohio. Its spokesman is Joseph W. Sharts, state secretary of the S. P. Let me give you a few samples of his new fascist program for the S. P.:

Frank recognition of the futility of all socialist efforts so long as we ignore or oppose those elemental emotional forces implied in "Americanism," "nationalism," and "patriotism," and therefore the need of utilizing or at least neutralizing them by a shift of attitude and propaganda so as to enlist national pride and love of country.

The socialist appeal which relies on a vague internationalism and a mythical working-class instinct of solidarity is easily crushed whenever it meets the elemental emotional forces roused under the name of patriotism.

These great traditions cluster around the Stars and Stripes and make it worthy to be fought for, regardless of the capitalist connections in recent years.

Not by the pacifist but by the patriotic approach lies our path to power and freedom.

It would be difficult to improve on Mr. Sharts by quoting directly from Hitler.

PROGRESS IN THE BOLSHEVIZATION OF THE COMMUNIST PARTY

What is meant by Bolshevizing the Party?

It means to master all the lessons taught us by that first Communist Party, the most successful one, created and led to victory by Lenin, and now successfully building socialism under the leadership of Stalin. It means to become a party of the masses; to be a Party with its strongest roots among the decisive workers in the basic industries; it means to be a Party whose stronghold is in the shops, mines and factories, and especially in the biggest and most important ones; it means to be a Party that leads and organizes the struggles of all the oppressed people, brings them into firm alliance with the working class; it means to be a Party that answers every question of the struggle, that can solve every problem; it means to be a Party that never shrinks from difficulties, that never turns aside to find the easiest way; that learns how to overcome all deviations in its own ranks—fight on two fronts; it means to become a Party that knows how to take difficulties and dangers and transform them into advantages and victories.

Are we such a Party? Not yet. We have a strong ambition to become such a Party. We are making progress in that direction. But when we consider the extremely favorable circumstances under which we work, when millions are beginning to move, to organize, to fight, when only our program can solve their problems, then we must say that we are moving forward entirely too slowly. Our task is to win the majority of the working class to our program. We do not have unlimited time to accomplish this. Tempo, speed of development of our work, becomes the decisive factor in determining victory or defeat.

The Bolshevik method of work necessary in this period was concretely outlined for the Party in the Open Letter of the Extraordinary Party Conference last year. It called for concentration of our forces upon the most important tasks, upon the workers in the basic industries, upon the biggest factories. It set certain minimum, practical tasks to be accomplished within a certain period; it called for periodical re-examination, check-up and control on the execution of these tasks.

This 8th Convention of the Party must make such a check-up and control for the entire Party. We must review the work of our Party since the 7th Convention and especially since the Extraordinary Conference, and establish what we have succeeded in accomplishing. Where have we failed, and where are our weaknesses? Upon this basis we can then correctly set ourselves the control tasks for the next period. We must forever put behind us that time when we wrote resolutions and set ourselves tasks on paper, then took this paper, carefully locked it up in the drawers of a desk, forgot about it and proceeded to drift along as best we could according to the exigencies of the moment without plan, without direction, and then at the next conference write another resolution like the one we wrote before and proceed to forget it like we forget the other one. When we write a resolution, this is the most serious binding of ourselves to carry it out. If it is not carried out we must know why, and in the next resolution we write we must take all necessary measures to guarantee that the resolution will actually be put into execution.

In 1930, at the 7th Convention, our Party had just emerged from a long period of relative stagnation and even retrogression, resulting from protracted inner party factional struggles, and the domination of the opportunist policies of the Lovestone leadership. The 7th Convention consolidated the unification of the Party, confirmed the throwing off of the opportunists, and turned the Party resolutely towards the correct Bolshevik policy of mass struggles and mass organization. But the Party was still very weak in practice. It had only 7,545 dues-paying members; its factory nuclei were few and functioned very weakly. The revolutionary trade unions had no more than 25,000 members, and were poorly consolidated; revolutionary work in the A. F. of L. was at its lowest ebb; mass organizations around the Party, mostly language and cultural organizations, were not politically active and a very generous estimate of all mass organization membership could not possibly exceed 300,000.

Since that time important changes have taken place. Consider firstly only the dues-paying membership of the Party. If we take this by half yearly averages, we obtain the following very instructive figures:

1931—First half	8,339
1931—Second half	9,219
1932—First half	12,936
1932—Second half	14,474
1933—First half	16,814
1933—Second half	19,165
1934—Three months	24,500

From these figures it is clear that the unification of the Party and its correct general political line from the 7th Convention and during the period of the crisis, has resulted in a constant increase in membership from half year to half year. Today our Party is more than three times its size at the 7th Convention. But it is also clear that it is the past six months which show the most decisive upward turn. This corresponds with the period when the main body of the Party began seriously to improve its work, that is, since the Party studied and began to master the Open Letter.

This becomes even more clear when we study the figures of our shop nuclei. At the 7th Convention, we had a little more than a hundred shop nuclei. At the time of the Open Letter there was still only 140. Even taking into consideration that the intervening period had witnessed the closing down of innumerable factories, and the consequent destruction of many nuclei, still it is clear that we only little more than held our own. Since the Open Letter, however, due to our concentration and improved work, assisted, of course, by the general atmosphere of struggle that has swept the factories, we can now report 338 shop nuclei. The proportion of total membership in shop nuclei has risen from 4 to 9 per cent, and the proportion of employed members is 40 per cent.

What kind of shops are these in? Last year, 68 of them were in basic industries. This year, there are 154, with a proportionate increase in membership. The majority of these shop units are in small factories. A growing number are in the larger and more decisive factories. We have shop units functioning now in our concentration points in the steel industry, the big mills of Pittsburgh, Youngstown, and Calumet Valley areas. We have nuclei in the important auto shops as well as in many of the smaller shops; we have a growing number of mine nuclei. In the shops where these 338 shop nuclei operate, there are at work a total of over 350,000 workers, showing a general average of about 1,000 workers per shop.

In these enterprises where our shop nuclei work, there was one year ago very little trade union organization. The total membership of all categories in the shops of the 140 nuclei was a little more than 7,000. Today in the 338 shops where our nuclei operate, there are over 10,000 members of the revolutionary unions, more than 5,000 members in independent unions, and over 21,000 members of the A. F. of L. These figures represent a very important increase, comprising more than 10 per cent of all the workers in these enterprises. That the Communists have had a great deal to do with this growth in trade union organization is demonstrated by the relatively high proportion of revolutionary and independent unions. The most serious weakness that these figures disclose is that as yet only a little more than 10 per cent of the workers have been brought into the unions.

It is clear that precisely at this point we have the key problem to the future growth of our Party and of the revolutionary trade union movement. The problem of our shop nuclei is to win the leadership of the overwhelming majority of these 350,000 workers, bring the best fighters, the most capable forces, into the Communist Party and the whole mass of workers into the trade unions. Is it utopian to set such a task for ourselves? No, it is not. Weak as our shop work has been, we already have examples showing that it can be done, and done quickly.

Let us take, for example, the case of a certain metal shop, the experiences of which I have personally examined. This shop is of medium size in the lighter section of industry. It employs in this period about 500 workers. A year ago we had a stagnant nucleus of three members. Following the Open Letter, the Party committeee in the section where this factory is located, assigned some politically capable comrades to work with and help the nucleus. In connection with the Metal Workers Union, the shop was drawn into a strike movement, together with many other small metal shops. The demands of the strikers were won, and the employers signed a contract with the union. The nucleus was still functioning very weakly. It had worked only as a fraction of the union, without showing the Party face. Consequently, it recruited very slowly. The workers in the shops didn't know the Party existed there. The union leaders were afraid that if the Party nucleus took any initiative it might disrupt the mass organization of the union in the shop. As a result of this political weakness, the shop committee of the union elected as its chairman one of the most reactionary elements in the shop, a very conscious supporter of the Socialist Party leadership, and an enemy of the union. The opinion prevailed that this was the way to secure full unity of the shop, but this shop chairman sabotaged the work of the union. The shop nucleus meeting every week with the personal participation of representatives of the section, and discussing all the problems of the shop and the union, gradually became conscious of these weaknesses and dangers. They saw the boss becoming very arrogant again and threatening to refuse to renew his contract with the union, or to consider the new demands the workers were formulating. They saw a spirit of passivity and defeatism spreading among the workers in the shop. The nucleus decided that it must become active and make its presence known in the entire shop. Its first move was to secure the defeat and removal of the sabotaging shop chairman. A shop paper began to appear regularly. It is interesting to note that our trade union leaders resisted the developing initiative of the shop nucleus. They were afraid of it; they even developed the theory that the shop nucleus was merely a fraction of the union, and subject to the directives of the leading fraction of the union as a whole. But the nucleus correctly and successfully overcame this resistance. At the crucial moment when it seemed that the union in the shop was about to be wiped out, the nucleus distributed throughout the shop to every worker a leaflet in which, speaking as a unit of the Communist Party, it pointed out the dangers to the workers, called upon them to rally their forces to the union and to win their demands. Within a day the atmosphere in the shop was entirely transformed; defeatism and demoralization vanished. The Communist who had been discharged for distributing the leaflets in the shop was quickly reinstated in his job by the action of the entire body of workers, who threatened immediate strike if this demand was not complied with. The employer quickly changed his tone, and instead of tearing up the union contract, he negotiated a new one, embodying additional gains for the workers. The union meeting in the factory thereupon invited an official speaker from the Communist Party to come and speak at their meeting; greeted the speaker with an ovation. It is the common talk of the shop that "our union is strong because we have an active, strong Communist Party nucleus among us." The Party and Y.C.L. membership in this shop now comprises 14 per cent of the whole body of workers. The shop is 100 per cent unionized in the revolutionary union. These workers are raw and inexperienced, the type usually known as "backward." The leaders of the shop nucleus and the shop committee of the union is now composed of new, active, capable forces in command of the situation, displaying strong initiative; the individuals who make up this leadership were three months ago looked upon as "backward workers," who rarely raised their voices in meetings.

Imagine the tremendous steps forward our Party would make if the experience of this shop was repeated in just half of our existing shop nuclei! Imagine how quickly we could develop a mighty mass Party when we get a few hundred strongholds like this throughout the country, especially in the basic industries! What a transformation would take place in the Chicago District! If the Packinghouse and Steel nuclei would repeat this experience, if the comrades had not forgotten their own good resolutions! What a new District Pittsburgh would become if a similar work were done in the Jones and Laughlin steel mill!

The greatest weakness of our shop nuclei is that they are not so much secret from the bosses as they are from the workers in their shops. They are afraid to speak to the workers in the name of the Party. They rarely issue leaflets. Less than 15 per cent of our shop nuclei issue a shop paper of any kind. We even find theories popping up—for example, in Cleveland and in some sections of New York—that Party shop papers are really a danger and a hindrance to penetrating the factories, that we must work by stages and have first only union papers; then later on, carefully begin to introduce Party shop papers. This opportunistic hiding the face of the Party in the shops is the most serious right danger.

Our street nuclei are also beginning in some cases to learn how to do mass work on their own account. We now have 1,482 street nuclei. What a tremendous power even these can become when they learn Bolshevik methods of work. That they are not such a power today is only because they still look upon themselves merely as dues-collecting agencies, as agencies to distribute leaflets handed down to them from above; at best, as political discussion clubs of a general character and a timid distributor of the *Daily Worker*. That is the picture of the average nucleus. But in these cases where a street nucleus begins to understand its independent political function as being *the Party* in its own neighborhood, as being the organizer and leader of the masses in that neighborhood, when it begins to set itself the task of winning the majority of the workers in its neighborhood, and to take the initiative in accomplishing this task, the results are simply tremendous. Street nuclei are finding out that very often with only a little attention they can, themselves, give birth immediately to important shop nuclei out of their own membership. They are finding that individual connection with particular shops can quickly be built up into a shop nucleus, and especially they are beginning to find the proper activity for a street nucleus, as such, rooting the Party among the masses in the neighborhood, building neighborhood strongholds for the Communist Party.

Above all, the street nuclei must become serious organizers and leaders of the unemployed. From 60 to 70 per cent of our members are themselves unemployed, but relatively few of them are active in building block committees and Unemployment Councils winning strongholds for the Party among the 16,000,000 unemployed. We must declare that just as it is the duty of every employed Communist to be a leader in his trade unions, so also is it the duty of an unemployed Communist to become the leader of 10 or 100 other unemployed workers in block committees and neighborhood councils.

Let me cite only one good example of a street nucleus which is beginning to get itself on its own feet, politically. This nucleus has no great achievements yet in factory work. A year ago it was a rather discouraged group of good, loyal comrades who didn't exactly know what to do. They began to apply the Open Letter to their neighborhood problem. They opened a neighborhood Workers' Club and kept it open at all hours, especially for the young people in the neighborhood. They introduced organization of a primitive sort among these people, giving them activities, games, music, etc. In another part of the neighborhood, with a considerable Negro population, they began to build a branch of the L. S. N. R., with white and Negro members. Some members of the nucleus took the initiative in launching a branch of the C. W. A. Workers' Union. The nucleus undertook action in support of strikes that affected the neighborhood, and rallied some support for picket lines. As a result of these activities, the unit began to grow, more than doubling its membership. It has drawn into the Party several excellent new Negro workers. At its last meeting, it spent a couple of hours discussing the most difficult problems that have arisen with the mass influx of raw young American workers from the streets into the neighborhood club. Large groups of such youngsters that had for months been avoiding the club as "disreputable red" headquarters, had suddenly changed their attitude, and presented themselves for membership in the club, and were making all sorts of demands upon the leadership for organization and activities. The life of this unit is now rich and intense with the problems of the daily life of the neighborhood. It has become a mass influence among thousands of people.

An interesting sidelight on our methods of work is given by an experience of this unit in conducting its neighborhood club. In order to raise the political level of the club life, they have been inviting speakers from various mass organizations and the Party from other parts of the city. They report almost invariably these speakers are absolutely unintelligible for the neighborhood crowd that attends this club. The speakers never find any point of contact with their audience. They talk over their heads, use long phrases which may have been very good in a thesis, but of which these neighborhood workers haven't the slightest understanding. As a result, the audiences grow restless; the young people get boisterous, and even contemptuous of these political spouters. This phase of politicalization has been a dismal failure, as it was bound to be with such an approach. Here is a lesson for the entire Party, in its work of mass agitation and propaganda, of political education of the new raw masses that are coming to us. It is the virtue of parrots and of,phonographs that they mechanically repeat the phrases given to them. But that is no virtue for Communist speakers. We must completely overhaul our methods of mass education; we must absolutely put a stop to this business of our Party speakers copying parrots and phonographs, putting forth the Party program in such unintelligible terms that it is just so much Greek to the audience and doesn't touch their lives in any way or arouse a spark of interest.

The next central point in Party building after the shop and street nuclei is the Party Section Committee, Section bureau. This is the real cadre of the Party's mass leadership. To the extent that this is broadened and strengthened, to the degree that it becomes the decisive and controlling force in our daily work, to that degree, the Party will become a mass Party. That means that our sections must be small enough for the committee to actually know the problems, find the solutions, and give direct leadership in carrying through the work. A Section Committee must be the general staff of the revolution in its territory. It must know every house, street, and factory. It must know the daily problems of life of its population. It must know all our enemies and learn how to defeat them. It must turn its section into a Communist stronghold. That means a larger number of sections, more careful selection of leadership, and a better quality of leadership to the Sections from the Districts.

We have made progress in development of Sections of our Party, but not nearly enough. Where in 1930 there were 87 Party Sections, there are today 187. The geographical extension of the Party organization is shown in the fact that these Sections include functioning Party committees in 463 cities. The works of these Section Committees have improved, but we must place before the leadership of the Party today as a decisive question for our future progress, much more decisive improvement of the quality of our Section leadership.

A most serious problem of Party growth is the fluctuation in membership. Since 1930, starting with a membership of 7,545, we had recruited up until February, 1934, 49,050 new members. If we had retained all old and new members, we would have had in February, 56,595 members. Instead of this, we have dues-payment of only about 25,000. Two out of every three recruited members have not been retained in the Party. Fluctuation is being reduced, but is still high. It is no explanation for us to cite the fact that organization membership is in America traditionally unstable and fluctuating. It is precisely the task of Bolsheviks to be different from everybody else. It is no explanation for us to cite the unsatisfactory character of this recruiting, which was largely from the unemployed, from open-air mass meetings, etc., and not the basic building of the Party through struggles and in the midst of struggles in the factories, in stable neighborhood organizations, in the mass organizations, trade unions, etc. It is precisely the task of Bolsheviks to improve the quality of recruiting itself, so that Party recruits are permanently assimilated into the life of the organization. The proper use of the new forces drawn to us, their activization and education in Bolshevism, is our basic task. This is the creation of the main instrument for building a socialist society in America. Every weakness, and especially such weakness as exhibited in this still high degree of fluctuation, signalizes a danger to the successful building of the revolutionary movement in America. The whole Party must be roused to a consciousness of this problem. All the forces of the Party must be concentrated upon the task of holding and consolidating every new recruit.

On Using Our Strongest Weapon, the "Daily Worker"

The Open Letter set a main task for the Party in improving and popularizing the *Daily Worker* and transforming it into a real mass newspaper. This problem has two distinct sides, which are, however, very closely interrelated. These are the editorial improvements of the *Daily Worker* contents and the creation of a mass circulation of the paper. In the first respect we have made a decisive step forward. Since last August the contents of the *Daily Worker* have been enlarged, enriched and improved in every respect. The paper has become of interest to its readers every day, and is more and more showing what an indispensable weapon it is in the building of a mass Communist Party, as well as for the conduct of the everyday struggles. It is still far from the ideal Bolshevik newspaper; the editorials are as yet weak, not simple and clear enough; it is not yet sufficiently decisive in its role as political educator of the masses; it is not yet sufficiently bound up with the daily life of the masses in the decisive districts and factories. We can say it has made important steps in the right direction.

Unfortunately we cannot say the same about the *Daily Worker* circulation. With regard to circulation the situation is really alarming. The number of copies printed daily (not taking into consideration the large special editions and the special Saturday circulation) still remains considerably below the level of 1931. True there has been a certain improvement even here, so far as payment to the office of the *Daily Worker* for this circulation. The amount of money received by the *Daily Worker* for its papers has slightly increased above 1931. It is also true that there has been an improvement in circulation from the low point of a year ago by about 50 per cent. But this has been almost entirely the product of the spontaneous response to the improved contents of the paper and only in a small degree the planned, conscious, systematic activity of our Party. Shall we wait until it costs us our head to be caught with a copy of the *Daily Worker* before we realize its inestimable value? We are only playing around with the *Daily Worker*, until we have given it a minimum circulation of 100,000 copies a day. We already have grouped around our Party, under its influence, far more than that number of workers who need a Communist newspaper and are not served by our language newspapers. To set the goal of 100,000 circulation is merely to reach with the *Daily Worker* those workers with whom we are already in contact. Until this goal is reached we must declare the circulation of the *Daily Worker* is the weakest sector in our battlefront.

CHECK-UP ON OUR CONTROL TASKS

The Open Letter set us the task of decisively strengthening our work in the A. F. of L. and other reformist trade unions. We can register some serious beginnings of improvement in this field. I have already spoken of the broad scope of the movement for the Workers' Unemployment Insurance Bill inside the A. F. of L. We can record that the work of the revolutionary oppositions under Communist direction is now the decisive leadership in approximately 150 local unions of the A. F. of L. with a membership of from 50,000 to 60,000. This opposition work is improving in the most important industries such as mining and steel. In addition to those local unions in which the revolutionary opposition has the support of the majority of the workers, there are serious minorities in a larger and growing number of unions. The weakest field in this respect remains the railroad industry. Here we cannot yet say that the Party has taken up the task with full seriousness, nor even made a considerable beginning. Throughout the work in the A. F. of L., the characteristic weakness remains the formal character of the opposition work, its tendency to remain content with participation in union elections and formal debates, the legalism of the work, its failure to orientate itself to the shops and establish its organizational base there, and its weakness in developing independent leadership of the daily struggles.

The most decisive advance in the trade union field in the past year has been the emergence of the revolutionary trade unions as real mass organizations, directly leading the struggle of 20 per cent of all the strikers in this period, and winning a far higher proportion of the victories won by the strike movement. Especially important has been the advances in steel, agriculture, marine, as well as the serious advances in lighter industries, such as, shoe, needle, furniture, etc. Over 100,000 new recruits, offset by fluctuation of about 15,000 gives us at present about 125,000 members in the revolutionary unions. The increased stability of these organizations is due to the fact that they were built in struggle, that they are mastering the art of trade union democracy, are developing their own responsible trade union functionaries and exhibit a growing and active inner life.

The Unemployment Council movement was only in its first beginnings in 1930. Four years of rich experience in local, state and national struggles and actions, the high points of which were the great March 6, 1930, Unemployment Day Demonstrations, the National Hunger Marches in 1931 and 1932, and the recent National Unemployment Congress in Washington in February, 1934, have crystallized real mass organizations on a nation-wide scale. In the Washington Conference, which brought together the Unemployment Councils, trade unions and all forms of mass organizations that support the struggle for the Workers Unemployment Insurance Bill, there was organized representation of about 500,000 workers. In the Unemployment Councils, C.W.A. Unions, Relief Workers Unions, etc., there is comparatively stable organization of from 150,000 to 200,000. In spite of the fact, however, that the Unemployment Council movement under our leadership is the predominant organizational expression of the unemployed on a national scale, we must say in many localities it exhibits the most serious weaknesses. These weaknesses are both political and organizational. Especially we have not fully involved the trade unions in unemployed work. The Party has answered in principle all the problems and found the solutions to these weaknesses, but due to insufficient, direct political and organizational leadership by the Party, from top to bottom, units, sections and districts, and the weak functioning of the Party fractions, the full benefit of our experience has not been carried to the movement as a whole. The result is a big lag behind the possibilities on a national scale, with the most dangerous weaknesses in the majority of localities. As a result, we see in many places new organizations of unemployed, in which the "left" social-fascists and renegade elements live off the capital of our weaknesses and neglect. The movement under our leadership is the only broad, unifying force, and the only section of the unemployed with a clear and consistent program. It has a growing cadre of the best leaders of the unemployed movement. If we will give it the proper guidance, with persistent, systematic support, it can in the coming year organize millions instead of the present hundred thousands.

Since the 7th Convention, we have made another important addition to the list of mass revolutionary organizations. This is the mutual benefit society, International Workers Order. Since the Open Letter, the I.W.O., through its membership campaign, has multiplied itself, and now contains about 45,000 members. Even more important, it has built strongholds among the workers in the basic industries and has extended beyond its foreign language sections by recruiting native-born American and Negro workers. The I.W.O. has before itself the problem of how to consolidate and further extend its mass membership, without lowering its previous high standard of revolutionary activity, of political education of its members, especially through involving them more directly in the class struggle.

Surveying the whole field of language mass organizations (including the I.W.O.), we find in 20 language groups that these mass organizations have grown from about 50,000 in 1930 to over 133,000 at the present time. Besides these organizations led by Communists, large gains have been made in building revolutionary opposition movements inside the reformist language organizations, on which it is difficult to give reliable statistics. The Party's foreign-language newspaper circulation has increased from 110,000 in 1930 to 131,000 in 1934. Most of this increased circulation has come within the past year. It is clear that the language press is by no means keeping up with the extension of the language organizations. We must set for our language bureaus and language newspapers the task of raising the political standard of their work, to draw their membership much more intimately into the main stream of the American class struggle, to activize it, to bring forward new leading cadres, and to speed the process of a Bolshevik Americanization—that is, the welding of a united proletarian mass movement that transcends all language and national barriers.

Especially important for stabilizing the lower Party organs and mass organizations has been the program for Bolshevizing our financial methods and accounting. A special sub-report will be made on this question. It is not a technical question. It is of first class political importance. Bolshevik planning, budgeting and a strict responsibility are being instituted. This must become the universal rule. There must be no loosening up on this question.

Scores of smaller mass organizations have arisen in the past year, each serving some special need, and each contributing to the general strengthening of the revolutionary movement. We have no time to review them all here, important though many of them are. Special mention must be made of the International Labor Defense, which has won many serious political victories in this period, chief among them the conduct of the Scottsboro case. The I. L. D., however, lags seriously behind in organizational consolidation and in the systematic development of its whole broad field of activities. Most serious political guidance must be given by the Party to the work of the Communist fractions in the I. L. D. to overcome these weaknesses. The Communists who participate in the broad non-Party organization of the Friends of the Soviet Union, have done good work here. Only a handful of Communists are in this organization, but they have rallied around it the most varied circle of sympathizers, individuals and organizations which was demonstrated in an excellent mass convention held recently in New York City. The many other organizations, which we will not go into in detail; one and all can find the road to strengthen themselves, to improve their work, by studying the methods of our Party in the larger fields of mass work, by mastering the art of Bolshevik self-criticism, and detailed study of their problems. Special sub-reports will deal with the problem of training new cadres and the related question of our growing system of Party schools. We have advances to record in dealing with these questions in a planned way, as special problems. But again we must say, this is not characteristic for the entire Party. Planned training and promotion of new cadres is the essence of Bolshevik leadership.

If we make a conservative estimate of the total membership of mass organizations around the Party, and under its political influence, allowing for possible duplications of membership, we will see that we have approximately 500,000 individual supporters in these organizations. Compared with the estimated 300,000 at the time of our 7th Convention, this is not quite a doubling of our organized supporters. The quality of this support we must say, however, is on a far higher level; it is more conscious, more active, more consolidated, and has been tested in the fires of four years of struggle against difficulties, against the sharpening attacks of our enemies. The largest part of this gain has come in the past year as the result of serious efforts to carry out the line of the Open Letter, and to execute the control tasks set by the Extraordinary Party Conference.

We have been able to make these advances because we have begun to learn how to apply Bolshevik self-criticism. We have learned to face our weaknesses and mistakes, boldly and openly.

On Learning the Art of Self-Criticism

We have learned to use the powerful corrective influence of collective self-criticism. Our enemies gleefully exhibit our self-criticism as the sign of a dying movement. We can afford to let them have what satisfaction they get out of this, when we know that it is precisely through self-criticism that we have begun seriously to overcome these weaknesses. We are beginning to master, according to our own weak abilities, the art of self-criticism, so ably taught to the Communist Party of the Soviet Union by Comrade Stalin. We can still, with great profit, read again and again the reports of Comrade Stalin to the Congresses and Conferences of the C. P. S. U. As one such contribution to our 8th Convention, I want to read a few pages from the report of Comrade Stalin to the 15th Party Congress in 1927, almost every word of which has a direct lesson for us in our work. Comrade Stalin said:

Let us take, for instance, the matter of guidance of economic and other organizations on the part of the Party organizations. Is everything satisfactory in this respect? No, it is not. Often questions are decided, not only in the locals, but also in the center, so to speak, *en famille,* the family circle. Ivan Ivanovitch, a member of the leading group of some organization, made, let us say, a big mistake and made a mess of things. But Ivan Federovitch does not want to criticize him, show up his mistakes and correct him. He does not want to, because he is not disposed to "make enemies." A mistake was made, things went wrong, but what of it, who does not make mistakes? Today I will show up Ivan Ivanovitch, tomorrow he will do the same to me. Let Ivan Ivanovitch, therefore, not be molested, because where is the guarantee that I will not make a mistake in the future? Thus everything remains spick and span. There is peace and good will among men. Leaving the mistake uncorrected harms our great cause, but that is nothing! As long as we can get out of the mess somehow. Such, comrades, is the usual attitude of some of our responsible people. But what does that mean? If we, Bolsheviks, who criticize the whole world, who, in the words of Marx, storm the heavens, if we refrain from self-criticism for the sake of the peace of some comrades, is it not clear that nothing but ruin awaits our great cause and that nothing good can be expected? Marx said that the proletarian revolution differs, by the way, from other revolutions in the fact that it criticizes itself and that in criticizing itself it becomes consolidated. This is a very important point Marx made. If we, the representatives of the proletarian revolution, shut our eyes to our shortcomings, settle questions around a family table, keeping mutually silent concerning our mistakes, and drive our ulcers into our Party organism, who will correct these mistakes and shortcomings? Is it not clear that we cease to be proletarian revolutionaries, and that we shall surely meet with shipwreck if we do not exterminate from our midst this philistinism, this domestic spirit in the solution of important questions of our construction? Is it not clear that by refraining from honest and straight-forward self-criticism, refraining from an honest and straight making good of mistakes, we block our road to progress, betterment of our cause, and new success for our cause? The process of our development is neither smooth nor general. No, comrades, we have classes, there are antagonisms within the country, we have a past, we have a present and a future, there are contradictions between them, and we cannot progress smoothly, tossed by the waves of life. Our progress proceeds in the form of struggle, in the form of developing contradictions, in the form of overcoming these contradictions. As long as there are classes we shall never be able to have a situation when we shall be able to say, "Thank goodness, everything is all right." This will never be, comrades. There will always be something dying out. But that which dies does not want to die; it fights for its existence, it defends its dying cause. There is always something new coming into life. But that which is being born is not born quietly, but whimpers and screams, fighting for its right to live. Struggle between the old and the new, between the moribund and that which is being born—such is the basis of our development. Without pointing out and exposing openly and honestly, as Bolsheviks should do, the shortcomings and mistakes in our work, we block our road to progress. But we do want to go forward. And just because we go forward, we must make one of our foremost tasks an honest and revolutionary self-criticism. Without this there is no progress.

The task of our Party today, the tasks of this Convention, have been clearly and systematically set forth in the documents before us for adoption, especially the Theses and Decisions of the 13th Plenum of the Executive Committee of the Communist International, and the Draft Resolution prepared for this Convention by the Central Committee. My report has been for the purpose of further elaborating these fundamental directives and discussing some of our central problems concretely in the light of these directives. All these tasks set forth in the documents before us are particular parts of the one general task to rouse and organize the workers and oppressed masses to resistance against the capitalist program of hunger, fascism and imperialist war. They are parts of the one task of winning the majority of the toiling masses for the revolutionary struggle for their immediate political and economic needs as the first steps along the road to proletarian revolution, to the overthrow of capitalist rule, the establishment of a revolutionary workers' government, a Soviet government, and the building of a socialist society in the United States.

It is the source of our greatest strength that in our work in the U. S. A., we are not isolated from our brothers in the rest of the world. We are organizationally united in one World Party with all that is most fearless, devoted, honest and energetic in the working class of every capitalist country, as well as of the toiling masses struggling for their liberation throughout the world. We draw additional strength and inspiration from the magnificent achievements of our brother Communist Party in China, which stands at the head of the powerful and growing Chinese Soviet Republic. We are proud and inspired by our unity in one Party with such fighters as George Dimitroff and his comrades, who, single handed, met and defeated the Nazi murder bands in the courts of Leipzig. It is our strength that we are of the same Party with Ernst Thaelmann, and the thousands of heroic fighters in the German Communist Party, who, through prison cells and concentration camps, defying the Nazi headsmen, maintain and carry on every day struggle for the overthrow of Hitler. We take special pride in the achievements of our brother Communist Party in Cuba, which roused and led the mass upheaval that overthrew the bloody Machado, and which is now gathering the forces of the Cuban masses to drive out Machado's successors and establish a Soviet Republic of Cuba. We are stronger in the knowledge that the Communist Party of the Philippine Islands stands shoulder to shoulder with us in the joint struggle to overthrow American imperialism. Our work in the United States gains additional power from the fact that, reaching across the border, both north and south, we grasp the hands of our brother Communist Parties of Canada and Mexico. Throughout Latin-America, our brother Parties are challenging us to socialist competition as to who can strike hardest and quickest against the imperialists and their agents.

When we contemplate the tasks of struggle against imperialist war, for the defeat of our own imperialism, our muscles are further steeled by the knowledge that our brother Communist Party of Japan is blazing the way for us by their heroic struggle for the overthrow of Japanese imperialism in the midst of war. Above all, do we arm ourselves with the political weapons forged by the victorious Communist Party of the Soviet Union, with the mighty sword of Marxism-Leninism, and are strengthened and inspired by the victories of socialist construction won under its Bolshevik leadership, headed by Stalin. Our World Communist Party, the Communist International, provides us the guarantee not only of our victory in America, but of the victory of the proletariat throughout the world. (*Prolonged applause.*)

SUMMARY

We have come to the end of the discussion of our Eighth Convention. In the main, these discussions have revealed a unanimity of political line in every essential problem before the Party such as our Party has never known before.

There are not many political questions to clear up in the summary. A few points that have been the subject of controversy must be dealt with. I take in the first place the questions that stand between us and Comrade Zack. I will not attempt to go into a catalogue of the deviations of Comrade Zack. That would take entirely too much time. I will take just three points on which Comrade Zack has not only been in the past resisting the line of our Party, but on which Comrade Zack still stands stubbornly defending his errors.

The question of work within the A. F. of L.: Comrade Zack declared that he is in complete agreement with the decisions of this Convention regarding the work in the A. F. of L., and then in the next breath he proceeded to declare that when the leadership of the Party removed him from New York they made an unwise and unjust decision, that his line on this question in New York was 100% correct. We have to tell Comrade Zack that evidently he simply does not understand the decisions of this Convention. He does not understand the line of the Party if he thinks he was carrying it out in New York. I will just cite the kind of thing that made it necessary for him to be removed as a warning that he had to correct his line, a warning which Comrade Zack did not take seriously.

Here is a circular gotten out in New York by the independent union of Alteration Painters, addressed to the members of the Painters Union of the A. F· of L.——

[Interjection by Zack: "Not written by me."]

——which Comrade Zack endorsed and defended——

[Zack: "Not true."]

——and which represented the influence of Comrade Zack in the leadership of this work, and this leaflet, in the midst of a struggle and the attempts on our part to develop a left wing in the A. F. of L. union, calls upon these members: "Come into our union—the doors of our union are open to every honest rank and filer, exchange your Brotherhood book for a membership book of the Alteration Painters Union." This kind of line has absolutely nothing in common with the line of our Party. Such a line is bound to result in pulling the militants out of the A. F. of L. unions at a time when the mass of the workers remains in them. Such a line means leaving the workers in the A. F. of L. under the complete influence of the reformists, instead of building a strong rank-and-file opposition to challenge the leadership of the corrupt A. F. of L. officialdom.

On the question of shop papers: Comrade Zack stated in his speech that he admits the mistake on the question of shop papers and stands corrected, but he said this only as a preface for a bitter denunciation of the article in *The Communist*, which polemized against his mistake. According to Comrade Zack, such a polemic against his mistakes is impermissible slander which cannot be allowed against such a leading comrade as Comrade Zack. It is clear that Comrade Zack has not corrected himself on this point in which his first formulation on the question was an apparent admission of his mistake.

Finally, Comrade Zack has been of the opinion that the Central Committee and its Political Bureau is unsound on the whole question of trade-union work, that it is in constant danger of heading off into the swamp of opportunism and becoming objectively counter-revolutionary. Comrade Zack came into the open with this opinion in the article he wrote in the discussion, printed in *The Communist*. Comrade Zack's contribution to the pre-convention discussion was a warning to the Party not to trust its Central Committee. Comrade Zack has repeated his accusations in the Convention, and further specified who he believes to be the source of danger to our Party. He looks upon Comrade Stachel as the would-be liquidator of our trade-union work and the rest of the leadership of the Party as under the influence of, and conciliatory towards, the liquidation tendency of Comrade Stachel. What is at the bottom of these accusations? What, but an obstinate resistance to the stress upon work in the A. F. of L.—a resistance that constitutes a downright opportunist deviation from the Party line on work in the trade unions? What can we say about such slander as this, which is at the same moment coupled with a verbal declaration of support for our resolution? Comrades, we have to characterize this as double bookkeeping, and the attempt to establish a factional platform in the Party—a kind of thing which cannot be tolerated and which must be eliminated from our Party life. This is not Bolshevik political discussion, such positions as these Comrade Zack has taken on these questions. Comrade

Zack has not spoken one word directed towards further strengthening the solid, firm unity of our Party, without which nothing can be achieved. Comrade Zack has yet to learn some of the first fundamentals of Bolshevik work, namely, the ability to collectively hammer out~a line, to arrive at unanimous decisions, and to proceed to turn all forces unitedly and unanimously into carrying out these decisions. (*Applause.*)

And let me repeat: One of the most important tasks of the incoming Central Committee as well as of every District and Section Committee will be to organize a broad revolutionary opposition inside the A. F. of L. unions—an opposition that shall be able to win the workers from the influence of the reformists, to lead and organize the struggles of the workers against the will and over the heads of the bureaucracy. And we will not tolerate a single comrade in any leading position who is not prepared to carry through with all his energy this important work. We mean business and not such phrasemongering as indulged in by Comrade Zack.

I pass on to the questions raised around the case of Comrade Nowell: I don't want to review the full discussion of our Negro Commission and the excellent contributions that we had there. We have had a rich discussion—a discussion that I am certain has been a help to everybody in the Party from the first to the last delegate at this Convention, and it will further serve the entire Party membership and the whole struggle for Negro liberation. The crushing convincingness of our correct line even forces Comrade Nowell to come before this Convention with an admission of the ·true character of his political tendency and his activities as petty-bourgeois, nationalist and factional, and a confirmation of the correctness of the Central Committee. Whether this statement by Comrade Nowell represents a true enlightenment on his part or whether it represents an additional maneuver, time and the work and activities of Comrade Nowell will demonstrate. The Party will be alert to see just exactly what this statement means in life.

And Comrade Nowell should not imagine that we shall believe him so readily! Too long has he indulged in underhanded maneuvers against the Party. One more attempt in that direction, and the Party, in the interests of our revolutionary work, especially as concerns our work among the Negro masses, will clear him from its ranks. The Party has far too long been patient with such methods of disintegration.

I pass on to the question of the activities of Comrade Harfield in Buffalo. Comrade Harfield has submitted a statement confirming the correctness of all the charges that we made against him. What are we dealing with, however, in the case of Comrade Harfield? We are not dealing with political unclarity or political differences. In this case we have an almost "pure" specimen of unprincipled factionalism. It is deliberate, demoralizing, corrupting work in the Party, based not on any political objective or political opinion, but upon the desire to make Harfield an important person in our Party. For this purpose he was ready to use the position given him by the Party to create doubts among the new members, and even among leading comrades in the District, as to whether the Party really, in all seriousness, supported its own program on the Negro question.

It is clear that we cannot be quickly convinced of the sincerity of Comrade Harfield's statement, not so quickly as Comrade Harfield found it possible to write his statement. It is clear that the least measure possible in dealing with such slimy poison as Comrade Harfield dragged into our movement is to provide safeguards against such a comrade holding any responsible position in the movement until he has proven in practice his ability to do Bolshevik work in the ranks.

I pass on to one further question that arose in connection with Buffalo. That is the question of whether the fraction in the Steel & Metal Workers' Union in Buffalo should have proposed a united front with the A. F. of L. union in the Buffalo mills. Comrade Johnson in his speech continued to defend the mistaken position of the Buffalo comrades that such a proposal would have been wrong because the A. F. of L. union has only a small group of old hardened reactionaries whom it is not possible to win over. But we must point out to Comrade Johnson that his argument betrays a still somewhat shallow understanding of the whole purpose and meaning of our united front actions. Our united front proposals are not directed towards the purpose of winning over the hardened reactionaries and officialdom of the reformist organizations; our proposals are directed to the mass of the workers and not only the workers inside the reformist organizations, but also to the workers outside the reformist organizations, in order to prove to them that if there is division in the ranks of the workers this division is not caused by the revolutionists; this division is brought there by the reactionaries, the reformists. (*Applause.*) Further, this argument shows too narrow an approach to the question. It is entirely limited to the effects of this tactic upon the particular locality. But the comrades in every locality must always remember that they are only a part of the whole national situation. Even from the point of view of the membership of the A. F. of L. unions only, there are in the steel industry not only a handful of hardened reactionaries, but some twenty to thirty thousand workers in some of the most important sections of the steel industry. Precisely because in Buffalo we were stronger organizationally, as compared to the A. F. of L. unions, for that reason it would be all the more necessary for us in Buffalo, because of the national effect it would have, helping us in those districts where we are weak, to make precisely this united front proposal to the A. F. of L. unions. Comrade Johnson should study questions over more fundamentally, avoid jumping to conclusions always on the basis of surface indications of the problem, to dig deeper into these problems, to grasp their essence. With regard generally to the contribution of Comrade Johnson to our work and to the discussion of this Convention, we must state that Comrade Johnson exhibits quite strongly both the strong points and the weak points of our rising new cadres, white and Negro, and, first of all, along with serious mass work, a lack of mastery of that most important Bolshevik art, the art of self-criticism. Our comrades must all study self-criticism. We none of us are good on this activity yet. All of us are just beginning really to learn the full meaning of self-criticism. We are just beginning to learn that Bolshevik self-criticism has nothing to do with tearing down ourselves or one another, but on the contrary, is the only possible source of strength. Just think for a moment how Comrade Johnson himself could have multiplied tenfold his positive contribution, which is valuable but could have been ten times more valuable, if it had been presented to this Convention with just a little more fundamental examination of his own weaknesses and errors. This is all said in the spirit of giving the utmost possible help to Comrade Johnson and making much stronger his contribution to our Party.

Now I want to say one or two words about certain questions that were involved in the whole Negro discussion. During the discussion in the Negro Commission there was incidentally brought forward by one of the speakers the proposal of the slogan, something like (I don't remember the exact wording): "Lynch the lynchers." I think it is necessary for us to point out that the whole trend of such proposals as this is to lead us into very serious traps of the bourgeoisie. Our struggle against lynching, our struggle against capitalist terror of all kinds, can be answered only by our taking up, not the forms of struggle of the bourgeoisie which are strong only when used by our class enemies, but by finding our own special proletarian forms of fighting—always based upon mass action. (*Applause.*) Our slogan must be: Against the lynchers, the mass united front action of whites and Negroes! To break down the influence of the bourgeoisie, of the lynchers, the intensification of mass educational work among the backward white masses in the South, the broadest possible popularization of the Comintern program on the national question as it relates to the struggle for Negro liberation. And we must always carefully distinguish our slogans, speeches—everything that we say—from our enemies. When we go up against the bourgeois state in the struggle for power, we don't put forward the slogan of dictatorship against dictatorship, but we put forward the slogan, proletarian dictatorship against bourgeois dictatorship. We must always carefully distinguish the class content and form of our action as distinguished from the attacks against us by the bourgeoisie.

One other incidental question in the Negro discussion which has already been very ably answered by Comrade Ford, but which I want to mention for the purpose of emphasis—that is the idea which has been smuggled into our movement by our enemies that we have one policy for the American Negroes, United States Negroes, and another for the West Indian Negro. What is this? It is clear the essence of this is introducing nationalism and national division into our ranks. It is of precisely the same political content as all forms of chauvinism. After all, what is all chauvinism, including white chauvinism, national chauvinism, the bourgeois nationalism of an oppressed nation? All of them are merely forms of the political ideology of the bourgeoisie, of our class enemy. We can't possibly breathe politically except in struggle against it. Our Party would be suffering from a dry rot in its very heart if it could for one instant entertain the slightest concession to national division among the Negroes, as between American and West Indian. It is of the same sort of chauvinism as is exemplified in that rotten poison that is more and more being spread in the United States today—anti-Semitism. We must understand that today the bourgeoisie is systematically exploiting and cultivating and pushing into every nook, cranny and corner it can, every form of chauvinism, nationalism, national division among the workers. White chauvinism is the most sharp and dangerous form for us, but. exactly the same political poison is contained in anti-Semitism and in such ideas as the division between West Indian and American Negroes. We are the Party of internationalism, against all forms of chauvinism. (*Great applause.*) We must answer the imperialist splitters of the Negro ranks with the revolutionary political slogans: For the independence of the West Indies! Demand the withdrawal of the armed forces of British, French, Yankee, and other imperialist powers from the West Indies and other Caribbean countries! For the abrogation of all slave treaties! For a united fighting front of West Indian and American Negroes in the joint struggle against imperialism! For the liberation of the Negro peoples throughout the world!

I pass over to a brief restatement of the question of our international tasks. Our Party is an international Party, even in its composition. Our Party responds to internationalism very keenly. This is expedited by the fact that it is difficult for chauvinist tendencies to find growth in a Party which itself is composed of some 22 nationalities. But that does not mean that we are by nature good internationalists in the Bolshevik sense. That never comes naturally, by itself; that has to be consciously cultivated and developed before it can possibly reach the plane of Bolshevism. We have not left our internationalism completely for resolutions, speeches, etc. We have many examples of *action* of directly international character. We have examples, such as the strikes of American seamen in support of the striking Cuban sugar workers, refusing to unload the cargoes. We have the recent beginnings on our part, even though belated, of organizing material aid from our Party to the German Communist Party. In this respect, by the way, we must say that the initiative which was taken in New York, and intended as an example for the entire Party to organize a series of special great mass meetings and demonstrations for the specific purpose of raising as much money as possible for the German Communist Party, must be followed up much more energetically by the other districts. Further, we must say there is not yet sufficient keenness of our entire Party from the bottom up to carry on the monthly assessment we have placed on ourselves for the benefit of the German Communist Party. This German assessment, comrades, this little red strip stamp we put in our membership books, every month—this should be one of the most sacred things, and every one of us should check up and see that we do this, and that every cent of that money gets to the Central Committee, and check up and see that the Central Committee sends every cent every month to Germany. (*Applause.*) We had actions in support of our magnificent comrades in the Reichstag fire trial. We carried on mass actions in the United States. We can be proud of them. We can be especially proud that in this protest movement against the Reichstag trial, one of the most important parts was taken by precisely these supposedly "backward" Alabama sharecroppers. (*Applause.*) We had right here in this Convention a telegram of greetings from Baltimore, which reported that their form of greeting this Convention was to announce that they had set up an Anti-War Committee on a ship in the harbor in Baltimore. These are certain examples of the positive side of our work. But comrades, if we can do these things with such a very weak and partial mobilization of our forces, then is it not clear that a serious effort could have had a far larger result? And isn't it, comrades, really a crime that holding such possibilities in our hands, we did not make use of them? Can we be satisfied with the campaign we are now carrying on for the freedom of Thaelmann? We cannot by any means be satisfied with it. It is still weak. It doesn't register. It does not even yet fully rouse all of our Party members. And yet we may find that if we would properly develop this movement—the movement for the freedom of Thaelmann may become of greater historic importance than that which saved our comrades Dimitroff, Popoff, Torgler and Taneff.

Then we must point out that every day from the United States there is being shipped munitions and war supplies of all kinds to Japan, for war against the Soviet Union, and to Kuomintang China, for war against the Chinese Soviet Republic. What is our activity against this? We do a little journalistic work, sometimes good and sometimes not so good, but we yet don't have serious actions, mass demonstrations of protest against these shipments of munitions, actions on the part of the workers on the ships, to stop the loading and shipping. That is our task.

We give a little support to the Cuban workers and their Party, but is this in any way representing adequate mobilization of mass support from the United States directly to the Cuban revolutionary struggle? In the Philippine Islands, the leaders of our brother Party there are in prison or exiled to the far and most barren islands, sent there directly by the government of the United States headed by that very "liberal" ex-Mayor Murphy of Detroit, now Governor-General of the Philippine Islands. We have passed a few resolutions of protest, we have sent them over to the Philippine Islands to console our comrades who are in exile, to remind them that somebody in America is thinking about them. But what have we done to rouse the masses of the United States to register a protest in Washington that will force attention from this regime, and win the liberation of Comrade Evangelista and the other leaders of the Philippine Communist Party? We haven't enough learned the necessity of these things, which is not merely the necessity of the Philippine Party, but is *our* necessity if we are to realize our ambition to be a Bolshevik Party in the United States. This is the root of the whole matter; we haven't enough taken this question of internationalism out of our Conventions and resolutions into the trade unions, shops, factories, mines, neighborhoods, the homes, out of the holiday atmosphere to bring it down to real everyday life. We haven't made our internationalism the property of the masses, an essential part of their lives as well as of our inner Party line.

I have already spoken, in dealing with Comrade Zack's deviations, of our A. F. of.L. work. I want to mention this again, not for further elaboration, but for additional emphasis. Comrades, we still have to carry through the task of making our whole Party understand that unless we do serious, stubborn, organized work inside of the A. F. of L. everywhere where it has any masses of workers, that we will not succeed in any other phase of our trade union work or in the main political tasks of our Party. There is still some resistance here and there in the ranks of the Party. There's still, in one form or another, the ideology that is expressed by Comrade Zack. We must liquidate it. We should endorse the proposals to the Convention by our trade union comrades, as the immediate tasks for overcoming our weaknesses:

1. Strengthen the existing A. F. of L. rank-and-file committees.

2. Arrange conferences of the A. F. of L. local unions for the Workers' Unemployment Bill, for the right to strike against compulsory arbitrations, for exemption of dues stamps for unemployed and for democracy in the union.

3. Each section to select local unions in which to build the Party

fraction and build the broad rank-and-file opposition based on the revolutionary program.

4. Establish national industrial centers in the following industries: mine, marine, needle, painters, carpenters, auto, cleaners and dyers, textile and machinist.

5. Increase the circulation of the *Rank-and-File Federationist* from 10,000 to 25,000 in three months. (The *Rank-and-File Federationist* to become a mass organizer of revolutionary opposition groups in the A. F. of L. unions.)

6. To secure the election of at least 10 delegates to the coming Convention of the A. F. of L. Half of these delegates to come from central bodies, the other half from federal locals.

7. Prepare resolutions for the coming state and international conventions which are being held in the near future. Secure delegates to these conventions who will bring forward the rank and file program at these conventions.

8. The A. F. of L. fraction to arrange a tour to cover the steel towns and mining field to strengthen our opposition work.

9. Build the fraction and the opposition in the Central Labor unions and fight for all elective posts.

10. Prepare a large rank-and-file conference in San Francisco to be held simultaneously with the 54th A. F. of L. Convention.

These proposals to become part of the control task in every district.

A central political task today is the struggle against fascism. The basic weapon of struggle against fascism is the development of economic struggles and, in connection with economic struggles, the sharpening fight to preserve and extend the civil rights of the workers, rights of organization, strike, free speech and free press, etc. Upon the basis of the growing proletarian movement and mass struggles, we must bring around the working class all other elements of the population suffering from the crisis and capable of being roused against fascism. We have had a very excellent discussion about the most important phase of winning these non-proletarians which becomes so important in the struggle against fascism, in the work of our Agrarian Commission. Because the entire Convention doesn't have yet the full benefit of the Agrarian Commission's work, all the more is it necessary for me to emphasize this here, so that every comrade will read the documents that will appear as the result of this work. We must make it clear that our work among the farmers is not a monopoly of our growing and valuable specialists in the agrarian work. Our Agrarian Department and its new and growing cadres is a very valuable addition to our army, but we are not going to leave the whole job of winning the farming population to them. We refuse to grant them a monopoly in this field; we insist that our District Committees and our District Bureaus and District Organizers have not only the right but the duty to do something themselves directly to win the farmers.

Just in passing, in dealing with these non-proletarian strata which we must win; just a word about the important and serious student movement: This was not mentioned in the Youth Resolution which was brought to this Convention, an oversight which must be remedied in the editorial work that this Convention will authorize, I hope, so that this question will be included in the final document.

In my report, I brought forward the question of the coming Congressional elections. I suggested perhaps we should set ourselves the task of electing a few Communist Congressmen this fall. I haven't been able to follow all the debates in the Convention, but so far as I can learn, nobody took up this challenge concretely. The Canadian Party told us about some important election successes. We have no such successes to report in the United States, and unfortunately we don't seem to have enough ambition in this line. We still underestimate the value of revolutionary parliamentarism. We are at a moment when it is quite possible for large masses to swing over very quickly to the support of the Communist Party, especially in the Congressional elections. There is therefore no utopianism in suggesting the possibility of many successful Communist candidates if we work correctly and if we make a serious campaign. But the condition of success is a serious campaign. The workers will not come to us and hunt us up, especially when they can't even find our offices; we have to go to them. They do not know our leaders yet. We must let them know that the Communist Party is in the election campaign, who are its candidates, show the faces of these candidates, with a very short, snappy election platform, with a few main principal demands that everyone suffering from the crisis wants.

After Comrade Hathaway's report on our work among the youth, there is nothing for me to add. Just a word of emphasis upon what he said, of the necessity to really carry through our resolution on this question, that is, that it must become a practical task which we have to work out in concrete terms of assigning certain jobs to certain people to be accomplished within a certain time, with check-up and control, to see that they are done, and if not, why.

Similarly with the work among the women. It does not do very much good for our work among the women for us to give them compliments whenever we meet. What we need now is to start serious work in the factories, in the trade unions, in the neighborhoods, around the high prices and rents, in women's councils; to develop cadres and bring them boldly forward and to use for that purpose every such opportunity as we have in this campaign for delegates from America to the International Women's Congress to be held in Paris at the end of July. These are not impossible tasks, quite within our power, and.

they will mean, if carried through, a serious beginning in women's work.

With regard to some general features of our task of Bolshevizing our Party: the discussions in this Convention have brought out the extreme importance of raising the political level of our Party. We are raising the political level. The level of this Convention is far higher than any gathering the Party ever had before. But we must take this into the life of our Party down to every unit. This raising of our political level, the mastery of Bolshevist theory and practice, concretely, in facing the problems of the life of the working class, this is the only possible weapon with which we can clean our house, sweep out completely all remnants of factionalism, unprincipledness, bureaucracy, from our movement from top to bottom. The weapon for this is self-criticism. I said before we haven't mastered this weapon yet and here I must say that our Polburo and Central Committee is far too weak in the self-critical examination of its own work. We have to develop effective self-criticism, beginning at the top and, by example, carrying it throughout the Party.

Our new Central Committee must work on a higher level than the old one. Every member of the Central Committee that we elect here must understand that he is personally responsible for carrying through the decisions of this Convention wherever he may work, and that the Central Committee as a whole is collectively responsible for the collective organization of all this work.

Our Party has grown materially in membership and politically in its grasp of politics and theory in the period since the Seventh Convention. We have become more a real leader of struggles. We have led successful strikes, unemployed movements, farmers' activities, movements of middle class elements. Through our activities since the Seventh Convention, four years ago, we have extended our basic capital of revolutionary experience and theory. But we made many mistakes, and many mistakes we made twice and three times, because of lack of sufficient understanding of the class relations in the country and the meaning of each particular struggle and situation. The only remedy for that is more systematic approach to the problem of mastery on a larger scale by a growing body of our cadres of the theory and practice of Marxism-Leninism. Our Party is largely new. The Credentials Committee report read to you showed 66 delegates of this Convention joined the Party since the Open Letter, since our Extraordinary Party Conference. A majority of our Party members are less than two years in the Party.

There is no miracle whereby workers become Marxist-Leninists by taking out a card in our Party. They will become Bolsheviks only to the extent that the Party organization sees to it that every Party member is interested in the study of theory as an essential part of the daily mass work. If every member is made to understand that the study of theory is not something which merely has to do with the improvement of his intellectual level, but is the forging of the weapons of struggle which have to be used every day in the fight, then we can not only train our membership but by training them we keep them in the Party and solve the problem of fluctuation and multiply manifold the force of the Party among the masses.

Bolshevism is a science and to master it we must study it. Study is a necessity of our Party life. We have excellent cadres that have come to us out of the struggles that we organized and led, have been developed by these struggles. In all the ordinary questions of life these are far more practical and efficient than our "old guard," but they still lack something. They haven't been equipped with that something beyond their own experience, with the tremendous treasury of the experiences of the entire world working class movement. That is what we must give them. When we give them that, we will have the force which will make the revolution in America and not before.

A main immediate and practical task before us is the question of the *Daily Worker* and its mass circulation. Every district and section of our Party must set itself the task of giving the *Daily Worker* a mass circulation, a task that can be carried out during the year 1934, which by the end of the year will give us a minimum circulation, to be a little conservative, of 75,000. This means to a little more than double the present circulation of the *Daily Worker*. Can that be done? I'm sure it can. I'm sure every district committee will agree that it can be done. If we put this question seriously throughout the Party it will be done. It must be done if we are in earnest about any of our tasks. Without that, the rest of all that we say and write becomes so much chattering.

Similarly with building our Party membership. Is it too much to say that we should have 50,000 members by the end of 1934? If you think it is too much we will compromise and say 40,000. But at least 40,000 members.

These tasks—*Daily Worker*, membership—these are not tasks which will take us away from the mass work of the Party. These will not interfere with our preparations for making May Day the greatest day of struggle that has ever been seen in America. In fact I don't see how we will make May Day a success unless we use the *Daily Worker*, especially the May Day special edition. I think that May Day will be something of a failure for us if we don't recruit many new members out of it. Similarly, with the preparations for Anti-War Day on August 1.

Just a few words, in summing up, on the strong sides and the weak sides of our Convention which expresses the whole life of the Party. The Convention shows that the Party has grown. That is fine.

Everybody feels good about that. But what about our fluctuation, and what about the hundreds of thousands ready for us whom we have not reached, and are not yet seriously trying to reach? The Convention does not show enough determination to remedy this weakness. If the figures of our growth cause any feeling of self-satisfaction, then it would be better to keep quiet about them.

The Convention shows the Party is leading struggles everywhere. Good! That is the strong side of our Party, it is a fighting Party, it is in daily struggles. But the Convention also shows very important places where the workers are fighting, where strike movements are rising, where all the forces of capitalism are brought to bear to prevent these struggles—and we are not there, or there so weakly that our influence is not yet a decisive factor in helping the working class to break through. That is the weak side of our Party in this Convention. Why haven't we been able to go forward at the head of these 200,000 auto workers who are burning with the desire to fight? Here we are weak. We haven't solved this problem yet. What is true of auto is true of many other key points. Our Convention shows, as one of its strong sides, the improving composition of our Party as a result of concentration, of leadership of struggles, of going into the factories, of beginning work in the A. F. of L., of building the militant trade unions, of winning Negroes, etc., but it also shows that we have only begun serious work in this respect. In many localities we have not yet a single important factory that we can call our stronghold. When we speak of our Party being the leader of these struggles, through our improving cadres, at the same time we must say our Convention discussion is still too much merely reporting on these struggles, not drawing the lessons of these struggles—the good lessons and the bad ones. We do not enough draw the conclusions, the directives that must be formulated from these experiences—the directives for ourselves as to how we must work better, and the directives for the masses as to how they must fight more effectively to win these struggles. The Party has a correct line of struggle against all varieties of social-fascism. That is good! We can be glad of that. But the discussions in this Convention have not enough shown that we are carrying on a stubborn unrelenting struggle every day among the masses against the concrete manifestations of this enemy ideology, in the midst of these mass struggles that we are leading. We could carry this analysis of our strong and weak points through a long list. And we must do this. We must have a perpetual and continually renewing self-examination of our work, a searching out of every weak point and finding the way to remedy it.

It is not sufficient to have a correct Party line. On this point I can't do better than to read what Comrade Stalin said at the recent Seventeenth Party Congress of the C.P.S.U. These words of Comrade

Stalin must become a directive for our daily work. They are meant for us just as much as they are meant for the Bolsheviks in the Soviet Union. Comrade Stalin said:

Some people think that it is sufficient to draw up a correct Party line, proclaim it from the housetops, enunciate it in the form of general theses and resolutions and carry them unanimously in order to make victory come of itself, automatically, so to speak. This, of course, is wrong. Those who think like that are greatly mistaken. Only incorrigible bureaucrats and office rats can think that. As a matter of fact these successes and victories were obtained, not automatically, but as a result of a fierce struggle to carry out the Party line. Victory never comes by itself, it has to be dragged by the hand. Good resolutions and declarations in favor of the general line of the Party are only a beginning, they merely express the desire to win, but it is not victory. After the correct line has been given, after a correct solution of the problem has been found, success depends on the manner in which the work is organized, on the organization of the struggle for the application of the line of the Party, on the proper selection of workers, on supervising the fulfillment of the decisions of the leading organs. Without this the correct line of the Party and the correct solutions are in danger of being severely damaged. More than that, after the correct political line has been given, the organizational work decides everything, including the fate of the political line itself, i.e., its success or failure.

Comrades, this must be the keynote of our Convention also. This must be the leading thought in all our work throughout the Party, throughout the mass organizations. We have the beginnings of this spirit in our Party. As an example I may mention that yesterday I received a little resolution that came from that shop nucleus I talked about in my report. This resolution declares the nucleus has met and discussed the fact that the National Convention of the Party is examining the work of this nucleus. The nucleus declares that this creates in them a feeling of great responsibility, and as a result they have come together and worked out control tasks for the next three months, to increase the number of Party members in the shop by so many, increase the circulation of the *Daily Worker* by so many, and so on and so on. This is an application of the line of Comrade Stalin's speech that I just read to you. (*Applause.*)

Comrades, I think I have said enough. The work of our Convention has revealed to all of us that we have a Party stronger than we ever knew. We have a Party that already has forces capable of doing tremendous things in the United States. If we haven't done these things already, it is not the fault of these forces we have; it is only because we are still so badly organized, and because we who lead the Party are still not the kind of leaders that we must be. This Convention has revealed such forces which we must properly use to seriously carry out among the masses more practical everyday work, collectively organized, collectively criticized, collectively checked up on, tightening our organization, cementing its unity, fighting against and eliminating every deviation, raising the theoretical level of the Party, always and everywhere in the forefront of the rising struggle of the masses. If we do this, if we make use of these tremendous opportunities revealed to us here in this Convention, comrades, then we can be sure that in a short time we will be a mass Party in the United States; we will be leading serious class battles in this country; we will be challenging the power of American imperialism; we will be seriously preparing the American workers for their revolutionary tasks. (*Prolonged applause.*)

III

The Fight for Bread *

OUR Convention meets in the midst of the greatest economic crisis ever known. The present ferocious attack against the toiling masses— that is the capitalist way out of the crisis.

While millions starve, Hoover, chief of the Republican Party, leads the fight to save capitalist profits at the expense of the lives of the workers, their wives, and children.

In this situation only the Communist Party rises and fights for the workers' demands for jobs, bread and peace. (*Applause.*)

For three years Hoover promised "prosperity in 60 days." This prosperity takes the form of cities of unemployed, homeless outcast millions living in packing-boxes, in cellars, under bridges, in sewers. Hundreds of these cities, all over the country, have very properly paid homage to the fame and glory of the great engineer in the White House by adopting the name, "Hooverville." The very name of this man has become a symbol of degradation and misery for the masses.

Fifteen million workers are unemployed, other millions have only part-time jobs, wage-rates for the employed have been cut by 25 to 60 per cent, millions of farmers are being evicted from their farms because they are unable to pay taxes and interest on their mortgages. Starvation and diseases are sucking the blood of men, women and children in every state, every city, every working-class neighborhood.

The issue of the elections is the issue of work and bread—of life or death for the workers and the farmers. (*Applause.*)

All this occurs in the richest country in the world. Our warehouses are bursting with unused food and clothing. Our cities are full of empty houses. There is plenty to spare of all things needed for life for all people.

Millions are starving precisely because there is *too much of everything*. That is what all the wise men of Wall Street tell us. That is the fundamental law of our economic and social system. That is capitalism. That is the inevitable result of a system in which the machinery of production and distribution is the private property of the small parasite class.

The Communist Party is the only Party which organizes the workers and farmers to create a revolutionary government which will confiscate

* Keynote speech opening the Presidential Nominating Convention of the Communist Party, Chicago, May 28, 1932.—*Ed.*

the industries, banks, railroads, etc., from the parasite capitalists who have proved they do not know how to run them, and to put the industrial machinery to work for the benefit of the masses of workers and farmers. (*Applause.*)

The question is not one of Hoover. It is of the system, of which way out of the crisis. Hoover's policies have been carried out by a coalition of the Republican and Democratic parties. Between these parties there is a fight only about who shall get the graft of office, but complete agreement that the workers and farmers shall pay all the costs of the crisis, complete agreement that the government treasury shall be used primarily for the benefit of the banks, the railroads, the great corporations.

The Reconstruction Finance Corporation that gave two billion dollars to the banks and corporations, was the joint work of Republicans and Democrats, and was endorsed by the leaders of the Socialist Party whose only complaint was that "it didn't go far enough."

The present projects before Congress supposedly for relief—from Hoover's billion, to Robinson's two billion, to Hearst's five billion, to the Socialist Party's ten billion—all differ from one another only in the degree of their demagogy. They all agree that nothing can be done except through restoring capitalist profits and placing the burdens of the crisis upon the masses.

Even the shameful charity doles, which prolong the starvation of a portion of the unemployed, are not taken from the rich capitalists who own everything in rich America, but from the masses who have nothing except a remnant of a job at part-time. A classical example of this is the New York "block-aid" system. Under this system each block is to take care of its own starving; down on the East Side where two thousand are starving together in one block, the few hundred with jobs in that block shall take care of others; up on Fifth Avenue, Morgan, Rockefeller and Company will take care of all the unemployed in their blocks.

In putting across this beautiful scheme, which includes a system of blacklisting all radical workers spotted by the "Block-Aid Committees," all those who support the capitalist way out of the crisis were brought forward: J. Pierpont Morgan spoke over the radio for it, and said: "You give a dime and I give a dime, and we all share equally": over the same radio Morgan was followed by Norman Thomas, leader of the so-called Socialist Party, who supported Morgan and attacked the Communist Party as "slanderers" of Morgan's pure motives.

There are only two ways out of the crisis. One way is the capitalist way. That way is the attempt to restore capitalism, to restore profits. But to restore profits means to cut wages, to throw millions out of work, to refuse unemployment relief, to refuse social insurance, to pile heavy taxes upon the masses and reduce the taxes on wealth, to refuse the bonus to the ex-soldiers. It means "to balance the budget," in the words of the slogan that now unites all three capitalist Parties, the Republican, Democratic, and Socialist Parties. And it means *war*.

The capitalist way out of the crisis is the way of misery, suffering, starvation, war, death for the workers and farmers. It is a way out only for the little parasite class of capitalists and their servants.

The capitalists have two main weapons, demagogy and terror, to put across their attacks upon the workers. They use these weapons through their three parties—Republican, Democratic and Socialist. These are, first, to confuse the workers' mind with demagogy, with false promises of "prosperity in 60 days" and later, with the hope that "Congress will do something before long." Thus they try to keep the workers quiet and patient under all miseries and attacks.

But when the demagogy fails to keep the workers from fighting for some relief, then police violence and terror, as well as illegal fascist attacks upon the workers.

The working class already has a long list of martyrs, of dead and wounded and imprisoned, in the fight to resist the capitalist attacks.

Melrose Park, in Chicago, where the underworld, the police and the American Legion opened machine-gun fire on an unemployed meeting, is only an outstanding example. Democrats in Chicago and New York, Republicans in Detroit at the Ford massacre, and in Pennsylvania "progressives" and reactionaries—it makes no difference for the workers. They all club, shoot, imprison, if they cannot keep the workers quiet with their lies.

In Kentucky they already have an open fascist dictatorship, which differs from capitalist "democracy" in Chicago, Detroit and New York only by its discarding of all pretences and bragging about what the others try to conceal.

And not to be outdone by its elder brother parties, the Socialist Party in Milwaukee (the only city it controls) sent the unemployed leader, Fred Bassett, to prison for one year for leading the demonstration of March 6, 1930, at the same time that Democratic Jimmy Walker of Tammany Hall, New York, who received gifts of a million dollars while in office, was sending Foster, Minor, Amter, and Raymond to jail for six months for the same "crime."

The officialdom of the American Federation of Labor is openly supporting the Hoover program. It fights against the workers and for the capitalists on every essential point. It fights against unemployment insurance, against the bonus for the ex-soldiers, it prevents strikes and signs agreements for broad wage-cuts, it fights for huge grants of money to the corporations and taxation of the masses, it supports new laws to help build greater giant monopolies, it helps imperialist wars, especially the war against the Soviet Union. Through its deceitful "non-partisan" policy of "rewarding friends and punishing enemies," it delivers the workers gagged and bound to the Republicans and Democrats, "progressives" and reactionaries, in order to further confuse and divide the working class. It decks itself out in "victories," like the so-called anti-injunction law, which fastens injunctions and yellow-dog contracts more firmly upon the workers than ever before.

The reactionary officialdom of the American Federation of Labor is an agency of capitalism among the workers for putting over the capitalist way out of the crisis.

Oppression of the Negro masses in the United States takes on the most bestial forms, rivalled only by the rule of the British in India, and by the Japanese and Kuomintang generals in China. Negroes are burned alive on the public squares of our cities, and their bodies mutilated in the most horrible manner by crazed and drunken agents of the landlords and capitalists. And it also takes on the most subtle forms, those of the "liberal" and "humanitarian" slave-owners, who with gentler means keep the black man "in his place" of servant—the ways of deceit and hypocrisy.

The Democratic Party is the party of the lynchers; the Republican Party is bidding for the support of the lynchers and has completely discarded its tradition as liberator of the chattel slaves; the Socialist Party at its convention last week rejected the Negro demand for social equality, and one of its chief leaders, Heywood Broun, has openly declared against enforcing the right to vote of Negroes in the South. The Socialist Party conventions was even more "lily-white" than the Republican Party in its most degenerate days.

It is clear that only the Communist Party fights every day in the year for equality of the Negro masses, complete equality without any restrictions, economic, political or social. (*Applause.*) Only the Communist Party comes forward with the demand for self-determination for the Negroes in the Black Belt where they constitute the majority of the population. Only the Communist Party fights every day for the unconditional freedom of the Scottsboro boys, and against each and every act of oppression of the Negro people. Only the Communist Party calls upon the white workers to defend their Negro brothers, and organizes the joint struggle of white and Negro toilers, side by side, in the closest fraternal unity. (*Applause.*)

The climax of the monstrous brutalities of the capitalist way out of the crisis is the preparation for a new imperialist war.

Hoover, at the head of American imperialism, is one of the chief organizers of the war against the Soviet Union. Secretly and openly instigating Japanese imperialism to begin this attack in the East, the Hoover government at the same time pushes on the French military system in Europe.

Hoping thus to destroy the Soviet Union, and at the same time weaken American imperialism's strongest rivals, Hoover and Company are dragging the American working class into a world slaughter for redivision of the world.

The new world war, which will claim millions of working-class lives, can only be postponed by the most energetic, fearless, self-sacrificing action of the workers of all lands, especially of America, to fight against and halt the whole capitalist offensive.

The Communist Party calls upon the workers of America to fight for the defense of the Chinese people, for the liberation of the Philippines and other colonies and semi-colonies, for stopping the shipment of munitions to Japan. We call for fraternal solidarity with and support of the heroic Japanese workers who fight for the overthrow of their semi-feudal ruling regime, and support the demand for the expulsion from this country of the representatives of Japanese imperialism. We call upon the workers to fight and defeat the war plans of American imperialism, and build a living wall of defense of the workers' fatherland, the Soviet Union. (*Applause.*)

Billions for the banks and corporations; hunger, starvation, oppression and war for the workers and farmers—this is the capitalist way out of the crisis.

Will American workers submit to this without a fight? No, they will not! (*Applause.*) This Convention, representing the most developed workers and farmers from coast to coast, is itself one of the most important signs that the workers will fight, that they are already beginning to fight.

There is no way out of the crisis for the workers and farmers except the road of militant class struggle. Against the united forces of the capitalist class, which, in spite of all differences swings into action against the toiling masses—against this the working class must build up a fighting front of its own class forces.

Class against class! That is the expression of the class alignment which the workers must fight for and secure in the elections.

The elections struggle is not something separated from everyday life and problems. The election struggle grows out of, and must help conduct, the daily fight for bread, clothing, shelter for the worker and his family.

That is why the election platform of the Communist Party places in the very first place the fight for the most burning, the most immediate, needs of the toiling masses.

Our six main planks in the election platform, represent the most pressing needs of the million-masses of America. They are:

1. *Unemployment and social insurance at the expense of the state and employers.*

2. Against Hoover's wage-cutting policy.

3. Emergency relief for the impoverished farmers, without restric-

tions by the government and banks; exemption of impoverished farmers from taxes, and no forced collection of rents or debts.

4. Equal rights for the Negroes and self-determination for the Black Belt.

5. Against capitalist terror; against all forms of suppression of the political rights of the workers.

6. Against imperialist war; for the defense of the Chinese people and of the Soviet Union.

It is the task of the Communist Party to make of the election campaign merely a part of the whole struggle of the working class for these demands, which is conducted every day in demonstrations, strikes, struggles of every sort, in which the widest class forces of the workers will be registered. The mass fight for these demands alone can build up effective resistance to the capitalist way out of the crisis.

Only the fight of the masses can win these demands. (*Applause.*) Every Party that tells the workers to depend upon representatives in Congress to give these things to them, is fooling the workers, is trying to keep the workers quiet while the capitalists continue to rob them and oppress them.

Especially important is the fight for *unemployment insurance.* There can be no security of life, to the smallest degree, until the workers force the capitalist class, the ruling class, to give them unemployment insurance. (*Applause.*)

Now, at a time when even if capitalist industry increased its production, still fewer workers would be engaged, because of labor-saving machinery and rationalization and speed-up—now, it is a thousand times more important that the workers shall force the capitalists to give a minimum guarantee of the means of life under all conditions.

The only project for such unemployment and social insurance which gives any guarantee to the workers, is the *Workers Unemployment Insurance Bill* which was presented to Congress last December 7th by the National Hunger Marchers who came from all over the country.

The Communist Party election struggle will be, before all, the fight for the *Workers Unemployment Insurance Bill.* And the Communist Party is the *only* Party that fights for this bill. (*Applause.*)

The fight for these demands is the first step to find the working-class way out of the crisis. The working-class way is, and must be, the revolutionary way, that is, it must be the way of a fundamental change in the whole system, it must take power out of the hands of the capitalist class and put it into the hands of the working class.

The struggles of the working class must have as their aim the setting up of a *revolutionary workers' and farmers' government.* (*Applause.*)

Only such a government can finally free the masses from starvation and slavery. Only such a government can open up every idle factory, mill and mine, and give jobs again to every worker and provide a decent living. Only such a government can immediately seize and distribute to the hungry masses the enormous stores of food now kept locked up in warehouses. Only such a government can open up the millions of houses, kept locked and empty by greedy and private landlords, and fill them with the homeless unemployed.

This is the only working-class way out of the crisis.

Of the three political parties of the capitalist class—the Republican, Democratic, and Socialist parties—the first two are open tools of Wall Street, while the third calls itself a "workers' party." But the Socialist Party is only the third party of the capitalist class. It is no more the party of socialism than is the Democratic party the party of democracy. It is the party of the betrayal of socialism. (*Applause.*)

A new socialist system of society is actually being built in a great country, one-sixth of the entire world. That is in the Soviet Union. (*Applause.*) There the working class, allied with the farmers, took political power away from the capitalists, chased the capitalists away or put them to work, and set up a new kind of government, the Soviet Government.

Today, finishing the Five-Year Plan of socialist construction with the most magnificent success, building giant new industries where there were none at all before, growing at a rate five to ten times as fast as anything the world ever saw before, the Soviet Union is the living example of the workers' way, the revolutionary way out of the crisis, the way to socialism and communism. (*Applause.*)

But the Socialist Party is the bitterest enemy of the Soviet Union. Its brother-party in Russia joined the capitalists in trying to overthrow the Soviet government. The leader of the Socialist Party in the U. S. A., Morris Hillquit, was the attorney for those ex-capitalists of tsarist Russia who owned the Baku oil fields before the Revolution. Morris Hillquit signed the documents of these capitalists who asked the United States government to seize the oil shipped to the United States and turn it over to them because the Baku oil fields had been "unlawfully and wrongfully seized" by the Russian working class and really belonged by right to their former capitalist owners.

Can the Socialist Party bring socialism in America, when its chief leader fights to restore capitalism in Russia?

The Socialist Party has the same program as its brother party in England, the Labor Party, which, when in office, was the most aggressive initiator of wage-cuts, reduction of unemployment relief, inflation, and the whole capitalist way out of the crisis. It has the same program as its German brother party, the Social-Democracy, which is in coalition with the monarchist Hindenburg, and is negotiating a coalition with the fascist Hitler, for the capitalist' way out at the expense of the workers.

What is true of the Socialist Party is equally true of its self-styled left-wing, the "militants" and Musteites, as well as their Lovestone and Cannon winglets. These groups use radical phrases, and put on sham fights like that against Hillquit in Milwaukee, but they are all agreed on fundamentals. They are united in struggle against the Communist Party of the United States and against the Soviet Union.

The Socialist Party puts itself forward as the champion of American democracy, capitalist democracy. It is for the democracy which puts Jimmy Walker in charge of New York City, to secure a million dollars graft by farming out the right to exploit the masses; it is against the dictatorship in the Soviet Union which shoots such grafters as Jimmy Walker.

But the workers of the United States are learning a great deal about the real meaning of capitalist democracy. They can no longer be fooled, as of old, so easily. The workers know that in the Soviet Union, the dictatorship of the working class means the first and only real democracy for the workers. (*Applause.*) That it is a dictatorship against the exploiters and their agents. They know that in the United States, the boasted democracy is a democracy of money, and a dictatorship against the workers. (*Applause.*)

Only the mass struggle for the demands of the workers contained in the platform of the Communist Party is an effective method of gaining concessions from the capitalist class here and now. (*Applause.*)

There is no other practical struggle for immediate demands except the class struggle led by the Communist Party. (*Applause.*)

A million votes for Foster and Ford and the Communist platform in the presidential elections will win many concessions for the workers from the capitalist class, who are filled with deep fear when the workers turn towards communism.

A million votes for the Communist platform will be the first long step on the road of the revolutionary way out of the crisis. (*Applause.*)

Forward to the revolutionary election struggle of the working class for its immediate needs and its ultimate goal!

Organize a mighty mass movement of the workers and farmers, Negro and white, men, women and youth, to vote Communist on November 8th, and to fight every day in the year against capitalism until it is destroyed and a Soviet government rules in the United States! (*Loud applause—ovation.*)

IV

Is Planning Possible Under Capitalism? *

I AM afraid that Mr. Soule has played a little trick on me. He has put me in the position of declaring that it is impossible under capitalism to make bad economic plans. It is impossible for me to defend this point of view. I will admit all the contentions that Mr. Soule makes about the existence of economic planning under capitalism. I don't deny that such plans are made. I don't deny that such plans are applied. I don't deny that such plans have ever growing effects. But I do deny that all of these efforts are in any way contributions toward the establishing of a planned economic system.

So I would wish to restate the question a little before I can take up the negative and say, not, is economic planning under capitalism possible, but *is it possible under capitalism to establish a planned economy, that is, a stable economy not subject to constantly recurring, constantly deepening crises?* **

It is, of course, entirely correct to say in one sense that the traditional rugged individualism of capitalism has been transformed into its very opposite, the denial of individualism by monopoly. That is, in

* Speech delivered at the debate with George Soule, January 13, 1933.—*Ed.*

** Competition, profits, the driving force of capitalist production makes social planning impossible. The growth of productive forces are for the manufacturers compulsory under competition. Planning takes place in the individual factory in order to make competition more effective. This planning in the individual factory is based upon greater exploitation of the workers engaged in production. In the words of Marx, ". . . within the capitalist system the methods for raising the social productiveness of labor are brought about at the cost of the individual laborer. All means for the development of production transforms this into means of domination over the exploitation of the producers. . ."

Thus we see that the greater planning in the individual factory, raising the productiveness of labor, is based upon greater exploitation of the workers. This sharpens the basic contradiction of capitalism, the contradiction between the social form of production and the private appropriation of the social product by the individual capitalist. The absence of social planning, the anarchy of production, with profit as a driving force, cause overproduction. Therefore the poverty of the masses is the basic cause for the recurrent crises under capitalism. This contradiction between the planning by the individual capitalist and the anarchy of production in society as a whole was referred to by Engels in his statement as the "contradiction between socialized organization in the *individual* factory and *social* anarchy in production as a whole." (Our emphasis.) The more the capitalists plan in their individual factories to increase productivity based on the exploitation of labor, the greater the development of "social anarchy in production as a whole."

reality, capitalism today is far from the original individualism (competitive capitalism) which remains only as a tradition from the days of the rise of capitalism.* The transformation of capitalism, however, has not been in the direction of peacefully transforming it into its opposite, in the sense of a planned society, but in organizing all of its contradictions on a higher plane. Thereby it intensifies all of these contradictions within capitalist society and brings closer by these very steps (the growth of gigantic trusts, monopolies, and all other forms of organization within the capitalist system), not a planned economy, but a catastrophic collapse of the entire present system.

Let us examine a bit more closely the planning that capitalism does. Of course it does lots of planning. I was in Philadelphia today and happened to pick up the *Philadelphia Ledger* and saw one of the latest plans. This plan comes from one of the "enlightened" capitalist statesmen, from Governor Pinchot of Pennsylvania. What is his plan? It is a new plan for feeding the masses of unemployed in the State of Pennsylvania. And what is the purpose of this plan? The purpose of this plan is to abolish cash relief, and to substitute planned distribution of food by the state directly to the unemployed. The motive behind this plan of direct feeding and substitution of food for cash relief, thus avoiding the price system, is that the State of Pennsylvania will be enabled to cut the cost of relief from $1.10 a week per person down to 41c for adults and 27c for children, per week. Of this kind of plan, of course, we have a tremendously growing crop. Every day gives us a few hundred new plans of this kind. That is one kind of capitalist planning.

Of course there are very important phases of capitalist planning that have to do with production. In the period of the rise of capitalism these planning efforts of the capitalistic system were generally summed up under the heading of scientific management. All of the plans of capitalism that properly come under this head are merely phases of the growth of the productive forces and by no means make any contribution

* The growth of trusts, of gigantic monopolies, does not do away with competition between the capitalists. On the contrary, it sharpens the struggle for markets. The competition between Ford and General Motors is very bitter. The competition between General Electric and gas companies over refrigerators is by no means gentle. The crisis, which has narrowed the home and world markets, has intensified competition between the trusts at home and has led to the breaking up of many of the international cartels.

"Marxists" of the type of Kautsky and Hilferding saw in the development of cartels and international agreements the beginnings of "organized" capitalism that will do away with crises and competition. But the present crisis has shattered all these theories into dust. The present talk of planning is merely an extension of the "new era" theories and of "organized capitalism" theories adapted to the present crisis and to meet the challenge of social planning which is making undisputed headway in the Soviet Union.

whatever to overcoming those fundamental clashes and contradic- .
tions existing under capitalism, that bring about crises and catastrophes
such as those at the present. On the contrary. What was the
effect of all the contributions of scientific management, of all the
achievements of the American engineers? It was precisely the achievements of this kind of capitalistic planning that brought the present
crisis and gave it its tremendous depth and duration. It is precisely
because of the achievements of rationalization, of scientific management, of engineering, which so enormously expanded the productive
forces and possibilities of American economy, that brought them to
such fundamental and violent conflict with the political-social super-
structure within which these forces had to work, and which paralyzed
these forces. So, we must say quite finally and definitely that when
Mr. Soule looks toward the further development of the processes started
by Taylor and the Taylor Society as a way towards solving the fundamental problems of the present economic system, that he is in a blind
alley; that same blind alley which the whole capitalist system is in.

There is another kind of planning. The planning of capitalism for a
crisis. Capitalists make plans for crises, too. Let us examine a little
bit some of the plans Mr. Soule mentioned, which are very much in the
public eye today, and which won an overwhelming support of the
electors on November 8.

We have the farm allotment plan of Mr. Roosevelt, of the Democratic
Party. What sort of plan is this? This plan has other characteristics
besides the fact that it proposes a certain state subsidy to certain
categories of farmers. It has the characteristic that it proposes this
subsidy on condition that the farmer reduces his production. This
supreme example of capitalistic planning today proposes that the
masses of the population who consume the products of the farmer are
to pay the farmer a double price, on condition that the farmer produces
less than before. This is planning! Yes, but it is the planning of
suicide—economic suicide! It is the planning of a society in decay
and in collapse, and further it is a kind of plan which will not postpone
this collapse, but will hasten it and will make the catastrophe of this
collapse even deeper. This kind of planning is possible for capitalism.
This kind of planning is being carried out every day. This kind of
planning, however, is not taking us step by step towards a future
planned economy, except in the sense that it is taking us step by step
towards a catastrophic collapse out of the ruins of which will rise a
planned economy.

No one concerned with capitalistic planning ever pretends even to
hope to overcome the basic contradictions of the capitalist system
which render a planned economy impossible. The basic factor of
capitalism is private ownership of the means of production, on the
basis of which is established a class division of capitalists and workers.

This division of society into two basic classes, in which a small para-site class controls the basic instruments of society, renders futile all attempts to establish a planned economy; renders impossible the mass participation in the planned economy; creates the kind of society that destroys its own markets; and which generates forces of civil disturb-ance in its very midst.

Not only are there these class divisions, but the capitalist class itself is incapable of acting as a class for planned economy, and even if we could presuppose the benevolent neutrality of the working class, the capitalist class would find it impossible to plan as a class because it is torn to pieces with the most intense rivalries, and the only way in which groups of capitalists can cooperate is through the defeat of one by the other. So that trusts are almost never built up through the process of friendly mergers, but are created through the process of the most violent struggle in which one group destroys the other. The very fabric of the capitalist system is a competitive struggle, war.

The capitalist class itself is the first to proclaim that a planned economy is impossible. That is why our gentle liberal friends who have gentle hopes for the gentle passing into a planned society, find a very convenient way of disposing of all those who proclaim the impossibility of this, by saying that extremes meet, that Communists who claim it is impossible, are equally reactionary with the capitalist class who claim it is impossible, and thus the revolutionary camp is thrown into the reactionary camp, and the gentle "revolutionaries" claim they are the only ones who stand for progress. (*Laughter by the audience.*) But they are the obstacles of progress.

These are some of the contradictions within capitalist society which make planned economy impossible. But I am afraid I will not cover my outline if I pursue that line of analysis further. I hope to elaborate on this some other time.

All of the contradictions which give rise to crisis and which bring home to the masses the fact that they are living in a chaotic society, in which plans have no large social significance, all of these contra-dictions rise out of the basic fact of private property in the means of production. There is no possible way toward progressing toward the establishment of a planned economy except when that progress begins with the basic step of abolishing private property in the means of production.

The abolishing of private property in the means of production will not come as the product of a long evolutionary development of planned economy. The abolition of private property is the precondition for the beginnings of the development of planned economy. Here we have the basic dispute between Mr. Soule and myself, which is the dispute between liberalism (or radicalism which it sometimes prefers to call itself) and Marxism-Leninism. There is no road toward socialism except the road of building up of the revolutionary forces within capitalistic society, which will overthrow the system.* That is, the building up of forces of the working class, preparing it through the experiences of the daily struggle for its immediate needs, preparing it for the revolutionary seizure of power in alliance with other oppressed sections of the population.

If capitalism can plan, and can begin the development of a planned economy, one would think that now is the time to do its stuff. Surely there are sufficient needs even from the point of view of the capitalists for some plan to be brought forward which will really convince the masses of the population that they have found some way out of the crisis. The final proof that capitalism cannot plan is the fact that capitalism is not planning. All the evidence brought forward by Mr. Soule to prove the capacity of capitalist planning merely proved the capacity of capitalism to plan new attacks against the working class, not its capacity to plan a way out of the crisis, a rehabilitation of the economic system. There is no plan for this purpose which is a serious plan, which faces the basic factors of the reestablishment of production. We have no such thing. There is not even a pretense to offer such a thing. When we say this, it applies not only to the Reconstruction Finance Corporation of Hoover, which is not and does not even pretend to be anything more than an emergency prop to prevent collapse, and is by no means something which promises to rehabilitate a system which cannot rehabilitate itself by its own inner forces; not only to the allotment plan of Roosevelt; but also to all of the other plans and theories about planned economy, including the new seven-day wonder, Technocracy. And one should say also, I think, even including the very intelligent discussions and proposals that have been made by Mr. Soule himself.

There are many kinds of advocates of capitalist plans and capitalist planning. Some of them are of the type we call social racketeers; that

---

* The Soviet Union is at the present time the only country where social planning is possible. What was the first step which the toilers of Russia took towards social planning? That was the proletarian revolution—the dictatorship of the proletariat—which abolished private property in the means of production. Engels many decades ago posed the question, when does "socialized production upon a predetermined plan become possible?" His answer is clear. "The proletarian revolution, solution of the contradictions, the proletariat seizes public power and by means of this transforms the socialized means of production, slipping from the hands of the bourgeoisie, into public property. By this act the proletariat frees the means of production from the character of capital they have thus far borne and gives their socialized character complete freedom to work itself out. *Socialized production upon a predetermined plan becomes henceforth possible.*" (My emphasis.) The Russian Revolution, the growth of socialist construction in the Soviet Union, is the living example of social planning. The Soviet Union by its first and second Five-Year Plan is the most effective reply to the fallacies of social planning under capitalism.

is, it is a racket with them—something they are selling as a business. I think that characterization should be given to the world-famous Technocrats. I don't think it is possible to take the contents of their proposals or theories very seriously.

With regard to the arguments of Mr. Soule, especially as expressed in his book, *Planned Society,* one has to examine these on a different plane. Mr. Soule is a serious person, who faces problems and argues about them on an intellectual plane. If he is wrong, it is not because he is deliberately prostituting his mental capacities to serve any section of the capitalist class. At the same time, even when we deal with the theories of Mr. Soule, we have to take into account the class meaning, the class significance, the class origin of such ideas. We never, if we wish to have a scientific understanding of social problems, can get very far away from the examination of the class forces that are at work.* The reason why Mr. Soule's analysis of the problem of planning results in so little of any practical significance is because his thought process is so far away from the class struggle.

A national plan requires a strong motive force behind it to put it into effect. A plan does not operate by itself. A plan is merely an instrument in the hands of some strong force. Where can we find the force capable of putting through a national economic plan for America?- There is only one class which has the possibility of providing this force—the working class. Not because we have some mystical conception of some force which has been placed by a mysterious god within these people, the workers, but because historical development is hammering out of this human material which constitutes the working class, that force which, because of the nature of its existence, finds it possible and necessary to carry society forward to its next stage. It is not necessary for us to confine ourselves to the broad generalizations of history that have been made by our great teachers, Marx, Engels, Lenin, Stalin, to prove this fact. We also have our own experience right here in America, for all of our "backward" American working class. Some people like to talk a great deal of the "backwardness" of the American working class. I think that in the course of a very few years of the capitalist crisis, the American working class is going to take such a leap forward politically, that all this talk of the "backwardness" of the American working class will be forgotten. (*Prolonged applause.*)

We had one experience in the changes recently in the National⁻

* What is the class meaning of all of the theories of planning under capitalism? The present crisis with its untold misery for the toilers dooms the capitalist system as a system which has completely outlived its historical usefulness and which only hinders the further development of mankind. The capitalists are trying through these theories of capitalist planning to hide the fact that "the bourgeoisie are convicted of incapacity further to manage their own social productive forces."

Hunger March. The National Hunger March showed the revolutionary potentialities within the working class. Here was a great national action carried through on schedule, carried through without any financial resources whatever, except those drawn out of the masses, pennies, nickels and dimes, by the political attractive forces of the beginnings of class action. Three thousand delegates coming together from different parts of the country, very few having ever seen each other or even worked together before, and presenting such an exhibition of organization and discipline as has rarely been seen before in the history of this country. Does anybody think these things are the creation of some mechanical organizational apparatus of the Communist Party? Not a bit of it. These things are the creation of the political class conscious-·ness of the workers of America who are beginning to wake up on a mass scale, and they demonstrated the tremendous creative power that is in the working class of this country. And by the way, this Hunger March was an example of a "planned" action.

I must say that (although I can't take sufficient time to develop it as it deserves) with regard to the planned economy the Socialist Party, although it uses many phrases about socialism, occupies exactly the same position—no, rather a position somewhat to the right of—that occupied by Mr. Soule. What Mr. Norman Thomas offers in the name of socialism is a planned economy which is merely more planned capitalism, that is, state capitalism.

Now I want to spend my last fifteen minutes with an examination of certain more fundamental questions involved in all of this debate. I am not exactly sure as to how to formulate this question. One could approach it from many angles. One could ask, for example, "Why is it that such a keen intelligence as Mr. Soule's, for example, can be so blind to certain very obvious facts in a field in which he has conducted prolonged and profound studies? Why is it that Mr. Soule, after all his study of the question, finally comes to such provisional conclusions as to make it even very difficult to debate with him?" One is not always sure just what he does believe after all. And in his book, which I studied in preparation for tonight, he tells us practically this: "Well, maybe the revolutionists are correct, maybe the reformists are correct. The only possible way we can know who is correct, is to let them fight it out and whoever wins is correct." Now, what significance does this attitude, which is not alone the attitude of Mr. Soule, have? It is an example of the typical philosophy of the typical American bourgeois, that is the philosophy of pragmatism, or, if one is to be "up-to-date," instrumentalism, which means the same thing. It is the typical attitude of the whole philosophy which is summed up in the expression, "Well, you will know what is the truth after the truth is established. There is no possible way to know it beforehand." That attitude is contained in the famous illustration that I think is to be referred to John Dewey (although I am not sure, not being an expert in this field, perhaps it is from William James) that the man who is lost in the forest cannot possibly know in advance the way out of the forest. He can experiment and try various ways out, and after he is out, then he can know the truth about the way out of the forest. This approach, by the way, is also typical of the Technocrats.

Mr. Soule has written some penetrating criticism of Technocracy and has asked the Technocrats some very embarrassing questions. I have only wondered why Mr. Soule did not answer the questions himself. Because, though they are very keen and embarrassing to Technocracy, they are just as embarrassing to Mr. Soule. This pragmatism that recognizes the truth only *a posteriori* (as the learned gentlemen say) only as something that has already arrived, cannot distinguish the face of truth amidst falsehoods and illusions. It has an inherent inability to recognize the face of the truth, it proclaims that the only possible way to recognize the truth is when you see it from the rear, when you see its backside, when it has already passed into history. This is a convenient philosophy for that bourgeoisie which is "sitting on top of the world," the bourgeoisie in ascendancy. But when bourgeois society falls into a crisis, this philosophy of pragmatism falls into crisis also along with the whole capitalist system. Where in the period of "Coolidge prosperity" it gave all the answers required to all of the problems of the bourgeoisie, today it begins to give the wrong answers to the bourgeoisie. Even if we judge the capitalist system today by that final criterion of the pragmatists, *Does it work?* we have the answer, "No, it does not work." So capitalism stands condemned by the standards of the philosophy of the bourgeois themselves. By the same standard, if we ask about the dictatorship of the proletariat in the Soviet Union, the new Socialist planned economy, and ask, *Does it work?* the answer is, "Yes, it does work. In the midst of a world that is going to pieces, it works." So pragmatism has failed its class creators in the crucial moment. It is unable to give capitalism any answer to the question, What way out? Because all the thinkers for capitalism are bound within the philosophical framework of pragmatism, they are unable to even formulate any proposals for a way out and are in the same position as the one who says, "Maybe the revolutionists are right, maybe the reformists are right, who knows? Let us wait and see."

But if pragmatism is of no use to the capitalist class to find a way out of the crisis, we must say it is no use to the working class, either. The only effect of the influence of this ideological system upon the working class is a very poisonous one, to create hesitation, indecision, hesitation again, more indecision, wait and see, wait and see.

The working class must have a different kind of philosophy, because the working class faces the future—not only faces the future, is already beginning to control the future. That is the essence of planning, *to control the future.* And you cannot control the future if your approach to the future is that it is impossible to know what is the truth until after the future has become the past. Those who are going to control the future have to be able to see in the future. Those who are going to control the future must know what is the truth before the event, before it happens, and by knowing it, determine what is going to happen and see that it does happen. That is the revolutionary working class, the only power that is able to put into effect a planned economy, and the only class that is capable of developing the whole philosophy and the understanding of society, which is necessary to put a plan into effect.

In conclusion: I would read a short quotation from Stalin, which in my opinion is one of the best short answers that has ever been given to the question, Can Capitalism Create a Planned Economy? Stalin speaking at the Sixteenth Party Congress, said:

If capitalism could adapt production, not to the acquisition of the maximum of profits, but to the systematic improvement of the material conditions of the mass of the people; if it could employ its profits, not in satisfying the whims of the parasitic classes, not in perfecting methods of exploitation, not in exporting capital, but in the systematic improvement of the material conditions of the workers and peasants, then there would be no crisis. But then, also, capitalism would not be capitalism. In order to abolish crises, capitalism must be abolished.*

* Joseph Stalin, *Leninism, Volume II,* p. 313.

V

Why an Open Letter to the Party Membership *

WHY ARE we holding an extraordinary Party conference at this time? And why are we proposing that this conference shall issue an open letter to the Party? It is not alone because of the extreme sharpening of the crisis and consequently of the class struggle and of the danger of imperialist war. Above all the reasons for these extraordinary measures lie in the fact that in spite of serious beginnings of revolutionary upsurge among the masses, our Party has not developed into a revolutionary mass Party.

This extraordinary conference and the open letter are designed to rouse all of the resources, all of the forces of the Party to change this situation, and to give us guarantees that the essential change in our work will be made.

The draft open letter, which is the central document in this conference, is the result of long discussions and examination of our work. It represents the most serious judgment of the situation and tasks of our Party by our leadership. It will undoubtedly be endorsed by the overwhelming majority of our membership.

BASIC TASKS OF THE 14TH PLENUM NOT CARRIED OUT

But we must recall that more than a year ago, at our Fourteenth Plenum already the Party had adopted all the essential features of the program of action here laid down. Yet, although we had some significant successes in our work since the Fourteenth Plenum—the Hunger March, the Detroit strikes, the Farmers' Conference, victories in the Scottsboro case, the veterans' movement, some important steps forward in applying the tactic of the united front and so on—yet the point upon which we must concentrate all of our attention is this: *that the basic tasks laid down at the Fourteenth Plenum have not been carried out.*

When we consider the especially favorable conditions for rousing and organizing a real mass movement around our Party, then it is clear that our small successes are important mainly to show the tremendous unused opportunities, to prove what could have been done everywhere and in the most important fields, if only we would seriously mobilize all our forces at the most decisive points.

* Excerpts from the Report to the Extraordinary Party Conference, New York City, July 7, 1933.—*Ed.*

What were these most decisive points? They were: (1) to win a firmer basis for our Party and for the revolutionary trade unions among the decisive strata of the workers in the most important industrial centers; (2) the strengthening of the Red Trade Unions, especially the miners', steel, textile and marine unions, and the organizing of a broad revolutionary opposition in the reformist unions—above all among the miners and the railroad workers; (3) mobilization and organization of the unemployed millions together with the employed for their most urgent daily needs and for unemployment insurance as the central immediate struggle of the Party; (4) the transformation of the *Daily Worker* into a really *revolutionary mass paper,* into an agitator and organizer of the masses; (5) wide development of new leading cadres of workers—the establishment of really collectively-working leading bodies and the improvement of these leading bodies by the drawing in of capable new working-class elements.

In the Fifteenth and Sixteenth Plenums of the Central Committee, we clarified certain fundamental questions upon which confusion had arisen. It is not necessary to revise any concrete decisions taken at the Fifteenth and Sixteenth Plenums. They were correct. But it must be recognized that these two last plenums of our Central Committee, in the face of continued failure to really concentrate the whole Party upon its basic task, did not arouse the whole Party to the seriousness of these tasks and did not let loose all the forces of the Party from below to secure the guarantee that the essential change would really be made.

To remedy these central weaknesses must be the central point of this conference, which must launch and carry through the profound deep-going transformation.

CLASH FOR MARKETS LEADS TO WAR

Before passing on to detailed examination of some of these problems, a few words must be said about the international situation. It is quite clear from the events taking place that the tempo of the war development is speeding up very fast. The practical collapse of the London Economic Conference has revealed how irreconcilable are imperialist antagonisms, how sharply their interests are clashing. The British-American trade war which is raging throughout the world, and which has for a long time been conducted in South America in the form of armed warfare between the South American countries, has by no means been softened as a result of the developments of the London Conference. On the contrary, in spite of the attempts which are made in the public press to indicate that in London a certain amount of general agreement has been established between London and Washington on the currency question and on other questions before the London Conference, the fact remains that the central antagonism upon which the whole conference was wrecked was precisely the war between the dollar and the pound. The British-American antagonism is coming forward sharper than ever before in the international scene. The Japanese-American antagonism is also assuming a very sharp form. Perhaps some of you already noticed that this afternoon's *World-Telegram* carries a big broadside editorial by Roy Howard, calling for building up the navy to full treaty strength as the "means of preserving peace in the Far East." These antagonisms among the great powers, and the measures being adopted for meeting the world problems of capitalism, make the development of the new world war a question of the day.

The danger of war is by no means expressed only in these sharpening main imperialist antagonisms. The sharper these antagonisms become, the stronger become the efforts of the leading capitalist statesmen to find a temporary solution in a common anti-Soviet war, to find a temporary solution of their antagonisms at the expense of the Workers' Republic. It is by no means an accident that precisely in the last days the relations on the eastern frontier of the Soviet Union have considerably sharpened. The attitude of the Manchurian "republic," puppet of Japan, has become extremely provocative. In Tokyo the newspapers are openly speaking about the necessity of annexing eastern Siberia. We can be sure that when Japan begins to take up seriously as a practical order of business the moving across Soviet borders, that they do so in certain agreement with at least some of the Western powers. We must not under any circumstances allow ourselves to become lax in our vigilance as to the necessity of rousing the masses for the defense of the Soviet Union merely on account of the diplomatic victories that are being won at this moment by the Soviet Union.

When we say this we do not by any means want to underestimate the importance of these diplomatic victories. The extension of the system of non-aggression pacts between the Soviet Union and France, and France's satellites in Eastern Europe, constitutes a definite victory for Soviet peace policy. The cancellation of the trade embargo of the British against the Soviets is another victory of Soviet diplomacy. The beginnings of organized large-scale trade relations between the United States and the Soviet Union and the perspective of a possible recognition of the Soviet Union by the United States in the near future are also victories. *But the winning of these victories does not soften the basic forces that are operating towards bringing together the imperialist powers for a desperate war of intervention against the Soviet Union.* It is necessary for us to weigh all of these factors in their proper perspective and to understand that the war danger is really an immediate question for the masses today, that we are really operating in a world situation more explosive, more pregnant with all of the factors of imperialist war of the most destructive character than July, 1914.

ROOSEVELT "NEW DEAL" AND FASCISM

This world situation is the outgrowth of the deepening of the crisis of world capitalism. This is bringing profound changes into the world relationships and into the domestic policies of the American bourgeoisie. In the United States these changes are expressed in the development of the Roosevelt "New Deal."

The "New Deal" represents the rapid development of bourgeois policy under the blows of the crisis, the sharpening of the class struggle at home and the imminence of a new imperialist war. The "New Deal" is a policy of slashing the living standards at home and fighting for markets abroad, for the simple purpose of maintaining the profits of finance capital. It is a policy of brutal oppression at home and of imperialist war abroad. It represents a further sharpening and deepening of the world crisis.

It has become very fashionable lately to speak about the "New Deal" as American fascism. One of Mussolini's newspapers declares that Roosevelt is following the path marked out by Italian fascism.

Norman Thomas has contributed a profound thought to the question and has written several long articles in the capitalist press, to point out that the "New Deal" is "economic fascism," and that it is composed of good and bad elements, many of them even "progressive" in their nature, if not accompanied by "political reaction." And a group of honest revolutionary workers in Brooklyn recently issued a leaflet in which they declared that Roosevelt and Hitler are the same thing. Such answers as these to the question of the essential character of the "New Deal" will not help us much.

It is true that elements of fascism long existing in America are being greatly stimulated, and are coming to maturity more rapidly than ever before. But it would be well for us to recall the analysis of fascism made at the Eleventh and Twelfth Plenums of the Executive Committee of the Communist International, both for the purpose of understanding the situation in Germany and for accurately judging the developments in America.

First, it must be understood that fascism grows naturally out of bourgeois democracy under the conditions of capitalist decline. It is only another form of the same class rule, the dictatorship of finance capital. Only in this sense can one say that Roosevelt is the same as Hitler, in that both are executives of finance capital. The same thing, however, could be said of every other executive of every other capitalist state. To label everything capitalist as fascism results in destroying all distinction between the various forms of capitalist rule. If we should raise these distinctions to a level of difference in principle, between fascism on the one side and bourgeois democracy on the other, this would be following in the line of reformism, of social-fascism. But on the other hand to ignore entirely these distinctions would be tactical stupidity, would be an example of "left" doctrinairism.

Second: the growth of fascist tendencies is a sign of the weakening of the rule of finance capital. It is a sign of the deepening of the crisis, a sign that finance capital can no longer rule in the old forms. It must turn to the more open and brutal and terroristic methods, not as the exception but as the rule, for the oppression of the population at home and preparation for war abroad. It is preventive counter-revolution, an attempt to head off the rise of the revolutionary upsurge of the masses.

Third: fascism is not a special economic system. Its economic measures go no further in the modification of the capitalist economic forms than all capitalist classes have always gone under the exceptional stresses of war and preparation for war. The reason for the existence of fascism is to protect the economic system of capitalism, private property in the means of production, the basis of the rule of finance capital.

Fourth: fascism comes to maturity with the direct help of the Socialist Parties, the parties of the Second International, who are those elements within the working class we describe as social-fascists because of the historic role which they play. Under the mask of opposition to fascism, they in reality pave the way for fascism to come to power. They disarm the workers by the theory of the lesser evil; they tell the workers they will be unable to seize and hold power; they create distrust in the revolutionary road by means of slanders against the Soviet Union; they throw illusions of democracy around the rising forces of fascism; they break up the international solidarity of the workers. They carry this out under the mask of "socialism" and "Marxism." In America this role is played by the S.P., "left" reformists and the A. F. of L. bureaucracy.

The development of Roosevelt's program is a striking illustration of the fact that there is no Chinese wall between democracy and fascism. Roosevelt operates with all of the arts of "democratic" rule, with an emphasized liberal and social-demagogic cover, quite a contrast with Hoover who was outspokenly reactionary. Yet behind this smoke screen, Roosevelt is carrying out more thoroughly, more brutally than Hoover, the capitalist attack against the living standards of the masses and the sharpest national chauvinism in foreign relations.

Under the New Deal we have entered a period of the greatest contradictions between the words and deeds of the heads of government.

Hoover refused the bonus to the veterans and called out the troops against them, causing Hushka and Carlson to be killed. Roosevelt gave the veterans a camp and food, and instead of sending the troops he sent his wife to meet them. But where Hoover denied the bonus, Roosevelt also denied the bonus and added to it a cut of $500,000,000 in pensions and disability allowances.

Roosevelt's international phrases have only served to cover the launching of the sharpest trade war the world has seen, with the United States operating on the world market with a cheapened dollar, with inflation, that is carrying out large-scale dumping.

Roosevelt's election campaign slogan of unemployment insurance and relief by the federal Government has been followed in office by refusal of insurance and drastic cutting down of relief, the institution of forced labor camps, etc.

Under the slogan of higher wages for the workers he is carrying out the biggest slashing of wages that the country has ever seen. Under the slogan of "freedom to join any trade union he may choose," the worker is driven into company unions or into the discredited A. F. of L., being denied the right to strike; while the militant unions are being attacked with the aim to destroy them.

With the cry, "take the Government out of the hands of Wall Street," Roosevelt is carrying through the greatest drive for extending trustification and monopoly, exterminating independent producers and small capitalists, and establishing the power of finance capital more thoroughly than ever before. He has turned the public treasury into the pockets of the big capitalists. While Hoover gave $3,000,000,000 in a year, Roosevelt has given $5,000,000,000 in three months.

As for the extra-legal developments of fascism, we should remember that it is precisely in the South which is the basis of power of the Democratic Party, that the Ku Klux Klan originated and is now being revived. It is the South that for generations has given the lie to all Democratic pretensions of liberalism by its brutal lynching, disfranchisement and Jim-Crowing of the Negro masses, and upon this basis has reduced the standard of living of the white workers in the South far below that of the rest of the country.

Large sections of workers in the basic industries in America, living in the company towns which are owned body and soul by the great trusts, have for long been under conditions just as brutal and oppressive as under Hitler in Germany today.

It is clear that fascism already finds much of its work done in America and more of it is being done by Roosevelt.

But it would be incorrect to speak of the New Deal as developed fascism. With a further rise of the revolutionary struggle of the masses, the bourgeoisie will turn more and more to fascist methods. Whether a fascist regime will finally be established in America will depend entirely upon the effectiveness of the revolutionary mass struggle, whether the masses will be able to defeat the attacks upon their rights and their standards of living.

What are the main features of the New Deal? Let us consider it as a whole, as a system of measures, and bring together all the various features embodied in new legislation and actions in Washington. We can sum up the features of the New Deal under the following heads: 1) Trustification; 2) inflation; 3) direct subsidies to finance capital; 4) taxation of the masses; 5) the economy program; 6) the farm program; 7) military and naval preparations; 8) the movement toward militarization, direct and indirect, of labor.

MAIN FEATURES OF "NEW DEAL"

First, *trustification:* Under the mask of the "radical" slogan of "controlled production," the Industrial Recovery Act has merely speeded up and centralized the process of trustification which has long been the dominant feature of American economy. There is now being carried out a clean-up of all the "little fellows." They are forced to come under the codes formulated by the trusts, which will have the force of law. The "little fellows' " doom is sealed and they are busy making the best terms possible for a "voluntary" assimilation before they are wiped out. Capitalist price-fixing has been given the force of law and the profits of the great trusts are guaranteed by the government. As for "controlled production," we have the word of an administration spokesman that "competition is not eliminated; it is only raised to a higher plane." That is quite true. The further strengthening of the power of monopoly capital is intensifying all of the chaos, antagonisms, disproportions, within American economy. "Controlled production" is impossible upon the basis of capitalist private property. There is only the growth of the power of the big capitalists and the intensification of all social and economic contradictions.

Second, *inflation:* The continuous cheapening of the dollar serves several purposes. First, it serves for a general cutting down of the living standards of the masses through higher domestic prices, and especially a reduction of workers' real wages (already over 20 per cent), and if we study the course of prices in the last few days, you will see that the reduction of real wages is now speeding up very fast. Second, inflation results in helping restore solvency to the banks and financial institutions by increasing the market value of their depreciated securities. Third, inflation carries out a partial expropriation of the savings and investments of the middle classes. Fourth, it results in the creation of a temporary expanding market to stimulate industrial production for a time, through the rush of speculators and profiteers to lay up stocks for higher prices. Fifth, inflation results in the launching of a tremendous commercial war of price-cutting and dumping on the world market. All of these results of inflation serve to strengthen finance capital, build up its profits at the cost of sharpened exploitation of the masses at home, and lead directly to imperialist war.

Third, the *direct subsidies:* This is only an enlargement of Hoover's policy of the Reconstruction Finance Corporation. Many billions of dollars as gifts, disguised as "loans," are being poured into the coffers of the big capitalists. It all comes out of the lowered living standards of the masses, the expropriation of the savings of the petty bourgeoisie, and out of mass taxation.

Fourth, the *taxation program:* There is being carried out under the New Deal an enormous shifting of even the present limited burdens of taxation on property and big income away from them and on to the shoulders of the masses, the workers and farmers. Almost all the increased taxation is in the form of sales taxes of all kinds, indirect taxation that falls upon the small consumers. All apparent measures of increasing income tax rates have merely fallen upon the middle class, while the big capitalists relieve themselves of all income taxes, as exemplified by the biggest capitalists of them all, Morgan, Otto Kahn, Mitchell, etc., who have gone for years now without paying any income tax.

Fifth, the *economy program:* While new taxes have been piled up and new billions of dollars given to the banks and trusts, "economy" is the rule for all government expenditure that reaches the masses or the little fellows. The government sets the example for the entire capitalist class with wholesale wage-cuts, with rationalization, mass discharges, etc., of government employees. The war veterans have their disability allowances cut by half a billion dollars; unemployment relief is substituted by forced labor camps; social services of all kinds is heavily slashed or discontinued altogether. That is the economy program of the New Deal.

Sixth, the *farm program:* While millions of workers are starving for lack of food, the Government turns its energies to cutting down farm production. Growing cotton is today being plowed under by direction of the Government. That is the New Deal. A 30 per cent tax is placed on bread in order that farmers shall get (at best) the same return for a smaller amount of wheat. Those farmers, in the best case, will still only maintain their bankrupt situation while the masses will have less bread at higher prices. The mortgage holders will absorb the great bulk of this government subsidy, at the expense of the stomachs of the masses. This year's wheat crop, already in the hands of the speculators, bought from the farmers at about 25 cents a bushel, sharply rises in price with enormous profits for the speculators. By the time the farmers can get 80 cents to $1 for the coming crop, the dollar will be so inflated that it will be worth just about that 25 cents they got for wheat last year. Farmers will be at an even greater disadvantage in buying industrial products at monopoly prices sharply

rising under the Allotment Plan provided in the New Deal which is
used as an attempt to divide workers from farmers and set them in
sharp rivalry, but the masses including the farmers pay all the bills.

Seventh, the *military and naval preparations:* This is one of the
chief features of the New Deal. The wild commercial war on the
world markets, sharpened to an enormous degree by the falling value
of the dollar, has already disrupted the London Economic Conference,
has brought all imperialist antagonisms to a critical point. British-
American relations are clashing in every field. Japanese-American relations are growing sharper. A government which carries out this
bandit policy of inflation and dumping, while at the same time driving
down the living standards of the masses at home, such a government
really should logically go heavily armed. An inevitable part of the
New Deal is therefore the tremendous building of new battleships,
cruisers, new poison gases, explosives, new tanks and other machinery
of destruction for the army, new military roads, the increase of armed
forces, increased salaries for the officers. Industrial recovery is thus
to be hastened by working the war industries overtime. Such war
preparations have never been seen before since 1917.

Eighth, and finally, there is the movement towards *militarization of
labor.* This is the most direct and open part of the fascist features of
the New Deal. The sharpest expression of this is the forced labor
camps with the dollar-a-day wage. Already some 250,000 workers
are in these camps. This forced labor has several distinct aims. First,
it sets a standard of wages towards which the capitalists will try to
drive the so-called free labor everywhere. It smashes the old traditional wage standards. Secondly, it breaks up the system of unemployed relief and establishes the principle that work must be done
for all relief given. Thirdly, it furnishes cheap labor for government
projects, mostly of a military nature, and for some favored capitalists.
Fourthly, it takes the most virile and active unemployed workers out
of the cities where, as government spokesmen have said, they constitute "a danger to law and order," and places these "dangerous" people
under military control. Fifthly, it sets up a military reserve of
human cannon-fodder already being trained for the coming war.

But the provisions of the Industrial Recovery Act regarding labor
provide a much more large-scale effort at militarization of labor, though
in quite different form from the forced labor camps. In the industries,
for the employed worker, the aim is to establish a semi-military
regime, in many ways similar to the old war-time legislation, under
government fixed wages, compulsory arbitration of all disputes with
the government as arbitrator, abolition of the right to strike and independent organization of workers. These things are to be achieved
through the industrial codes worked out by employers and given the
force of law by the signature of Roosevelt, supported when and where

necessary by the American Federation of Labor and the Socialist Party, who have already entered wholeheartedly into this pretty scheme.

In the labor section of the New Deal are to be seen the clearest examples of the tendencies towards fascism. It is the American brother to Mussolini's "corporate state," with state-controlled labor unions closely tied up with and under the direction of the employers. Here we have also the sharpest American example of the role of the Socialist Party and the trade union bureaucracy, the role of social-fascism as the bearers among the masses of the program of fascism, who pave the way for the establishment of fascist control over the masses.

SITUATION IN OUR PARTY

New let us consider what is the position of our Party for facing and solving all the enormous problems that arise out of this situation. What is the basic situation of the Party? During 1932 our membership was doubled. But in the first half-year of 1933 it has remained stationary. We decided that recruiting should not be a special campaign, but should be an every-day activity. That was a very nice decision. But the way we carried it out was that we abolished the campaign feature of recruiting but we failed to replace it with serious day-to-day recruiting work; the result was that our Party has stopped growing. *This is a most serious and alarming fact.* It is clear that tens of thousands of workers are ready for membership but we do not bring them in. We do not consolidate those we bring in. The membership remains around 20,000 with average dues payments of 17,000 to 18,000 per week. We cannot claim any serious growth in membership and we will not be able to claim serious growth of membership under present conditions until we reach and surpass 50,000 members.

Secondly, our membership consists in its majority of unemployed workers, and the proportion of the unemployed constantly rises. What recruiting we do is mainly among the unemployed; partial figures available for some districts show that fully 80 per cent of the new members have no connections with the shops, mills or mines. Of course we want all these new members from among the unemployed, and more of them—but if this is not accompanied by simultaneous recruiting of employed workers, then a most serious danger arises that we may become a Party of unemployed; that we may find the very composition of our Party becoming an obstacle to the basic task of building unity of employed and unemployed workers. It is clear that in this respect we are following, not our plan of work, but are drifting along the line of least resistance.

Thirdly, those new members we recruit are not, except to a small degree, brought from the most important strata of workers—from the basic industries, from mines, from among the steel workers, the railroad workers, etc. We have no serious planned recruiting work among these most important sections. Here again we drift and become the victims of spontaneity.

Fourthly, our shop work remains disgracefully weak. Only four per cent of our members are in shop nuclei; no serious improvement can yet be seen. Hundreds of nuclei have been organized only to disappear, and very few leading committees are enough interested to even be able to tell us how and why they were destroyed and how they could have been saved and built up. In the main these shop nuclei have died because of lack of leadership, lack of concrete help, from the Political Bureau, from the Central Committee, from the District Committees, from the Section Committees. We did not learn how to obtain the necessary activity in the shop—without which a nucleus exists only in form and will dry up and blow away—combined with the necessary safeguards against victimization, without which a nucleus is destroyed by our enemies. We did not seriously study the methods of combating spies, exposing and driving them out of the shops by the mass pressure of the workers. We did not take up seriously the problems of conspiratorial work in the shop, did not seriously understand that shop work is illegal work, and that here we must find the most skillful combination of legal and illegal work. There was laxness in the Central Committee and in the Political Bureau in systematically pushing these questions forward and finding the way to lead the whole Party to their solution. There was too much mechanical pressure from above for unprepared, unplanned activity; there was insufficient attention to concrete shop issues and the combination of these with the larger political questions. There were no steps taken to strengthen the weak inner political life of the shop nuclei.

Fifthly, all our lower units suffer from lack of concrete tasks and concrete, planned work, based upon an examination of the situation of each one. Abstract, general plans, worked out above, are mechanically applied to the life of each and every local organization. The result is lack of contact with real life, undirected general activities without results, therefore dampening the enthusiasm of the membership. This again results in surrendering to spontaneity, the line of least resistance; unplanned work, uncontrolled activity.

That, briefly is the situation of the Party. . . .

STRUGGLE FOR SOCIAL INSURANCE—A CENTRAL TASK

Let us turn to an examination of our central struggle for social insurance, where we have most serious weaknesses. These weaknesses have been examined in detail in the article of Comrade Gussev published in the *Communist International* and in the *Daily Worker*. We must all agree with the fundamental correctness of that article. We must search for the causes and remove them.

While in theory we all agree that social insurance is the business of all workers, of all organizations, yet in practice we assign all concrete measures in the fight for unemployment insurance to the Unemployed Councils. In resolutions, we speak of unity of the employed and unemployed, but in practice our Red unions often ignore the whole question of social insurance. They do not undertake any concrete actions which show they understand it is their very central task to fight for social insurance also. We have the beginnings of a good movement for social insurance in the A. F. of L. local unions, but it is left isolated, working by itself. The districts and sections neglect their task of building the whole broad movement.

Above all we have a general underestimation of the historical aim of the fight for social insurance, even within our Party, and yet worse among the leading cadres. We have not won mass support as it is quite possible to do because we have not been able simply and clearly to explain to the workers the need for struggle for social insurance. We will win the masses when every Party member and every Party leader can explain in the simplest terms that mass unemployment of millions of workers is a permanent feature of American society as long as capitalism lasts; and without unemployment insurance this condition results in degrading to a starvation level, not only the millions of unemployed but the millions who are in the shops. We must explain the difference between the real social insurance as proposed in the Workers' Unemployment Insurance Bill and the fake schemes of the reformists. . . .

WORKERS' UNEMPLOYMENT INSURANCE BILL AND BILLS OF OUR OPPONENTS

I will list ten points that distinguish the Workers' Unemployment Insurance Bill, points upon which we can win the masses to us, to work with us, fight with us, to support our struggle, to join our organizations. These ten points are:

First. Whereas the fake schemes of the employers, reformists and social-fascists, direct themselves only to *future* unemployment, the Workers' Bill provides for immediate insurance for those *now* unemployed.

Second. While the fake schemes all exclude some categories of workers, the Workers' Bill covers *all those who depend for a living upon wages.*

Third. While most of the fake schemes place burdens upon the employed workers, the Workers' Bill places the full burden of the insurance upon the *employers* and their *government.*

Fourth. While all of the fake schemes contain provisions that could and would be used for strike-breaking, wage-cutting and victimization, the Workers' Bill protects the unemployed from being forced to work below union rates, at reduced wages, or far from home.

Fifth. While all fake schemes place the administration of the insurance in the hands of the employers and the bureaucratic apparatus controlled by them, the Workers' Bill provides for administration by representatives elected from the workers themselves.

Sixth. While all the fake schemes provide for benefits limited to a starvation level, a fixed minimum which is also the maximum, and this only for a few weeks in a year (thereby being in amount even below charity relief), the Workers' Bill provides for *full average wages* for the entire period of unemployment, determined according to industry, group and locality, thus maintaining the standards of life at its previous level.

Seventh. While the fake schemes establish a starvation maximum above which benefits cannot be given, the Workers' Bill establishes a living minimum, below which benefits shall not be allowed to fall, no matter what the previous condition of the unemployed worker.

Eighth. While all the fake schemes refuse benefits to all workers who still have any personal property, forcing them to sell and consume the proceeds of home, furniture, automobiles, etc., before they can come under the insurance, the Workers' Insurance Bill establishes the benefits as a matter of right, without investigation of the workers' other small resources.

Ninth. While the fake schemes limit their benefits to only able-bodied unemployed, the Workers' Bill provides for every form of involuntary unemployment, whether from closing of industries, from sickness, accidents, old age, maternity, etc.; in other words the Workers' Bill is an example of true *social insurance.*

Tenth. Whereas the fake schemes all try to turn attention of the workers to the 48 different state governments in an effort to split up and discourage the movement, the Workers' Bill provides for federal insurance, one uniform national system, financed through national taxation and all proposals to the state legislatures contain the provision that the state bills are only temporary, pending the adoption of the Federal Bill demanded in the state proposals.

These ten points all protect the most vital interests of the entire working class. Each and every one of them is absolutely essential to protect the working class from the degrading effects of mass unemployment. All that is necessary to win millions of workers to active struggle for this social insurance is to make these proposals clear, show how the fake schemes violate these fundamental interests of the workers, and show how mass struggle can win real insurance.

With this Workers' Bill we can then proceed to smash the influence of the social-fascists and employers who claim that it is impossible to finance such a system of insurance. The Hoover and Roosevelt administrations have already shown that tens of billions of dollars are available to the government whenever it really decides to get the funds. But Hoover and Roosevelt got these billions only to give to the banks and trusts. We demand these billions together with the hundreds of millions used in war preparations to be used for social insurance.

We really must begin a mass campaign along these lines, conducted in the most simple form with a real concentration of attention by all of our organizations and all leading committees. Such a campaign will rouse a mighty mass movement for the Workers' Bill. And this movement will be under the leadership of the Communist Party. The fact that our mass struggle for social insurance has been so weak, politically and organizationally, is largely to be attributed to neglect arising from serious underestimation of this issue; and also to lack of detailed understanding of our own Workers' Bill, and the vital differences between it and the other bills.

OUR UNITED FRONT POLICY—A LEVER TO WINNING THE MASSES

In the last period of the struggle for a united front against the capitalist offensive, which began with the manifesto of the Communist International and the rise of fascism to power in Germany, our own Party has made some improvements in this field. The manifesto of our Central Committee in March was on the whole a correct and effective application of the united front to our conditions. We made some concrete extensions on these good beginnings. But can we say that we have decisively overcome our former weaknesses in our struggle against social-fascism? No, we cannot say it. These weaknesses still remain and some of them in even more serious form just now.

First is the lack of serious sympathetic approach to the rank-and-file members of the reformist organizations. Literally hundreds of our lower organizations still take a certain pride in the fact that they have no contact whatever with the workers of the Socialist Party, A. F. of L. or the Musteites. They make no effort whatever to reach them. They organize meetings only for "our own" workers, those who already agree with us on everything. If they happen by accident to meet a Socialist Party or A. F. of L. member, these comrades assume a very high and scornful attitude. They appear very superior to these people. They are very free to speak of them as "social-fascists," applying the term to the workers and not the leaders. They think it is beneath their dignity to explain carefully, patiently and sympathetically how the Communist Party, or our various mass organizations, propose united struggles of all the workers for their most burning needs; to explain how the split among the masses arises because the social-fascist leaders sabotage and obstruct the struggle and thereby help the capitalist class.

They do not see that it is absolutely necessary to convince each worker in the Socialist Party, Musteites or A. F. of L., through his own contact, that the Communists are the only sincere, active and efficient fighters for unity in the struggle for their own daily needs. Above all our comrades do not understand the need for sympathetic approach to these rank-and-file workers. Unless we really overcome this weakness in a more decisive manner we will not make the progress that is required for us towards winning the majority of the working class.

Second, we have a tendency to neglect or slur over differences in principle between the Communists and the social-fascist leaders. We can never win the workers to a united front of struggle, which means winning them away from the social-fascist influence, unless we meet squarely and explain sharply the basic differences between us and them.

Many comrades think that we will build up the anti-fascist front by keeping silent about the betrayal of the German Social-Democracy and its open going over to Hitler. But an anti-fascist front which keeps silent about this basic fact is no anti-fascist front at all. It is already beginning to go on the same route as the Social-Democracy—surrender to fascism. An anti-fascist fighting front must be built—and can only be built—through exposure of, and fight against, those who helped Hitler to power, who voted for Hitler's policy in the Reichstag.

Third, there is a rising tendency, which we must very sharply fight against, to accept conferences, nice resolutions, new united front committees with all sorts of fancy names—as a solution of our problem. These things become not a means of reaching, organizing and activizing the masses but an excuse for stopping work. This tendency must be smashed. Words must be checked up against deeds. Action must be demanded and carried out. New masses must be reached. Everyone who hinders this, everyone who sabotages or neglects this must be exposed, no matter who it is, and fought against. Every committee which does not work must be resolutely liquidated as an obstructor of progress and discrediting the united front.

For example, we have a committee which was set up to collect aid for the victims of fascism in Germany. This committee has been allowed to drift along and spend most of the little money that it has collected for the expenses of the collection. This situation is a scandal. We cannot tolerate such things. It makes the situation not one bit better, rather all the worse, that the Communists who should be the most active in the committee sometimes leave the responsibility to non-Party elements who for some reason or other are unable to function. Thus, on this anti-fascist committee we placed Muste as chairman, without any question as to whether he would or could give active leadership, but merely as a "united front" decoration. Such a united front is a miserable parody which discredits the idea of united front. It should be in the archives of the past history,

Every united front must be active, testing all its participants, including ourselves—above all ourselves. It must provide the masses with the opportunity of really forming their own judgment as to who is a really devoted, capable leader and fighter, who is a slacker, who is sabotaging and who has a tendency to surrender and collaborate with the enemies.

Such weaknesses as these that we have just briefly described will become all the more dangerous in the coming months if they are not quickly and energetically overcome. We are entering a period of large-scale united front efforts and actions, of which the August 26 conference in Cleveland is only a beginning, which must be given the most solid roots and foundations down below among the masses. If we do not have a correct approach to the masses, if we do not keep our attention upon the masses, if we surrender to this game of playing around with leaders, then we are not serious revolutionaries at all, then we are surrendering to social-fascism, then we deserve the contempt of every revolutionary worker. . . .

NEED FOR A CORRECT POLICY OF CADRES

Another serious weakness in our work is the general lack of a well prepared and energetically executed policy of cadres—how to develop cadres, new leading forces, how to make use of them. This applies also to the question of the proper utilization of old cadres, the promotion of new forces and the establishment of collective leading bodies in such a way as to strengthen our connection with the masses, to consolidate our organization, give more guarantees for the execution of all our complicated and difficult tasks. We do not give the necessary attention to the developing of new forces among the Americans, and especially the young Americans and the Negro Americans. The distribution of old forces has usually been according to the needs of the moment, without plan. Many excellent comrades, good material for leadership, have been misused, shifted around so many times they don't know where they are at, and lose the capacity for serious planned work. And many old comrades also have simply been neglected and left to one side without the assigning of serious work. Comrades with long standing and training in the movement and great capacity of work, through the lack of systematic cadre policy, are left in passivity and their capacities wasted. We must really insist upon every leading committee in the Party and every fraction in the mass organizations discussing this question and beginning to build up a conscious policy of how to deal with leading forces, how to provide the conditions so that comrades can really go into their work and master it, how to help in the education of these cadres and especially how to develop new cadres and bring in fresh elements.

We must above all emphasize that there cannot be the old surrender to spontaneity. We must really plan this work and direct it to the most important points, *i.e.*, we must give our main attention to new cadres and the proper use of old cadres, especially in the mining industry, in metal, in railroad, and the heavy industries generally. And in these industries, to 'concentrate upon the biggest shops, the most important shops. There is where we must find our most important new cadres. If we do not find new cadres, we will not get new masses; and if we do not get new masses, we will not solve any of our problems.

IMMEDIATE DEMANDS—THE REVOLUTIONARY WAY OUT

In the election campaign last year our Party made its first big effort to place before the masses the struggle for the revolutionary way out of the crisis, and its connection with the fight for the immediate needs of the workers. Our election platform placed this question correctly. But we have not yet learned how to make this connection in life among the masses so that large numbers of workers will understand the revolutionary consequences of their immediate struggles and become convinced Bolsheviks through these struggles. This is a weakness which has been further emphasized by our tendency to neglect the agitation and propaganda for the revolutionary way out.

More energetic development of the struggle for immediate demands (shop struggles and strikes, fight for unemployment relief, against evictions, for social insurance, fight for civil rights, etc.) is the basic feature of all our tasks in the U.S.A. We must understand, and must bring this understanding to the masses, that under the conditions of the crisis, even the smallest of these struggles takes on a political character; places the workers before state power in the hands of finance capital; and raises the question of the struggle for power. This question, arising even spontaneously in the minds of backward workers, calls upon the Party to give the masses a more full understanding of the problems of the struggle for power, and of the program of the Party for the time when the workers hold power, the program of the revolutionary solution of the crisis and the building of a socialist society.

There is no contradiction between the needs of the immediate struggle, and the propaganda of the revolutionary way out. On the contrary, the latter strengthens the former.

Of course, it is the tactics of the S.P. and the A. F. of L. to shout that they represent the immediate interests of the workers, and that the C.P. subordinates these immediate interests to a far-off revolutionary goal. But the social-fascists betray not only the revolution, but even the smallest wage-struggle. Immediate demands can be won, even under the worst conditions of crisis, but only through revolutionary struggle and with revolutionary leadership. The more clear the leadership and the masses on the revolutionary implications of the fight, the more chance of winning immediate demands.

Any failure to understand this leads towards submission to the social-fascists and agents of the employers. We had a clear illustration of this during the Detroit auto strikes. Due to our own lack of vigilance, agents of the bosses came into leadership of the strike committee in the Briggs Mack Avenue plant. After they had established their positions by using the prestige of the Auto Workers' Union among the workers, they turned against the Union, claiming it was led by Communists and they didn't want the issue of communism to prejudice the winning of their strike for wage increases. Our comrades hesitated in front of this "red scare"; they tried to avoid the issue. By this weakness they actually failed to avoid the issue, but on the contrary made it effective against the Union, instead of making it favorable to the Union. The results of the strikes proved that it was precisely the anti-Communists who betrayed the strike for higher wages; the Mack Avenue plant, which broke away from the Union, lost the strike; those plants staying with the Union and Communist leadership won their strikes.

We should, can and must make this clear to the masses with detailed facts and not leave it to them to learn this lesson by their own bitter experience. We must face the issue of a "red scare." We must explain, not in the language of high politics but in simple, clear language, what is our aim. We must not shout empty phrases about hanging the red flag over the white house or over the factories, but quietly in every-day language explain that while we put all energy into the winning of immediate struggles, we know that strikes must go on and be broadened and deepened until the workers put their own representatives into a position of power, to open factories and give everyone work, to open closed apartments, to open to the hungry and ragged the warehouses that are bursting with food and clothing. That can only be carried out by a workers' government which has driven the capitalists from their seats of power. To see and know these things in advance makes every worker a better fighter. The Party which sees these things in advance is the only party which is capable of leading the workers to successful fights for their immediate demands. The S.P. and A. F. of L. sell out, betray and sabotage the smallest struggles, precisely because they are against the revolutionary solution of the crisis; precisely because they want to restore capitalism, precisely because, in the last resort, they always take their orders from the capitalist government which they are opposed to replacing by a workers' government.

HOW TO FIGHT AGAINST THE N.I.R.A.

The fight against the Industrial Recovery Act—how shall we organize it? This is not a simple task. The illusions about the New Deal as a road back to prosperity are still strong among broad masses. To expose and disperse these illusions will require more experience and above all requires the active, ceaseless, carefully thought-out intervention of the Communist Party. These illusions are based not only upon the "newness" of the Roosevelt regime, the demagogy of Roosevelt, but also upon two other important factors. These are, first: the appearance of "concrete results," as they say, in the increase of industrial production, and second: the active efforts of the A. F. of L. and the S.P. in support of the Roosevelt program.

Let us be very clear about the significance of the increase in industrial production. It has been a big increase in certain industries. It would be the greatest stupidity to deny this fact. It has been greatly exaggerated in the capitalist press, and we may point this out. What is really important, however, is that in most industries rationalization and speed-up have made such strides in the past year that even with increased production, the total number of workers employed is less than it was a year ago. A classical example of this was brought out in the auto workers' convention, with regard to the Ford plants, where production has increased 10 percent over last year, and the number of workers declined by 20 percent. This is a striking example of the truth, now generally admitted even by the capitalists, that even the return of full capacity of production in all industries would not put the unemployed back to work but would leave eight to ten million permanently unemployed. When the masses understand this fully, and realize that this will determine their conditions even if they are among the lucky ones who get jobs, then a large part of their illusions about the New Deal will be undermined.

Further, the increase in production does not represent an improvement in the consumption market. On the contrary, many of the most important indexes of consumption show a decline. Thus department store sales for June, one of the most important indications in the retail market, declined five percent from a year ago. But if consumption is not increasing (and it is not), then whence comes the demand that brought about increased production? Equally clearly, this production is for a speculative market caused by inflation. With the value of the dollar declining, that is, with increasing prices, all the speculators and profiteers are piling up goods in warehouses to speculate on the higher prices. Accumulated stores are increasing. In other words, overproduction, a greater amount of commodities than can be absorbed in the effective market, is more pronounced than ever. The stopping of inflation would immediately send the market crashing into a deeper crisis than ever before. That is why Roosevelt was ready to insult every imperialist nation and broke up the London Economic Conference rather than stabilize the dollar. But even continued inflation, continued indefinitely, cannot hold up this false market for more than a time. Sooner or later, probably sooner, the accumulated stores of materials will break down this speculative market. The indefinite storing of unlimited quantities of unused goods cannot continue. Even this limited revival of production, produced by inflation, cannot last very long. The end will be worse than the beginning.

EXPOSE CONCRETELY A. F. OF L. AND S.P. SUPPORT OF N.I.R.A.

The American Federation of Labor and the Socialist Party are playing a very important part in building up and supporting the mass illusions about Roosevelt. The bourgeoisie is very anxious that the masses shall not resist their attacks. Workers and farmers, however, resist the attacks (this is already shown in the rising strike wave) thus making it difficult for Roosevelt to put across his program. The administration can be forced at least to make concessions to the mass resistance. Roosevelt's problem is how to keep the masses from struggle. His most valuable helpers in this task are the American Federation of Labor and the Socialist Party.

The A. F. of L. unconditionally accepts the Industrial Recovery Act and has pledged itself not to allow members to strike but to accept, without protest, whatever decisions are made by the employers and Roosevelt. These leaders cooperated with the bosses in working out the codes, as in the textile industry, with a wage scale lower than the present average, and 35 percent below four years ago. They make glowing promises to the masses of benefits under the Industrial Recovery Act if only they would join the American Federation of Labor. Great recruiting campaigns are being carried on; the workers are led to think that they are joining a "trade union" which will conduct "collective bargaining" for higher wages. They do not yet realize that the "wage codes" are not even an imitation of collective bargaining, not to speak of struggle and that these "trade unions" are not a means of action but a means whereby employers obtain guarantees against any action by the workers.

The Socialist Party has been very active in support of the New Deal. Already in the first days of the Roosevelt regime, Norman Thomas and Morris Hillquit paid a formal visit to Roosevelt in the White House and afterwards issued a public statement to the newspapers praising Roosevelt and recommending his program to the workers. At the recent meeting of the Socialist Party National Executive Committee at Reading, Pa., it was decided to cast their lot without reservation with the American Federation of Labor in putting over the industrial slavery law. The "Left" reformists, the Musteites, are wavering between the position of the Socialist Party and the class struggle, under pressure of their own radicalized followers. They are forced, to hold their following, to pay lip service to the united front, and even sometimes take practical steps for concrete struggles. Our task is to win these masses for clear and unhesitant policies. *The social-fascists are the shock troops of finance capital in pushing the New Deal into the camp of the workers.*

The first stage in arousing and organizing workers against the industrial slavery law is to thoroughly understand what it means in actual life and explain this to the broadest possible number of workers. Even this very necessary educational work, however, requires actions and maneuvers in order to make the issue clear and understandable to the broadest masses. That is why the Trade Union Unity League and the National Textile Workers' Union sent a delegation to Washington to appear at the hearings on the Textile Code. This delegation spoke and made proposals in quite a different sense from that of the representative of the A. F. of L. and the Socialist Party. Comrade Croll, spokesman for the delegation, exposed the whole purpose and effects of the Recovery Act as an enslavement and impoverishment of the workers. She declared that the workers would not surrender the right to strike against any conditions unsatisfactory to them. Then she proposed amendments to the labor code, the complete rejection of which exposed the true nature of the Code to all workers who followed the proceedings. The rejected amendments called for the establishment of a guaranteed wage not below $720 per year based upon a guarantee of not less than 40 weeks' work a year and not less than 30 or more than 40 hours' work per week. The fact that the administration refused to consider any provision directed towards really raising the standards of living of the textile workers, or to give any guarantees about employment, exposes the whole purpose of the Act as being merely a guarantee of bosses' profits and to stifle any resistance by workers. In addition to the wage provision, the Trade Union Unity League proposed other safeguards to the workers that were also rejected.

In line with this excellent example given by the Trade Union Unity League and the Textile Workers' Industrial Union at the hearings, it is absolutely necessary that every revolutionary trade union and group shall develop, each in its own industry, similar actions, and to bring those actions to the largest possible number of workers. The presentation of our demands at the time of the formulation of the Industrial Recovery Code must be made an instrument of mass agitation and organization of the workers, the beginnings of organization of these workers for these demands and making these hearings one of the incidents in a battle for the organization of the workers for the direct struggle for these demands as presented for the Codes.

The role of the A. F. of L. in the textile hearings is very instructive for the entire movement. We must study and learn how to expose these tricks before the masses. It is not enough merely to state that the A. F. of L. is helping the government and employers. We must prove it, and this means we must learn concretely how to expose all their maneuvers. The A. F. of L. bureaucrats are not so stupid as to think they can get away with their treachery without masking it with all kinds of clever and flexible tricks. Thus in the textile hearings, William Green, who helped formulate the code, succeeded in getting himself into the newspapers as in opposition to the Code, on the grounds that the wage-scale was not high enough, demanding $16 instead of $12. Then McMahon, President of the Textile Workers' Union, also found it necessary to speak, but more modestly, demanding only $14.40. Then one of the commissioners, Mr. Allen, who evidently was inexperienced and hadn't learned to "play ball" with the leaders of the A. F. of L. and allow them their necessary freedom to appear as a loyal opposition, let the cat out of the bag by indignantly exclaiming that McMahon had worked with him in the preparation of the Code and expressed his agreement with every feature of it.

This revealing little incident is particularly valuable and should be carried to every worker in every industry. In the future we can expect that this will not be repeated. Undoubtedly Mr. Allen, and all the other commissioners, were called into a private conference and explained that they must not expose the collaboration of the A. F. of L. leaders behind the scenes, but give them liberty to make a fake opposition in the public hearings.

It is also necessary to learn concretely how to expose the maneuvers of the Socialist Party, typified by Norman Thomas. Mr. Thomas is one of Roosevelt's most valuable assistants in putting across the New Deal. Of course, this does not mean that Thomas comes out openly to endorse it. If he did, then he would be no more valuable than any of Roosevelt's direct secretaries. On the contrary, he says he is opposed to the underlying philosophy of this bill, but goes on to say that these politicians in Washington are so stupid, so poorly prepared to draw up a bill that would really execute the wishes of the big industrialists, that they left a lot of loopholes for the workers to change it into something entirely different from what the capitalists intended it to be. Mr. Thomas assures the workers that they can turn this law into something for their own advancement instead of the enrichment of the capitalists. These golden opportunities, Thomas assures the workers, much more than offset the bad effects which the bill is intended to have in driving down the standards of the workers, destroying the right to strike and herding them into company-controlled unions. This propaganda of Thomas and the Socialist Party is accompanied by declarations of 100 percent cooperation with the A. F. of L. which openly supports the bill in its entirety.

UNITED FRONT MOVEMENT AGAINST N.I.R.A.

It is highly important in the very first stages of the Industrial Recovery Act to secure the broadest possible crystallization of opposition against it and preparations for the development of mass struggles which are sure to come in the immediate future. On this vital issue affecting every phase of the workers' every-day life, we must crystallize a real united front of struggle. Here, if anywhere, are the need and opportunity for applying the united front.

From this point of view there has already been launched a serious move for united action. In the next days there will be distributed a public manifesto against the Industrial Recovery Act which will have signatures of 70 or 80 leaders of various economic organizations of the workers. The signers will include the T.U.U.L. and various unions affiliated with it; Muste and various unions associated with his particular tendency; National Unemployed Council, and unemployed leagues with a Musteite leadership; a series of A. F. of L. local unions, the A. F. of L. Committee for Unemployment Insurance and some unattached independent unions. The manifesto gives a politically satisfactory characterization of the new deal, exposes the falseness of the promises of returning prosperity and lays down a six-point workers' program against the Roosevelt program. It then proceeds to outline methods of struggle against the capitalist offensive. This program contains the following points which are the very center of every united front action today, and to the extent that we can mobilize workers and workers' organizations around this, we can really build a united front:

(1) Initiate and support all efforts of the workers to organize in shops, mines, stores and offices; strengthen the existing class unions to carry on the class struggle of the workers against the bosses and boss-controlled government agencies; immediate conferences of all genuinely militant elements in steel, in mining, textile and other industries to unite the masses for struggle.

(2) Agitate and organize in all unions and other economic organizations for the adoption of a fighting policy in line with the program here set forth and against those who follow the dangerous and deceptive policy of "cooperating harmoniously" with the bosses.

(3) Intensify the struggle against autocratic, corrupt and racketeering elements in the unions and against the A. F. of L. officialdom which supports or tolerates such evils.

(4) Build up the mass organizations of unemployed workers, bring them into close cooperation with the employed; promote the unification of all mass organizations of the unemployed, locally, state-wide and nationally.

(5) Organize and support strikes and demonstrations of employed and unemployed workers.

(6) Organize a broad campaign for federal social insurance through conferences, meetings, collection of signatures, etc.

This United Front Manifesto concludes with a call to all workers' economic organizations to meet together in a general conference in

Cleveland, August 26-27, to work out measures for organizing the broadest possible mass fight.

One of the important features of this Manifesto is the agreement to work for a unification of the unemployed, locally, state-wide and nationally. Serious progress is already registered in the unification of the unemployed. It is clear that in this broad movement, with strong representation of Musteites, the road to unity on the basis of class struggle will not be a simple and easy matter. It is easier to get agreement on a sound manifesto than to get bold and energetic action to carry it out. Only the most persistent and careful checking up on the actual performance of all those who claim to support the united front program, only the most fearless criticism of every failure to properly apply it, can provide a guarantee that the unity movement will consolidate the forces of the class struggle and not paralyze this struggle.

Our Party will be put to the test in this united front movement. If we are to succeed it will be necessary for us to make a basic improvement in all our methods of work and our approach to the masses. The nature of our criticism must be very clearly thought out, moderate and restrained in its tone and at the same time fearless in raising the necessary questions. We must learn to arouse mass criticism of every weakness and hesitation. Where arguments do not convince, mass pressure will often win. . . .

ROOTING PARTY IN BASIC INDUSTRIES

It is clear that the working class in America, and the Communist Party, are entering into a period of decisive events which will determine for many years to come the whole history of our movement. Whether the toiling masses of America will go upon the path of determined class struggle, whether they will take the road toward the revolutionary way out of the crisis of capitalism, or whether they will be turned into the channels of social-fascism or fascism—this question will be decided by the work of the Communist Party. If our Party can gather all its forces for a profound change in its work and really make a Bolshevik turn to the masses, can assume the full responsibilities of leadership of the growing strike movement, the struggle of the unemployed; really build a solid base for itself among the most decisive strata of the working class, the workers in basic industry; if our Party can really gather around it the non-proletarian masses who are suffering under the crisis—only then will the Communist Party of the United States really have measured up to its historic responsibility. Only then will we really have shown that we understand the basic teachings of Lenin.

When we search for the reasons of our previous failures to make this decisive change, we must emphasize one key question which explains most of our failures. The Open Letter states this very sharply. It clearly establishes that among all our weaknesses, *the central point is the failure to understand the decisive role played by the workers in basic industries,* in the most decisive industrial centers, in the most important big shops and mines. Without securing a solid foundation among these most decisive workers, all successes in other fields of work, no matter how important they may be, are built upon sand without any guarantee of permanence.

Because of our weak understanding of this central question, the Party and its leadership, first of all the Central Committee and Political Bureau, has not been able to drive forward along a firm course determined according to plan. It has as yet been unable to make use of the most favorable possibilities for moving forward steadily from point to point, consolidating the growing forces of a rising mass movement. We have surrendered our planned work to the pressure of incidental problems of every-day life. We have become captives of spontaneity instead of masters of the development of events. We have surrendered to our weaknesses instead of overcoming them. Because the main body of our membership are unemployed, we allowed the growth of our Party to accentuate this one-sidedness, instead of decisively driving toward the recruitment of employed workers. Because our members are mainly in small shops, we have surrendered to the difficulties of penetrating the big factories. Because it is easier to win small temporary victories in light industry, we have allowed ourselves to be driven back in coal, steel, railroad, etc. The practical work has been determined not by our plan, but by the pressure of the events of the day.

When we give this most sharp emphasis upon the central importance of winning a solid foundation among the workers in the basic industries, we must warn against the interpretation that this means we are doing too much among the unemployed workers. Such an interpretation would be a serious distortion of the Open Letter. We do not have too many unemployed, we only have too few employed. It is not that our Unemployed Councils are too strong. On the contrary, they are seriously weak. It is only that our revolutionary trade union movement and the leadership of strike struggles in the basic industries are still stagnant.

The decisive strengthening of our base and our activities among the employed workers in basic industry will not weaken our unemployed movement. On the contrary, it will give it an enormous impetus forward. At the same time our Unemployed Councils will grow in membership and power, if they are also orientated mainly upon the workers who have been thrown out of the most important factories and industries, thereby able to contribute to the growth of the revolutionary trade unions in these industries.

Similarly, our emphasis upon winning the decisive proletarian masses must not be interpreted as in any way turning away from the task of winning allies among the non-proletarian masses. One of the important results that will follow from a decisive widening of our proletarian base will lie precisely in the strengthened abilities of the Party to lead the struggles of the farmers, of the Negro masses, the veterans, the students, etc.; to really bring them into the revolutionary struggle against the rule of finance capital. It is not a weakness of our Party that it has played an important role in the rising mass struggles of the American farmers. But our leadership of these militant farmers has suffered from the obscuring of the role of the Party and the Party's distinctive program. This leadership will always be under the danger of being broken by some clever demagogue until and unless our Party finds its proper foundation in strong organizational roots among the basic proletariat and until it works among the farmers as a strong, flexible, proletarian mass Party. Especially we must emphasize the importance of the agricultural workers, the part of the working class who are at the same time engaged directly in agriculture with the farmers, in close contact with the farming masses. Agricultural workers, many millions of them in the United States, beginning to ripen for organization, will give us a proletarian base among the farmers, the binding link between the workers and farming masses.

With regard to the work among the women, we have very important experiences in this field which should be fully brought out, especially in the reports from the districts. I have in mind especially the strikes of the Negro women, the nut pickers in St. Louis and the needle workers on the South Side in Chicago. These are really historical strikes. The strikers were mostly young Negro women who were striking for the first time; they carried through struggles, established their own leadership, won battles and built up unions—these are things which certainly should fill us all with enthusiasm and confidence for a real tremendous mass movement in this country. When' we see young Negro women doing these things while we are sitting around complaining that we were not able to do them, among miners, steel workers, etc., we must blush for shame. In this connection it is very interesting to note that these Negro women are doing good political educational work. In St. Louis they have just sent in an order for 500 copies of every issue of the *Working Woman.* They are carrying on a systematic campaign of education, distributing literature, holding discussions, etc.

ORGANIZING BROAD NEGRO LIBERATION MOVEMENT.

With regard to Negro work I will only make a very brief observation. The latest victories of the Scottsboro Case have carried the influence of our program for the liberation of Negro masses far and wide and have created for us tremendous opportunities. We must say, however, that we are handling these opportunities clumsily, hesitatingly, not exactly knowing how to go about it, how to crystallize organizationally this movement of struggle around the Scottsboro case. Sometimes it seems we are afraid to admit that victories have really been won by our activities, there is sometimes the impression that these victories are merely diabolical maneuvers of a super-clever enemy who is outwitting us by making concessions to us. This kind of nonsense must be ended. Most important of all we have failed to find organizational instruments capable of embracing this broad mass movement of Negroes. Of course, it is necessary to give first attention to drawing Negro proletarians into the revolutionary trade union movement. The two strikes I spoke about are of significant importance in this respect. The fact that the same thing does not take place in other industries is not satisfactory however. Both of these successful strikes take on similar importance because they both resulted in building the trade unions and in creating leading cadres from the strikers. We must also emphasize the drawing of Negro unemployed into the Unemployed Councils, into leading positions and the progress that has been registered by this. We must recruit the best fighters among the Negro masses into the Party, training cadres for future important work. It is possible and necessary to build a bigger Negro membership in the I.L.D. and other organizations. When all these things are said and done the question still remains unanswered, what are we going to do about these broad masses of Negroes who have been awakened by our struggles in their behalf and by our activities, but who cannot as yet be drawn into the Party, Unemployed Councils or I.L.D.? Every day this question is pressing upon us more sharply. Over two years ago we tried to find an answer in the League of Struggle for Negro Rights. Is it not possible that the time has now ripened, that the L.S.N.R. can be successfully brought forward as the answer to the problem of organizing the broad Negro liberation movement?

SHIFT CENTER OF GRAVITY TO LOWER ORGANIZATION

· In order to carry out the profound change in our work called for in the Open Letter, it is necessary to make profound adjustments in the inner life of the Party. It is necessary to shift the center of gravity of Party life to the concentration points down below. This also means that the Section Committees of the Party must play a much more responsible role than they have ever done before.

The very heart of all the work which we are speaking about lies in the Party section and its leadership. It lies in the building of capable, energetic, responsible section committees. It is one of the most basic tasks of our Party. The sections must be developed to the point where they have more initiative and more sense of responsibility and power.

Where sections are now assigned big territories which they cannot effectively cover, they must be broken up into a number of sections of workable size. The section committee must have much more material resources with which to work. This must begin with a basic redistribution of Party finances. The present distribution of dues income where half the Party funds come to the national office must be radically revised. This system had justification in the past when only the existence of a relatively strong central apparatus guaranteed the correct political line of the Party. Today the point of emphasis must be changed. Only the building of strong section committees of our Party can give the guarantee for our growth and the firmness of our political line. The strengthened Party sections can in their turn concentrate upon the most important factories in their territory and give serious leadership to all mass activities.

In connection with the shifting of emphasis to the lower organizations it will be necessary to carry out a serious review of the apparatus of paid functionaries throughout the Party and mass organizations. It is clearly necessary to move decisively towards reducing the proportion of paid workers in the apparatus in relation to the size of membership which is served by it. Especially in all the national offices it is necessary to reduce the paid apparatus to a minimum. Many times in the past we have moved in this direction. After a few months, however, old habits get back and the apparatus grows again. It will be necessary now to take measures that will really make these changes permanent.

REORGANIZATION OF OUR FINANCES

The whole system of finances of our movement requires a thorough re-examination and re-adjustment. It is necessary to have from top to bottom an improvement of our financial system carried through by every responsible committee, applying the following principles:

(1) The sources of financial support must be broadened out, must be placed upon a mass basis. Every organization must, in the first place, rely for its finances upon continuous and growing mass contacts and mass support.

(2) There must be established with the utmost firmness, a strict system of accounting for all finances and the establishment of guarantees that they are expended for the purpose for which they were intended. Auditing and reports to the membership must be made.

(3) The personnel handling finances must be carefully selected from among the most trusted comrades and the financial apparatus should be small with the strict fixing of personal responsibility. This is especially important in the mass organizations where organizational looseness often results in unreliable elements drifting into positions of financial responsibility, and by their misuse of these positions discrediting the movement.

(4) Methods of making money collections in mass meetings must be seriously revised. The existing tendency to make long general collection speeches as the main feature of the meeting without any clear explanation of what the money is for, must be decisively done away with. The collection of money at mass meetings must be politicalized. The purpose of the collection must be very definitely stated. The audience must be moved to contribute by arousing its interest in the purpose of the collection and not by intellectual bludgeoning which defeats its own purpose. The carrying through of this change in methods of money-raising will be such a relief to our audiences, they will be so thankful to us, that they will be more generous than ever before. Our present methods drive them away from us and seal up their pockets to our appeals.

(5) The Party organizations must absolutely respect the independence and integrity of the financial systems of the mass organizations. The Party can place no tax upon these organizations. When it needs financial support, it must approach these organizations and independent bodies, stating the definite purpose of its needs and requesting these bodies to make voluntary donations for the stated purpose. The financial relations between the Party and non-Party organizations must be known and approved by the non-Party membership.

(6) The distribution of finances must be reviewed and revised according to the principle of concentration. Unproductive overhead expenses must be drastically reduced. First consideration must be given to the needs of the lower organizations which are closest to the mass work. The needs of finances for mass agitation, our papers, leaflets, pamphlets, schools, etc., must be given preference over the maintenance of unproductive apparatus. The most serious economies must be carried through, especially by the elimination of unnecessary traveling expenses, long telegrams that can well be substituted by air mail letters which will arrive two or three hours later; and this is a very serious question for the *Daily Worker*, comrades. When it is necessary to send a telegram, there is such a thing as telegraphic language. Some people think they are too important to consider such things, but everyone must consider them.

(7) The whole financial policy must be directed toward the aim that each organization shall build and maintain its own sources of revenue, to cover its own expense. It is clear that with the diversion to the lower organizations of much of the present revenue now received by the national office, the Center must make a very sharp cutting down of the present subsidies it gives to the weaker districts. This will have to be done gradually, while these weaker committees will, with the assistance of the Center, build up their own sources of revenue. We must take always into account certain organizations, which by their very nature require help from the other organizations. Here I refer

particularly to the National Committee of the Unemployed Councils, which is a very important strategic organization for us, and now plays an important role. The Unemployed Councils always and necessarily will for a long period, consume all the revenue they can raise in the local organizations. The National Office cannot depend upon them for money. For such an organization as this we must work out a regular system, a continuous system, which operates month after month, of all the organizations which support the program of the Unemployed Councils giving a very small amount each month to the National Committee of the Unemployed Councils. If our organizations would give, for each member, five cents a year to the Unemployed Councils, this would support the whole national organization of the unemployed movement.

(8) The system of financial responsibility and accounting must also be applied to the departmental activities within the Party which have their own financial systems. Funds for literature must everywhere be maintained intact; literature bills must be paid. This is not a business question, this is a political question, and you cannot have a serious mass educational movement until literature is sold, literature is paid for, literature funds are established and grow by the accumulation of the profits of literature sales. The proceeds from *Daily Worker* sales and collections must be strictly accounted for to the *Daily Worker* and not diverted to any other purpose. Sometimes our comrades take advantage of the business management of the *Daily Worker* continuing to send them papers although the bills are not paid; they sell the papers and then they use the money for whatever purpose happens to suit the fancy of the moment. Sometimes they want to start a new business, so they take the money of the *Daily Worker* and open up a book store, or further replenish the stock of the literature. By what right do they take the money of the *Daily Worker* to build the book shop? "Well, it doesn't make any difference—take it out of one pocket and put it in another, what difference does it make?"—"It all belongs to the movement anyway!" But, comrades, this is the kind of attitude that destroys our organization, destroys system, destroys responsibility and prevents us from building up anything.

We must have the most strict, intolerant attitude towards any kind of irregularity in the handling of finances and we have got to begin to make the entire movement understand this in unmistakable terms. And if it is impossible to carry through these measures otherwise, we must begin to make examples out of people who violate these principles before the entire movement.

HOW TO DISCUSS AND APPLY OPEN LETTER

The carrying through of the re-orientation of the entire Party toward the decisive proletarian masses presupposes a stirring up of the entire

Party from below, the release of all the Party's forces to expression and activity; the development of a healthy Bolshevik self-criticism; the development of collective leadership and collective work in every unit and committee of the Party. To make the Open Letter the instrument to bring about this change, it will be necessary to discuss the letter in every unit and committee of the Party, in every fraction of the mass organizations. This discussion must not be abstract. It must be directed toward reviewing the work of that particular unit, fraction or committee in the light of the Open Letter and formulating on the basis of this discussion a resolution on the next tasks in which each one of these bodies sets itself a certain minimum set of control tasks, that we must do within a certain time, and that we will check up on every week to see whether we are doing it or not. Copies of these resolutions must be sent to the section, district and national office and furnish the basis for the further concretizing of the work of the higher bodies. The higher committees must base themselves on this work of concretization that is done in the lower units and fractions of the Party; the Central Committee setting certain minimum control tasks for the principal concentration districts.

What we are calling for is not merely a change in the work of the Central Committee but of the entire Party. We can build a mass Bolshevik party only through the conscious participation of every Party member. We can build it only through controlling the execution of our decisions, checking up on them, placing definite responsibility for particular work on each particular member—by helping the nuclei from the section committees, from the district committees and from the Central Committee to overcome their difficulties and solve their tasks.

The Central Committee is proposing that the Eighth Party Convention, originally intended to be held in May, shall be called together only toward the end of October. The motive of this proposal is in order to have time to really carry through the stirring up of the Party from the bottom, thoroughly review the entire work of the Party in every unit, committee and fraction, to formulate new plans on the basis of this review and have our first experiences in the serious attempt to carry through the turn to the masses started in the convention period.

On the basis of this discussion, these experiences, we can expect to be able to carry through a real refreshing of the leadership of the Party from bottom to top. We can expect to draw into all leading posts those comrades who have distinguished themselves in mass work. We can draw the fires of serious Bolshevik mass criticism against all those who remain passive or resist the necessary transformation of the Party's work in its turn to the masses. We can carry through a consolidation of all the healthiest and most energetic and most devoted forces of the Party in all the decisive points of Party leadership. The carrying through of this discussion does not mean a moratorium on practical work—on the contrary, it can only be fruitful if it is done in the midst of an intensified taking up of all the every-day tasks of the entire movement. The test of every comrade shall be not so much can he speak well about these problems, but can he work well in carrying out this line. How well can he put the Party Open Letter into practice in daily work?

All of the many-sided and often complex tasks which confront our Party will be carried through with greater success than ever before, if we learn the methods of concentration, if we learn to gather our forces for the most important tasks, if we learn to rouse and organize new forces among the masses, if we learn to draw in the basic proletarian elements into the fight, if we achieve a correct approach to the masses, apply a correct united front policy, if we learn to promote fresh proletarian leading cadres and train them politically, if we carry on a relentless struggle against "Left" and Right deviations, and if we develop collective work and politically activize the entire Party.

Are we able to carry through this change? Has the Party the necessary forces within itself to establish contacts with the masses and transform itself into a Bolshevik mass party? Of course we can do it. With all of its weaknesses, we have a Party which is proletarian in its composition, which is composed of the most loyal, devoted, energetic and enthusiastic elements, who are really the vanguard of the American proletariat. Our weaknesses can all be overcome, provided we really mobilize all of our forces, remove every obstruction, with the fullest utilization of every comrade, maintain Bolshevik unity of purpose and effort, establish a real inner Party democracy and fight energetically for the real carrying through of the turn to the masses. It depends upon us. The only guarantee for the carrying through of the line of this Open Letter is an aroused and active Party membership. We have faith that the Party members will unitedly respond to this call. That is why we called this special conference. That is why we propose to issue this Open Letter to the Party.

CONCLUDING REMARKS

This special conference of our Party reflects the growing upsurge of the masses and the growing activity of our Party. This is its first characteristic. This conference constitutes additional proof of the ripeness of the situation for our Party to make some decisive steps forward in winning the masses and it also gives evidence of the growing efforts of the Party to accomplish this task.

Now to proceed to some of the questions of our discussion. The center of our discussions here has been how to understand, expose and combat the big offensive which the capitalist class is making upon the toiling masses, how to fight against the New Deal. We have considerably clarified this question for ourselves and have laid down the correct approach to the problems of carrying out in life the struggle against the New Deal. It was correctly said in the course of the discussion that the effects of this general attack upon the working class also provide us with an opportunity to make use of the broad uniform sweeping character of this attack to rouse the class-consciousness of the masses of America. Whether we will make this use of the situation, however, depends upon whether we can learn to get away from abstract slogan-shouting, down to very concrete work among the masses on the basis of their immediate needs, mobilizing them for struggle for these needs on the basis of the united front.

Shop Base for Fighting N.I.R.A.

First of all it is clear that the central point in this struggle lies in the shops, around the shops, the penetration of the shops, the development of the struggle in the shops; upon this will depend the whole development of every phase of the resistance to the capitalist offensive and the development of a counter-offensive of the workers.

In the shops the fight against the New Deal must be taken out of the clouds of high politics and expressed in terms of the immediate working conditions in the shops, the smallest issue, the question of wages and hours; making use of every special circumstance that arises out of any situation, to raise these demands among the workers and organize them in struggle for these demands. That means making the fullest possible use of every step of the government and of the employers in applying the Industrial Recovery Act to transform it into the opportunity to mobilize the masses against the application of the Recovery Act. That means making use of the formulation of the codes by the employers, and the hearings upon these codes by the government, to bring the demands of the workers, to fight for them, and to spread the knowledge of these demands among the broadest masses and rouse them to expressions of support and to concrete organizational measures.

Second, this means taking some further steps. In the development of the Textile Code, for example, which has been cited in our reports here as a model for the other industries, we must declare that this is a model only in the sense that it is the best attempt in this direction and indicates the general line which all of the other counter-codes that we present and fight for will have to take.

However, this was not a model *how* to work out the demands. Perhaps I can betray a little secret and tell you that on the day before these demands were to be presented we did not as yet know what they were to be, concretely, and certainly the broad masses of textile workers did not know. A few leading comrades sat down a couple of hours before train time and hammered out these demands in an office.

Under the circumstances it is quite extraordinary how successful they were. But please don't take this, you comrades in the mining industry, steel and marine industry, as an example of how to work out these demands. Now we have sufficient time to take at least the first steps in the drawing in of the masses of workers into the formulation of further demands and spread them, broadcast them, among the masses before they are presented in public hearings. And only when we do this will we really begin the proper method of mobilizing mass struggle against the New Deal.

It is unfortunate that in all our discussion there was so little attention paid to the question of the concrete demands contained in the Textile Code as we presented it.

Comrade Stachel in his excellent report went into great detail on this question. The fact that the comrades did not react to discussion of these things proves that the comrades have not really faced all of these issues yet down among the workers where all these questions of formulation of codes become an object of the most intense discussion and attention.

We cannot take these formulations lightly. They are of the most serious importance to the workers and only if we engage the workers in a discussion on these things and also prove to the workers that we can intelligently discuss these things will we be able to mobilize them in this fight.

Third, it must be made very clear that while our central attention is given to crystallizing our organizations in the shops and building up the revolutionary trade unions, in every case where the employers are carrying through their company union system—the system of employers' representation organized by the companies—we do not boycott those elections but put forward, encourage and lead the most active and best elements, our members and sympathizers and everyone that we can reach, to put forward our demands in those elections and within those systems of employees' representation, fight for the codes and demands that we work out. We already have experience showing that this is possible and also proving the excellent results that we can achieve by making use of every opportunity of this kind.

Next, we must emphasize the necessity to make use of every one of these issues from our shop basis and from outside the shop when we have no direct connection with particular shops, to raise these questions inside the A. F. of L. unions where they exist whether these are old established unions or whether these are the most recently called meetings of the A. F. of L.; to go into every such meeting and every union of the A. F. of L.; to raise very concretely all these issues around the fight for conditions, for wages and hours contained in our counter-codes and to crystallize the Left opposition.

All of this work must be orientated around the central problems of building trade unions in all those industries where we are building the Red unions now. We must make use of the very illusions among the workers, the illusions that they have some opportunity to organize, the illusions that they have some sort of choice as to what organization they shall join, and crystallize struggle to realize these things. And although we know that the purpose of the law is exactly to defeat these things, we can, by making use of their resentment against the denial of any of these rights, rouse and organize them into struggle and realize this by their own strength

A tremendous role will be played in this process by making use of this activity that is going on, especially in the basic industries, to crystallize small struggles, to crystallize the dissatisfaction of the workers around the small demands for improvement of conditions, sanitary conditions, and every little victory that is gained will be a crystallization of class struggle organization inside the shops.

And finally on the basis of all of this detailed work, agitation, propaganda, organization within the shops and around the shops upon the basis of the smallest questions leading up to the largest questions, to systematically bring before the workers the perspective of big mass strikes in order to realize their larger demands.

FURTHER TASKS AMONG THE UNEMPLOYED

Next in importance in the development of mass struggles is the fight around the question of the forced labor camps and public works. It must be said that we have not given sufficient attention to this. This work has tremendous possibilities and is directly connected with the shop problems and especially with the building of the trade unions. It is precisely the forced labor camps and public works that constitute one of the most direct and easily recognizable blows which the capitalists are giving against the workers' conditions, hours and wages, especially in the basic industries. The central point in this fight is the demand and struggle for trade union wages on all public works, the fight against forced labor and for the establishment of trade union wages. In the forced labor camps it is also the fight for cash payments, the elimination of all payments in kind and the withholding of money for long periods. We must put forward against the government plans for public works our own proposals; we must formulate definite proposals which we can place before the masses for a public works program, to provide housing for the workers, hospitals, schools, etc., as against the government proposals which are directed towards military purposes or the service of big corporations. We must develop in the forced labor camps the struggle against the military regime within them. We must make a fight for self-government, the regulation of these camps by elected committees within them to break down the military discipline. We must make a struggle for better food, housing and sanitary conditions. We must make mass exposures of the conditions that exist in these labor camps by letters from inside the camps, by leaflets based upon these inside exposures, the concretizing of these exposures in definite reports by those inside the camps, by sending delegations elected on the outside to go into the camps, by holding meetings to report on these conditions, and so forth. And finally, by directing the efforts within the forced labor camps towards large-scale strikes to realize these demands.

Among the unemployed masses, the struggle is being exceptionally sharpened by the latest phase of the New Deal and we must develop a counter-offensive through our unemployed organizations, developing a real mass fight against those relief cuts which are taking place almost everywhere throughout the United States today, intensifying the fight for cash relief, against the system of food vouchers, etc. We must organize on a broader scale against evictions which now in the summer months have again greatly intensified. The problem of evictions is becoming an acute mass problem again. We must give more attention to the struggle for conditions in the flop houses. We have largely ignored the fact that this summer when relief generally is being cut down the flop houses are growing, the number of inmates is swelling and there is a definite program to force larger numbers who formerly got relief into the flop houses. It is one of the essential features of the struggle against the New Deal that we shall counter this move by real movement amongst these large masses, who have been forced into the flop houses by the cutting down of relief. Our experiences have proven that everywhere in these flop houses we are not dealing with *lumpen*-proletarians, we are dealing with workers who come from the basic sections of the American working class, and everywhere where we have touched these flop houses, we have been able to find live elements among them, capable men, natural leaders. A little bit of attention will bring forward splendid cadres.

Further, we must give more attention to the development of the work for taxation of the big companies to pay relief to the workers discharged from the factories. It should be recalled what an important part is being played by mass resentment against Ford's throwing of the tax burdens onto the small people, the home owners, property owners and the masses in Dearborn. This has roused the greatest impetus to struggle against Ford and has created the conditions whereby we have been able to emerge from illegality in the city of Dearborn. The same thing can be developed in every company town, provided we study every case very carefully, develop the issues very concretely and prove to the masses that we know what we are talking about.

At the present moment we must very sharply bring forward a demand of the unemployed for the diversion of war funds for unemployment relief. At the present moment when hundreds of millions of dollars have been appropriated for the construction of war ships and other military purposes, this is most important for tying up the struggle of the unemployed masses with the anti-war struggle, deepening the understanding of the whole class struggle.

We must make much more effective use than we have hitherto of the fact that the government, while cutting down the funds for unemployed, is increasing tremendously the direct subsidies to the big capitalists. We must follow up every development of the operations of the Reconstruction Finance Corporation and, for example, every time another $50,000,000 is given to the banks of Detroit, the comrades must make known through the masses of Detroit, that while the government is giving these millions of dollars to the banks, Detroit relief has been cut down below what it was in 1931. The demand to divert these government subsidies to the relief of the unemployed is an issue on which we can really rouse the masses. We must take much more energetic steps to bind together the struggle of the employed and unemployed, to bring expressions of support from the workers in the shops to every struggle of the unemployed, even if it is only a resolution or leaflet, even the smallest expression will grow and develop into something bigger. At the same time, more carefully and more systematically and energetically bring the unemployed workers into active participation in every struggle that takes place in and around the shops in support of the demands of the employed workers.

In every city there is a whole maze of concrete issues surrounding relief funds, of graft and favoritism which mark their administration. It is a shameful thing for us to admit that the capitalist gutter press has done more to expose and exploit the graft in relief funds than the Communists have done, than the Unemployed Councils have done. We must take up this issue in every city and put up the demand for workers' inspection and control of all funds for unemployment relief.

ADDITIONAL PROBLEMS IN OUR STRUGGLE AGAINST REFORMISM

Now just a few words about some of the problems connected with reaching the masses in the reformist organizations. We have emphasized in the report and in the discussion that the very first prerequisite for success in winning of these workers who are in organizations hostile to us is a creation of a sympathetic approach to them. This is the main significance of our maneuvers on the united front; the calling of conferences, the sending of letters; issuance of manifestos, etc., directed to these organizations. It is to create the approach to these workers and provide the opportunity to raise these issues concretely.

This requires not only the proper kind of documents and conferences. Above all it requires an active and sympathetic contact with these workers down below. The offering of joint actions for concrete demands, the methods that must be carried through at every step and especially in the development of the united front below, the development of such joint actions is the only possible basis for a real building up of a fighting united front. Our united front is a united front of struggle.

The greatest weakness which we have in carrying through our united front policy is that our comrades carry over the very bad habits of commandeering workers, of not taking carefully into consideration all special organizational peculiarities and habits and traditions, of ordering about workers as soldiers in an army, of which we are the officers and in which we direct their activities. All these habits of commandeering, of arbitrary approach to non-Party workers, will mean death to every effort of the united front. Especially if we go down among the basic sections of the American working class, we will find every trace of this old military approach; this old commanding approach will not only hinder any progress among these workers, but even more, these workers will throw us out on our necks when we try to use these methods among them.

In the building of united front committees with these workers, a few little directives, if always kept in mind in the practical carrying through, will be of great help. For example, let us always remember that we want big committees and we will find the social-fascist leading elements will always want little committees. We want the biggest possible committees because the bigger they are, the more likely they are to have healthy proletarian elements among them who will join with us on the concrete issues that we raise.

Second, never have secret negotiations on the united front. Let every step of the negotiations of the setting up of united front committees always be reported to our members and to the workers generally.

Third, we must absolutely break down this idea that the establishment of a united front means the stopping of criticism. It is true that we have to learn much more effective methods of criticism. We have got to be restrained in our language in the development of criticism within these united front efforts. But we must be unhesitating, we must be bold in the raising of every issue on which criticism is required. Every hesitation of the leading elements of these reformist organizations, to carry through struggles that have been decided upon, every hesitation to join in a mass action that is initiated by other organizations, every sabotage, every holding back must be criticized. Failure to criticize these things on our part means to surrender to the social-fascists in the name of the united front. A committee which does not make fighting conclusions is not a united front. It is a sabotage of the united front.

We must give very careful examination to all of the problems around the penetration of A. F. of L. unions, Socialist Party and Musteite organizations; study the special prejudices that all of these workers have, and concretely develop our issues suited to the special circumstances within each organization.

The united front is not a peace pact with the reformists. The united front is a method of struggle against the reformists, against the social-fascists, for the possession of the masses. It is necessary to emphasize this, because it was not clear in the discussion that all the comrades understand it. Some of the comrades in the discussion here have given an argument like this: "Well, maybe you fellows in New York know what you are doing when you enter into a united front with the Muteites. We have our doubts, but we won't venture to criticize this much at the moment, but we want to tell you that this united front doesn't apply to our district. In our district, these Musteites are betraying the working class." But, comrades, whoever told you that the Musteites don't betray the working class in New York City? Did you think we are making the united front with the Musteites because we have suddenly become convinced that they are good class-conscious fighters, good leaders of the working class? Have you forgotten that precisely the reason why we make the united front with them is because we have got to take their followers away from them? And if you want to enter into a struggle, you must get within striking distance. It is quite remarkable that we are told, for example, that down in the Carolinas, I think it is, a Musteite is systematically betraying the workers down there, and therefore this Musteite who has signed some of our joint manifestoes can't have a united front with our comrades in the Carolinas. Why didn't the comrades make a campaign against this fellow before? If our united front with the Musteites has brought sharply before the comrades in Carolina the necessity of conducting a mass campaign against all the betrayals going on down there, that is a proof then of the correctness of our application of the tactic of the united front with the Musteites. Our united front with the Musteites is not a means of silencing our criticism of any one of their betrayals. It is a means of making our criticism more effective by making it reach their own followers and winning their workers to a line of class struggle.

It is necessary to emphasize that the unorganized workers are also a proper subject of approach with the tactic of the united front. Just because a worker is not in an organization doesn't mean that we don't have to use special means to reach him and bring him into struggle. Hundreds of thousands of workers who are unorganized yet have a mentality which is determined precisely along the same lines as those of the workers within the A. F. of L. or the Socialist Party. They have the same prejudices to be overcome and they have to be approached in much the same way.

We must emphasize all of these things in connection with the calling of the conference in Cleveland on August 26 and 27, a United Front Conference for Struggle Against the "New Deal." This conference call which will be issued in a few days is a joint call by Communists, Musteites, leaders of Unemployed Councils, etc., quite a heterogeneous gathering of names that are signed to it. Let us again ask the comrades to assure all of our workers out in the field that when they get this manifesto, they are not to understand it as a declaration of peace between us and the reformists. On the contrary, this manifesto which sets down all of the basic proposals of our struggle against the New Deal must be taken as a test of the activities of every leader in every district, in every town on all questions about the Industrial Recovery Act, all questions about trade union struggle, all questions of the unemployed, and if any of these leaders don't go along with the struggle and really contribute to the struggle for these things, then it is our duty to begin immediate criticism, sharp criticism, rouse the masses against their violation of the program to which they or their leaders have affixed their signatures and use this as a weapon to destroy their influence among the workers among which they operate.

The movement for unity of the Unemployed Councils together with the Unemployed Leagues, and other unemployed organizations, must receive very careful attention. Let us again remind ourselves that this unity movement of the unemployed is not a love-feast, it is a struggle. We are fighting for unity, and we are fighting for the masses. We are fighting to win the masses to the support of our program. All of the elements in these other organizations, no matter who they may be, we welcome if they really support and fight for this program of struggle, but we will fight against them to the extent they hesitate, sabotage or oppose this basic program of struggle.

In the development of the unity movement of the unemployed, we must concentrate on unity from below, the bringing together of the different unemployed organizations on a neighborhood, city, township and county scale, and try to create a solid foundation to actually achieve unity from below. On the basis of this, we can proceed to larger unity moves on a national scale.

The concrete efforts towards applying this tactic to unify the trade union forces in each industry, especially in coal, textile, etc., are one of the essential features of this whole movement. In the August 26 Cleveland conference, we hope to be able to have the central role played by the trade union and the trade union questions—the questions of the struggle for shop conditions, hours and wages and the unification of the existing militant trade unions.

In this whole struggle against the New Deal, the central unifying issue around which everything else is organized is the struggle for social insurance. In reviewing our discussion of the past days, social insurance and the concrete questions of how we are carrying through the campaign for social insurance in each industry and in each district, did not occupy a sufficiently central place. This reflects that we have not, even in the last weeks since we have begun to write good resolutions and articles about it, really taken up in a serious fashion the struggle for social insurance.

SPECIAL PROBLEMS OF SHOP CONCENTRATION

Now I want to speak of some of the special problems of shop concentration. The first point in shop concentration is picking out the shop to concentrate on. There are three guiding lines for the picking out of a shop. First, we must make our main points the biggest, most important key shops in each industry and each locality. If we do not do that, we are running away from the main problem. The main important forces, the most able forces must be directed towards these, which are usually also the most difficult points.

At the same time, let us keep in mind what the Detroit comrades described as picking out the strongest and weakest links for concentration. Some of the first successes of our Auto Workers Union came from concentrating not only on the biggest plants, but simultaneously also on some of the weaker and smaller plants. And especially when these can be combined in one region, one town, this combination will often be found very valuable. Of course, where we have forces on the inside, this is often a good reason for beginning some concentrated work on the factory.

One of the problems of shop concentration is always the relation of outside and inside work and whether an outsider can do work in a shop or in a particular industry. In this respect I want to refer to the speech of Comrade Ray of the Marine Workers. I noticed particularly that Comrade Ray said that what he was interested in was that the people who are going to do marine work must study the problems of the marine industry. He complained that this position of his had been misinterpreted as meaning that nobody could go into the marine work except marine workers themselves. This is very important for us. Comrade Ray is correct when he says nobody can do marine work who goes in with a know-it-all attitude, to run the marine workers' business like he once ran a cooperative store, or like a branch of the I.W.O. or the I.L.D.

Every factory is to be studied concretely and a concrete plan of campaign mapped out. All that we can learn from other experiences is the general principle, to learn the mistakes to be avoided, to learn how to direct our forces towards these concrete questions. Different factories have different problems—big factories different ones from the little and all the experiences we have gained help us in all factory work. We have to work out special problems of approaching different kinds of industry.

We must at the same time not forget that in all of the shop work the question of conspiracy is more and more important, the question of illegal work, how to get open organizations and at the same time protect our organization on the inside.

In this connection the problem of winning new forces among the masses and giving them the opportunity of developing in the struggle is of growing importance. We have many good examples of this given to this Party Conference. One especially good thing is in the speech of Comrade Abraham of Connecticut. This is an example of real mass work and the development of new forces.

Comrades, in all of this work one of the things that we must learn is how to make use of small successes, to proceed further. We are often in this fix: as long as we are not successful in an immediate objective we always know just what to do. But when we win, we don't always know what to do next.

The problem of penetration of the shops and the problem of the development of the strike movement, the problem of building the trade unions, is the problem of how to develop confidence *among the masses in our leadership,* by showing them we know how to do things, by winning one thing here and winning one thing there, always make one thing lead to another, to a higher stage of struggle, or broadening out the struggle, or deepening the political character of it. Moving from success to success, making of every success the foundation of immediately moving forward to another one. In this, we have one of the basic principles of concentration.

Why do we concentrate on one key shop? Is it because we think that this big shop is important, but the whole industry is not important? By no means! Our concentration is no narrowing down. Our concentration is to win a strategic point precisely because a success there will move the entire industry, or move at least the entire locality, whereas if we concentrate on the whole locality and the whole industry, it will take us so long to move it that the workers will be somewhere else by the time we get anything done.

The whole principle of concentration is to throw all the forces into one point, and win a success there, and by that success you double your forces, and can go on to move the entire mass. The very example of a success in a strategic locality, in a shop or organization, will very often set the whole mass into motion, bring them either under our leadership, or in the direction moving towards us.

In this respect, we have to give the most serious attention to the problems of consolidating the organization during and after an action. One of the most important contributions to our movement in this whole last period, has been the nut-pickers' strike in St. Louis, precisely because it gave us a living example of the consolidation of a mass organization in the course of the struggle, maintaining it after the struggle. This problem as we have seen very clearly from the reports on the nut-pickers' struggle, the needle trades workers' strike in South Chicago, and more in the negative sense, although not negative entirely by any means, our experience in the auto workers' strike. We see that this whole problem is one of involving the new members in tasks within the organization, inside the shop, and also giving them tasks outside the shop, in spreading the organization into other shops, and even into other industries. I am certain that one of the main reasons for the successful consolidation of the nut-pickers' union is the fact that this union immediately set itself the task not only of organizing all of its own industry, but of organizing the needle trades shops in the vicinity in St. Louis, and even beginning to organize the men folk of these women, who work in basic industries, railroads, metal shops, etc.

I think that perhaps the best example of a very systematic, conscious carrying through of this approach to all of the practical problems of struggle, in the building of organization, was contained in the speech which Comrade M—— made, in which he told us about his work in the Black Belt, about the building of the Sharecroppers' Union. I felt as I listened to that report, that I was watching the working out of the theses written by Lenin. I don't know how much of Lenin's writings Comrade M—— has read, but one thing is certain, that he applies the teachings of Lenin in life better than most of our scholars in the American movement. Comrade M—— gave us a picture of a movement developed in what is usually considered the most backward section of the American toiling masses, and the astonishing completeness of each phase of this work is shown by the fact that in his short report of the activities of the past several months, we had every feature of the international class struggle, developed concretely in life from the smallest problem up to the largest problem in the fight against German fascism, imperialist war, and support of the Soviet Union.

If there is anybody who thinks there is a contradiction between the struggle for the immediate demands and the highest politicalization of this struggle, just take a lesson from the work of Comrade M——, who has politicalized the sharecroppers in the South, and made them an integral, conscious part of the international revolutionary movement.

A few words about the concentration industries and districts. Here I want to utter just a little word of warning against some tendencies of crystallizing some brother theories to go along with the theory of concentration. Some comrades want to emphasize that concentration on one thing means the neglect of another. Now it is often true that we are so badly organized ourselves, and so badly prepared to concentrate that in our first beginnings of concentration, we will tend to neglect other things. But let's not make a theory of it and justify that neglect. No. And especially let's not only avoid, but let's set ourselves the task of stamping out any tendency, such as was described by Comrade Ben Gold this afternoon, when he said that some comrades sneer at the needle trades work, the needle trades work is some kind of inferior work, that the only thing a respectable Communist would consider doing is the work among the miners and steel. It is true, and must be emphasized, that it is more important and a greater achievement to organize 500 workers in a steel mill than it is to organize 5,000 workers in a multitude of small shops in light industry; that it is a basic guiding principle for us, the central feature of concentration. But that does not mean that we are going to neglect the needle workers or that we are going to put work among the needle workers in a sort of second class citizenship.

The building up of our forces in the basic industries is our first and central concentration not because we do not want workers in light industry, or because it is not important, but because we can more quickly win the masses and can consolidate the revolutionary organizations among the masses by making our base the heavy industry. Precisely the importance of heavy industry is that a little organization there will swing into action a broad number of workers in light industry, but a little organization in light industry will not swing heavy industry into motion. That is, we concentrate on heavy industry because it is a lever by which we can move the whole mass. The whole mass of workers are "our" workers, and every one of them is equally important for the revolutionary movement. Factories in light industry can also be made to help serve the task of conquering heavy industry, although the main feature is the other way around, that heavy industry gives us a lever by which we can move more workers in light industry into action.

THE INSTRUMENTS OF CONCENTRATION

What are our instruments of concentration? Our concentration point for all our work is the unit and the section of the Party. The section organizations are going to be the backbone of the Party, and if the sections are weak the Party will be weak. If the sections do not have strong consolidated collective leadership with political initiative with capacity and self-confidence, then the Party will not move forward. We must make use of every means of concentration, every feature of our work must carry through the principle of concentration: Party organizations, the trade unions, Unemployed Councils, workers' clubs, I.W.O., I.L.D., language clubs, language press, all of these are tremendous instruments for us. We often forget that the language organizations and the language press are still our greatest mass instrument or could be if we would make intelligent use of it. But the point we must continue to emphasize is that the central instrument for carrying through the turn to the masses is the Party section and the Party unit. . . .

The cry for forces must be turned away from the center and down to the units and the sections. The cry for forces must be turned into the shops and we will get our forces from down below, and these forces gotten right out of the work and out of the movement will be worth a hundred times as much as the forces taken out of the ice-box of the national office and shipped around by mail order! (*Laughter, applause.*)

Our task, comrades, is the task of the creation of new cadres—the building of a mass trade union is the building of cadres. If you don't build these new cadres you haven't built any union, you have only created the appearance of a union—you have built a paper house, a house that will fall down with the first wind that blows. And the reason why our unions that we rebuild and rebuild, year after year, don't stay built is because we are doing it always with outside cadres, importing the cadres, giving no attention to the building up of new forces down below that have a solid foundation there and will stay put year after year, whose only possibility of living is the building up of the union right there. If you do not do that you have not built anything. This is true of every mass organization. The only real solid building of anything is the building of stable cadres from among the masses, the membership of this organization. The role of the office in all of the work of building an organization is a very small one. You need a national office for a union to provide all of the organization with uniform organizational materials, to provide the apparatus for bringing together the consultations and conferences of all the various parts, you require a leader who works collectively with a larger group, a group that meets from time to time to work out the basic principles and tactics of the organization, and at least one national leader who makes it his responsibility to keep in touch with all the parts of this organization, to respond on the new issues, to advise for the various parts, but between this bureau and lower organizations, the masses, is about this ratio, one per cent the bureau, ninety-nine per cent the lower organizations.

The approach to the problems of building an organization from the point of view of an office is bureaucracy and the only time when the office does not become a danger to the organization is when it is the product of the effort of an organization from below.

Work Among Negro Farmers and Colonial Masses

Some of the Negro comrades criticized my report for a lack of sufficient emphasis upon the importance of Negro work. I accept that criticism because I am sure that we have failed to get sufficient political emphasis upon the importance of the proper solution of all of our problems of work among the Negroes. We have not yet made a decisive change in our work in Harlem. We have not yet consolidated our political influence in Harlem into an organization which knows its tasks, which feels itself as an integral part of our Party, and which is proceeding boldly to the solution of its mass tasks in Harlem. Nor have we achieved this anywhere else, unless we except the South where the work that has been done by Comrade M——— with the Share-croppers' Union seems to be a real solid base about which we do not have to have any uneasiness at all. But Harlem, Chicago, and the other big cities with a Negro population, we have not yet really consolidated our Party among them. At the same time we have really made enormous progress in extending our general political influence among the Negroes. Basically this question is a question really of overcoming the distrust that the Negroes have for white workers, a distrust which they also bring towards our Party, a distrust which will continue just as long as they see any remaining influences within our Party of the ideology of white chauvinism. The struggle against white chauvinism by the white comrades of our Party is the basic means for the liquidation of the distrust of the Negroes. At the same time there is another necessary task to be followed, and that is that especially our leading Negro comrades shall take it as one of their first tasks to try to instil confidence in our Party among the Negro masses, especially by giving examples to the Negro masses of Negro Party members and leaders who have the most complete confidence in the Party. A big step will be made in solving this problem by us when we really find the road to a mass organization of the Negro liberation struggle.

The large part of the dissatisfaction among the Negro comrades arises from the fact that they feel that some important problems have not been solved. They may not be conscious of it but in the first place it is the feeling of the necessity that this Negro liberation struggle shall have a broad mass organizational expression, and this is one of the most important features of the consolidation of the Party among the Negroes.

One criticism that has been made by some Negro comrades in Harlem with regard to the leaders of the Party we must declare is correct. We have not given sufficient attention to the solving of the problems of Harlem and have not given enough direct leadership from the leading comrades of the Center to Harlem. Harlem is certainly important enough for us to give our best forces as its leadership. We have discussed this question, we have taken up the spontaneous mass proposals that came out of this conference to have Comrade Ford go into Harlem as the Section Organizer.

One of the weaknesses of my report was that I gave little attention to the question of our work among the farmers. It is now so late that I can't remedy this weakness in my summing up either. Let me just say very briefly that Comrade Puro's report here at this conference and especially the very detailed resolution on our agrarian work which goes into the most minute examination of our basic problems must receive the attention of the entire Party. This resolution you are going to be asked to vote on and adopt at this conference. If you adopt it, it becomes a basic decision of the Party that there must be a discussion on the agrarian work in every unit of the Party, in every committee of the Party. The problem of the farmers, work among the farmers, is not merely a problem of those organizers that we send out among them. It is a problem of the entire Party, of the allies of the proletariat, a problem which is of importance to everyone who is seriously looking forward to the struggle for power in the United States.

We can also accept the criticism that was made by our Latin-American comrades that this conference and that the Party generally gives insufficient attention to the colonial work, that is, to the work for the support of the liberation struggle in the colonies in Latin America, in the Philippine Islands, and also to our work among the colonial emigrants in the United States. That is certainly true.

We must begin to find a way to remedy this weakness. We must especially strengthen our work among the colonial emigrants here. We must especially begin to have systematic work and a mass paper for the Latin-American emigrants, we must have a leading bureau among the Latin Americans. In this respect we should by all means at this conference send a message of greetings to the new Communist Party in the Philippine Islands (*applause*) whose leaders are under long prison and exile sentences, sentences which are being put into execution by the new "liberal" Governor-General of the Philippine Islands, Frank Murphy, from Detroit; and the sentence will be executed now, this moment, largely because the Philippine Party was not able to finance the court proceedings to carry these cases higher to the United States Supreme Court. And due to our slowness here we did not raise money quickly enough to get these papers. Certainly the least we can do is provide some support to the colonial movement, to at least carry through the appeals of the comrades to support them against the imprisonment. . . .

Open Letter Is Open Mass Criticism

Now, comrades, how are we going to carry out the Open Letter? If there was one questioning note that was sounded in the discussion it was not about the correctness of the Open Letter, but some comrades were still doubtful as to whether we are really going to carry it through or not. Well, I think that we can say that we have more reason for expecting to make the change today than we had before. I received this afternoon some evidence of this. You remember, I think it was Saturday night, this conference heard the speech of a representative of a certain shop nucleus engaged in a government enterprise. Well, this comrade had no sooner made his speech to the special Party Conference, but the next day his unit met, took up the question of his report to the conference, discussed it, examined it, brought out the weaknesses of this report, and the nucleus itself worked out a resolution and sent it to this special Party Conference correcting all of the weaknesses of the report of its delegate and declaring its determination to really carry out the Open Letter of this conference. (*Applause.*) I think we have got quite a few units that are ready to work like that. This is the guarantee, and especially if we give them a little bit of leadership, if we begin to mobilize them from the bottom for this turn, then we will have a real guarantee that we will make the turn. And that is the reason for the Open Letter. It is to build a fire under all of our leading committees so that they can't sit comfortably on their chairs.

This Open Letter is open mass criticism and open mass criticism is a powerful force that can change even the most stubborn habits and can even break down the worst sectarianism and bureaucratism. We have had a certain loosening up of the forces of the Party right here at this conference. We have had a little freer and more healthy development of self-criticism than we have had before, and that is also a guarantee for the execution of our decisions. I think that we can characterize most of the speeches in this conference as a step forward in the development of self-criticism. Of course, we have to distinguish between the self-criticism and the methods of developing criticism of the more responsible leading comrades and that of the comrades from the lower organizations. We demand much more of the leading comrades in the way of accuracy, care, serious preparation of self-criticism beforehand, than we do of the comrades from the nuclei, from the sections. In this respect, I think we must say that the kind of criticism made of the center, of the Political Bureau and its work, by, for example, Comrade Johnstone from Pittsburgh, is a very healthy contribution to the work of the Political Bureau. If we had more of this serious, healthy criticism for the center, I am sure the center would work much better. The center must work under the constant criticism of the entire Party organization. The districts must also work under the pressure of this criticism, and the sections must, because this criticism is the Bolshevik weapon for the steeling of the Party, for the correction of all our weaknesses, for securing the real guarantee that decisions will be carried out and not left on paper.

The carrying through of the decisions, however, is a fight. It is a fight for the line of the Party. It is a fight against deviations. However, when we say "fight," let us warn the comrades. There are some comrades who might have an inclination to think, "Well, if it is a fight, it has to be a fight against somebody and if it is a fight against somebody, that means that we have to organize those that are against them. That means that in order to fight for the line of the Open Letter, we must form an 'Open Letter group' within the Party. (*Laughter.*) All the sincere friends of the Open Letter will band themselves together to fight against the enemies of the Open Letter." That is not what we mean, not that kind of fight. There has been a little experience in the international movement with that kind of a fight and experience has proven that this is precisely the way to prevent the carrying out of the Open Letter. This is the surest way to sabotage the turn to the masses. Perhaps we can remember that our French brother Party had a sad experience with the organization within its ranks just a few years ago of a group that called itself "the group to fight against Right Opportunism" in the French Party. And this "group to fight against Right Opportunism" became a very handy instrument in the hands of the French police to disrupt the French Party.

At the same time, comrades, I have heard that around the fringes of this Conference, there are a few comrades who are still addicted to political speculation and who are whispering to one another, "Doesn't the paragraph in the Open Letter mean that there are serious struggles going on in the Political Bureau of our Party?" and beginning to build all sorts of stories out of their own minds about this alignment and that alignment and that our Party leadership is divided into factions. Comrades, I want to assure you that all of these speculations are baseless. There is no such condition in our Party leadership. We have had difficulties in our Party leadership last year. These difficulties were already largely solved and removed even before this Open Letter was written. And when the Open Letter warns the Party against the danger of any revival of factionalism it is not because there are any factional divisions or groupings in the leadership of our Party today. I hope the comrades will take that statement as the truth and will really put a quietus upon all remaining gossip mongers in our Party. (*Applause.*)

Comrades, in conclusion, let us point out this, that although our report has emphasized the very precarious nature of the present industrial production increase that is taking place, the nature of the inflation stimulus as a part of the New Deal, and we have emphasized the imminence of a fresh collapse of industry and emphasized the sharpening of the crisis in every respect—let us be very careful not to develop the idea of waiting for collapse to come in order to bring about the change in our Party. If we wait for something outside of ourselves to bring the change in our Party, the change will not take place. There is only one thing that can make this change and that is— you and I and every member of the Party. A conscious determined struggle is the only thing that will put into effect the Open Letter, and that is what we have to secure in the Party today. We must realize the truth pointed out in the Twelfth Plenum of the Executive Committee of the Communist International by Comrade Gussev where he spoke particularly in regards to America of the immediate future holding the prospect of very quick developments and changes in the situation. That is more true today than ever before. The American social contradictions and economic contradictions have reached such a proportion, have such explosive possibilities in them, that tremendous historical events may break out about us at any time. We must prepare our Party for its revolutionary role in the great upheavals coming in the United States. This role which is placed upon us by history will be really performed by us only if we prepare ourselves for these tremendous tasks.

We can prepare ourselves only if we will actually carry through in life this course laid down by the Open Letter before this conference. Comrades, we can take up this task with greater confidence when we see how our brother German Party has met more serious tasks than this, and has overcome a thousand-fold more difficulties than we have, even in the conditions under which they are working in Germany at the present time. If the German Communist Party, with such determination and heroism, succeeds in meeting the conditions of struggle against the Hitler regime, certainly we also will be able to meet the offensive of the Roosevelt New Deal and establish our Party as a mass leader in America. Certainly, when we understand that the program of our Party is worked out on the solid foundation of the teachings of Lenin, upon the same foundation which has produced that marvelous revolutionary organization that has brought about the tremendous achievements of the building of a socialist society in the Soviet Union, when we understand that our Party is a part of the same world Party as the Soviet Union Communist Party, then we can feel real confidence in the ability of our Party, in the determination of our Party, to boldly, fearlessly, ruthlessly carry through the line laid down in the Open Letter of this conference.

VI

What Every Worker Should Know
About the N.R.A.*

EVERY NEWSPAPER is writing about the National Recovery Act and the industrial codes. Every radio carries speeches and propaganda. Speakers hold forth on the streets about it. Even our homes are visited by N.R.A. advocates to talk to us. The Blue Eagle stares at us from every window and signboard.

But what is it all about? What does it all mean in the daily life of a worker? It is not easy to learn the answers to these questions from all the mass of writing and speaking.

Let us try to get at the truth in a simple, easily understood way.

Why was the N.R.A. made a law by act of Congress?
Because the economic system of America had broken down. Four years of crisis, closed factories, millions unemployed and starving, banks unable to pay and closing their doors, wages being slashed, strikes breaking out—these things forced everyone to see that something was fundamentally wrong with the whole system. The thing simply wouldn't work any more.

Nobody believes any more in the old system. Everybody demands a new system. Everybody demands that a way out of the crisis shall be found.

The N.R.A. was the official recognition that the old system was smashed, that the masses of people who work, when they can get a job, and who depend upon a job in order to live, must be given something new.

That is why we have the New Deal and the N.R.A.

What does the N.R.A. promise to give to the workers?
It promises to remove the cause of the crisis. It promises to reopen the factories, restore production, bring back prosperity. It promises to remedy the disorder, the chaos, the anarchy of the economic system, and put in its place a planned economy without crises. It promises higher wages, shorter hours, and the right of the workers to organize according to their own desire.

All these things would be very fine, if we could get them. They

* Pamphlet, October, 1933.—*Ed.*

would make life easier, they would remove the terrible conditions which today make life a horrible nightmare for millions of people.

These are wonderful things that have been promised. Even the simple promising of these things, before any of them are realized, made Roosevelt a popular hero with millions of people.

The masses want these things. They need them in order to live.

Therefore it becomes a very important question as to whether these things are being realized through the N.R.A.

· We don't want to be fooled again, as we were fooled with the promises of Herbert Hoover, when he was President and promised us "prosperity in 60 days."

We have a right not to trust in anybody's words any more. We have been lied to so much, that we will be stupid fools to believe in any words that cannot be proven by facts.

So let us examine what facts we can find.

When we look for facts, it is no longer enough to read the newspaper headlines and front pages, or listen to the speeches of "big men." In such places we don't find those facts which show the true conditions. We must turn to the financial and business pages, read the economic journals, and get reports from the workers in the industries all over the country.

Newspaper headlines tell us: "Roosevelt and the N.R.A. have started the factories to producing again. Prosperity is coming back."

Is it true? Millions of workers wish it to be true, but if it is a lie, then it is a cruel one, raising high hopes only to dash them to the ground again.

To judge this question, one must study the collected figures of the business of the entire country. Such figures are collected by organizations supported by the big capitalists; we can be sure that they will show the situation as favorably as possible. Such an institution, for example, is the Index Numbers Institute, Inc., whose figures are published in big newspapers all over the country. At random we pick up the Pittsburgh *Post-Gazette*, for September 11, which publishes these figures. What do they show?

Economic activity for August, 1933 (production, business, etc.), is represented by an index figure of 79. This means that if all economy of 1926 is represented as 100, then August, 1933, would be 79, or 21 per cent less. Or if it is compared with a five-year period of pre-crisis times, which showed a combined index of 125, that means we are 40 per cent below "normal."

That is certainly not "prosperity," as yet, is it?

"But things are better than they were," say the newspapers. "No matter how bad they are now, they get better, and move towards prosperity."

Is that so? True, things were going up for a while; now they are going down again; up and down, up and down, that is the way the capitalist system is always going. But how far up?

Remember last year, during the presidential election, Herbert Hoover also told us things were getting better. And they were—in the same way as in April to July this year. Hoover's boom rose almost as high as the Roosevelt boom this year—up to the index of 76. But that did not mean that we were approaching prosperity again; instead we were coming to a new crash, which followed in December, January and February, the worst the country ever saw.

Remember also, that Hoover's boom (which went almost as high as Roosevelt's boom this year), was brought about without much effort. Hoover did not do much of anything. Roosevelt's boom cost a thousand times the effort, and required inflation, going off the gold standard, the N.R.A., the Agricultural Adjustment Act, the new banking law, the codes, the Blue Eagle, and so on—and still it went only 3 points higher than Hoover's, and now is already dropping below.

We cannot say, with any truth, that "things are getting better" until, at least, things get better than in the last year of Hoover's administration.

"Overproduction, which caused the crisis, is now being overcome," say the newspaper headlines.

Is it true? Has the N.R.A. reduced the extent of "overproduction"?

Unfortunately, the facts do not show it. On the contrary. No one will deny that last December there was "overproduction," that is, great stocks of unsold goods with nobody to buy them, which was the reason that more factories than ever closed down last winter.

Are things any better in this respect as we approach the winter of 1933-34? No, things are worse. *Today there is twice as much goods in the warehouses as in December,* 1932.

Production did go up in April to July. But instead of making things better, it made them worse, because most of the goods went into storage, increased "overproduction." The goods were not being sold for consumption.

But why would anybody buy and store up goods, if the markets were not expanding? Why did production increase, when the warehouses were already full?

The answer is: Because of *inflation,* the cheapening of the dollar, the going off the gold standard, which caused a tremendous *increase in prices.*

When prices began to go up, every speculator and profiteer rushed to buy and store up goods, in order to make gamblers' profits. With the prospect of prices going up 30 per cent, or 50 per cent, or even 100 per cent, they bought at the old prices, being willing to wait many months before selling until the much higher prices came into effect.

Now the warehouses are filled up. Prices are high. The speculators want to "cash in" on their speculative profits. They must sell their goods. But the real market, the consumers' market, is very little larger than it was before, and is shrinking again. The goods moving out of the warehouses therefore begin to squeeze out the goods coming from the factory. There is more than enough, already manufactured, to fill all demands. The factories are beginning to close up again.

"Overproduction" is with us again, stronger than ever. The N.R.A. which was promised to cure "overproduction," we now see, really caused it to be worse than before. Inflation and higher prices, which were a part of the whole plan of the N.R.A. and "New Deal," have prepared a new crash.

Roosevelt's boom lasts only a little longer than Hoover's.

The N.R.A. forced up the figures of production for a few months, but since July 15 they have been dropping faster than they went up before. We can trace these facts, for example, in the weekly business index figure of the New York *Times*. This shows the high point of 99 was reached on July 15, and then a drop, drop, drop, every week, until at the beginning of September it is below 85.

Clearly, the engine of the N.R.A., which promised to pull us out of the crisis, is missing fire, it is backfiring. It is the same old engine trouble that wrecked the Hoover administration.

"Even if all this is true," objects the spokesman of the N.R.A., "yet still some good has been accomplished; we are forcing the capitalists to pay higher wages for shorter hours, and thus improving the conditions of the workers."

Is that so? Again we can trust more the statistics of the capitalists than we can their newspaper ballyhoo. Looking at their figures, we find that they tell a different story.

Wages are worth what they will buy in food, clothing, and shelter. What they will buy depends upon prices. And prices are shooting upward like a skyrocket—this feature of the N.R.A. has been very successful. But the higher go prices, the lower go real wages—wages turned into the things which the wage-earner needs.

How much have prices gone up? Different authorities give different figures, depending upon which particular items of goods they base their figures on. Retail prices move more slowly than wholesale prices, but it is only a question of time when the higher wholesale prices will be passed on to the workers in higher retail prices.

The retail price of *food*, chief item in a worker's expenses, went up about 20% between April and the beginning of September, 1933. The *Consumers' Guide*, issued by the Agricultural Adjustment Administration, admits that a family market basket, containing meat, eggs, milk, butter, cheese, rice, potatoes, flour, bread and macaroni cost only $14.68 in April; but by the end of August, the family was paying $17.74 for this monthly basket-load. Potatoes went up 120%; flour, 66%; navy beans, 49%; evaporated milk, 29%; lard, 27%. Bread rose 19%.

Total cost of living, including food, clothing, rent, fuel, lighting, and other necessaries, went up at least 8.5% during the first six months of the "New Deal," according to the most conservative estimates, while the Labor Research Association estimates that the correct figure is at least 14%.

What lies ahead is admitted by the employers' journals, in such statements as the following:

. . . *the advance in retail prices has not been exhausted.* Many consumers will be surprised when the ultimate advance has reached its height. (*Daily News Record,* October 9, 1933.)

. . . there is ample evidence to substantiate the statements of manufacturers that opening prices for spring, 1934, will be anywhere from 33 1-3%, most conservatively estimated, to 40% or more, compared with wholesale and retail prices prevailing last spring. (*Daily News Record,* October 13, 1933.)

If at the same time the total amount of wages paid to the workers (in terms of dollars) also rose by the same amount as the cost of living, then the total amount of real wages (in terms of what the worker buys) would be exactly the same as before, neither higher nor lower. If wages did not rise so fast, then real wages were being cut down.

Everybody knows wages have not risen so fast. At the very most wages rose only by 6% between March and September, according to the official figures of the U. S. Department of Labor and the Interstate Commerce Commission. This little 6% increase has been eaten up in the increased living costs—8.5% to 14% as we have seen. Thus, even if we use the more conservative figure of 8.5% for increase in living costs, the worker finds his real monthly income in September actually below March by 2.3%. What has actually happened, then, is a cut in real wages.

The situation was described in the businessmen's newspaper, *Daily News Record,* for August 30, as follows:

The latest index number (of prices) is 43 points higher than it was at this time last year. Textiles, house furnishings, and like commodities are increasing. The increase is having its effects in two ways: helpful for the producers [capitalists—E. B.], but not any too good for the consumer, for the reason that purchasing power has not increased proportionately.

Roosevelt promised that the N.R.A. would increase the purchasing power of the toiling masses, the workers and farmers. But in reality the opposite has occurred. There has been a tremendous cut in real wages. Under Roosevelt and the N.R.A., the millions of workers are getting less food, less clothing, less shelter, than they did under Hoover.

Illusions are stubborn things. We showed the above facts to an enthusiastic supporter of Roosevelt and the N.R.A. He said:

Maybe all you say is true. It is hard to deny, because these figures come from the Government and the big capitalists themselves, who have every interest to show things not worse but better. But still the N.R.A. has given more jobs by reducing hours, and increasing production even temporarily.

Again we will play safe and ignore the newspaper ballyhoo, in order to take a look at the facts shown by official statistics.

Production in July was 30 points higher than a year before. But employment was less than 12 points higher.

What does this mean?

It means that a terrible speed-up has been put across on the workers in the factories. It means that every worker must produce more than ever before, even with shorter hours. It means more workers displaced by machines. It means constantly fewer and fewer jobs for the same amount of production.

It means a great increase in permanent unemployment.

It means more starvation and catastrophe for the workers.

That is what Roosevelt and the N.R.A. have given the workers in the matter of jobs. The reality is the opposite to the promise.

But at least the N.R.A. has given one thing to the worker—argues the enthusiastic supporter of the Blue Eagle—it has given the worker the right to organize and fight for better conditions.

In law and in theory, the workers have for many, many years had the full right to organize and strike. When this is written into a new law, and proclaimed again by big politicians, this still doesn't give the workers anything they didn't have before. It is still only a law, worth not one cent more or less than previous laws.

Do you remember the War Labor Board, under President Wilson? Do you remember how it worked to strangle the strike movements of 1918-19, and hold down wage rates? Perhaps you do not remember that it conducted its work under a declaration of government policy, stated in almost exactly the same words as Section 7 of the N.R.A. The War Labor Board declared:

The right of workers to organize in trade unions and to bargain collectively through chosen representatives is recognized and affirmed. This right shall not be denied, abridged, or interfered with by the employers in any manner whatsoever.

What was this worth to the workers? Just exactly nothing. Under it they had the rights they always had, to organize and defeat their enemies if they could, the right to take what they were able to get with their own power. Strikes were prevented or strangled by "arbitration." Under this declaration the steel workers, for the first time in history, organized and went on strike to enforce the "collective bargaining" guaranteed by the War Labor Board. But the U. S. Steel Corporation "denied, abridged, and interfered with" their rights, fired the workers who joined the union, and broke their strike with armed force, both with private police and government forces. No one ever heard of Judge Gary, the president of the Steel Trust, being arrested and tried for this crime against the law. But thousands of workers were jailed, and many killed, for trying to get these rights "guaranteed by law."

The same thing is being repeated today.

The N.R.A. "grants" the rights which the workers already have, in order to establish control over their organizations, tie them up in "arbitration," squeeze out or crush the militant trade unions, and in general to prevent strike movements by all possible means.

But the N.R.A. has given the opportunity for organization, which the workers can take advantage of by organizing into the American Federation of Labor. William Green is even on the National Labor Board. Give it credit for that much.

Thus pleads the advocate of the N.R.A.

What is this "opportunity," whose is it, and how has it been used? These are interesting questions.

The A. F. of L. officials had the opportunity to help work out the industrial codes before Roosevelt signed them. How did William Green utilize this "opportunity"?

Green and his A. F. of L. fellow-bureaucrats signed a steel code, which fixed the existing wage-scales and hours of labor as the legally approved ones without any change whatever. This was done at a moment when rising prices and strike movements had succeeded in forcing wage increases in most other industries. This was at a moment when steel workers themselves, in Buffalo, in McKees Rocks, in Cleveland, had shown by example that it is possible now to *strike and win* substantial wage increases also in the steel industry. But the leaders of the A. F. of L. signed away this movement to the Steel Corporation and the N.R.A.

Clearly, the "opportunity" in the steel industry was grasped by the Steel Trust, with the help of the A. F. of L., to prevent either a wage increase or a strike movement.

In the automobile industry, Mr. Green put the name of the A. F.

of L. to the Roosevelt code which gives government approval to the "open shop."

Truly, this was a wonderful opportunity—but for General Motors, and especially for Henry Ford, who gets all the benefits without even signing the code, and for the whole "open shop" movement of the Chamber of Commerce of the U. S.

Or take the coal code. Before it was adopted, after months of jockeying about, already it effectively was used to choke the strike of 60,000 Pennsylvania miners, and actually prevent even such wage increases as the workers are winning by their own actions in other industries under the pressure of rising prices.

The coal code was thus also an "opportunity"—for the coal barons to stifle the fighting movement of the miners. The miners will win better conditions, not through the code, but through fighting against the code.

Or look at a smaller but equally illuminating example: The Radio and Television Workers of Philadelphia seized the "opportunity" to organize into the A. F. of L., in Federal Labor Unions Nos. 18368 and 18369. Mr. William Green used the "opportunity" personally to supervise the negotiation of a "contract" with their employers, "establishing their right to collective bargaining," with the personal collaboration of General Hugh Johnson. This wonderful contract also deals with wages. To obtain an increase? No, no, not at all! On the contrary, to guarantee to the employers that the workers *will not demand any increase!* The contract declares that the unions:

will not demand an increase over present scale of wages rates unless such increased rates are incorporated in the N.R.A. code for the radio industry accepted and approved by the President of the United States.

Yes, indeed, this was a wonderful "opportunity"—for the radio employers to secure the A. F. of L. guarantee that the N.R.A. "minimum" code shall also be in reality the maximum, without any inconvenient strikes by the workers!

And if the workers go on strike anyway? Then the N.R.A. also gives a great "opportunity"—for the capitalists to fight the strike with material and moral support from the government, from the A. F. of L. and also from the Socialist Party, whose leader, Norman Thomas, has declared that, in view of the "New Deal" and the N.R.A.: "This is not the time to strike."

Truly, the N.R.A. creates many "opportunities"—for the capitalists!

But the N.R.A. gives the right to join any union the worker wants— say the Blue Eagle boys.—If you don't like the policy of William Green and the A. F. of L. join another union, such as the fighting unions of the Trade Union Unity League, or an independent Union. The N.R.A. will protect you in that right.

Yeah? You don't say! But take a look at what the government and the employers, with the help of the A. F. of L., try to do to those who would exercise these "rights."

The tobacco workers of Tampa were organized in the Tobacco Workers' Industrial Union, affiliated to the T.U.U.L. The government of Florida came in, destroyed its headquarters, sent its leaders to prison on frame-up charges so flagrant that even the U. S. Supreme Court was forced to reverse the verdict, and turned hundreds of its members over to the Washington authorities who deported them out of the country as "undesirable citizens" for daring to take their rights of organizing a union.

Later, when the N.R.A. became law, the Tampa workers' faith in their legal rights revived—enough to organize an entirely independent union of their own on a local basis. They sent a delegation to Washington to talk with the N.R.A. administration. General Johnson and his aides refused to talk with them. When the delegation returned to Tampa, they were arrested, turned over to the Ku Klux Klan, who beat them up severely and ran them out of town. The union headquarters were again wrecked, and the members dispersed by police terror.

That is the reality of the "freedom to join any union," as the Tampa tobacco workers found it.

Or consider the case of the miners of Utah and New Mexico. In these two fields the miners, by overwhelming majority and secret ballot, decided not to join the United Mine Workers of the A. F. of L. They didn't trust it, because its officers came into the field as the personal friends of the coal operators and government officials. Instead they joined the National Miners' Union. They went on strike and won wage increases and union recognition. Then came word from Washington, from the N.R.A. administration, that the local employers made a mistake to settle with the union. The employers broke their agreement. The union went on strike again. The governors of Utah and New Mexico, with the open help of the U. S. Army, of which Mr. Roosevelt is Commander-in-chief, declared military rule, martial law, arrested all leaders of the N.M.U. and hundreds of its active members, holds them incommunicado without trial, while the A. F. of L. officials openly issue calls for scabs to come in and break the strike.

These are typical examples of what is going on, in one form or another, all over the country, in all industries. "Unions of their own choice!" What a mockery!

But even if everything you say is true—argues the blind follower of Mr. Roosevelt—that only means that we must all make some sacrifices for the common good that will come from an organized planned economy under the N.R.A.

It is true that sacrifices are being demanded—and taken—under the "New Deal" and the Blue Buzzard. But who makes the sacrifices?

First, the working class, whose income has been cut by two thirds, to less than one third part of what it was five years ago, and is being further reduced by higher prices every day.

Second, the poor farmers, whose income has been reduced about the same as that of the workers, and who are losing their farms to the bankers and other mortgage holders, thus being turned into tenants or wage-workers.

Third, the veterans of the World War, who are not only denied payment of the bonus (a debt acknowledged by the government by formal certificates) but who have further had taken away from them by Mr. Roosevelt and the "New Deal," a half-billion dollars per year from their pensions and disability allowances which they received under Hoover.

Fourth, the Negro people, most of whom suffer as workers, poor farmers and veterans, and suffer further as an oppressed nationality, whose wage-rates are omitted from even the N.R.A. codes, or deliberately set at figures from 25 to 50 per cent lower than the general starvation level, who are more than ever being Jim-Crowed and lynched in this time of N.R.A.

Fifth, the small bank depositors (some workers and many middle-class people) whose savings have been confiscated by the so-called "bank failures" (which is only another name for the process of big banks eating up the little banks). Many billions of dollars have been "sacrificed" in this way—to go into the vaults of J. P. Morgan, John D. Rockefeller, Andrew Mellon, and the rest of the little group of "rulers of America."

Sixth, the small business men are also making sacrifices. The abolition of the anti-trust laws has removed the last small restraints upon chain stores, monopolies, and big trusts. They are free to use their mass resources to the full to crush and absorb the little fellows. At the same time these monopolies are writing the "industrial codes" under the N.R.A., in such a way as to guarantee monopoly profits while squeezing out entirely the little fellows.

On top of all these sacrifices, which all go to swell the treasuries of monopoly capital, of Wall Street, further billions of dollars are being taken by the government through taxation of the masses, and through the operations of the Reconstruction Finance Corporation, are being passed on to the banks, insurance companies, railroads and great industrial corporations.

These sacrifices made by the broad masses of the people for the benefit of Wall Street, of monopoly capital—these are called, with a grim humor peculiar to the N.R.A., *establishing a planned economy*.

But this is nothing else than a gigantic *trustification of capital* at the expense of the masses and of economy.

This increased trustification does not and cannot overcome the crisis. It was the previous trustification that made the crisis so deep-going and protracted. It does not organize economy to overcome those features which bring about crises and catastrophes. It only deepens the crisis and drives the world even faster to the further disaster of a new world war.

But the N.R.A. has nothing to do with war—says our faithful supporter of Roosevelt—the New Deal means more friendly relations with other nations. Therefore, why do you talk about war?

So, Roosevelt is also going to abolish war? Yes, much the same as he is abolishing the crisis! Just as the N.R.A. talks higher wages but actually cuts real wages, so does the New Deal talk about peace but really prepares for and carries on war.

The N.R.A. established a three-billion dollar fund, supposedly for "public works." This is being expended mainly to launch the greatest navy building and military program the world has ever seen.

All these warships, bombing planes, tanks, poison gases, army camps, etc., these are the means for establishing "more neighborly relations"? Yes? Tell that to Japan and England, and see how much they believe it!

Japan and England, France, Germany, and Italy—all are feverishly making the same sort of preparations for "more neighborly relations"! All arm to the teeth against each other—and all try to unite for a moment for war against the Soviet Union.

How strange, how typical of the topsy-turvy times in which we live, that such blatant hypocrisy can fool anyone even for a moment. And such a moment, when the whole world knows that it is faltering on the brink of the most destructive war the world ever witnessed!

Even the most "constructive" measure of Roosevelt's "New Deal," the Tennessee River development around the Muscle Shoals hydroelectric plant, is a senseless thing until it is seen as a part of a war program. At the same time that Roosevelt pays out many hundreds of millions of dollars (taken from the masses by special sales taxes) to the farmers in order to persuade them to *reduce production,* to plow under every fourth row of cotton, to leave stand idle every fourth acre of wheat land, to slaughter six million pigs to reduce the production of meat— at this same moment he spends more hundreds of millions to complete and put into operation the Muscle Shoals fertilizer plant. To produce fertilizer is useful to *increase production in agriculture,* the opposite of Roosevelt's program. But the method in this madness can be seen when we recall that Muscle Shoals is a fertilizer plant only by afterthought. In the first place it is a monster *munitions plant, to produce explosives for war.*

The N.R.A. is from beginning to end a part of the program of war and preparations for war!

Yes, the selfish, bad capitalists are doing all the things you describe—admits our Rooseveltian enthusiast—but Roosevelt himself is a good, well-meaning man who is doing his best for us, and fighting against all these bad things.

That reminds me of a story. An old Scotchman had for many years been a member of a savings and loan association. Came the day when he wanted to obtain a loan. He went to his old friend, the Chairman of the Board, with his application. The chairman said: "Sandy, I'd do anything in the world for you personally. But this is something that must be decided collectively by the entire Board." Sandy visited each member of the Board and got the same reply from each. Contentedly he waited for the Board to meet, sure of the support of each member as his loyal personal friend. After the Board meeting, the astonished Sandy was informed by the chairman that his application had been turned down. "Well," said Sandy, sadly disillusioned; "personally each member of the Board is a good man and my personal friend, but collectively I must say that you're the worst bunch of bastards I ever met."

And so it is with that "good man" Roosevelt, who is such a firm "friend" of the workers and all the oppressed. He is at the same time the chairman of the Board that must make all decisions "collectively." He is the chairman of the executive committee of the capitalist class. That is what the job of President of the United States means.

How childish it is to think that the "goodness" or "badness" of the individual Roosevelt can make the slightest difference in regard to the policies of government!

The government, with Roosevelt at the head, is trying to save the capitalist system. To save the system makes it necessary to put the burden of the crisis upon the workers, farmers, and middle classes. They follow the class logic of their class position.

In order to improve the situation of the masses, of the workers and farmers and impoverished middle classes, it is necessary to start out from the position, not of saving the capitalist system but of changing the system, of moving toward substituting for it a socialist system.

Such an issue is above all questions of personal virtue or lack of it. It is a *class issue.* Roosevelt is bad for the workers because he is the leader of the capitalist class in its attacks upon the working class.

To be a "friend" of the working class in any real—that is, political—sense, requires being against the system of private ownership of the means of production by the capitalist class. It requires building up the organized power of the working class in struggle against the capitalist class. It requires helping the working class to take governmental power out of the hands of the capitalists, and establishing a Workers' Government, which takes the means of production away from the capitalists and organizes them on a new socialist basis, as the common property of all.

Oh, so you're a radical, a Red—exclaims our defender of the Blue Buzzard—you are one of those anarchists who want a bloody revolution in America, who preach force and violence. You are opposed to Americanism. That's why you criticize the N.R.A.!

What is a "radical" or a "Red"? Read your capitalist newspaper again and you will see that this name is applied to everyone and anyone who calls upon the working class to organize and fight for its rights, who helps to lead this fight, who refuses to trust in the promises of the class enemy, who exposes their tricks and maneuvers, who fights with all energy for better conditions *now* and who points the way to the final solution of all the problems, the revolutionary solution, the revolutionary way out of the crisis.

You see, then, it is not so terrible to be a "radical" or a "Red."

But we are not anarchists, we are not for disorder. The only real anarchists are the capitalists, who by their wild competition, their ruthless grabbing for individual profits, create this world-wide disorder and chaos of the crisis, of the many wars going on, of the bigger war preparing.

We are not for violence and bloodshed! It is the capitalists who every day carry out the violent and bloody suppression of strikes. It is the capitalists who bring upon the world that supreme example of violence and bloodshed—imperialist war. We fight against all such violence and bloodshed with all our power. The abolition of all such violence and bloodshed can only be achieved by the accomplishment of our aim, the overturning of capitalist power and the establishment of a Workers' Government.

We are not for the destruction of goods and houses! It's the capitalists and their government which is destroying wheat, cotton, milk, fruits—all the things people are dying for lack of—which destroys the productive forces by keeping them standing idle, rusting away, which keeps the buildings standing empty while millions freeze for lack of shelter. We are against all this destruction. We want all the wheat and cotton given to the people to feed and clothe them with. We want all the factories to open to make more things for the masses to consume. We want the houses opened up for the homeless to live in!

We are not un-American! Since when has it become un-American to revolt against oppression and tyranny? Since when is it un-American to call for revolutionary struggle to overthrow a tyrannical and destructive system? The United States was born in "treason" against King George and the British Empire. The United States was born in revolutionary struggle. It was born in the confiscation of the private property of the feudal landlords. That good old American tradition of revolution is today kept alive *only* by the Communist Party. We are the only true Americans. The Republican, Democratic and Socialist Parties are all renegade to the basic American tradition of revolution.

These fundamental features of Americanism were explained long ago by that eminently American historian, John Lothrop Motley, in the following words:

No man on either side of the Atlantic, with Anglo-Saxon blood in his veins, will dispute the right of a people, or of any portion of a people, to rise against oppression, to demand a redress of grievances, and in case of denial of justice to take up arms to vindicate the sacred principles of liberty. Few Englishmen or Americans will deny that the source of government is the consent of the governed, or that any nation has the right to govern itself, according to its own will. When the silent consent is changed to fierce remonstrance, the revolution is impending. The right of revolution is indisputable. It is written on the whole record of our race. British and American history is made up of rebellion and revolution. Many of the crowned kings were rebels or usurpers. Hampden, Pym, and Oliver Cromwell; Washington, Adams and Jefferson—all were rebels. It is no word of reproach. But these men all knew the work they had set themselves to do. They never called their rebellion "peaceable secession." They were sustained by the consciousness of right when they overthrew established authority, but they meant to overthrow it. They meant rebellion, civil war, bloodshed, infinite suffering for themselves and their whole generation, for they accounted them welcome substitutes for insulted liberty and violated right. There can be nothing plainer, then, than the American right of revolution.

Americans have always been able to solve a basic crisis by revolutionary means. In 1776 we smashed the fetters of reactionary feudal rule by the European absentee landlord. In 1861 we smashed the feudal remnants of Negro slavery. With the same resolute and revolutionary determination we must, in 1933, turn to the task of smashing the oppressive and destructive rule of the Wall Street monopolist capitalists who have brought our country to the brink of destruction.

"If that be treason, make the most of it!"

That's a beautiful dream—admits our admirer of General Johnson and his blue bird—but it's Utopian. It wouldn't work. We can't get along without the capitalists.

That used to sound like a crushing argument. But that was long ago, when the capitalist system was working, after a fashion, and there was no other example of social organization except the feudal, pre-capitalist societies. But today such an argument falls very flat.

It is exactly capitalism that doesn't work. The whole system has cracked up so completely that nobody pretends to deny the fact any more.

The only country in the world that has no crisis today, is that country where they got rid of all their capitalists. That is Soviet Russia, the Union of Socialist Soviet Republics.

Russia, when it was ruled by the capitalists and feudal landlords, under the Czar, was the most backward country of Europe. But after the Russian workers and farmers defeated the old government and its landlord and capitalist class supporters, after they set up their own government of Workers' and Farmers' Councils (Soviets), after they chased out the capitalists or put them into overalls—since then that backward old country has made amazing strides forward.

Just look at a few things they were able to do, at a time when our capitalist system was falling about our ears and threatening to destroy us.

In Soviet Russia production has increased three-fold over the pre-war figure. Meanwhile, our production dropped more than one-half.

The Soviets abolished unemployment entirely. In America we threw 17 millions out of their jobs.

The Soviets multiplied their schools and cultural facilities by five or six times, and turned billions of dollars into this development. In America our school system is falling to pieces, its revenues are drying up, our school teachers are unpaid, our culture is stultified.

In America all is confusion, uncertainty, chaos, disaster.

In the land of the Soviets, all is orderly advance, progress, certain planned economy, and an ever-growing socialist prosperity.

Why this contrast? Why did we fall behind? Why do they forge ahead?

A few years ago America was the richest, most prosperous land; Russia was the poorest, most backward.

We had everything, they had nothing.

So it seemed. But in reality it was *our capitalists* who had everything—*we* really had nothing.

The Russian workers, because they had abolished capitalists and capitalism, while they seemed to have nothing, yet had everything required for a glorious development of a new working class society—of socialism.

Because it was *our capitalists* who had everything in America, that is why we have fallen into starvation in the midst of riches.

The Soviet Union proves that there is a simple and quick way out of the crisis.

Push aside the capitalists, open the warehouses, distribute the goods to all who need them. They will soon be consumed. No overproduction any more.

Then open up all the factories. Give everyone a job. Produce all we need to fill the warehouses up again as fast as they are emptied. Nothing needs to be destroyed, and the unemployment problem is solved, and everyone has enough of everything.

In America there are such enormous productive forces, such a wealth of factories, mills and mines, that if they work only eight hours a day in two shifts of four hours each, they will produce twice as much as we need in this country and the rest we can give to our less fortunate brothers in other lands until they catch up with us.

There is no reason to be pessimistic about our country. What the Russian workers accomplished in a poverty-stricken land through years of painful efforts, we can accomplish in this country in a few weeks. We already have all the productive forces they had to create from the ground up. And our working class will prove to be just as capable when it becomes conscious of its power and its tasks.

The Russian workers had the tremendous advantage of the leadership of Lenin.

But we also have the teachings of Lenin to guide us, and of Lenin's teachers, Marx and Engels, and of Lenin's outstanding disciple and successor, Stalin, organized in our American section of the international Communist Party.

We have a working class that is learning to fight for its interests, even against Roosevelt and the N.R.A. It is learning how to build up its own fighting trade unions to win higher wages and better conditions, by successful strikes; to build up powerful Unemployed Councils and to win adequate relief and Unemployment Insurance.

As we learn how to expose the fakery of our class enemies, such as the ballyhoo around the Blue Eagle, as we learn to win the daily struggles for bread and the right to live—by this road we are also moving forward to defeat not only the N.R.A. attacks, but also to defeat the whole capitalist system, to overthrow it, and to establish a Workers' Government, a socialist society.

There are only two roads before the working class. One is the road of the capitalist class, the road of Roosevelt and the N.R.A., the road of wage-cuts, starvation and war. The other is the working-class road, the road of revolutionary struggle for our daily needs, and the ultimate overthrow of capitalism, the road to socialist prosperity and peace.

VII

The Situation in the United States *

THE SITUATION of the United States confirms most strikingly the correctness of the draft thesis before us, when it speaks of "the tremendous strain of the internal antagonism . . . as well as of the international antagonisms." The policies of the Roosevelt administration, known as the "New Deal," called into being by the crisis and by these "tremendous strains," have by no means softened these strains and antagonisms, but on the contrary have intensified them. Precisely the period of the Roosevelt regime has marked not alone the sharpening of the international relations of the United States, but also the internal class relations.

Roosevelt's policy called for "national concentration" and "class peace." But in spite of the apparent surface successes of his regime, even the "honeymoon period" of the New Deal has been marked by rising mass struggles, by great class battles, by a radicalization of large sections of all the toiling masses of the population. The protracted strikes of 70,000 or more miners in Pennsylvania, Utah and New Mexico; the long strike of 60,000 silk workers in New Jersey and Pennsylvania; the many strikes of steel workers, penetrating into the heart of the steel industry around Pittsburgh; and the hundreds of smaller strikes, in almost all industries and regions, increasing in numbers and intensity from March to October—all disclose the hollowness of the "civil peace" of the Roosevelt New Deal, resulting from the fact that N.R.A., while promising wage increases, actually made a general wage-cut of exceptional severity. The mass struggles of the bankrupted farmers, quieted for a few months by the promises of the Agricultural Act and a moratorium on debt foreclosures, are breaking out again on a large scale and with full sharpness with the disclosures that the Roosevelt "allotment plan" has failed to meet a single one of the problems faced by the poor farmers. Even the middle classes are stirring with unrest, under the pressure of continued expropriations carried out by the closing of many hundreds of small banks, by the rapid progress of trustification in all lines, and by wholesale inflation. Never before in modern times has the "strain of internal class antagonisms" in the United States been so sharp and so general.

Characteristic for the whole system of policies known as the New

* Speech at the Thirteenth Plenum of the Executive Committee of the Communist International, December, 1933.—*Ed.*

Deal is their nature as preparations for war. The economic contents of these measures are those of war economy. The famous three-billion-dollar building program turns out in reality to be a program of Navy building, mechanization of the Army, building of military roads, and the putting into operation of the Muscle Shoals explosive plant abandoned at the close of the World War. The "unemployment relief" program turns out to be first of all the setting up of a network of military training camps, under the direction of the War Department, where 300,000 young men are being prepared for the Army. The National Recovery Administration follows the pattern laid down by the War Industries Board of the World War. Never before has there been such gigantic war preparations at a time when the "enemy" is as yet unnamed. Simultaneously, United States oppression of the colonies and semi-colonies takes on sharper forms, as the resistance of the colonial masses grows—witness the fifty-million-dollar loan to Chiang Kai-shek to finance the anti-Soviet campaign, the naval concentration in Latin-American waters, and especially in Cuba, where the anti-imperialist revolution has already partially broken through the chain of American imperialist puppet-governments.

If we witness all these developments during what may be called the "honeymoon" period of the Roosevelt regime, when the illusions created by an unprecedented demagogy were bolstered up for a time by a rapid rise in production stimulated by an enormous speculative market (the flight from the dollar)—then we have every reason to expect the growth and intensification of class conflicts, and of all the contradictions of capitalism, now when the Roosevelt program has already exposed its inability to improve the condition of the masses, when production again declines precipitately, when rising prices and inflation cut further sharply into the living standards of the masses, and when demagogy is rapidly being reinforced with a sharp development of fascist ideology and terror directed against the struggling masses.

International social-fascism has hailed the Roosevelt policies as "steps in the direction of socialism." The British Labor Party and Trades Union Congress have adopted the Roosevelt program as their own, demanding that it be imitated in Britain. In this way they are but continuing, in the period of crisis, that complete ideological subordination to the bourgeoisie which, during the period of American prosperity, created out of the figure of Henry Ford the reformist "saviour." The American Socialist Party has not lagged behind in this respect; Norman Thomas and Morris Hillquit hastened to pay a public visit to Roosevelt, upon his assumption of office, to congratulate him upon his policies, which they hailed as nothing less than a "revolution" in the interests of the masses.

But the fascist direction in which the Roosevelt policies are carrying the United States is becoming clear to the whole world. Nowhere is this more manifest than in the efforts to merge the reformist American Federation of Labor into the machinery of government, under the avowed banner of the fascist conception of the "corporate state," prohibition of strikes, compulsory arbitration, governmental fixing of wages, and even control of the inner life of the trade unions. For the edification of the masses this was spoken of as a "partnership of capital and labor, together with the government." Under this program the A. F. of L. is given governmental support and even financial assistance, and a determined effort is made to control and eventually choke off the strike movement, by driving the workers into the A. F. of L. where it is hoped the official leadership will be able to bring the masses under control.

THE A. F. OF L. AND THE T. U. U. L.

During 1933 over a million workers have engaged in strikes. From six to eight hundred thousand workers have come into the various trade unions; of these, between four and six hundred thousand were recruited into the A. F. of L., about one hundred thousand into the Red Trade Unions of the Trade Union Unity League, and one hundred thousand into newly formed independent unions opposed to the A. F. of L. but not yet prepared to enter the Red Trade Unions.

Of outstanding importance to us is the fact that the A. F. of L. has grown by about a half million members, placing very sharply before us the urgent task of organizing a mass revolutionary opposition and overcoming all hesitations in our ranks towards this work. This growth has resulted from the mass illusions built up around the N.R.A., from the direct support of the government, which looks upon the A. F. of L. as its main support within the working class. The A. F. of L. was able to capitalize these illusions and the mass faith in Roosevelt. It must be said, however, that the bourgeoisie has been disappointed by the performance of the A. F. of L., which could not control the masses nor prevent the strike movement, nor recruit such masses as was expected of them.

The comparative failure of the A. F. of L. to recruit the great masses or control the strike movement arises from a number of factors. First, not all capitalists accepted the government policy, and especially in the basic industries most employers preferred to establish "company unions" instead of the A. F. of L. or even to continue to refuse to have any kind of union at all in their plants. Second, the crude and open strike-breaking policy of the A. F. of L. repelled large numbers of workers ready to join but disillusioned by their first contacts. Third, the A. F. of L. bureaucracy, which is of tremendous size, with 15,000 full-time paid officials, has, to a great extent, become so parasitically corrupted and degenerated by their past life, that it is incapable of the energetic activity demanded by a mass recruitment campaign, to the great disgust of the more virile leaders in the Roosevelt administration. And fourthly, the A. F. of L. unions have, in many places, been captured by the underworld gangs, turned into typical American "rackets," dealing in blackmail and bribery on a huge scale, and become incapable of conducting mass policy on the scale contemplated in the Roosevelt program. It is interesting to read, for example, the complaints in the stenograms of the last A. F. of L. Convention, voiced by the leader of the Chicago teamsters' union, who revealed that his union office must be fortified with steel plate and constantly protected by armed guards to prevent the dues payments from being seized by underworld gangs and even to prevent these gangs from taking possession of union elections and assuming the union offices. Revolt among the two and a half million members of the A. F. of L. against these primitive, semi-feudal conditions, not to speak of the more complicated betrayal of the no-strike policy and the New Deal, has been stimulated by the rising wave of mass struggles and by the influx of the half million new members. This, combined with the beginnings of more systematic and energetic work by the Communists inside the reformist unions, has played a great role in the development of the strike movement among the A. F. of L. workers, and begins to crystallize again into a broad revolutionary opposition movement. This becomes even more important when we see the determined policy of the bourgeoisie to bring forward the A. F. of L. especially in every case where the workers are mobilized in struggle and organized into the Red trade unions.

The growth in the trade unions, and in the strike movement, after four years of decline during the first years of the crisis, is of tremendous significance to our Party. This is all the more true when we see the character of the strike movement. With only a few exceptions, these strikes were directed not only against the employers for economic demands; they were also strikes against the official leaders of the American Federation of Labor, they were against the operations of the N.R.A. and the Labor Boards set up by the government—that is, they were also political strikes. This was true of almost all the strikes, whether of A. F. of L. members, of the Red unions, or of the independent unions. From this situation it followed that, when our Party (after some hesitations) began boldly to develop work inside the A. F. of L. as oppositions in combination with the independent building of the Red unions, even in the same industries and fields, and also to build independent unions where the workers hesitated to join the Red unions, our Communist and sympathizing forces played a constantly growing role in the whole strike movement. Thus it is that we have 45 per cent of all strikers (during 10 months of 1933) members of the A. F. of L. but fighting in opposition to their officials and the government, and to a growing extent openly following the lead of the Red unions, even while remaining in the A. F. of L.

THE STRIKE MOVEMENT AND THE RED TRADE UNIONS

Very significant also is the comparatively large role played in the strike movement directly by the small Red unions. With about 40,000 members at the beginning of July, they rose in membership to 70,000 by September, and now stand at approximately 125,000, having recruited about 100,000 and having lost about 15,000 during the same period. The Red unions are thus about 5 per cent of the volume of membership of the A. F. of L. But these small unions directly led 20 per cent of all strikers, and indirectly influenced in a decisive manner more than half the struggles of the A. F. of L. members and the independent unions.

During the strike movement, conditions often changed very quickly, making necessary quick changes of tactics on our part. At first we were very slow in recognizing the changed situation and adjusting our tactics. Thus in the Pennsylvania mine fields, our Red miners' union led the strike struggles of April and May directly, but after the establishment of the N.R.A., the reformist United Mine Workers' Union (A. F. of L.) swept through the field with a broad recruitment campaign, and our Red union members (without even consulting us) went along with the masses, and together with them organized the strike movement of July and thereafter through the local unions of the U.M.W.A. We were slow in reorientating ourselves to work mainly through the reformist union, and therefore were weakened quite seriously for a period, and we are only now beginning to reestablish our forces organizationally in that field. During the same period, the coalfields of Utah and New Mexico were completely organized in our Red miners' union, which led long strikes, holding the miners solidly in the face of military rule and the jailing of most of our leaders. Even in these fields, however, we were also forced to maneuver, as for example in Utah; there, the protracted strike and military persecution caused some of these new and untrained forces to weaken and hesitate and to consider the possibility of settling the strike by joining the reformist U.M.W.A. Just as we left America it became necessary to give directives to our Utah comrades, that if a split of the miners became a serious threat, we should avoid this by taking the entire body of miners unitedly over from the Red union into the reformist U.M.W.A.

The silk textile strike furnished most interesting and valuable experiences, in a different form. In the beginning, the workers were also entirely unorganized. The strike began in Paterson, New Jersey, called by local leaders of the A. F. of L. as a means of organization with expectations of a quick return to work and settlement through arbitration of the N.R.A. Both the A. F. of L. and the Red textile union began with only a few hundred members. The employers threw in their influence to drive the workers into the A. F. of L., telling the workers that only the A. F. of L. could ever gain a settlement with them. As a result, the workers in their large majority joined the A. F. of L.; among them was a considerable sympathy for the Red unions, but they lacked confidence that they could win a favorable settlement, while they were influenced by the illusions that the A. F. of L., through its support by the government and bourgeois press, created for them more favorable conditions. We maintained our Red union throughout the strike, however, even though a minority, and fought for unification of the strike committees and picket lines. The open efforts of the A. F. of L. leaders to sell out the strike, repeated several times, were each time defeated by almost unanimous votes of all workers, in each case under the leadership of the small Red union. The result was that the influence of our Red union continued to grow in the ranks of the A. F. of L., who more and more looked to the Red union for a lead on all questions, even though they remained formally within the A. F. of L. This influence became so decisive that when a large mass delegation was elected to go to Washington, to place the demands of the strikers before the National Labor Board, even the A. F. of L. leaders were forced to accept Ann Burlak and John Ballam, the two main leaders of the small Red union, as the leaders and spokesmen of the mass delegation, while the bourgeois press and employers openly declared that it was impossible to settle the strike unless they dealt with the Red union at the same time. The A. F. of L. leaders were forced by the workers to discontinue their attacks upon the leaders of the Red unions, and at the most decisive meeting the workers drove their leaders off the platform and invited our comrades to speak to them. These events were a revelation of the tremendous possibilities of a correct application of the united front tactic in strike struggles; they also showed how work within the A. F. of L. can be combined with building the Red unions, and can be strengthened thereby, provided a correct united front policy is carried out.

Since June, all trade union questions have been dominated by the questions of policy regarding the N.R.A. For a time we had to conduct a sharp struggle within the Party on two fronts, against the tendency represented by the idea of "boycotting" the N.R.A. and against the tendency to surrender to the illusions concerning the N.R.A., to drag at the tail of the A. F. of L. and the Socialist Party. The latter, the open Right opportunist tendency, was the most serious and the most stubborn. Comrade Kuusinen has already in his report mentioned a few of the most crass examples. Some comrades were convinced that we would succeed in organizing mass unions only if we made them look before the workers as much like A. F. of L. unions as possible, in name, program and daily policy. Our fight to liquidate this tendency was helped considerably by the fact that as quickly as our comrades built unions in this fashion, they were immediately taken over by the reformist leaders, our people were kicked out of them without even any serious support among the workers.

Our Party and the Red unions came out openly and boldly against the N.R.A., and exposed it as a general attack against the workers' standards, and as a movement toward fascism. In this we had to go sharply against the stream of mass illusions that had been aroused by the Roosevelt demagogy. These illusions were bolstered up for a few months by the rise in production, the opening of more factories, the appearance of "returning prosperity" brought about by the speculative market created for a time by inflation. When this speculative production broke down, when the factories began to close again, when it began to be clear that the N.R.A. itself had cut wages instead of raising them, the disillusionment of the workers which set in greatly increased the prestige of our Party and the Red trade unions which had from the beginning told the workers what they now see to be the truth.

Our work to build a broad united front of struggle against the N.R.A. led to the calling of the Cleveland Conference in August. This was called jointly by the Red unions, the Muste group of "Left" reformists, and a few independent union leaders and various unemployed organizations. This conference was very valuable to us, although it failed to build a real broad united front. The great body of the conference was composed of our own forces; besides ourselves and close sympathizers, only a small group of Muste leaders came. For us the conference was valuable, however, in that it was a good mobilization of our own forces for struggle against the N.R.A.; it was a broad school in the tactics and policies of the struggle; it was a public proclamation of our program; and it was a rehearsal for our forces in the problems of building the united front. With those Muste leaders who came, we had agreement on the most important questions of policy so long as it was writing general programs against the N.R.A., for unification of the unemployment movement, etc. But we quickly came into conflict with them on the question of organizing the strike struggles in the steel industry, where the Red steel workers' union was already leading and winning strikes. This question already was too close and burning for the Muste group to commit itself to revolutionary responsibilities; we had an open clash with them in the Conference which cleared the air greatly, and educated our movement better than a hundred resolutions could have done.

THE ANTI-WAR AND ANTI-FASCIST MOVEMENT

Our most successful application of the united front has been in the anti-war and anti-fascist movement. We led a highly successful United States Congress Against War, which brought together 2,616 delegates from all over the country, and unanimously adopted a manifesto and program which is politically satisfactory. The composition of the Congress was overwhelmingly proletarian with a core of 450 trade union and shop delegates; it contained a very satisfactory youth delegation of about 500, a majority from reformist and Socialist organizations, which in a special meeting openly accepted the leadership of the Young Communist League in the Congress; a considerable delegation of farmers; representation from every important pacifist organization in the country; a group of local organizations of the Socialist Party and mass organizations under its influence; and a few important A. F. of L. trade unions with about 100,000 members. We also had a delegate from the United States Army. The Congress from the beginning was led by our Party quite openly but without in any way infringing upon its broad non-Party character, with the Party members at all times in a minority numerically, and leading by the quality of their work. This success was, of course, largely due to the very favorable situation, and the position of our Party as almost a monopolist of the anti-war movement in the United States. After the Congress a broad mass campaign has been launched to popularize its results, a campaign which has been highly successful, greatly helped throughout by the assistance of Henri Barbusse and Tom Mann, from France and England, whose presence added force and political significance to the Congress and the mass campaign carried on afterwards to popularize its work. The Congress set up a permanent organization on a federative basis, called the American League Against War and Fascism, which is publishing a popular monthly paper.

Our campaign of solidarity with the German working class and against German fascism has been growing and involving new circles of workers. The American workers have been filled with enthusiasm by the magnificent defense, or rather counter-offensive, of the Communists in the Leipzig trial led by Comrade Dimitroff.

Especially effective for the U. S. A. was our exposure of the work of the Nazi organization in the United States, which was even taken up by bourgeois organizations and resulted in a criminal indictment of the Nazi leader in America, Heinz Spanknoebel, and his disappearance into hiding. We secured and published a secret Nazi letter, written from New York to Berlin, a document which has been placed in the records of New York City, and now in the last days before a Committee of the Congress of the United States, with expert testimony which substantiates its genuineness. The character of this document is so sensational that I understand there has been some hesitation in publishing and using it in Europe. I can assure you that the document is genuine. It is a letter written by W. Haag, adjutant to H. Spanknoebel, leader of the Nazi organization in the United States, addressed on September 23 to *"Uschle Berlin Alexanderplatz."* The letter contains the following paragraph which I read:

I cannot find a place for Van Der Lubbe here, it is best if you throw him overboard into the ocean while enroute to another country. Whom do you intend to hang in his place in Germany? I agree with you entirely that it would be good to give the damned Communists in Leipzig an injection of syphilis. Then it can be said that Communism comes from syphilis of the brain.

The leading Nazi committee in New York held a special meeting, with one of their important American friends, Congressman Hamilton Fish (a leading enemy of the Soviet Union) and discussed the question whether they should not bring a court action against the *Daily Worker* for publishing this letter. Unfortunately they finally decided against bringing suit against the *Daily Worker*, evidently understanding that we would be able to establish its genuineness. After two months the document is now accepted as genuine by the bourgeois press of America, but they consistently refuse to publish the paragraph about Van der Lubbe, which I have quoted above, and confine themselves to the other parts of the letter which show the Nazi violation of American immigration laws, and the crganizing of anti-Semitic agitation in America.

Our Party work among the farmers, leading their mass struggles and raising their political understanding, has improved in the past period. We now stand at the head of a growing mass movement, which marches under the chief slogan of cancellation of debts and back taxes, and which actively fights against the dispossession of the bankrupt farmers, and which establishes the closest unity with the city workers, employed and unemployed. This farmers' movement has just concluded its second national conference, with 660 delegates from 40 out of the total 48 states of the United States of America.

THE INNER SITUATION OF THE PARTY

A few words about the inner situation and growth of our Party. The Party leadership is fully united in carrying into effect the *Open Letter*, expressing the policy of the Communist International, which was adopted at our Extraordinary Party Conference in July. The efforts of the Party to concentrate on the basic industries has given us the beginning of a growing trade union movement in almost every district. About a hundred new shop nuclei have been formed in the past five months, of which two-thirds are in the concentration industries; the proportion of Party membership in the shop nuclei has been raised from 4 per cent to 9 per cent. The Party membership which in 1932 rose from 12,000 to 18,000 dues payments per week, with 21,000 members registered in March, 1933, remained at about the same level until September when it began to rise again after the question had been sharply raised in the Party, and at the present moment the dues payments have risen to more than 20,000 per week, with more than 25,000 registered members. Our *Daily Worker* has broken out of its stagnation, improved its contents, and begun to grow in circulation, selling 45,000 copies daily in October, with 100,000 on Saturdays when the paper gets out a special edition. Our eight other daily newspapers in various languages have all registered some improvement politically and some growth of circulation, and the same can be said for most (although not all) of our eighteen foreign language weekly newspapers.

Our Party has made certain beginnings in carrying into effect the *Open Letter*, in becoming a mass Bolshevik Party. The beginnings have been uneven, and are not yet consolidated. The Party still lags far behind the objective possibilities. The danger of Right opportunism, especially opportunism in practice, still shows itself in our work, and requires a constant struggle, a constant education of the new Party members and especially of the new cadres that are gradually being built up. Examples of "Left" opportunism, also, are often seen.

The last Central Committee meeting of our Party stated the immediate most pressing tasks of the Party as follows:

Special emphasis must be laid upon the daily tasks of every Party unit, fraction and committee to (a) recruit immediately into the Party the broad surrounding circle of supporters and especially the most active fighters in the struggles now going on; (b) a real drive to establish mass circulation of the *Daily Worker* as an indispensable weapon of all struggles of the working class; to consolidate the improvements already made and to strengthen the *Daily Worker* as an agitator and organizer, and as an instrument to carry out the *Open Letter;* (c) build the revolutionary trade unions and opposition in the reformist unions, develop them as the real leaders of the growing struggles, paying special attention to the masses newly recruited into the A. F. of L., prepare for the coming convention of the T.U.U.L., clarify the role of the Communists and the Party fraction in the trade unions; (d) give serious attention to carrying out the Party decisions on building a mass youth movement and Y. C. L.; (e) develop and extend the mass movement of the unemployed, build the Unemployed Councils as the leading fighters for one united unemployed movement, and develop a broad mass campaign for unemployment insurance; (f) strengthen the work among the Negroes, especially for winning them into the trade unions, unemployed councils, share-croppers' union, etc., and organize a broad national liberation movement in · the L.S.N.R.; (g) more serious extension of the Party among the farmers, leadership and support to their struggles, and practical assistance to the successful carrying out of the Second National Conference of the Farmers' Committee of Action; (h) to extend activities among working-class women and draw them into struggle against the N.R.A., in factories, among unemployed and against the increased cost of living; (i) build the united front movement against war and fascism on the broadest basis.

The weakest point in all our Party mass work, from which most of our other shortcomings spring, is the weakness in bringing forward the revolutionary goal of our Party, the program of the revolutionary way out of the crisis. The deepening crisis, the growing misery of the masses, forces the wrokers to look for a way out. They want a leadership which can connect their daily problems with a wider perspective, with a possibility of final solution of their problems, with a program of building a new workers' state.   They more and more realize that such a new society is being built in the Soviet Union.   This opens their minds to what the Communist Party has to say to them.   They want the Communist Party in their own country to give them the answers to all their questions, the question of power, the question of building the new society under American conditions, as well as the problems of the trade union and unemployed struggles.   As we learn how to fulfill these demands of the American workers, we are succeeding, and we will more and more succeed, to build a mass movement of struggle around the Communist Party, building solid cadres which are more and more Bolshevized, which will place on the order of the day in America, perhaps not as the last capitalist country in the world, the question of Soviet power, of proletarian revolution.

VIII

New Developments and New Tasks in the United States *

I. THE ECONOMIC SITUATION

THE THIRD year of the depression, following the lowest point of the economic crisis reached in 1932, completely bears out the characterization of the depression as a "depression of a special kind which does not lead to a new boom and flourishing industry, but which, on the other hand, does not force it back to the lowest point of decline."

The short-lived spurt upward of industrial production in the first months of Roosevelt's administration (April-July, 1933), was quickly cancelled by the declines of the last months of the year, while 1934, beginning also with a rise in production, is also ending on the downgrade, which more than wipes out all gains in the first part. The zigzag line representing the high and low points of the depression is indicated in the following figures:

1929 average	100	July, 1933	82
July, 1932	50	December, 1933	60
November, 1932	58	July, 1934	72
March, 1933	51	October, 1934	60

(Based on Federal Reserve Bank index.)

It would be hard to find signs of recovery in these figures.

The above quoted figures show not only the present difficulties hindering the going out of the economic crisis on the basis of the mobilization of the inner forces of capitalism, but on the whole they reflect the results of the economic policies of the N.R.A. and New Deal. These policies have not succeeded in keeping industrial production above the level already reached under Hoover. It is true that Roosevelt's 40 per cent inflation of the dollar created a four-month inflation "boom," but this ended at the same moment that the N.R.A. with its system of industrial codes was established, and almost all those gains from inflation are again wiped out.

A sober estimate from the point of view of finance capital, from the *Business Bulletin* of the Cleveland Trust Company (November 15), is the following:

* Written in November, 1934, as a report to the Executive Committee of the Communist International: published in *The Communist*, February, 1935.—*Ed.*

All the advance of the earlier months of this year has been cancelled, and most of the advance of last year.

The financial journal, *The Annalist* (October 19, 1934), speaking of the September figures, declared editorially:

This is the lowest level reached by this index since April, 1933. Only in the worst months . . . from April, 1932, to April, 1933, has this index stood at a lower level. . . .

And concludes:

We are entering the sixth year of depression with business activity almost at its extreme depth.

Employment, wages and earnings have all declined for the working class as a whole, during Roosevelt's regime. Official statistics on employment show an increase, but this is accomplished by spreading part-time work (which is no increase in employment for the working class) and by listing as employed the workers forced to render labor services of non-productive character in return for unemployment relief. Official statistics show an increase in wage scales, but this is in terms of the dollar, which has itself been depreciated 40 per cent, so that real wages have actually declined. Weekly earnings of workers have declined even more than real wages, due to the shortening of working time through the spread-the-work system. Even the organ of finance, *The Annalist*, is forced to admit this (October 26) when it says:

Factory employment, seasonally adjusted, was slightly lower than last December, though factory payrolls were slightly higher. If, however, allowance is made for higher living costs, the real wages of factory workers were no higher than last December.

Such conservative sources as Hopkins, national relief director, and William Green, president of the A. F. of L., have publicly admitted that this winter will bring the largest relief lists ever before seen in America. More than 20,000,000 people will be directly dependent upon relief, while an additional 20,000,000 will be supported by relatives, friends, and their own last accumulations. A total of 40,000,000, or 30 per cent of the population, will be without normal current income.

II. SIGNIFICANCE OF THE NATIONAL ELECTION RESULTS

Results of the national Congressional elections on November 6, which greatly strengthened Roosevelt's control of Congress, were generally interpreted (both in the United States and abroad) as showing a big wave of mass sentiment in support of Roosevelt and the New Deal. This interpretation will not, however, stand up under analysis.

Total votes cast declined under the figure of 1932, by over 10,000,000. This mass abstention from the polls was greater than in normal times, indicating mass dissatisfaction with the programs of the major parties.

This mass abstention was even greater among the followers of the Democratic Party than among those of the Republican Party. While the Republican vote declined by 3,000,000, the Democratic vote declined 7,000,000.

Despite their greater loss of votes, the Democrats increased their strength in Congress. This is because, wherever it appeared that the Republicans had a chance of election, there usually the abstentionism was overcome—the votes turned out *to defeat the Republicans*. That is, large masses were supporting Roosevelt on the theory of "the lesser evil," in spite of their discontent, disillusionment, and even a growing, though vague, mass radicalization.

This mood among the masses was even more sharply and clearly expressed whenever it had the opportunity to rally around candidates, factions or new party formations which appeared before the masses as being "to the Left" of Roosevelt, and which yet did not, in the estimation of the masses, represent a revolutionary departure from the present system. Wherever such "Left" alternatives to Roosevelt were offered, they gained unprecedented mass support. We need mention only four outstanding examples among a great number of lesser ones:

1. Upton Sinclair, with his EPIC program, running on the Democratic ticket, with his promise to "end poverty" without disturbing capitalism, received 800,000 votes out of a total of 2,000,000, and was defeated only by the intervention of the Roosevelt administration against the California Democrats in favor of the Republican candidate.

2. Huey Long retained control of the Louisiana Democratic Party, against the Roosevelt administration, on a program of a two-year moratorium on debts, taxation of the circulation of the capitalist daily newspapers, struggle against the bankers, etc., and legalized for the next two years his one-man dictatorship of the state.

3. The LaFollette brothers in Wisconsin, sons of the late leader of the third-party movement of 1924, split away from the Republican Party, established an entirely new party (called "Progressive"), and carried all important state and congressional posts in the elections.

4. Floyd Olson, heading the Farmer-Labor Party of Minnesota, carried the state with an increased majority, on a vague but radical-sounding platform calling for "the cooperative commonwealth."

In these events we have the characteristic feature of the November elections. Without being prepared as yet to come out in support of a revolutionary challenge to the capitalist system, the masses were seeking something new, something more radical, something which promised more definitely relief from their miseries. They rejected decisively all appeals of the Republican Party to return to the era of Hoover, appeals based upon the traditions of the two-party system in America—that discontented masses always vote out the party in power and put its established rival in office again. Where they had no other alternative, they apathetically, without enthusiasm, supported Roosevelt as the "lesser evil." Where a "progressive" faction or party emerged, it at once gained enthusiastic mass support.

We must conclude from the elections that among the broad masses strong currents to the Left have begun. These currents have already paralyzed the normal operation of the old two-party system, begin to present manifestions of its break up, of mass desertion of the old capitalist parties, and indicate the probability that in 1936, with the continued absence of economic recovery, with continued prolonged depression, there will emerge a mass party in opposition to and to the Left of Roosevelt.

III. SOCIALIST AND COMMUNIST PARTIES IN THE ELECTIONS

The Socialist Party vote in the elections was, on the whole, stagnant. In a few localities it succeeded in becoming the "progressive" opposition, and elected state legislators in Pennsylvania and Connecticut. Its national vote will probably fall below that of 1932. (Information on the smaller party votes is not yet completely available.) This stagnant condition was primarily due to its inner condition, which was one of partial paralysis, resulting from a deepening division which has split the Party into two main warring camps—one, which wants to take the Party to the Right and merge in the Progressive movement, and the other, which moves to the left under the general influence of the Communist united front activities, and a part of which operates under the slogan of united front with the Communist Party.

The Communist Party vote increased over 1932 by 80 to 100 per cent. The total will be about 225,000. (These figures do not take into account exceptionally large votes for individual candidates, like the 80,000 votes for Anita Whitney in California, but only that cast for the whole or major portion of the Party ticket.) In New York City the vote increased from 26,000 to 45,000; in Ohio, from 8,000 to 14,000; in California from 8,000 to 24,000. In Arizona, the C.P. came second, the comparative vote being: Democratic—45,000; Communist —11,300; Republican—2,500.

In a number of small communities in the mining area of Illinois, the Communist and Socialist workers put up Workers' Tickets on a united front basis; in Taylor Springs, such a ticket was elected to office, including most of the county posts. In Trumbull County, Ohio, a united front between the local Socialist and Communist Parties, which had been formed in a series of struggles, was carried over into the elections, in a joint appeal to the workers to vote for the Socialist local ticket, and for the Communist state ticket (this was facilitated by the fact that the C.P. was not on the local ballot, while the S.P. was absent from the state ballot).

In general, neither the Socialist nor Communist Parties succeeded in engaging in its support the masses who were tending to break away from the two traditional capitalist parties. In the case of the S.P., this is to be attributed primarily to its inner contradictions, to its inability to make up its mind decisively in what direction it wishes to go. In the case of the Communist Party, the subjective weaknesses of insufficient contact with these masses, remnants of sectarian approach, are supplemented by the still low degree of consciousness among the Leftward moving masses, the main part of which is by no means prepared as yet to go boldly upon the path for the revolutionary solution of the crisis, which was given major emphasis by the C.P. during the election campaign.

IV. THE STRIKE MOVEMENT AND THE ROLE OF THE C.P.

The major manifestation of radicalization of the working class was, in 1934, the strike movement, which has already involved well over 2,000,000 workers this year, has taken on political character in the growth of general strike sentiment and actions, and represents the strongest revolutionary upsurge seen in America since the first post-War period.

These strike actions, in their great majority, were carried through under the banner of the American Federation of Labor. This already is a great change from 1931-32, when most strike struggles were initiated and led directly by the independent revolutionary unions; and even from 1933, when the strike movement was initiated by the Red unions, which led the first successful strikes in the crisis period, in auto, mining, textile, steel, and other industries, and in which the A. F. of L. only came into the strike movement later, when its membership surged out of its control under the influence of the successful strikes led by the Red unions.

In 1934, the Red unions definitely passed into the background in the basic industries, and to some extent also in light industry. The main mass of workers had definitely chosen to try to organize and fight through the A. F. of L. organizations, even though that meant also struggle against the official top leadership.

The chief feature of the strike wave was the sudden crystallization of a movement for general strike and solidarity strike actions. The first important movement of this sort came in Toledo, Ohio, in May, when a small strike in an auto-equipment factory, on the verge of defeat, was suddenly brought to life again by the surging onto the picket line of ten thousand sympathetic workers, mostly unemployed, who had responded to a call by the Unemployment Councils led by the Communists. The mass picket line, continuing for some days, was attacked by state troops, one worker killed, many wounded, hundreds gassed and arrested. The response to this attack was a vote in every union in the city on the question of an immediate general strike; out of 91 unions, 83 voted for the strike. Before the hour set for the general strike, the employers and union leaders hastily patched up a settlement of the strike, granting the striking workers some of their demands and giving guarantees against victimization.

Within a week or two of the Toledo events, a similar solidarity movement took place in Minneapolis, Minnesota, in support of the teamsters' strike, where also lives were lost, where masses came onto the streets and took possession of them, and where also the general strike was only prevented by a hastily conceived settlement which could be paraded before the workers as a victory.

Again within a few weeks, a strike of street car workers in Milwaukee, Wisconsin, which seemed about to be broken, was suddenly made 100 per cent effective by the surging onto the streets of 40,000 workers, who prevented a single street car from moving. Again the use of violence against the workers, and the killing of a picket, so roused the masses that a general strike vote swept through the unions; within 12 hours the threat of general strike had secured the granting of most of the demands of the original strike and a quick settlement with the union.

During all this period of May, and on into June, the Pacific Coast marine workers (longshoremen, sailors and harbor workers) had been carrying on their general industrial strike over a 2,000-mile stretch of coastline. Early in July, the employers decided to smash the strike by violence, attacking the pickets on the streets of San Francisco, and killing two of them, one a member of our Party. Again the masses responded; at the funeral, 100,000 workers took possession of the main streets of the city. A general strike vote swept through the unions. The Central Labor Union leadership, which had been standing firmly against the general strike, suddenly changed front when they saw the movement going over their heads, came out for the general strike and took the leadership of it, and then proceeded in four days to betray the strike, hoping in crushing the general strike to smash at the same time the marine strike which was under revolutionary leadership.

For four days, however, the City of San Francisco was in the hands of the workers, until the strike committee itself had step by step surrendered the strategic positions and then called off the strike. Only the betrayal of the San Francisco general strike stopped the development of general strikes in Portland, Oregon, and Seattle, Washington.

This wave of local general strike movements and solidarity mass actions is unprecedented in modern American labor history. I will not go into an analysis of these strikes, their strength and weakness, the role of the C.P. in them, etc. This has been done at some length in a special resolution of our Central Committee which has been discussed and approved in the Comintern.

What is important here to establish, is the characteristic of the passing over of even small economic struggles into great political class battles; of the engaging of entire communities in solidarity actions; of the winning of factory strikes by means of the solidarity actions of the unemployed; of the growth of class consciousness and the feeling of class power among the workers, the breaking down of fears and hesitations, the prompt mass responses to go on the streets as the answer tŏ police and military violence.

Within six weeks after the ending of the San Francisco strike, came the great general strike of the textile workers, involving about 400,000 workers. This again was the expression of a great upsurge from below; the strike was forced by the membership against the wish of their leaders; when the strike call was issued, it was met with response far beyond the limits of the organized textile workers, tens of thousands of unorganized workers streaming into the union during the period of strike; entirely new forms of mass action were spontaneously developed from below, outstanding among which were the so-called "flying squadrons," consisting of 50 to 100 motor cars full of strikers, going from town to town to call out on strike the mills still working, and which met with tremendous successes.

Troops were called out in eleven states against the textile strike; the Governor of Rhode Island called upon the Legislature to declare a "state of insurrection" and ask Roosevelt to send Federal troops; the State of Georgia erected concentration camps on the style of Nazi Germany, herding several thousand textile pickets into the camps. Some 18 or 20 workers were killed, hundreds wounded, tens of thousands gassed and arrested.

In spite of this extraordinary terror, the strike was growing stronger every day, extending to new mills, when suddenly it was called off by the leaders on the basis of a request from a Board appointed by Roosevelt, with loud claims of victory but without a single demand conceded by the employers.

It is undoubtedly necessary to characterize this wave of struggle as a revolutionary upsurge of the American working class. This upsurge defeated the efforts of the A. F. of L. bureaucrats and the government to bring the trade unions under governmental control and transform them into semi-official agencies of the N.R.A. It defeated the efforts of the leaders to drive the Communists out of the unions, and opened up a broad field for revolutionary work where before it had been impossible to penetrate. It gave the masses vivid and clear lessons in the practical benefits of class struggle, when the only considerable gains conceded to any group of workers in this period were those given to the longshoremen who had followed Communist leadership throughout their struggle and afterward, and who continued the fight by always new forms even after their strike was ended. As a result of these battles, there is a new relation of forces, a new social atmosphere, a new spirit among the masses, a new confidence and readiness to fight.

In characterizing the strike wave of 1934, it can be said that its most significant features are: first, that for the first time since 1919 have we witnessed such a great wave of struggle, developing on a continually rising level; directed against the effects of the Roosevelt New Deal policies; second, the masses have been aroused to an unparalleled fighting spirit and desire for unity in action, as expressed in the development of solidarity actions and movements for local general strikes, and the participation of the unorganized workers, the unemployed, and even the poor farmers; third, the mass urge of the unorganized workers for organization, and struggle against the company unions, which breaks through all the barriers which the trade union bureaucracy of the A. F. of L. attempt to put up.

The struggles for the most elementary economic demands develop into struggles of highly political character. Every effort of the reformist leaders to prevent or sidetrack these struggles did not succeed, and they were forced to go along with the strike movement in order to avoid being swept aside and be in a better position to betray the struggle through arbitration. In this they were ably assisted by the Trotskyites (Minneapolis), the Musteites (Toledo), and the Socialist leadership (textile). .

This strike movement took place mainly through the channels of the reformist unions, and the Communists in the main were unable to exercise a decisive influence in the leadership of the workers because we were not entrenched as yet inside the A. F. of L. unions which the masses were entering for the purpose of carrying on struggles for their daily interests.

Nevertheless, the Communists played a growing and effective role, in some instances relatively weak as in Minneapolis (but even here of decisive importance at certain moments), in other cases of great influence though unorganized, as in the textile strike, and were able to issue timely slogans which were seized upon by the masses and translated into action (mass picketing, general strikes, solidarity actions).

Where the Communists were firmly established inside the A. F. of L. unions and had strong position, as in the Pacific Coast longshoremen's strike, we played a leading and decisive role from first to last, and were instrumental in forcing the calling of the San Francisco general strike.

What is of supreme importance is this, that out of the strike wave the A. F. of L. bureaucracy emerged weaker, the S.P. emerged weaker, the Muste group and the renegades emerged weaker—but the Communist Party emerged stronger in every instance without exception.

V. THE CHANGE IN TRADE UNION POLICY

Serious changes in our current trade union policy were found to be necessary, in order to achieve these positive results in our work. In all the basic industries it was necessary to shift the main emphasis to work inside the A. F. of L. This we proceeded to do, at first with some hesitation, but, with our growing satisfactory experience, with increasing boldness. Among the longshoremen in San Francisco we threw all forces into the A. F. of L. union, with excellent results, not only establishing leadership of the most important strike, but winning victories for the workers, and maintaining our organizational positions after the strike; the big majority of all offices in the union in San Francisco were filled, in the September elections, by Communists and sympathizers.

In the textile industry, we joined the small and scattered locals of the National Textile Workers' Union into the United Textile Workers' of the A. F. of L., thereby multiplying our organizational base by four or five times, and becoming an influential minority in the great strike movement of 400,000.

In the steel industry, we withdrew our Red union, the Steel and Metal Workers' Industrial Union, and confined it to the field of light metal and machinery, sending all our steel workers into the A. F. of L. union, the Amalgamated Association of Iron, Steel and Tin Workers, with the result that in a few weeks we have begun to crystallize a great national rank-and-file movement to prepare for strike in the spring, a movement which already has serious organizational strongholds in the union, basic American cadres of leaders, and excellent prospects for a great mass movement.

In the auto industry, we have dissolved the Red Auto Workers' Union, sending the members into the A. F. of L. federal local unions, and already have under way a serious movement for the uniting of the 80 to 90 locals in the industry into an industrial union within the A. F. of L., a movement which forced the recent national convention of the A. F. of L. to grant industrial union form of organization to the auto industry, as well as to others.

Even in light industry, we had circumstances where it was necessary to send our forces into the A. F. of L., as in the case of the New York dressmakers, and here again with the excellent results of considerably strengthening our influence over large masses of workers.

The resolution before us today proposes to confirm these changes in our trade union policy, and to set the Party even more firmly and energetically upon this path.

At the same time we do not propose a general and immediate abandonment of all independent revolutionary trade unions. While generally, in all industries, putting forward the line of trade union unity, we recognize that in some cases the cause of unification can be best advanced by strengthening the Red unions, or the independent unions not directly under our leadership.

There are still some seven national unions in the Trade Union Unity League, as well as a whole series of local unions, with a membership of about 75,000, for whom the perspective for the immediate future is continued independent existence; there are three or four unaffiliated national independent unions of which the same must be said.

That these unions have big possibilities of growth is demonstrated, for example, by the Metal Workers' Union, about which news has just come that it has held a unity conference with 12 smaller independent unions, of about 10,000 members, which decided to organize a joint council for common action.

The independent United Shoe Workers' Union (in which we merged our Red shoe union a year ago) is much larger than the A. F. of L. union, and must talk unity with it in much different terms than in other places where we are relatively weak.

At our Eighth Party Convention, we put forward the perspective of the organization of an Independent Federation of Labor, which would unite the Red trade unions with the then growing independent unions, and with the expected movements of splitting away from the A. F. of L. of those newly-organized workers who rejected the plans of the A. F. of L. to split them up into craft unions. This was a realistic perspective, a possible development, at that time; but now we must say that this project has receded into the background for the next period.

When we are sending a number of our unions into the A. F. of L., when the independent unions are not growing as they did last year, and when the split movements from the A. F. of L. have been halted by the concessions granted at the last convention for industrial unions, it is clear that a new situation has arisen, in which immediate organizational steps for the Independent Federation of Labor would not serve to strengthen the movement. Whether this issue will again come to the foreground will depend upon future developments.

VI. FINDING NEW ORGANIZATIONAL FORMS

In our latest resolution the concepts of "minority movement" and "opposition," as the organizational forms for our work in the A. F. of L., are sharply rejected, as tending to limit the movement to Communists and their close sympathizers; the task is set to find such forms which will lead to the Communists becoming the decisive trade union force, winning elective positions, becoming the responsible leaders of whole trade unions, and bringing the decisive masses behind them in their support. This position is fully confirmed by our experience in recent months.

Our most successful work has, in every case, found organizational forms which arise out of the established life and work of the individual

union, in most instances having as its main center one of the union
organs, either a local union in which we gain a majority, or a district
council or other body of elected delegates.

We have rejected the proposal to attempt to transform into a general
"opposition" center the A. F. of L. Rank-and-File Committee for Unemployment Insurance. This body has a specific role to perform,
which would only be hindered and perhaps destroyed by trying to make
it an all-embracing "minority movement." Its influence extends far
beyond its active participants, as shown by the fact that it has won to
the support of the Workers' Unemployment and Social Insurance Bill
more than 2,400 local unions and seven national unions, with a very
large part of the members of the A. F. of L. It furnishes a broad
recruiting ground for the gathering of new forces into the revolutionary
movements in the different industries and unions, which is a much more
valuable function than to try itself to become the form for the revolutionary movement in the unions.

An increasingly important role will now be played by revolutionary
delegates in trade union conventions and conferences and councils.
Even in the A. F. of L. National Convention, which is very tightly
controlled by the top bureaucracy, it is possible to develop effective
"revolutionary parliamentarism." These possibilities we are now beginning to use; thus, while in 1932, there was not a single revolutionary
delegate to the A. F. of L. Convention, and in 1933, there was only one,
in 1934 we had 15 delegates standing on our revolutionary program and
fighting for its adoption in the Convention, putting forward our various
measures before the whole working class through the participation in
the Convention.

VII. SOME UNITED FRONT SUCCESSES

An outstanding feature of our united front efforts was the Second
United States Congress Against War and Fascism, held in Chicago at
the end of September. At this Congress were 3,332 delegates, from
organizations with a total membership of 1,600,000. That represents
an extension of the influence of our movement over about a million
organized persons *more* than we have ever before had gathered around
us. The quality of this representation was higher than ever before;
it came after a year of the most intense attacks against the American
League against War and Fascism by the A. F. of L. and the S.P., who
denounced the League and its Congress as a "Communist innocents'
club."

In spite of these attacks, the Congress represented considerable
expansion in both the A. F. of L. and the S.P. For example, among
the 350 trade union delegates was an important delegation of A. F. of L.
union leaders, all workers from the mills but influential officials of the
union, representing a district which a few weeks later in its convention

voted to confirm its affiliation to the League. Further, there were 49 S.P. members present, headed by Mrs. Victor Berger, widow of the former Socialist Congressman, who formed themselves into a national committee to fight for the united front of the S.P. with the C.P.; since the Congress this Committee has gained notable victories. For instance, the Milwaukee S.P. organization, which had threatened to expel Mrs. Victor Berger for attending the Congress, and which actually did expel a member, Compere, has in the past days been forced to participate in a united street demonstration and march, headed by the expelled Compere, together with the secretaries of the local S.P. and C.P., and addressed by Mrs. Berger, among others.

The League Against War and Fascism also made significant advances among women's organizations, in connection with the campaign to send a delegation to the Paris Anti-War Congress of Women. Having set itself the task of getting 15 delegates to Paris, it surprised everyone by obtaining twice that number in a short campaign of 60 days, including that most difficult of all tasks, the raising of sufficient money to cover the heavy expenses of such a long trip for a large delegation.

An autonomous Youth Section of the League held a separate Youth Congress in connection with the main gathering in Chicago, with over 700 delegates. In this Youth Section are included all organizations of youth in the United States who in any way consider themselves "to the Left" of Roosevelt.

A unique achievement of the youth united front movement was the building of an anti-fascist bloc inside the American Youth Congress, which was called together by a certain young woman named Viola Ilma with the backing of Mrs. Roosevelt, Anne Morgan, a half-dozen State Governors, members of the Roosevelt Cabinet, etc., with the purpose of adopting a program for American youth which was distinctly fascist in its tendencies.

To this Congress came delegates of all varieties of youth organizations, including Y.M.C.A., Y.W.C.A., Boy Scouts, Girl Scouts, church youth organizations, trade unions, student organizations, the Socialist youth, the Young Communist League, etc., representing a membership of 1,700,000. The anti-fascist bloc in this Congress took control of it at its opening, adopted an anti-fascist program which included the immediate demands of the working youth, consolidated the overwhelming majority of the delegates behind this program, set up a continuation committee to which almost all the participating organizations continued to adhere after the Congress, conducted a series of conferences and meetings over the whole country, captured away from Ilma various state conferences which she tried to organize afterwards, and gathered another Youth Congress in Washington in January, to present the youth demands to Congress and to President Roosevelt.

Our united front approaches to the Socialist Party have been involved in the divisions within that Party which came into the open in the fight for and against the Detroit Convention declaration of principles. Two distinct camps have crystallized, which already have many of the characteristics of two separate parties (separate national committees, headquarters, funds, etc.), and which conduct negotiations with one another like two parties.

The so-called "Left," headed by Norman Thomas, is very heterogeneous, and really is a bloc of several distinct groups. The Right wing is very militant, while the "Left" with Thomas, the Centrist, at its head, is very conciliatory, although it controls the Party. In the Detroit Convention the Right wing wrote the trade union resolution which was adopted with the vote of the "Left" majority. The Right wing still dictates or decisively influences many of the current decisions of policy of the National Committee, of which Thomas nominally has a big majority. Thus on the issue of the united front with the C.P., Thomas swings back and forth with the wind of the moment, following no consistent line.

Shortly after Thomas had made a public speech hailing the French united front, and expressing the belief that it could be duplicated in the United States, he participated in the action to reject the united front by the S. P. National Committee. This action was itself a classical study in hesitation and equivocation. On a Saturday the Committee debated the question, coming to a decision *favorable* to opening negotiations with the C.P., by a vote of 7 to 4. A few hours after the meeting closed for the day, a capitalist newspaper appeared on the streets with big headlines announcing, "S.P. Decides to Join the Reds." Some of those who had voted for the united front went into a panic at the sight of this capitalist newspaper publicity on their action, and without a full or formal meeting of their committee, decided to reverse their vote, hastily wrote a statement to this effect and gave it to the newspapers, which came out with the news of the *unfavorable* vote two hours after they had announced the *favorable* vote.

The conflict was smoothed over later by a compromise decision, that the question of united front was only *postponed* until December, to obtain the advice of the Second International, to see the further development in France, and to have the results of the Seventh Congress of the Communist International (at that time expected in September); and further, to send a delegation of "observers" to the Chicago Anti-War Congress to report back with recommendations as to whether the S.P. should affiliate or not.

All the conciliation and waverings of Thomas, however, and all his concessions to the Right wing, have not served to bridge over the split, but seem, on the contrary, only to drive it deeper, to make the struggle develop more sharply. This is because in the lower organizations the controversy is raging, with the adherents of the united front becoming ever stronger, more organized, more clear and effective in their demands. In this the "committee for the united front," formed at the Chicago Congress, has been a decisive influence. The Revolutionary Policy Committee, while containing many energetic advocates of the united front, has been singularly passive and irresolute as an organized group. It is too heterogeneous in composition to become a forceful leading center in the inner-Party struggle.

Present indications are that the National Committee of the S.P. will try to obtain a temporary settlement of the conflicts on the united front by a decision to enter into the American League Against War and Fascism, with a series of conditions, such as the addition of a list of leading S.P. members to its leading committees, certain limitations upon criticism by the C.P. against the S.P. leaders and policies, etc. Our policy is to facilitate so far as possible, without concession in principle, the entry of the S.P. into the League; but at the same time to use this to raise even more sharply than before the question of direct negotiations between the two parties for a general united front on all the most burning questions of the class struggle, including the fight for the Workers' Unemployment and Social Insurance Bill, the Negro Rights Bill, Farmers' Relief, and the current strike movements.

VIII. THE QUESTION OF A LABOR PARTY

The political changes taking place among the American masses already require that the Communist Party shall again review the question of the possible formation of a Labor Party, and its attitude toward such a party if it should crystallize on a mass scale. The correct basic approach to this question was formulated at the Sixth World Congress in 1928, which said:

On the question of organizing a Labor Party, the Congress resolves: that the Party concentrate on the work in the trade unions, on organizing the unorganized, etc., and in this way lay the basis for the practical realization of the slogan of a broad Labor Party, organized from below.

Since 1929 until now, this correct orientation has necessitated unqualified opposition by the Communist Party to the current proposals to organize a Labor Party which, in this period, could only have been an appendage of the existing bourgeois parties.

Developments in 1934, however, begin to place this question in a new setting, in a new relation of forces.

The decisive new features are, in brief:

1. Mass disillusionment with the New Deal and Roosevelt administration, shown by the development of the strike wave *against* the codes, and *against* the Government conciliation and arbitration boards, also shown negatively in the fall of the Democratic Party vote from 22,000,-000 in 1932 to 15,000,000 in 1934.

2. The bankruptcy of the Republican Party policy, which attempted to utilize this disillusionment and turn it into openly reactionary channels, according to the traditional two-party system, but without success.

3. The mass support given in the election to groupings and leaders within the old parties and to new and minor parties standing (in the eyes of the masses) to the Left of Roosevelt (Sinclair in California; LaFollette and the new Progressive Party which captured the State of Wisconsin; Olson and the Farmer-Labor Party who won Minnesota with an unexpectedly large vote; Huey Long faction of the Democratic Party in Louisiana, with its two-year moratorium on debts, etc.; and a number of less significant examples all over the country).

4. Renewed mass interest in the trade unions in all forms of proposals that the workers' organizations engage directly in political struggle against the capitalists and their parties, whether through a Labor Party, through workers' tickets, or in other forms.

It is clear that mass disintegration of the traditional party system has begun; masses are beginning to break away from the Democratic and Republican parties. There are all probabilities that the discontented, disillusioned masses will already be moving during the next two years sufficiently to give birth to a new mass party, to the Left of and in opposition to the existing major political alignments.

As to the character of such a new mass party, the major possible variants are the following: (a) "Peoples" or "Progressive" Party, based on the LaFollette, Sinclair, Olson, Long movements, and typified by these leaders and their program; (b) A "Farmer-Labor" or "Labor" Party, with the same character, differing only in name and extent of demagogy; (c) A Labor Party with a predominantly trade union base, with a program of immediate demands only (possibly with vague demagogy about a "cooperative commonwealth" à la Olson), dominated by a section of the trade union bureaucracy assisted by the Socialist Party and excluding the Communists; (d) A Labor Party built up from below, on a trade union basis but in conflict with the bureaucracy, with a program of demands closely associated with mass struggles, strikes, etc., with a decisive role in the leadership played by militant elements, including the Communists.

The major task of the Communist Party is to build and strengthen its own direct influence and membership, on the basis of the immediate issues of the class struggle connected with its revolutionary program for a way out of the crisis. It cannot expect, however, that it will be able to bring directly under its own banner, and immediately, the million masses who will be breaking away from the old parties.

At the same time, it cannot remain indifferent or passive towards the development of these millions, nor the organized form which their political activities will take. It must energetically intervene in this process, influence the development towards assuming the form of a real Labor Party based upon the working masses, their struggles and needs, ally itself with all elements willing to work loyally towards a similar aim, and declare its readiness to enter such a mass Labor Party when the necessary preconditions have been created.

At the same time, it must conduct a systematic struggle against all attempts to capture this mass movement within the confines of a "Peoples" or "Progressive" Party, or within a Party of the same character masquerading as a "Labor" Party. This will at the same time be the most effective basis for struggle against a Labor Party bureaucratically controlled from above by Right-wing reformists with the exclusion of the Communists and rank-and-file militants.

In this situation the simple slogan "For a Labor Party" is not an effective banner under which to rally the class forces of the workers. This will be also the main slogan of a section of the reformist bureaucrats, who will transform its contents into that of a mild liberal opposition; its undifferentiated use by the Communists would therefore play into their hands. Every effort must be made, therefore, to bring a clear differentiation into two camps of those who are trying to turn the mass movement into two different channels, on the one hand of mild liberal opposition masking class-collaboration and a subordination of the workers' demands to the interests of capital, of profits and private property, and on the other hand of an essentially revolutionary mass struggle for immediate demands which boldly goes beyond the limits of the interests of capital. In this struggle for differentiation, care must be taken to avoid all sectarian narrowness, which would only play into the hands of the reformists; that means, first of all, that the basis of unity of the working-class camp must be the immediate demands with the broadest mass appeal. At the same time the Communist Party energetically conducts its own independent political mass work for the revolutionary way out of the crisis.

All premature organizational moves should be carefully avoided. The Communist Party should not itself and alone initiate the formation of a new Party. In the various states this problem will present itself with all variations of the possible relation of forces. It will be necessary to study carefully the situation in each state, and the tempo of development, adjusting our practical attitude and tactics in accordance with these differences. There is much greater possibility of the final crystallization of a mass Labor Party in certain states, in the immediate future, than upon a national scale where the contradictions and complications are more intense.

It is necessary to strengthen systematically all mass connections of the Party, and the Party itself, politically and organizationally, preparing to face and to solve without undue hesitation the various practical phases of this question that will present themselves in life, and which will be especially subtle and intricate in the earlier stages of development. The basic means to this end is the bold and energetic expansion of our united front work in all fields, but before all in the trade unions, especially in the A. F. of L.

Every phase of the struggle for the political leadership of the masses now breaking away from the Democratic and Republican parties is dependent upon the constant growth and strengthening of the Communist Party as an independent revolutionary force, with its full program made familiar to ever broader masses. It depends upon, and must always be subordinated to, the daily mass struggles of the workers, before all, of strikes and other economic struggles, the struggles of the unemployed, of the farmers, the movement for Unemployment Insurance, etc.

Under the conditions of the crisis, in its present phase of protracted depression, with sharpening and broadening mass struggles, of growing difficulties of the bourgeoisie, the only forces capable of leading a mass struggle really to win the immediate demands of the toiling masses of the United States, is the revolutionary vanguard of the working class under the leadership of the Communist Party.

IX

Three Main Policies of the Communist Party *

TRADE UNIONS, LABOR PARTY, UNITED FRONT

FIRST OF all on the developments of the international situation. It is one of the signs of the times that yesterday the newspapers reported the speech of Senator Nye, in which he declared that "it is safe to say we are closer to war today than we were thirty days before the World War." Senator Nye is not talking as a private individual, not only as Senator, but as the head of the munitions investigation which has led him very close to the question of the imminence of war. His utterance is not an isolated one. Where a year or two ago the Communists were the only ones to talk about the war danger, today everyone speaks of it much in the same terms as those used by Senator Nye.

Since the last meeting of our Central Committee there has been a series of outstanding events to underline this question. There was in the first line the assassination of our Comrade Kirov, one of the outstanding leaders of the Communist Party of the Soviet Union, one of the closest co-workers of Comrade Stalin. This assassination was without question part of a highly organized conspiracy of international ramifications, designed to answer the tremendous achievements of our socialist fatherland in the construction of the new order by not only attempting to throw confusion into the ranks of the Russian workers, but at the same time to encourage and provide the imperialist attack against the Soviet Union. It is a definite part of the drive towards war.

The events surrounding the Saar plebiscite, the results of which are just announced this morning, are by no means ended with the announcement of the poll. The Saar remains one of the points of greatest strain in the imperialist system around which forces of imperialist war are revolving. The break-up of the naval negotiations further emphasizes this situation and brings forward in the center of the war danger, especially in relation to the tasks of the American Party, the sharpening of the Japanese-American antagonisms, which play a decisive role on the whole process of the regrouping of the imperialist forces of the entire world. There is no doubt that but for the threat of revolutionary upheavals and the enormously growing defensive powers of the Soviet Union, backing up the aggressive peace policy of the Soviet Union, that war would long ago have broken out.

The rising tide of revolutionary struggles—outstandingly the battles

---

* Report to the Central Committee of the Communist Party, January 15-18, 1935.—*Ed.*

in Spain and the growing revolutionary crisis in Cuba, right at our own doorstep, strengthen the forces of the struggle against war, but at the same time bring it closer to the point when some event, more or less casual or accidental, may explode the powder barrel of imperialist antagonisms.

All of the work of our Party has to be conducted in the light of this world situation. It is not necessary for us to give again a detailed analysis of all of these problems, but it is necessary to remind ourselves of these as the foundation for all our treatment of the daily problems of our work.

Now I want to say just a few words about the developments of the economic situation since the last meeting of the Central Committee. During this short period, there have been ups and downs of the economic trends. In October and November the economic activity of the United States had reached the bottom of a new decline, which was approximately about the same level which had already been reached under Hoover in November, 1932, two years before.

Now there is again a slight upturn. We cannot say definitely how far it will go, the exact moment at which the decline will again come, but we can establish the fact that all of the fluctuations, up and down, in the last year and a half have taken place within the limits below the high point of the inflation policy of the first months of the Roosevelt Administration and above the low levels of the Hoover Administration. That is, all of these ups and downs serve to emphasize that characterization given by Stalin a year ago when he pointed out that the crisis has entered a period of depression, but it is a depression of a special kind —a prolonged depression which gives no hope for a return to boom prosperity. Everything that is happening confirms this analysis.

It is necessary to say just one or two words about new features of the policy, as carried through by the Roosevelt Administration. Since our last meeting the Administration has definitely moved to the Right. It has definitely set itself to bridge the gap between itself and the policy of the Liberty League. The policy on unemployment and the so-called "security" program fully confirms this.

It hardly even has a demagogic value any more. The labor policy, the policy towards the American Federation of Labor unions has moved even further, more definitely away from the demagogic promises of Section 7A, more decisively towards the possibility of company unions, necessary to prevent the organization of real trade unions and against any unionism at all where that is possible.

This first policy of the Roosevelt administration is particularly important for us to note because it serves to emphasize greatly the favorable opportunities for our work among the broadest masses, especially in the organization of the A. F. of L., because this development brings out before the masses in much sharper form than ever before the contradictions between the immediate interests of the masses and the policies of the leadership of the A. F. of L. Circumstances under which the bureaucracy carry out the policy today are much more difficult, and the maneuvering ground has been narrowed, and all possibilities of leading the masses and winning them to our class struggle policy in much broader numbers have been greatly increased.

Coincident with this whole development, which serves to emphasize the economic results of the year 1934 for the bourgeoisie, which has been one of increasing profits for the capitalists and a decline in the living standards for the masses, we have the concurrent development of fascist mass movements in their first stages. The concerted attack against the living standard of the masses is necessarily, more and more, supplementing the methods of demagogy with that of open fascist violence. Not that demagogy is passing out of the picture, but rather that it is incorporating within itself more and more the direct physical attacks against every manifestation of revolutionary mass organization and action.

The revelation of Smedley Butler throws an interesting light on all of these things which are going on underneath the surface, and by no means has revealed the most important facts. The rising of the figure of the half-fascist Huey Long as a major national political figure has also an important connection with this problem.

The beginnings of a national mass organization around the radio priest Father Coughlin are also a symptom of this development. And above all we must note the open fascist campaign of Hearst in the Hearst press which is already in the case of Hearst's attack against all even liberal tendencies in universities and schools in the United States, taking on all the characteristic features of the first stages of Hitler's campaign in Germany.

We have already in documents, and in articles which have been made available for the whole Party, analyzed the main features of the upsurge of the working class, the toiling masses generally, which has developed during 1934, as the response to these attacks by the bourgeoisie. It is not necessary for us to take the time of this meeting to go over all of this ground again. We will note here these things as basic to our further discussion.

We must emphasize that as a result of all of these developments, profound changes have taken place in this country in the recent period. We have been adjusting ourselves to these changes step by step during the course of the year. We have been modifying and hammering out our policy, trying at every step of the development to keep our feet firmly upon the ground, not going off into any speculations, testing the ground as we go along, and making the further steps in the developments of our policy, the correctness of which has been proven not only to the Central Committee leadership of our Party, but to the Party membership as a whole and to the broad masses surrounding our Party, and the correctness of the decision after that development. We can say that the most successful feature of the work of the Central Committee of our Party in this past year has been precisely this feature: that we have carried the Party and the workers who are with us almost 100 per cent without the slightest doubt being left in their minds as to the correctness of these policies in connection with every change and every shift of emphasis that we have made.

I will speak first about the new development in our trade union policy. This is basic to all of our work. We have made important changes in our trade union tactics in the course of 1934. Some of these we discussed at the Eighth Convention of the Party. We developed this further in the two following meetings of the Central Committee. The general direction of these changes has been clear to the Party from the beginning. It consisted of a shift of emphasis away from the independent organization to the work within the larger mass organization, in the American Federation of Labor. It is clear, the forces that predetermined this shift were the influx of many hundreds of thousands of new workers from the basic industries, including large numbers of unskilled and semi-skilled, including mass production plants as well as basic industries, into the A. F. of L. unions and the growing radicalization of the old membership in the reformist unions.

These factors opened up new and greater possibilities of mass work within the larger reformist unions, opened up a field which had not existed for several years. Now as a result of our concrete developments in carrying through this shift of policy we are able to summarize the results of our last year's work now at this meeting of the Central Committee and to give a general clarification of the whole question in much more precise and comprehensive terms than before. The line is clear. The problems have been worked out in principle, we have proven in action among the masses the correctness of the policy which we have developed. We are now able to say very clearly and definitely that the main task of the Party in the sphere of trade union work must be the work in the A. F. of L., so as to energetically and tirelessly mobilize the masses of their members in the trade unions as a whole for the defense of the everyday interests, the development of the policy of class struggle in the mass unions of the A. F. of L., fighting on the basis of trade union democracy, for the independent leadership of these struggles in spite of the sabotage and treachery of the reformist bureaucrats.

We have established unquestionably an enormous increase in strength which we are getting from taking the initiative boldly, aggressively for the struggle of the unity of the trade unions, the struggle for one united trade union movement, for their industrial structure, for the organization of the unorganized, for amalgamation of the craft unions along industrial lines; the struggle for trade union democracy within these unions, within the general framework of the A. F. of L. We have established that in this development a very serious and important role is played by the revolutionary unions. I don't think it is necessary for me at this meeting again to go over the ground of establishing the historical justification of the revolutionary independent unions. They proved themselves in the class struggle as necessary instruments without which we could never have had the present situation of great advance within the A. F. of L. And also at this moment, the independent revolutionary unions have a great role to play in the fight for the general unification of the trade union movement and for the establishment of class struggle policies within the A. F. of L.

The revolutionary unions which have taken the initiative in leading this struggle have strengthened themselves and not weakened themselves, and where there has been the merger with the A. F. of L. unions, it has not been at the cost of weakening the revolutionary movement, but greatly broadening and deepening the mass roots of the revolutionary trade union movement.

An outstanding example of this has been the Paterson silk workers and dyers, which gives an answer that should convince the most skeptical of our comrades, that should convince everybody except the incurable egomaniacs and renegades like Zack. We have established the fact that while practically we will for a long time be faced with the problems of the necessity of independent unions in one field or another, that we cannot have utopian hopes of quickly securing the immediate unification in the trade union movement within the A. F. of L., yet in principle even the maintenance and strengthening of these independent unions, which must continue independent, are best served by the approach to the questions that in principle we are for the complete unification; that the independent existence of smaller trade unions is a temporary thing and not in any sense a question of principle with us. We have proven that this approach does not weaken the work in the independent unions. Those who have tried to come forward against these changes, against this trade union line, who have put themselves up as the champions of the independent unions and declare that we now want to mechanically liquidate them, have been fully answered by the fact that these independent unions, which are growing and strengthening themselves, are precisely those which are closest to the Communist Party. And we have proven in life that the policy of the C.P. is the best protection of the interests of those workers and the best defense against any liquidation tendencies. We have learned in the carrying through of these changes that the change that we are in the process of making, must be much more profound and deep-going. So far this change has not been completely carried through. So far it has not yet sufficiently penetrated and affected and changed the habits and methods of our work of our comrades down below. This is reflected especially in the question of our daily response to the daily questions of our relations with the A. F. of L. unions.

At this meeting it is necessary for us to see that we must from top to bottom in our movement change the tone with which we approach and deal with A. F. of L. unions. We must not have the tone of an approach toward enemy organizations. While criticizing and exposing more concretely, more effectively, the treacherous leadership of the officialdom, we must make it in a manner that is really convincing to the broadest rank-and-file, and with the tone which gives not one single worker the excuse for believing that in us he finds an obstacle towards the building and strengthening of his union—what he regards as his union. We must have the approach not of fighting against the functionaries in the trade union movement, but of drawing in all of the honest functionaries—and there are thousands of them down below— and winning them for our movement, and making these lower activists of the A. F. of L. real forces for the revolutionary trade union movement.

And we must establish that we are not an irresponsible criticizing opposition within the union, but that we are the most active and most responsible section of the union; ready ourselves to take the full responsibility for the leadership and the administration of the union as a whole and responsible to the whole mass of the membership. And in this connection we must speak very concretely against old habits of thought and old methods of work in the reformist unions which have crystallized around the conception of opposition and minority movements. Around these two terms there have crystallized whole sectarian habits of thought where we have withdrawn ourselves from the life of the union, with no expectations and hopes of ever becoming the leadership and administration, but become a small group of opposition on principle, whom the membership always expects to be against everything and never doing responsible work in the unions for the solution of the problems.

The same thing applies to the conception of minority movements, of a permanent minority. We come in the unions not to be the minority, but to win the majority in the shortest possible time, to break down the whole ideology of our forms and habits which we have.

This means that while we must give the struggle an organized form, that this must not be a blue-print uniformly and mechanically applied everywhere, but that the organized form must grow out of the intimate life of this union so that all the members will understand that this is not an outside body, but even those who are against us must see that it is something natural and legitimate that grows out of this union, the members of the union.

These are the main features that we establish in our Resolution, before you, on the trade union question. We take a further step in this

Resolution. But a step which is logical and inevitable, summarizing and rounding-out all of the steps we have been taking in the past year. With this Resolution, I think, we can say that the evaluation of our trade union policy to meet the present situation has now been completed, that our problem from this becomes the finding of the concrete roads through which we can establish everywhere and in every industry such powerful foundations by our movement as have already in a few short months been developed in the few places in textile, some beginnings in steel, in mining, etc.

Now a few words about some of the special problems of the united front. The trade union question is, of course, basic to the whole problem of the united front. The signs of the development of the united front moves and movements among the workers are above all demonstrated in the trade unions. Precisely in this connection we have spoken about the various industries and such phenomena as the rebuff given to Green's circular for the expulsion of the Communists.

In the United States more than in most of the leading capitalist countries, the problem of the united front is broader than winning the workers in and around the Socialist Party. The problem of the united front is, first of all, the problem of the trade unions, of broad circles of non-party workers or followers of the old parties, and of the non-proletarian strata. However, we must not on this account underestimate the importance of the question of our relation to the Socialist Party workers. The Socialist Party has in spite of its weak and demoralized condition at the present time, enormous potentialities for harm for the working-class movement, which can only be countered and overcome by us with the correct united front approach and the winning of the followers of the Socialist Party for united front actions. The central question which we have not yet sufficiently solved in practice in the development of all phases of our united front activity is the carrying out throughout various united front work of a very broad mass agitation and propaganda about the role of our Party. This problem we used to express in the caution against hiding the face of our Party. But that old phrase has perhaps become too much of just a label which is mechanically applied to certain situations and mechanically answered. Let us restate this problem. Let us place this question from the point of view of the tasks of our Party to make use of the united front activity to educate the broadest masses as to what our Party is, what our program is, what our practical program is, to bring this through our united front activity, not merely in touch with our membership, but giving them knowledge of our Party as the organized driving force within the united front.

We have been in the past year trying to teach the Party by example how this can be done and how there is no contradiction between this talk of educating the masses on the role of our Party, with the simultaneous task of building the united front on the broadest possible basis. Any attempt to broaden out the united front, by putting into the background this task of teaching the masses about our Party, is a fatal opportunist error, which not only places our Party in the background and hides it from the masses, but defeats and destroys our efforts to broaden and build the united front of struggle for important and immediate issues.

I think that in the recent Washington Congress on Unemployment Insurance, we gave an example of how the sharp bringing forward of the Party and its role and its whole revolutionary program not only doesn't endanger the broadest united front, but serves to cement it, to crystallize it together as a conscious, organized movement which cannot be shattered and dispersed by any casual event of the day.

We must make the whole Party conscious of the problem, and on the basis of the best examples of our Party work, carry this method of work down into every neighborhood, down into every trade union and into every workers' organization. We must make a determined effort now to liquidate the still-strong sectarian tendencies in the daily work of our Party.

We have talked a great deal about the struggle against sectarianism; we have been struggling against sectarianism quite consciously in an organized way for several years. But now we must bring this struggle against sectarianism and methods and habits of sectarianism to a new stage, which does not mean increasing the amount of our talk against sectarianism.

Now it is the question of bringing the whole Party actively into mass work and liquidating through practical experience every old habit, and every old idea that stands as an obstacle between us and the masses. That means, of course, getting the whole Party active in carrying through these trade union tasks, these tasks of the united front, getting every Party unit, every Party committee, every Party member daily facing and solving concrete problems of contact with broad masses of workers; to throw the whole life and attention of the Party from the inward orientation, to the outward, so that their whole life is dominated by the problems of the masses around them and not by their own inner difficulties and discussions.

We have in the past year made a whole series of approaches to top leadership, especially of the Socialist Party, in the development of our united front activities. We will have to make such approaches in the future. At this moment, however, it is necessary to emphasize this point—that whatever advances the united front is able to make through these approaches from the top, in the final analysis, it always depends upon our work down below among the membership of the Socialist Party and the American Federation of Labor unions.

The united front from below—this remains basic to everything that we are doing in this field. It is impossible to think that we could have built up the various organized phases of our united front activities even to the inclusion of these leading strata which we have drawn in, except upon the basis that we had below a growing mass pressure upon these leaders, so that they are not moving independently; they are being carried along in mass streams of thought and activity of their own membership and of the surrounding population. This is the thing that changes minds of leading elements, activists, in the various organizations.

Our arguments may help to change their minds. But much more potent to change their minds than our arguments is the pressure of the masses. Our arguments, the development of the explanation of our position on every question—this is basic for the gaining of the masses down below. But basic for the gaining of the leading cadres and top leadership is not our arguments to them, but the fact that the masses have taken our arguments and bring pressure against them. That is why we will continue on appropriate occasions the approaches from above. But here again we emphasize that all united front activity is basically the building of the united front from below. . . .*

Finally, let us again emphasize what we made the main note of the last Party Convention, which we have a tendency to forget, the making of decisions is only the first step to the solution of a problem. If we make a decision we have to organize the execution of that decision, control its execution, control its carrying out, and unless we do that, it is better not to make the decision in the first place, because a decision which is not carried through has a demoralizing effect in the life of the Party. It disorganizes, discourages, demoralizes the whole Party membership. We see continuously decisions being made and not being carried out. We have got to establish the most strict attitude throughout the Party to the question of decisions—and be not so ready to accept decisions. It appals me sometimes when I sit in on committee meetings to see the light-hearted way they make the most far-reaching decisions. Why do they make so many excellent decisions on paper? Because they have no intention of carrying them out; because they are interested only in expressing their excellent intentions. There is such a light-hearted approach to the question of whether a decision is to be carried out or not. These are remnants from a non-Bolshevik past. This is the enemy of Bolshevism, the enemy of the Bolshevization of our Party, and we must guard ourselves and make a rule against it.

We must demand that every decision be carried out, and if it is not, a formal explanation why, and a registration of our failure. Only if we approach our problems with this strict Bolshevik standard can we seriously expect to meet the tremendous burdens and difficulties that are

* Here is omitted a discussion of the Labor Party question and other matters which are fully covered in other documents in this book.—*Ed.*

going to fall upon us. It is true that we are expanding and growing, and strengthening ourselves. This not only multiplies our problems, but it requires a higher degree of organization and responsibility.

Unless we improve the quality of our leadership, the quality of our daily work, and the quality of our execution—the more we get among these moving masses, the more certainly we are going to be lost among them, broken up and disintegrated, unless we concentrate all attention on the supreme instrument without which the whole movement cannot go forward a single step.

This instrument is our Communist Party. The building of the C.P. is the building of responsible leading cadres. The committees and organs of our Party should never make decisions except that they carry them out in life; every line we write into our minutes has an immediate repercussion among the masses, and we can control and direct events among the masses, move these masses towards revolutionary struggle, towards the transformation of society, because we are able to control and guide our own inner-Party life, control the execution of our own decisions.

X

The Communist Program: Only Way Out for Labor Now *

THE SAN FRANCISCO GENERAL STRIKE

THE EFFORTS of the Industrial Association, the shipowners and Chamber of Commerce to whip up a frenzy against the Communists, is a part of this drive to destroy the trade unions, to keep down wages, to build up their monopoly profits. Such shameless lies and slanders as filled the columns of the San Francisco daily press have rarely been seen before. This campaign is from the school of Hitler.

These gentlemen know full well that they are lying, and that their slanders cannot stand a moment's investigation. That is why they carry on a terror campaign which has converted San Francisco into a kind of "Little Germany."

While the vigilantes, organized by the police and paid by the shipowners, are raiding private homes, burning libraries and printing plants, chopping up pianos and smashing typewriters in workers' halls, it is such a moment they choose to charge the Communists with advocating violence.

But they have been unable to bring one single definite case of a single act or word to support their charge. All concrete cases of violence are those where violence is used against the workers.

Why this frenzy of hate against the Communists? Are the Communists proposing to make a revolution now, beginning in San Francisco? No, that is absurd nonsense. The Communists do not propose to make a revolution until, by comradely discussion and conviction of the toiling masses, they have majority support securely behind the Party. We have not yet got this support. But we will get it, and the more the bosses rage, the earlier. And the terror, suppression by the shipowners, the police, the vigilantes, the gunmen, will only help us to convince the toiling masses quicker that this system of misery, starvation, suppression of the poor, has to be changed as quickly as possible in the interest of the overwhelming majority of the population of this country, against the handful of bankers, against Wall Street and their lackeys, Rossis, Vandeleurs, etc.

* Statement by Earl Browder and Sam Darcy, District Organizer of the Communist Party and Communist candidate for governor of California, issued at the height of the campaign of terror and repression against Communists during the San Francisco general strike. Reprinted from the *Western Worker*, August 1, 1934.—*Ed.*

WHAT WE FIGHT FOR

Now, the Communists are fighting to help the poor farmers who are being crushed beneath the burdens of mortgage charges, taxes, marketing monopolies and drought.

Now, the Communists are fighting to protect the small home-owners whose taxes are being doubled to pay the strike-breaking bills of the rich shipowners.

Now, the Communists are fighting to recover the savings of the small depositors, which have been confiscated by the big Wall Street banks who closed down the little banks.

Now, the Communists are helping the veterans to fight for their back-wages [the bonus].

The Communist Party alone fights with all its energy for these things.

The monopoly capitalists fight against these things. That's why they hate the Communists. That's why they lie about us. That's why they raised a fund of five million dollars to "drive the Reds out of California." But gentlemen, you won't succeed in making California yellow.

That is why the Luckenbacks and Fleischackers give such high praise to Vandeleur, Ryan, Lewis, Casey and their kind. These fakers, who pretend to be trade union leaders, use their position to break strikes, to defeat the demands of the workers. It is true these strike-breakers are not reds. They are also yellow.

"LABOR LEADERS" SELL OUT

For the same reason that the capitalists praise the "labor leaders," the Communists fight against them and expose them. They are yellow. They are paid stool-pigeons of the capitalists. So long as the workers follow them, defeat is inevitable. When they stand at the head of a strike, it is not to win it, but to smash it—just as they did in the San Francisco general strike. Just as the British labor fakers did in the British general strike.

But every time these gentlemen hit the workers, and every time they hit the Communist Party, they are only furnishing new proof to the workers that what the Communist Party told them is correct.

The Communist Party has pointed out to the longshoremen and sailors how arbitration was used to smash and defeat the auto workers, the Minneapolis drivers, and the steel workers. By soldiers, police, clubs, gas, bullets, terror, the employers have forced the workers to accept arbitration. Now, they will have to prove to the workers that the Communists were right when they warned them against arbitration.

The workers are learning by bitter experience that if they do not want yellow leadership, then they must choose Red leaders, and the fully militant workers.

The shipowners boast that they will drive out all Communists. It can't be done. Hitler tried it in Germany and failed. So also the little Hitler imitations in California will fail. The Communist Party is of the bone, blood' and flesh of the working class. The capitalists must always have the workers to feed them—that's why they can never get rid of the Reds.

It is to be regretted that free speech and civil rights in California are so crushed at the moment that it was impossible to obtain a hall for a meeting so Comrade Browder could publicly discuss these questions. But this will not always be so. California workers will not be content until they regain freedom of speech and sweep aside the fascist assemblage.

We are certain that many tens of thousand of California workers will register their indignation at the Hitlerism of the powers that now are in California by voting for the Communist ticket in the coming elections—and that this will be the first step for thousands of them to join the Communist Party.

Long live the brave longshoremen and seamen of California!

Long live the heroic battle of the California workers!

California workers! Forward to victory against the capitalists and their yellow helpers!

(Signed) EARL BROWDER,
SAM DARCY.

San Francisco, Calif.
July 24, 1934.

XI

Make Betrayals of the Workers Impossible!

THE GENERAL TEXTILE STRIKE

To Every Communist Party Unit: *

Every revolutionist must be filled with indignation at the base betrayal of the textile workers' strike.** What a heroic struggle of hundreds of thousands of workers was here stabbed by the treachery of the Gormans and Greens!

But our hatred, our indignation alone are not sufficient. It is one of the most important lessons of this struggle that it was because there were too few Communists in the locals of the United Textile Workers, because we Communists were too weak in our influence in the U. T. W. locals, that it was possible for the U. T. W. officials to betray the strike. In their treachery, the U. T. W. leaders did not sufficiently encounter the resistance of workers firmly organized in the U. T. W. locals by revolutionaries. We Communists must face this truth squarely if we are going to make progress.

To those reactionaries and renegades who try to do business and think to make capital on the basis of our self-criticism, we answer: "Yes, gentlemen, we plead guilty to having failed to drive you from the ranks of the working class with sufficient speed." To drive these treacherous leaders from the ranks of the workers and the working-class organizations in the interests of the labor movement, in the interest of the liberation of the entire working class—this is our task! Whoever does not understand this, and does not bend all his energies to achieve it with far greater speed than has been the case up to now is not yet a fully conscious revolutionary. This is the task not only among the textile workers, but it is now more than ever the task of the whole working class.

Not only to agitate, but to plunge into the *practical work of organizing the workers in the A. F. of L. unions to resistance* against the treacherous policies of the A. F. of L. leadership is now one of the most vital links in the chain of our revolutionary policy. The experiences in the textile strike proved this again, for the hundredth time, and with even greater urgency. We must quickly prove in our practical work that we understand this, that we know how to work better among the workers in the A. F. of L.

What is to be done? In the next two weeks, every unit must take

* From *The Daily Worker*, September 26, 1934.—*Ed.*
** The general strike of 600,000 textile workers, September, 1934.—*Ed.*

up one central question: the work in the trade unions and especially the work in the A. F. of L. unions. At the unit meeting the buro must have each member report as to whether he is organized in a trade union, and where he is organized. If the comrade is not organized in a trade union, the reason must be found out, and he must be assisted to find his place in the proper trade union. If any comrade refuses to do this work, he must be convinced in a firm, comradely way of the urgent need for work in the trade unions.

But this is not enough. In addition, every comrade in the unit must report on the work that he is doing in his union, whether he belongs to a fraction, and what the possibilities are for organizing a fraction in his work. He must report to the unit on how he connects his Party work in the shop with the work in the shop organization of his trade union.

These will not be dull discussions. This is to take measures to make impossible future betrayals by the A. F. of L. leadership. This is to organize, more successfully and with greater speed, our revolutionary forces against the reactionary forces among the masses of the working class. This means to learn the lessons of the textile strike, to prepare for coming struggles, to make, at once, the necessary preparations for the approaching struggles of the seamen and longshoremen. *In short, this means to act as a revolutionary, to organize the revolution.*

This must be done within the next two weeks. Every unit must report directly to the District and to the Central Committee on the carrying out of this work and on the results. These reports will be published in the *Daily Worker*.

The quickening of our tempo of work is indispensable if we are to defeat the betrayers. It is indispensable if we are to organize the tremendous mass of workers who are eager to struggle, eager to resist the attacks of the employers. We must draw the practical, revolutionary conclusions from the tremendous indignation which the textile workers feel at the unparalleled treachery of the U. T. W. leaders.

Comrades, to work! Every unit must become an instrument for the organization of victorious struggle among the workers organized in the A. F. of L., as an organizer of victorious mass struggles of the working class.

*   *   *

To Every Party Member: *

Is there a single Communist who would not have wished that our Party had been five or ten times stronger among the tetxile workers to prevent Gorman's betrayal? Is there a single Communist who would not have wished that there had been more organized groups in

* From *The Daily Worker*, September 27, 1934—*Ed.*

the thousands of mills, that there had been more organized Communist fractions in the locals of the United Textile Workers, in close contact with the textile workers? Is there a single Communist who would not have wished that there had been twenty times as many Communists in the mass meetings and on the picket lines than there were?

There is no such Communist. And every Communist worked in the strike for the victory of the strike, to help the workers in the best possible manner to organize themselves, to overcome the bosses' resistance, to organize the picket lines, to warn of the betrayal—in a word: every Communist tried his best to help the strike to victory. It is therefore evident that every Communist wishes that twenty or thirty times as many Communists had worked among the strikers.

Just as among the textile workers, so it is in the other industries, in the struggle of the unemployed, in every section of the exploited population.

This is why we have before us the burning problem: We must have more, many more Communists among the steel workers, among the marine workers, among the longshoremen, among the railroad workers, among the miners.

If we Communists share the indignation of the hundreds of thousands of textile workers over the despicable treachery, we must draw these conclusions.

And, comrade, this depends on you.

Do not thousands of workers in every one of these tremendous struggles show capabilities, heroism? Are there not thousands of Communists of tomorrow among the fighters? Thousands of workers, where only very little is needed, to break them away from the links that still chain them to the capitalists, to the forces still under their influence.

Who can deny this? And this is why your personal work is needed, comrade, the utilization of all your connections in the shop, in the house in which you live, in the club which you visit, your personal friends, in order to make these Communists of tomorrow Communists today.

Every comrade should ask himself personally: Have I done everything by strengthening the Communist Party to make betrayal impossible for the betrayers? Every active worker brought into the Party, as a part of the organization, strengthened by the organization of the revolutionaries, and strengthening the organization of the revolutionaries, makes it easier to make these betrayals impossible for the reactionaries and to lead the workers victoriously.

Comrade, your answer and the answer of every individual comrade must be: In answer to this base betrayal of the textile worker we must bring thousands of workers into the Party, strengthen the ranks of the Party, strengthen the Party's connections with the workers.

That means, strengthening the capability of the Party, in the ranks of the workers, to lead the struggles against the attacks of the bourgeoisie and against the base treachery of the labor lieutenants of the capitalist class.

To bring the best fighters from the ranks of the strikers into the Party is the task of every individual comrade. It is a task of honor of every revolutionary.

The unit, the section, the district, the Central Committee, our press, our literature will help you, comrade. But every comrade must transform his indignation over the treachery into organizing action. The Party's offensive to prevent such betrayals must be sharpened.

Can anybody deny that if the Communists had had more well-organized Communist nuclei of groups in every textile mill, or at least in the most important textile mills, in every U. T. W. local, or at least in the most important U. T. W. locals, that then it might have been possible to prevent this betrayal?

He who really is a revolutionary can draw only one conclusion from this treachery of the textile workers: Make the absolutely firm decision for himself, the plan to bring within the next three or four weeks at least five workers, five active fellow-fighters into the Party.

Comrades, to work!

XII

Unemployment Insurance—The Burning Issue of the Day

1. THE WORKERS' BILL BELONGS TO THE WHOLE CLASS *

THE WORKERS' Unemployment and Social Insurance Bill, which is the main concern of this Congress, has the active and unconditional support of the Communist Party, for which I am speaking. (*Applause.*)

I want to express my appreciation for the support that was expressed by the previous speaker, Mr. Mitchell, a leading member of the Socialist Party. We Communists are very glad to extend a hand to all Socialists who join with us in this fight, together with all of the other workers of all parties who are rallying around this workers' bill. (*Applause.*)

It is also good that we should have had the letter of good wishes to the Congress from the principal leader of the Socialist Party, Mr. Norman Thomas. We can express the hope that this letter may help to bring the whole Socialist Party into this movement in the not distant future. (*Applause.*)

The President of the American Federation of Labor, William Green, has denounced this Bill, in a letter to all trade unions of the A. F. of L., which cites two main arguments in opposition. These are, first, that the Bill was written and proposed by the Communist Party; and second, that it is unconstitutional.

As to the first charge: It is true that the Communist Party worked out this Bill, after prolonged consultation with large numbers of workers, popularized it, and brought millions of Americans to see that this bill is the *only* proposal for unemployment insurance that meets their life needs. But that is not an argument against the Bill; that is only a recommendation for the Communist Party—for which we thank Mr. Green most kindly even though his intentions were not friendly. We Communists have no desire to keep this Bill as "our own" private property; we have tried to make it the common property of all the toiling masses; we have tried to bring every organization of workers (and also of farmers and the middle classes) to look upon this Bill as "their own." Thousands of A. F. of L. locals, scores of Socialist Party organizations, dozens of Farmer-Labor Party locals, claim the Bill as theirs. That is good, that is splendid; the· Communist Party, far from

* Speech delivered at the National Congress for Social and Unemployment Insurance, Washington, D. C., January 6, 1935.—*Ed.*

disputing title to the Bill with anyone, agrees with everyone who claims the Bill. We are ready to support any better proposal, no matter who should make it. Of course the Bill is yours; it belongs to the entire working class, to all the toiling masses of America. In this fact we find our greatest triumph.

Mr. Green's second charge, that the Bill is unconstitutional, is a more complicated question. This is a legal point, on which the last word will be said by the Supreme Court, a small body of elderly gentlemen who are famous for their obstinate defence of capitalist property and profits rather than for the defence of the vital interests of the masses. But we can warn the Supreme Court and the capitalist class for which it speaks, that on the day when the Court declares the Constitution forbids the *only* measure that promises to remove the daily menace of starvation from over the heads of millions, on that day it has struck a blow against the Constitution far deeper and more effective than anything revolutionists have ever done. If the Constitution prevents the principles of the Workers' Bill from becoming law, then millions will conclude, not that the Workers' Bill must be given up, but that the Constitution must be changed. They will remember the words of the Declaration of Independence, that "whenever any form of government becomes destructive of these ends (life, liberty, and the pursuit of happiness), it is the right of the people to alter or abolish it, and to institute a new government, laying its foundation on such principles, and organizing its power in such form, as to them shall seem most likely to effect their safety and happiness" . . . "It is their right, it is their duty, to throw off such government, and to provide new guards for their future security."

This revolutionary spirit which gave birth to the United States, still lives and grows in the working class. Never was security more shattered for the masses of the people than today; never were new guards for security more needed. If the Constitution stands in the way, then the Declaration of Independence points out the right, nay the duty, to "throw off" this Constitution and write a new one in keeping with modern needs. The toiling masses must prepare a new Declaration of Independence—this time independence from the capitalist class.

Of course, the real obstacle is not the Constitution but the greedy interests of the profit-makers, of the capitalists, of Wall Street. Unemployment and Social Insurance must be paid for; it will cost great sums. There is plenty of wealth in this great, rich country to pay for it—but it is all in the hands of the rich, the bankers, the monopolists. These gentlemen know full well that the poverty-stricken masses cannot pay, because they have stolen all the accumulated wealth and natural resources of the country. That fact is itself the cause and basis of the crisis, of unemployment. These gentlemen are determined not to pay one cent; instead, they wriggle out of paying even the present legal taxes, and indeed obtain hundreds of millions of dollars in tax refunds.

The Workers' Bill, and the Communist Party, declare that the cost of full insurance for all must be paid by the only ones who can pay—by the rich. Instead of the Roosevelt New Deal policy, which is taxing the poor in order to further subsidize the rich, which increased profits while lowering living standards, we demand that the government shall tax the rich to feed the poor.

It is not alone the unemployed and their families who need and demand the Workers' Bill. Also the workers in the factories, in the trade unions, need it just as much, to remove the pressure of the starving millions, to prevent their recruitment into the factories at lower wages, to prevent strikebreaking, to help build powerful trade unions, to hold up the whole standard of living of all the masses as the precondition of holding up the standards of even a part. It is needed by the farmers, who cannot sell their produce to millions without income, and who are therefore told to destroy their crops while these millions go hungry. It is needed by the middle classes, professionals, small business men, who are also being crushed into poverty because the impoverishment of the masses destroys their own field of business. Everyone needs the Workers' Bill except the bankers, monopolists, big capitalists, Wall Street.

President Roosevelt, when appealing for election in 1932, promised unemployment insurance. Two years have passed, and nothing has been done about it. Last summer he renewed his promises, in anticipation of the Congressional elections, and broadened it into the high-sounding phrase of "social security." But with the elections over, he has discovered once more that "social security" must wait upon the security of private profits of the rich. Once again we are given the mockery of the Wagner Bill and forced labor for a part of the unemployed at subsistence wages, the systematic forcing down of the living standards of the whole American people; once again we are told that insurance can only be in the form of "reserves" collected from the workers by the various States for *future* unemployment, ignoring the 16 million now out of work. They forget that if *present* unemployment is not met by real unemployment insurance, all their measures for the *future* will also become meaningless, for the masses will rise and throw off their power and write a whole new set of laws.

The Democratic Party, controlling Congress, is *against real unemployment insurance*. The Republican Party, which would like to control Congress, is even more unanimously opposed to it. Both these parties are owned, body and soul, by the capitalist class. They will do nothing—until we convince them that the masses of the people are "fed up" with their old two-party system, and are preparing to "vote with their feet" by walking out of the old parties in million masses.

Millions of toilers already showed, in the great strike wave and in the November elections, that they are getting tired of the old game.

It is not an accident that seven million who voted Democratic and three million who voted Republican in 1932, stayed away from the polls entirely in 1934. Millions of voters could see nothing in either Party to justify the effort of walking to the ballot box. And some enthusiasm in the elections could only be found (aside from the followers of the still small Communist Party) only where the voters thought they could see something "more radical" than Roosevelt. That is the meaning of Sinclair and his EPIC program in California; of LaFollette and the "Progressive" party in Wisconsin; of the Farmer-Labor Party victory in Minnesota in spite of the vicious record of Olson; and even of that half-fascist demagogue, Huey Long in Louisiana, with his moratorium and similar measures. Dozens of similar though smaller examples could be cited. The strikes of marine and textile workers, the Toledo, Milwaukee and Minneapolis strikes, and above all the great San Francisco general strike, point the same road. Millions of toilers are beginning to look for a new path. They are taking the first steps to break away from the old two-party system which denies unemployment insurance and every other measure in the interests of the toiling majority of the people. A mass break-away from the old parties is in preparation. It is this great movement of strikes and demonstrations, and the break-away movement from the old parties which give promise of forcing the adoption of the Workers' Bill.

This great mass movement is still confused and ineffective. It has not yet found itself. It will have to go through many bitter disappointments and disillusionments before it finds the right way. It will have to see how the Progressive Party of LaFollette clings in practice to the Roosevelt apron-strings, and uses its "radicalism" to catch votes but not even to write laws. It will see its Farmer-Labor Congressmen voting with the Democrats against their demands, and its Olsons calling out the National Guard against strikers. It will learn that it must find a program and a leadership which frankly and openly comes out in struggles against the big capitalists who own 90 per cent of the country, in the interests of the toiling masses, the 90 per cent of the people who do all the work. It will find that it must become an anti-capitalist party, a Labor Party.

Just imagine what a different situation in Congress we would have on Capitol Hill if the millions of workers had been organized to vote for their best strike leaders, the unemployed to vote for the builders of the Unemployed Councils, the farmers to vote for those who led their picket lines and "Sears-Roebuck penny sales," the Negroes to vote for those who lead the fight against lynching and jim-crowism and for freedom of the Scottsboro boys. Just imagine in the U. S. Congress a strong group of these leaders of the masses, supported by a mass movement, and imagine how much quicker we could force Congress to enact the Workers' Bill into law. How different such a Congress would be from this one composed entirely of lawyers, bankers, and the hired men of Wall Street!

Every honest fighter for the Workers' Bill must realize that precisely this is the only sure road, the road of mass struggle supporting parliamentary action, to the enactment of real unemployment insurance.

The Communist Party is a Party of Labor, of all those who toil. And it is not an ineffective Party. In comparison to its membership and vote, it is the most effective Party that ever existed in the United States. A vote for the Communist Party registers deeply; just think, for example, how much easier it would be to "persuade" even the present Congress to adopt the Workers' Bill tomorrow, if they had been frightened to death by the ghost of a few million Communist votes last November, and by a greater mass strike movement, by greater street demonstrations, by growing mass organizations!

But the Communist Party is a particular kind of a Labor Party. Our program goes far beyond Unemployment Insurance, which after all is only an emergency measure. We propose a revolutionary solution of the crisis of capitalism, by abolishing the whole rotten capitalist system, by setting up in its place a socialist system which would put everyone at work, not at the New Deal slave-labor, but with the most modern machinery producing the goods we all need for our own use and not for capitalist profits. We propose to travel the same road already shown by the glorious victories of the Russian working class and with the rapidly expanding socialist system. It is unfortunately true that the millions now preparing to break away from the old parties are not yet prepared to go the whole way now with the Communist program.

We Communists are often accused of being "unrealistic" and "sectarian," because we bring forward such a far-reaching revolutionary program. But we are convinced that our program is the only realistic one, the only program which can solve the problems now vexing humanity. We are sure that all of you, all the broad masses, will be convinced in the not distant future, by experience. We do not propose to "make a revolution" by ourselves, as the fantastic lies of the Dickstein Committee and Hearst tell you, not by absurd conspiracies, by "kidnapping the President," not by bombs and individual terror, all of which we denounce as police provocation, but only with the majority of the toilers, by mass action, when they have been convinced of the Communist program.

And we do not sit idly waiting until the masses are convinced of our program. We Communists work and fight together with all of you, among the broad masses, for all these partial demands, for the daily life-needs of the masses which are already understood. It is not an accident, for example, that it was left for us, the Communists, to formulate the Workers' Bill which is the center of the great mass movement represented in this Congress.

So, also, when it comes to the mass break-away from the old Parties, which will play such a great part in finally forcing the adoption of the Workers' Bill. We would welcome these masses at once into the Communist Party. But we are realists. We know that for a time they will stop short of the full Communist program. We do not separate ourselves from this mass movement for that reason. We encourage and help the movement in every way. We call upon all of you to do the same thing. We propose that all of us get together in a great effort for unity, unity in struggle for immediate demands against the capitalists, unity upon the broad basis of the class of those who labor against those who exploit our labor, unity on the basis of every-day needs, unity of the poor against the rich, of the producers against the parasites.

We Communists are prepared to join hands, with all our force, all our energy, all our fighting capacity, with all who are ready to fight against Wall Street, against monopoly capital, in the formation of a broad mass party to carry on this fight, into a fighting Labor Party based upon the trade unions, the unemployment councils, the farmers' organizations, all the mass organizations of toilers, with a program of demands and of mass actions to improve the conditions of the masses at the expense of the rich, for measures such as the Farmers' Emergency Relief Bill, the Negro Rights Bill, and the Workers' Unemployment and Social Insurance Bill.

The Congress on Capitol Hill, to which you will tomorrow present the Workers' Bill, is packed against us. It is composed of the paid agents of the bankers and monopolists, of Wall Street, and the parties controlled by them. You cannot convince them by arguments. You can change their votes only by threatening their power, by more unity, more organization, more *powerful* organization of the workers. The mass movement in support of the Workers' Bill is potentially such a threat. We must, from this Congress, go out to the country to rally millions for the necessary next step—to build a great, broad, united front of Labor, economically and politically, which will begin to take up the question of state power, of control of the government, which will begin to fight to end the power of Wall Street, to realize the political power of labor—which will launch the struggle that, though it begins with the Workers' Bill for Unemployment and Social Insurance, can end only with a complete Workers' Society that will abolish forever even the terrible memory of hunger, misery and unemployment.

2. ONLY THE WORKERS' BILL MEETS THE IMMEDIATE NEEDS OF THE MASSES *

THE BILL under consideration, H. R. 2827, has the unqualified support of the Communist Party. This bill embodies the principles which alone can provide any measure of "social insurance" for the workers, and, thereby, also alleviate the condition of impoverished farmers, professional and middle class people.

It is noteworthy that among all political parties, the Communist Party alone has a clear, definite, unequivocal position on this question.

Enemies of the Workers' Bill have failed to present their arguments against it, relying rather upon an attempt to smother it with silence. To make this more plausible, there has been trotted out, as the main alternative to the Administration program, the Utopian "Townsend Plan" which provides an ideal straw-man for administration supporters to knock down. But, as many workers have told this committee, the only real alternative to the administration's Wagner-Lewis Bill is H. R. 2827, the Workers' Bill.

The enemies of real unemployment insurance have, however, prepared carefully to attack the bill should it come up for vote in the Congress. They would be acting more in good faith if they presented their arguments to this Committee. Their absence thus far makes it necessary to answer them without having in hand the definitive text of their arguments.

It is known that the main argument against the Workers' Bill is that it costs too much, that the country cannot afford to pay such a tremendous sum as would be called for. This argument ignores the fact that the country must pay the full costs of unemployment, that there is no way to avoid it. The only question is, what part of the population shall pay, those who now pay with the lives of their women and children, the price of degradation and misery, or the rich who still evade payment, whose profits are going up while mass starvation increases, who alone can pay in any currency except the life-blood of the country.

We Communists are accused of being the enemies of our country, of being a menace that demands, in the language of Hearst and *Liberty* magazine, unceremonious hanging, "shoot first and investigate afterwards," or, in the more decorous proposals of the spokesmen for the McCormack-Dickstein Committee, the legal prohibition of the Communist Party *after* its "investigation" refused to hear the official spokesmen of the Communist Party.

Allow me to denounce all these current slanders against the Communist Party. We Communists yield to no one in our love for our

* Statement made at the Hearings on the Workers' Unemployment, Old Age, and Social Insurance Bill, H. R. 2827, conducted by the Sub-committee of the House Committee on Labor, February 12, 1935.—*Ed.*

country. It is because we love our country that we fight for the Workers' Bill, which alone can save millions of men, women and children from utter degradation. When we declare our love for our country, we mean we love these millions of people who are being reduced to an Asiatic standard of living; we must seriously doubt the quality of that love for country which says that profits must be maintained even though these millions starve.

This country has half of the accumulated wealth and productive forces of the entire world, with much less than ten per cent of the population. Yet we are told that "the country cannot afford" to guarantee its workers a minimum standard of decent living! It is clear that this phrase, "cannot afford," has a special meaning. It does not mean that the country has not the necessary resources; it means that those who rule the country, that small, infinitesimal fraction of the population which owns all the chief stores of wealth and means of production, considers it contrary to their selfish class interests.

This ruling class, monopolists, the Wall Street financiers, have dictated the administration program. They do not hesitate to condemn tens of millions to a degraded standard of life, just too much to die on but not enough to live on. These are the real enemies of America; here is the real menace faced by our country.

If revolution, or the threat of revolution has become a major problem of this country, this is only secondarily the result of the work of the Communist Party. In the first place, it is because millions have lost their last hopes of relief after being disillusioned with all promises, one after another, based upon the present system. Communism, and the threat of revolution will not be crushed by outlawing the Communist Party; it will grow in spite of everything, unless the conditions of life of the masses are improved, unless real social security is provided.

Precisely because those who rule are determined not to grant any real measure of social security, that is the reason for the attacks upon the Communist Party. These attacks are designed to prepare rejection of any real unemployment insurance. When the ridiculous charge is made that the Communists are "plotting to kidnap the President," that is only a cover for a real charge that the Communists are arousing a great mass demand for the Workers' Bill, H. R. 2827, that is only a cover for the "open shop" and the company-union drive, exhibited in the renewal of the auto code and the Wolman anti-Labor Board, which threatens destruction to the American Federation of Labor. Even those staunch servants of the President, the Executive Council of the A. F. of L., have been forced to recognize in these events the beginning of fascism in the United States. Germany taught the whole world to understand that fascism, beginning with the demand to crush the "Communist Menace," ends with the crushing of all trade unions, all civil rights, even all religious liberties. Fascism can only be halted if determined resistance is made to its first steps. That holds good for the U. S. A. as well as it did for Germany.

The demand for enactment of the Workers' Bill, H. R. 2827, the fight for the only proposal of real social security, is the front-line trench today in the battle for preserving a measure of life, liberty and the pursuit of happiness in this country. It is the essential foundation for preservation of a measure of civil liberties, for resistance to fascism and war. It is a fight for all those good things of life, which the masses of the people, as distinguished from the professional patriots, mean when they speak of "Americanism."

If real unemployment insurance is denied, this will only add fuel to the fire of discontent, sweeping through the working population today, rising into waves of struggle and radicalization. The American masses are approaching that mood and temper, in which our ancestors penned those immortal words of the Declaration of Independence. These words have been outlawed in many states of this country, but I hope that it is still possible to quote them before a sub-committee of Congress. The declaration contains the following words:

Whenever any form of government becomes destructive of· these ends (life, liberty and the pursuit of happiness), it is the right of the people to alter or abolish it, and to institute a new government, laying its foundations on such principles, and organizing its power in such forms, as to them shall seem most likely to effect their safety and happiness. It is their right, it is their duty to throw off such a government, and to provide new guards for their future security.

This fundamental right of revolution, inherent in the masses of the toiling population and represented today by the Communist Party and its program, is the ultimate guarantee that the principles of the Workers' Bill, H. R. 2827, will finally prevail. If not enacted into law by the present Congress, or if refused entirely by the rulers of the present system, they will appear again and again, and finally will be enforced by a new government representing a new social-economic system, that of socialism.

3. THE WAGNER-LEWIS BILL CANNOT STILL THE DEMAND FOR REAL UNEMPLOYMENT INSURANCE *

MR. CHAIRMAN AND GENTLEMEN OF THE COMMITTEE: Speaking for the Communist Party, for the approximately 600,000 organized workers who have endorsed our program, and for the several millions who have endorsed our position on unemployment insurance, I want to oppose

* Statement made at the Senate Finance Committee Hearings on the Wagner-Lewis Bill, February 19, 1935.—*Ed.*

the Bill before this Committee which embodies the Administration conception of unemployment, old-age, and social insurance.

It is the position of the Communist Party that it is the responsibility of the national government to provide, against all those vicissitudes of life which are beyond individual or group control, a guarantee of a minimum standard of decent livelihood equal to the average of the individual or group when normally employed. This, always a vital necessity, has now, due to the economic crisis and the protracted depression, become literally a matter of life and death for millions, and for the main bulk of the population a basic factor for maintaining standards of life.

Any proposed legislative enactment which claims to forward this aim of social security must be judged by the degree to which it embodies the following provisions:

1. It must maintain the living standards of the masses unimpaired. Anything less than this is not "social security," but merely institutionalizing the insecurity, the degradation, of the masses. It must provide for benefits equal to average normal wages, with a minimum below which no family is allowed to fall.

2. It must apply to all categories of useful citizens, all those who depend upon continued employment at wages for their livelihood.

3. Benefits must begin at once, when normal income is cut off, and continue until the worker has been re-employed in his normal capacity and re-established his normal income.

4. The costs of social insurance must be paid out of the accumulated and current *surplus* of society, and not by further reducing the living standards of those still employed. That means that the financing of the insurance must come from taxation of incomes, beginning at approximately $5,000 per year, and sharply graduated upward, with further provisions for taxation of undistributed surpluses, gifts, inheritances, etc.

5. Social insurance legislation must provide guarantees against being misused by discriminations against Negroes, foreign-born, the young workers never yet admitted into industry, and other groups habitually discriminated against within the existing social order.

6. Guarantees must be provided against the withholding of benefits from workers who have gone on strike against the worsening of their conditions, or to force workers to scab against strikers, or to force workers to leave their homes or to work at places far removed from their homes.

7. Administration of insurance must be removed from the control of local political machines, to guarantee that the present scandalous use of relief funds to impress masses into support of the Democratic Party shall not be made permanent under pretext of "insurance"; this means, that administration must be through the elected representatives

of the workers involved, making use of their existing mass organizations, relying upon democratic self-activity and organization.

The Communist Party opposes the Wagner-Lewis, Administration Bill, because it violates each and every one of these conditions for real social insurance. It does not provide for any *national* system at all, and the systems *permitted* for the various 48 States in effect *prohibit* the incorporation of any of the above-mentioned seven essential features.

The Wagner-Lewis Bill prohibits benefits of more than a *fraction* of average normal wages. It specifically excludes from its supposed "benefits" whole categories of workers, such as agricultural and domestic workers and those employed in small establishments, who need insurance the most because they are the most insecure, the most exploited and oppressed, and which include the majority of the Negroes. It provides for a benefit period which is only a *small fraction* of the average period of unemployment.

Examining only these three phases of the Wagner-Lewis Bill, the conclusion cannot be escaped that the result of the Bill would be to provide even *less* than is now being given in relief, miserably inadequate as that amount is, and to cut off from even this reduced amount the great masses now unemployed. The plain intention of this Bill is to *reduce* the volume of governmental aid to all those suffering from involuntary unemployment.

When it comes to provisions for financing this parody of insurance, it becomes even more clear that the intention is to relieve the rich and to place all burdens upon the poor. *Nothing* is to be taken from the social surplus, which exists only in the form of the higher-income brackets, undistributed surpluses, etc.; *everything* is to be taken directly out of the meagre and decreasing wage-fund and indirectly from the same source by a tax on payrolls which inevitably is passed onto the masses of consumers in a magnified amount.

Instead of guaranteeing against further intensification of discrimination against Negroes, the foreign-born and young workers, the Wagner-Lewis Bill does the opposite; it provides explicitly for such further discrimination, by excluding from benefits those who need them most, agricultural and domestic workers.

Instead of guarantees against the use of insurance as a strike-breaking machinery, this Bill in application would become an elaborate black-list system for the destruction of the trade unions. The only system of organization that could flourish under the Wagner-Lewis Bill would be the "company unions," those menacing forerunners of fascism in the United States.

Instead of providing for democratic administration of the insurance system by the workers, the Wagner-Lewis Bill would impose an enormous bureacracy, entirely controlled by appointment from above, which would make into a permanent institution that system which in present relief administration has already shown itself as the greatest menace to our small remaining civil liberties and democratic rights. We already have enough examples in the Labor Boards which are doing tremendous damage to organized labor.

These are the reasons, in concentrated outline, why the Communist Party opposes the Wagner-Lewis Bill. These are the reasons why we declare this Bill is not even a small step toward real insurance, but, on the contrary, a measure to *prohibit, to make impossible,* a real social insurance system.

The alternative to the Wagner-Lewis Bill is before Congress for its consideration, in the form of the Workers' Unemployment, Old-Age, and Social Insurance Bill, H. R. 2827, introduced by Congressman Ernest Lundeen of Minnesota. This Bill, H. R. 2827, while still suffering from a few defects, embodies in the main the principles which we support energetically and unconditionally, and for which we have been fighting for many years. Only the principles embodied in H. R. 2827 can provide any measure of real social security for the toilers of the United States.

It is one of the symptoms of the irrationality of our present governmental system, from the point of view of the interests of the masses of the people, that this Committee is considering legislation on unemployment insurance without having before it the Workers' Bill, the only project which has organized mass support throughout the country based upon intelligent discussion involving millions of people. The Workers' Bill is supported not only by the Communist Party and its 600,000 supporters for whom I speak, but by several million other organized workers, farmers, and middle class people.

There is a fashion, nowadays, for every upstart demagogue to try to impress Congress and the country with fantastic figures of tens of millions of supporters for each new utopia, each quack cure-all, which exploits the misery of the masses. I have no desire to compete in this game, the paper-counters of which cannot be checked against any reality. The figures which we cite of organized supporters of the Workers' Bill are verifiable membership figures of established mass organizations, almost all of them of long standing and including a great section of the American Federation of Labor.

An attempt is being made to smother in silence the Workers' Bill, both in Congress and in the newspapers. To make more plausible this silence on the Workers' Bill, which is the only practical alternative to the Wagner-Lewis Bill, there has been trotted out as the "alternative" a straw-man in the shape of the so-called Townsend Plan. It is very easy to tear to pieces this straw-man, in spite of its very praiseworthy desire to care for the aged, and to consider that this disposes of the Workers' Bill, which makes really practical provision for those over working age. But it will not be so easy to get the masses to accept this verdict. Even such loyal servants of the Administration as the Executive Council of the A. F. of L., who have swallowed one after another the injuries and insults dealt the workers for two years, and who have bitterly opposed the Workers' Bill, have been forced to draw back before the discredit and mass revolt against them which must inevitably be the lot of all who identify themselves with the Wagner-Lewis Bill.

The Workers' Bill is before the Congress and before the country. You have not answered it. Your present Bill is no answer, but only a new insult to the suffering millions. You cannot continue to answer only with silence.

We know, of course, that the enemies of the Workers' Bill have prepared and are preparing their arguments against it, when it shall finally force itself upon the floor of Congress. It would be more honest if they would at once place their arguments, and the comparison of the two alternative programs, before this Committee and others, and before Congress as a whole.

All arguments against the Workers' Bill finally resolve themselves into one, the argument that "it costs too much," that "the country cannot afford it."

What does this mean, the statement that "the country cannot afford it"?

Does it mean that our country is too poverty-stricken to care for its own people at a minimum decent living standard? Does it mean that in our country we do not have enough productive land, natural resources, plants, machinery, mines, mills, railroads, etc., or that we lack trained, skilled people to operate them?

Such an answer would be, of course, only nonsense. All the wise men and authorities of the country are wailing that we have too much of these things and of the commodities they produce. The Government has been exerting all its wits to reduce the supply, to destroy the surplus which it claims causes all the trouble.

Does it mean that the Government is unable, is too weak, to raise vast sums of money on short notice? That answer, too, is excluded. Our memories are not so short that we fail to recall how, in 1917-18, the Government raised tens of billions of dollars for participating in a destructive war; if we can afford to sink tens of billions in explosives, poison gases, battleships and other materials to destroy millions of people abroad, why cannot we spend similar sums to provide food, clothing and shelter to save the lives of millions of people at home?

No, that phrase "the country cannot afford it," can only have one meaning, that the small group (an infinitesimal fraction of the population) which owns all the chief stores of accumulated wealth and productive forces, and which dictates the policies of government, *refuses to pay,* while the masses of people who need insurance precisely because they have been robbed of all, *cannot pay.*

But our country cannot and does not avoid paying the bill for unemployment, old-age, maternity, and other hazards. *Now* the country pays, not in money but in the lives of men, women, and children. This is the price which, above all other prices, the country *really cannot afford to pay.*

We propose that our country shall begin to pay the bill in that only currency we can afford, in the accumulated wealth and productive forces, by taxing the rich.

We propose to reverse the present policy, which taxes the poor in order to relieve and further subsidize the rich; we propose to tax the rich to feed the poor.

Those gentlemen who argue that, despite our country's immense wealth, it cannot afford real unemployment insurance because the cost would dig into profits, and that our present system cannot operate if it touches these sacred profits, are really pouring oil on the fires of radicalization that are sweeping through our country. Millions of our people, the useful ones, those who work, are sick and tired of being told about the sacredness of profits, while their children starve. They are more and more getting into that mood which, in a previous crisis of our national life, produced the Declaration of Independence. The direction of the masses now, as then, is a revolutionary one, with this difference, that then it was independence from King George and a dying feudalism that was required, while today it is independence from King Profits and a dying capitalism which tries to prolong its life at the cost of denying social insurance.

We Communists have been denounced in this Congress, as well as in the daily press, as enemies of our country, as a "menace," because we speak of the possibility and necessity of revolution to solve the problems of life of the great majority of the people. We have been accused of all sorts of silly things, such as "plots to kidnap the President," of being bombers, conspirators, etc. All that is nonsense, but very dangerous nonsense—it is a screen of poison gas to hide the attacks that are being made against all democratic rights, against the trade unions, against the living standards of the people. History has shown beyond dispute, that such attacks, beginning against the Communists, never end there, but in a full-fledged fascist dictatorship which destroys all rights of the people.

The Communist "menace" really means that those moneyed interests which finance this great campaign against Communism, knowing that millions of people are in a really desperate situation and a desperate frame of mind, are afraid that these millions will go over to the Communist Party and program.

But those gentlemen who really want to remove this "menace"

should listen to the advice which we, the Communists, give you gratis. Remove the desperate situation of these millions, grant that minimum measure of real social security such as is provided in the Workers' Bill, prove in fact, in life, that it really is possible for the masses to continue to live under capitalism. We are accused of making political capital out of the misery of the masses, but in reality we are fighting to improve the living standards of the masses; when revolution comes, it will be, not because we Communists have "plotted" for it, but because the rulers of this country have proved that there is no other way out, that there is no other way towards a secure life.

It is worth remembering that after 1776, when our Declaration of Independence acted as the spark that set fire to the democratic revolution in France and thoughout Europe, the reactionary forces of the world fought against the "dangerous" ideas that were supposed to be "imported from America." Today the same comedy is repeated, but this time the revolution is said to be "imported from Moscow." In both cases, the deep reality behind the nonsensical slogan is, that the country attacked is the one that is showing the way to the solution of the problems of the people. "Moscow," that is, the Soviet Union, has adopted complete social insurance, has solved unemployment, is improving the living standards of all the people, is enormously expanding its economic life. Do a better job, or even just as good, and "Moscow" will be not the slightest danger.

Present proposals which, while denying real unemployment insurance, would enact some new Alien and Sedition Laws, to crush down the growing demand for a better life, also recall moments in the past history of our country. We had a period of Alien and Sedition Laws in the early 1800's, also adopted and carried out in the interests of established property and designed to crush a democratic movement arising from the masses of the people. The Party which sponsored those laws went down in disgrace and defeat, the laws were repealed after long suffering and struggles, those against whom the Alien and Sedition Laws were directed came into direction of the affairs of the country. Any attempt to solve today's problems by Alien and Sedition Laws will be as futile as those of the times of Madison and Jefferson.

There is no substitute, there is no way to avoid, the demand for full unemployment, old-age and social insurance. Its denial will only accelerate the growing revolutionary mass unrest, intensify the social struggles. The Wagner-Lewis Bill is a transparent attempt to sidetrack this demand. The new legislation against the Communist Party is only a futile attempt to silence the movement. Neither can succeed. Only the Workers' Unemployment, Old Age and Social Insurance Bill can satisfy the aroused masses of the useful people, the working people, of the United States.

XIII

The United Front Against Fascism and War *

THIS meeting, and the Congress which opens tomorrow, are promising signs of the rise of a great united movement against fascism and war.

Surely such a united movement is sorely needed. The United States is driving rapidly toward fascism and toward a new imperialist war.

Revelations of the Senate Armaments Investigation Committee have slightly lifted the lid of exposure; the resulting stink of corruption shocked the world. The governments of our own and other countries were shown as participants in a gigantic game of mass murder for profits.

These extreme nationalists, these 100 per cent Americans, these fighters against the Reds, are disclosed as international murderers, they arm the United States against Japan, and Japan against the United States; they sell munitions impartially to both sides in the South American wars; they rearm Germany and help rouse fear at this rearmament. The stink of this cesspool of murder and bribery has frightened our statesmen. They conclude that what is dangerous is not the condition, but its exposure.

Now the lid has quickly been clamped down again; the Senate investigations expressed fear that their revelations, if continued, would cause upheavals and revolutions.

It is very easy to shout complaints against the war preparations of other countries. But that does not help to stop war, that only strengthens the hands of the war-makers, who live on the fears of what the "other fellow" may do. The only way to fight war is to begin by fighting the war-makers in our own land, to extend this fight into the factories, especially in munitions factories, docks, etc., to bring this fight into every mass organization, trade unions, fraternal societies, clubs, farmers' organizations, churches, among the Negroes, soldiers, veterans, women and youth. The Roosevelt administration is carrying through the greatest war program ever seen in peace time. The very "recovery appropriations" for relief of the starving are turned into war appropriations, into gigantic naval expansion, into army mechanization, into poison gas, bombs, tanks, airplanes. Every person and party who helps this program is helping prepare the new

* Address at the opening of the Second U. S. Congress Against War and Fascism, Chicago, September 28, 1934.—*Ed.*

World War. The only way to fight war is to begin by fighting the war program being carried through by Washington.

A part of the drive toward war is the rising wave of fascist violence against workers, farmers and the discontented middle classes. Concentration camps already exist in Georgia, hailed by Hitler himself as following the Nazi model. National Guards have been called out in twelve States in the past months, to shoot down strikers and demonstrators. More than fifty workers have been murdered, hundreds wounded, thousands sent to prison. In California, the so-called vigilantes have burned, destroyed, tortured, maimed, openly violated every item on the Bill of Rights, on the call of General Hugh Johnson, speaking for the Washington administration, and with the active cooperation of local police and officialdom, on the best model of Hitler.

Already they are taking the Communist Party off the ballot, and in some places even the Socialist Party also. Now comes the self-styled American Liberty League, which is furnishing a political and financial center for fascism, which demands yet more and quicker fascist violence. As in Germany, fascism in America becomes a serious problem because it is being organized and financed by big capitalists, by monopoly capital, by Wall Street.

Also as in Germany, fascism rises here under the slogan, "Drive out the Reds." It is no accident that Hearst, whose yellow press leads the anti-red campaign, visited Hitler a few weeks ago, and now campaigns in his support. The first and fiercest attacks are against the Communists. But let every trade unionist remember Hitler Germany, where the suppression of the Communist Party was followed in a few weeks by the destruction of all trade unions. Let every Socialist remember that even the surrender by the German Socialist leaders could not save their party also from destruction. Let every church member recall that German fascism trampled down the churches a few weeks after the Reds and trade unions. Let every writer, liberal and professional remember the burning of the books, the banishment of every fearless and intelligent person, that followed the outlawing of the Communists. Fascism can be defeated only if *all* who suffer from it rouse themselves *now* to unhesitating, energetic *united action against fascism and war.*

I am speaking as a representative of the Communist Party of the U. S. A. We Communists greet this great united movement against war and fascism represented at this Congress. We are happy to see the growing numbers of American Federation of Labor unions in it. We are happy to see increasing numbers of Socialists and Socialist Party locals; we hope the whole Socialist Party will soon end its hesitations and come into the united front. We are happy to see the great youth movement, firmly rejecting the attempts of fascism to take leadership of it, and moving solidly into the anti-fascist united front.

We are happy to see the most important peace organizations, and women's organizations, the churches and religious societies, coming into the American League Against War and Fascism, and its Congress. We are happy to see the outstanding intellectuals, writers, artists, supporting this movement. *This great, progressive people's movement against fascism and war is looked upon by us Communists as the most promising development in America today.* We pledge our full, most loyal and energetic support and participation in all its work.

This movement already has a program, approved unanimously one year ago at the great First Congress in New York, with 2,616 delegates. This program has stood the test, has proved its correctness, has made it possible for this greater Congress to gather in Chicago. This program is not a Communist program; it is a minimum united front program, to which every honest fighter against war and fascism can subscribe. We support this program wholeheartedly.

We can do this with all the more enthusiasm, because we are sure that finally, in the course of the struggle to save civilization from fascist barbarism, every honest progressive is going to learn that, in full earnestness, the choice before the whole world really is the choice between fascism or communism. What fascism offers the human race has been demonstrated by Hitler Germany; what communism has to offer is shown by the triumphant construction of a new socialist society of peace and prosperity for the masses in Russia, in the Union of Socialist Soviet Republics of Marx, Lenin, Stalin. We know what the final decision will be. Today the first steps toward a better society are taken in the first steps of organizing a broad united mass struggle against fascism and imperialist war, against "our own" war-makers and fascists in the United States.

XIV

The Struggle for the United Front *

COMRADES, I want first to give you a few words of news about the health of Comrade Foster. I just received a letter from him in which he gives us a detailed report on his condition, in which I am sure everyone is interested. Comrade Foster, you will be pleased to hear, has made substantial health gains since he left New York, but the process is slow. He now has a feeling of complete confidence that he is getting well.

He further informs us that he will be returning to New York in two or three weeks, and expects gradually to get in touch with the work again, and gradually, over a long period, resume his work.

I take it for granted that this meeting of the Central Committee will send a message to Comrade Foster, hoping for his quick recovery, and hoping that he will be present at our next meeting.

*   *   *

I will now take up the report of the Central Committee, of the development of the work of the Party since the Eighth National Convention.

THE DEEPENING CRISIS AND THE DIFFICULTIES OF THE NEW DEAL

All the events since the Eighth National Convention confirm the Party analysis of the course of the crisis, of the direction of the New Deal policies, of the regrouping of class forces that is going on, the rising wave of mass struggles and of the developments towards fascism and war. In these past three months the difficulties of the New Deal policies, the development of their inner contradictions, have come to a head. Precisely out of the successes that have been achieved in accomplishing the central objectives of the New Deal—the restoring of profits to monopoly capital at the expense of the workers and farmers and small capitalists—comes this maturing of the contradictions of the Roosevelt policies. All of these contradictions are sharpening, many of them are coming into open head-on conflict between strata of the bourgeoisie, between various tendencies within the bourgeoisie, and

* Report to the Central Committee of the Communist Party, September 5-6, 1934.—*Ed.*

above all, between the two basic class forces, the capitalist class and the working class.

Dissatisfaction with the New Deal is becoming a general phenomenon throughout all classes. Among the capitalist class, including the highest strata, this dissatisfaction is expressed through, for example, the recently formed Liberty League, a coalition of leading Tory politicians of both old parties; it is shown in the attitude of Hearst and his chain of newspapers, which are leading the attack against the New Deal, although a few months ago Hearst was a declared supporter of Roosevelt.

The dissatisfaction among the petty bourgeoisie found its classical expression in the report of the Darrow Committee on the effects of the N.R.A. on the development of monopoly capital. The facts of the dissatisfaction among the farmers are well known, and even well publicized, being admitted in the administration circles, and tremendous masses of farmers are now in motion against the A.A.A., the crop reduction program, etc.

The dissatisfaction of the workers is expressed primarily in the growing strike wave, and even in the maneuvers of the A. F. of L., which is a most direct lackey of the Roosevelt administration, but is forced, in order to maintain its hold over the masses of members, to join in the general demand for the *reformation of the New Deal*.

The central conflict upon which the New Deal has, one can almost say, broken down, is the question of regulation of labor relations in the industries; the question of Section 7a, problems of the relation of the A. F. of L. and company unions, the contradiction of the decline of earnings in face of rising prices, which has aroused upheaval among the masses. This is typified by outstanding strike struggles in this period in Alabama, in Toledo, Minneapolis, Milwaukee, the Pacific Coast marine strike, the San Francisco general strike, and now the national textile general strike. Other great mass battles are maturing in the immediate future. This was spoken of in a recent issue of the Kiplinger Letter, confidential advice for business men, which remarked that "it would be hard to exaggerate the worry caused Washington officials by labor troubles. The government will not be able to prevent the spread of strikes."

The tempo of this development is accelerated by the economic trends. The whole course of economy in this period has served to emphasize the correctness of Stalin's explanation of the depression into which the capitalist class had entered at the end of 1933, as a special kind of depression. We examined this in some detail at the Eighth Convention of our Party. We can now declare that all developments since then confirm the correctness of our thesis.

There has not been a single sign of development towards recovery. On the contrary, everything points to long-continued depression with ups and downs and unevenness between different industries, localities, etc. This perspective of a long-continued depression is also recognized now by the bourgeoisie. Again I quote from the Kiplinger Letter, often the frankest spokesman of the capitalists:

> Business sentiment has taken a turn for the worse. Prospects for business have dimmed a bit, even allowing for excessive business jitters. Earlier belief that recovery would resume in a healthy fashion this fall is now giving way to fears that any marked revival of business will be delayed until spring of 1935 at the earliest. Relative low level of business will continue through the fall and early winter. High rate of industrial production reached in July, 1933, will not be reached again until sometime in 1935.

Some specific features of the present depression as analyzed at our Eighth Convention are now accentuated—the stimulation of industries through government subsidies has reached into the basic industries very weakly, no expansion of capital investment has taken place, new capital issues are overwhelmingly non-productive in character. Accumulated stocks are again rising, whereas at the Eighth Convention we noted a declining tendency in accumulated stocks. This is especially true in raw materials, due to the relative narrowing of the inner market by the restoration of profits at the expense of the masses. Business indices as a whole are considerably below July, 1933, at the time of the inauguration of the N.R.A. There has been a 30 per cent decline in economy since the N.R.A. went into effect and all indications are that the economic indices are not again reaching the point where they were in July, 1933.

A new economic feature is the drought. This natural disaster which has brought whole sections of the country face to face with famine, has in fact carried out the objectives that were set for the Agricultural Adjustment Act. The A.A.A. had been facing failure due to the off-setting features of many evasions of the crop reduction program carried through by fertilization and mechanization of reduced acreage. But the Roosevelt administration has been seriously embarrassed by the tremendous revelation that the aim of their effort was precisely the same as that condition which was brought about by the drought, which must be recognized as a calamity. The Roosevelt regime declares that while the drought was beneficial, they fear its effects in destroying illusions in the A.A.A.

Unemployment is again heavily increasing. This increase is more rapid than the decline in production, due to the heavy stretch-out and speed-up. Even during the period of the upward movement of the economic index, the increase in employment always lagged behind the increase in production and the lagging continually grew. Now that production is going down and unemployment increasing at a greater rate, the problem of unemployment and all the attendant questions of relief, relief methods, unemployment insurance, etc., are becoming again outstanding problems of millions. Official spokesmen of the administration predict 5,000,000 families on the relief rolls this winter, with approximately 4,000,000 families on relief at the present time, with an average of four to five to a family. Problems of maintenance of the unemployed are even further intensified by the progressive exhaustion of the resources of those who have been long unemployed, with larger proportions of the unemployed claiming relief.

And, to quote the Kiplinger Service:

Unemployment relief next winter will cost more than last winter. Number on rolls will be greater.

While all of these authorities and the capitalist press try to minimize the extent of the problem, they are all forced to recognize the direction in which it is developing. The crisis in the New York relief plans is duplicated more or less intensively everywhere.

The tremendous growth of the movement for the Workers' Unemployment and Social Insurance Bill, H.R. 7598,* which is carrying strongholds of conservatism in the A. F. of L., Y.M.C.A.'s, etc., has forced a general acceptance of the principle of unemployment insurance in words by employers.

Big efforts are being made to direct mass sentiment behind this movement to some scheme based upon actuarial principles, as they call it, for protection against *future* unemployment at the cost of the workers. The rising wave of local struggles around relief issues, revival of unemployment councils, unions of relief workers, reflect the crisis in unemployment relief and the bankruptcy of all present relief plans now in operation.

On the basis of these economic and political trends, we must note that the radicalization of the workers, farmers and middle classes is coming to a higher stage, finding newer, broader, more political modes of expression. The basic feature of this is the *general strike* and *solidarity strike* movement that sweeps the industrial localities and even whole industries, like the textile strike. From strikes around small economic issues, it broadens out into political class battles that even raise the whole question of state power, as in San Francisco. The elemental force of the workers' movement sweeps into the broadened stream of this radicalization representative strata of undifferentiated masses such as churches, Y.M.C.A.'s, small home-owners, small depositors, as well as definite middle-class groups, intellectuals and professions. To keep this upsurge in safe channels, new forms of demagogy are arising, such as Upton Sinclair's EPIC movement and the Utopians in California. Sinclair's sweeping of the Democratic

* Later introduced as H. R. 2827.—*Ed.*

Party primaries is a distorted reflection of mass radicalization, which obtained a clearer, more direct expression in the phenomenal vote of 180,000 * for Gallagher, running openly as an independent associate of the Communist Party.

A distinct new feature of the radicalization of the masses is the sharply favorable response that is arising and rapidly spreading to the call for a united front against the capitalist offensive, against fascism and war. We must immediately note that this is accompanied by the equally sharp and rapid spread of measures of fascist suppression of the mass movement which are especially directed against the Communist Party. In the center, as the conscious moving and directive force of the united front movement in all its phases, stands the Communist Party. Our position in this respect is clear and unchallenged. That is why the main fascist attack is against us. Thus, the fascist repressive movement must be judged dialectically. It is a blow against the working class and its vanguard; increases our difficulties, but at the same time it registers the growing effectiveness of our work in mobilizing the masses, in building the united front of struggle, and stimulates the development of the united front.

The A. F. of L., in its open leadership of the anti-Red campaign among the workers, is trying to buy its recognition by the employers through putting itself forward as the bulwark against communism among the workers. Our great movement for H.R. 7598, the Congress Against War and Fascism, the unexampled Leftward movement of the Youth Congress under Communist influence, the numerous united front actions with locals of the S.P., the successful leadership in vast strike struggles and in innumerable small ones—these are the reasons why the bourgeoisie and its agents, General Hugh Johnson, the Liberty League, William Green and the A. F. of L. bureaucracy, the Elks and Eagles, the American Legion, launched the present nationwide offensive against the Communist Party. This is a characteristic feature of the development of fascism in its first stage. Every political party and grouping in America finds it necessary today to define its attitude towards, or its relation with, the Communist Party as a major question of its whole orientation. Our Party by its correct policy and the growing effectiveness of its work has become an inescapable factor in the political life of America.

The fascist concentration against the Communist Party in the anti-Red drive cannot hide the growing disintegration, confusion and conflicts within the camp of the bourgeoisie. The bi-partisan coalition of the Tories in the Liberty League to the Right, the Sinclair development to the "Left," the breaking away of LaFollette from the Republican Party in Wisconsin, and also the crisis in the S.P.—these are all

* Later revealed as being over 200,000.

symptoms of the flux, disintegration and regroupings of the whole bourgeois camp. The rising mood of revolt among the masses, their radicalization, the mass struggles growing broader and deeper in combination with the impact of the world situation, have shattered the whole foundation of the bourgeoisie. We can say, without trying to draw any exact analogies which would lead us astray, but roughly comparing the stages of development, that the situation in the United States in this respect, the atomization, the breaking up into cliques and groups, and the organization of fascist groups among the bourgeoisie, are comparable to the pre-fascist atomization of bourgeois parties in Germany in the period of Bruening.

THE INNER DIFFERENCES WITHIN THE BOURGEOISIE

Serious dissatisfaction with the development of the N.R.A. has arisen in the past few months in the ranks of the big bourgeoisie. This centers around two points.

First and most important, there is a growing fear that the demagogy in connection with Section 7a, which tended to smother the big strike movements in automobile and steel, is now no longer effective, or is even having the opposite effect. There is a growing demand that the government come out more decisively to prevent strikes before they happen, that the government shall end the ambitions of the A. F. of L. to enter the basic industries. This is not at all because they distrust the good intentions of the A. F. of L. leaders or their desire to prevent strikes. It is rather because the bourgeoisie begins seriously to question the ability of the A. F. of L. leaders to control the mass upsurge of their members. This doubt has grown since the San Francisco and textile strikes.

Secondly, there is a growing conviction that of all of the New Deal policies only three points have seriously contributed to restoring the prosperity of finance-capital, namely: (1) inflation; (2) repeal of the anti-trust law and the institution of the control of the big monopolies; and (3) the government subsidies to big business. These sections of the big bourgeoisie became acutely conscious of all of the inner contradictions of capitalism in the form in which they are expressed through the New Deal institutions, the N.R.A., the A.A.A., etc., and the other new structures that have been built up like mushrooms from the New Deal. The idea grows among them, therefore, that inasmuch as these contradictions appear in the building of this new machinery, they can be abolished by doing away with this machinery, and handing the code authorities over directly to big industrialists. Roosevelt undoubtedly sympathizes with them and finds it daily more difficult to find a way out, although he has made many moves and more gestures in that direction.

The emergence of the Liberty League under the slogans "protect the Constitution," etc., is an attempt to influence the Roosevelt administration more sharply toward fascism in this period of reorientation. It is also a preparation for more serious action in the way of political realignment for the presidential elections in 1936. It is, of course, not a demand for restraining fascist developments. Neither is it concerned with cutting down governmental expenditures which go for big business, for this is considered protection of private property, but it is deeply incensed against the growing expenditures for unemployment relief, even though the amount of relief to the individual unemployed family is steadily going down.

Closely connected with the Liberty League is the position of Hearst and his big chain of newspapers. Hearst openly charges that Roosevelt's administration is more Bolshevik than the Communist Party itself. He attempts to turn the anti-Red crusade, of which he was pioneer and remains the sustained leader, into a mass movement to force the administration sharply to the Right. Approximately the same position is taken by the official Republican leadership, although in many localities the Republican policy is not followed by local leaders wishing to keep more friendly relations with the New Deal.

We must avoid the error of seeing in these divisions merely a "division of labor" carried out by agreed-upon plans by the decisive strata of the bourgeoisie. They are real differences over which the most bitter controversy rages, controversy which may have serious consequences. They cut through all the main bourgeois groups. They seriously impede the development of a united bourgeois policy.

But it would be equally wrong to consider these differences as going any further than the question of how best to throw the burden of the crisis upon the masses for the benefit of finance capital. These differences do not go beyond the policy of monopoly capital.

The pressure to increase the demagogy rather than to decrease it is applied upon those sections of the ruling apparatus which deal most intimately with restraining the mass upsurge and in those places where the problem is hottest for the moment, as, for example, in the LaGuardia Progressive administration in New York, where the number of unemployed workers in New York exceeds the number of unemployed in most capitalist countries—one-fourth of the population depending on the city dole. It is seen in the LaFollette Party in Wisconsin, which is the center of a storm of agrarian unrest; it is seen in Sinclair's capture of the Democratic nomination for Governor in California, as a result of the strikes and the extent of the mass unemployment.

The Roosevelt administration tries to be flexible. It will give way to both forms of pressure. It tries to give the Liberty League and the Hearst elements the essence of what they demand, while giving the masses the old demagogy in ever new forms. Spokesmen for the administration give repeated pledges that "private profits" and "business confidence" are their innermost motive and heart's desire. At the same time, Roosevelt agrees to meet Sinclair, and the New York *Herald Tribune* could write, without contradiction, the following frank analysis of the situation:

> Prior to the primary 'yesterday, Mr. Roosevelt, it is known, received communications from prominent California Democrats which took Mr. Sinclair's nomination for granted and urged that the national administration be prepared to get behind him. The tenor of this advice was that Mr. Sinclair should be surrounded with practical New Dealers who could keep him from going too far or too fast. It was pointed out that he was bringing into the Democratic Party a great many thousands of votes which otherwise would go to more radical candidates outside of both major parties. . . . According to this analysis of the California political situation which was circulated several days ago among important members of the administration, Mr. Sinclair is a powerful deterrent to the breaking away of large blocks of votes, especially among the unemployed, into the arms of communism.

That this analysis of Sinclair's role is absolutely correct is proved beyond all doubt, by the fact that over 180,000, most of whom voted for Sinclair, also voted for Gallagher, who was running with the endorsement of the Communist Party. Without Sinclair in this field, most of these votes should have gone for the straight Communist ticket.

Roosevelt, and the bourgeoisie generally, try to draw some advantages out of their mounting inner differences and difficulties. Both the Liberty League and Sinclair are used to try to reburnish the dulling halo of "Savior" about Roosevelt's head. Roosevelt, while yielding to the pressure of the Liberty League, poses as its antagonist; while yielding nothing in deed to the "Left" Sinclair he gives a carefully chosen flow of soft words to bind Sinclair's followers to the New Deal. It is our task to make use of these developments in the opposite way, to expose the inner political unity of finance capital behind all these differences, at the same time showing the unsolvable contradictions of capitalism which they express; especially to expose the reactionary utopianism of Sinclair's program; and to bring forward sharply and clearly the revolutionary way out of the crisis, given by the Communist program, upon the basis of an ever more energetic unfolding of the daily struggle for the most immediate needs of the workers.

LESSONS OF THE MOST RECENT STRIKES

The strike wave which began early in 1934, the first period of which was examined by the Eighth National Convention, has since that time risen to new heights. The strike movement not only grew in number of strikers, intensity and duration of strikes, but also qualitatively entered a higher stage with the emergence on a nation-wide scale of a general strike movement. This general strike movement came to the verge of realization in Toledo, Minneapolis, Milwaukee, Portland, Seattle. It was realized in San Francisco in a four-day general strike of solidarity with the Pacific Coast marine workers' struggle of twelve weeks involving the overwhelming mass of all workers in the San Francisco Bay region. At the same time the strike movement further penetrated the deep South and the basic industries. At the present moment a great movement for a nation-wide industrial strike of textile workers has forced their A. F. of L. leaders apparently to submit for the moment to the fighting determination of the rank-and-file and issue a general strike call for September 4. These struggles, and especially the San Francisco general strike, mark a new high point in the development of the American working class and are of historic significance even on a world scale. The lessons of these struggles are of first importance for the development of the entire revolutionary movement. The history of these battles must be thoroughly studied and their lessons assimilated by the entire revolutionary movement and the whole working class.

Already at the Eighth Convention the first manifestations of the tendency to mass solidarity strikes were noted particularly in the local general strike embracing all workers in the small industrial town of Centralia, Illinois.

In May the same tendency rapidly grew in Toledo, Ohio, around the relatively small strike of the Auto Lite Corp. This strike, on the point of being crushed, was suddenly revived by a great solidarity action of mass picketing, initiated and led by the Unemployment Council, involving principally unemployed workers, which completely tied up the plant and made the strike again 100 per cent effective. The declaration of martial law and the throwing of several companies of the Ohio National Guard into the strike area with the consequent killing of two picketers, aroused the entire Toledo working class to action, and a sympathetic attitude even in broad circles of the lower middle class. The slogan issued by the Communist Party for general strike to answer the declaration of martial law, was quickly seized by the trade union membership, which in a period of ten days had forced the adoption of general strike resolutions in 83 out of 91 trade unions in Toledo. The general strike was prevented only by a hasty last-minute settlement of the strike demands, on a compromise basis, engineered by the local A. F. of L. bureaucracy after being aided by Muste & Co. to regain the ear of the masses; by the National Labor Board, and put across on the masses with the help of Socialist Party leaders hastily brought from the S.P. Convention in Detroit.

Similarly in Minneapolis a general strike movement arose in May as a response to the Employers' Association's effort to break the truck-men's strike by the violent attack of a force of deputized business men against the strikers, which resulted in two deaths. Here also the solidarity action was halted by a hastily-contrived settlement, heralded by the Farmer-Labor leaders and their Trotzkyite lieutenants as a glorious victory, but actually a return to the pre-strike conditions while leaving hundreds of strikers victimized.

In Milwaukee a strike of street railway men to stop the dismissal of union members, a movement which seemed hopelessly weak on the first day of the action, was in the second day suddenly swept into 100 per cent effectiveness by a mass solidarity action of 40,000 sympathetic picketers mobilized by the Party and Unemployment Councils, who went to the car barns and into the streets and forcibly stopped all street car movements. The efforts of the police of this Socialist Party-administered city to suppress this mass picketing brought, on the fourth day, the decision of the power housemen to go out in sympathy and an insistent demand in dozens of local unions for a general strike. The tremendous pressure of this mass movement brought the sudden capitulation of the street railway management on the evening of the fourth day of the strike, which halted the general strike movement.

From these three experiences the general strike slogan had spread throughout the country. The outstanding lesson, that the mobilization of the class forces of the bourgeoisie against strikes could only be answered by a similar mobilization of working-class forces in defense of attacked strikes, even small ones, had spread through every industrial center among all the most active and intelligent workers.

It was with this experience and against this background that the San Francisco general strike of July came about. This historic action was the climax of the protracted Pacific Coast general marine workers' strike, the special problems of which we examine later on.

The marine workers' strike, which began on May 9, tied up all ports on the Pacific Coast except San Pedro, which was partially operated by scabs. In the beginning of July, after almost two months of complete tie-up of the ports, the Industrial Association and the Shipowners' Union of San Francisco, decided to "open up the port by all means." These means were a planned massacre of striking workers on the streets, in which two strikers were killed and many dozens wounded, in a premeditated firing upon an unarmed crowd. Even previously the solidarity movement had begun in the decision of the truck drivers not to transport scab cargo from the docks. The massacre of July set off a veritable explosion of working-class indignation and the demand for solidarity action. At the funeral of the slain strikers (one a Communist) a spontaneous procession, estimated as high as 100,000 workers, marched behind the coffins, taking possession of the main streets of San Francisco, causing the police to be completely withdrawn from view in fear that another collision might put the mass movement completely beyond the control of the bourgeoisie. From this demonstration, the slogan of general strike swept through the unions. But not entirely spontaneously. We must emphasize, it swept through the unions with the assistance of organized visits of the unions by representatives of the basic central strike movement, the Marine Workers' Joint Strike Committee.

Against the open opposition of the A. F. of L. local officials of the Central Trades Council, union after union in overwhelming majority was voting for the general strike. Unable to stem the tide, the local A. F. of L. leaders suddenly took a new tack. Announcing that the general strike would be considered, they appointed a specially chosen Committee of Strategy composed of the most hard-boiled reactionary officials, who placed themselves at the head of the movement. It was this committee, together with the so-called General Strike Committee, composed not of elected delegates, but of appointed officials, which issued the official call for the general strike.

In the San Francisco general strike, as in the other strikes spoken of, we have a classical example of the Communist thesis, that in the present period of capitalist decline, a stubborn struggle for even the smallest immediate demands of the workers inevitably develops into general class battles, and raises the whole question of state power and the revolutionary solution of the crisis. Beginning in a typical economic struggle over wages and working conditions of longshoremen, there took place, step by step, a concentration of class forces in support of one or the other side which soon aligned practically the entire population into two hostile camps: the capitalist class against the working class, and all intermediate elements towards support of one or the other. It became a well-defined class struggle, a test of strength between the two basic class forces. The economic struggle was transformed into a political struggle of the first magnitude. The working class understood that if it allowed the concentration of capitalist forces to defeat the marine workers, this meant the defeat of the entire working class, general wage-cuts, speed-up and worsening of conditions. The capitalist class knew that if the marine workers should win their demands, this would launch a general forward movement of the entire working class which would defeat the capitalist program for their way out of the crisis, a program based upon restoring profits by reducing the general living standards of the masses. It was the capitalist class, which, in panic before the rising giant of the class action of the masses, cried out that this strike, which they could have settled very quickly at any moment by the simple expedient of granting the workers' economic demands, was actually a revolutionary uprising organized by the Communist Party to overthrow the whole capitalist system in San Francisco. Of course, this strike did not have revolution as its objective, certainly not a revolution in a single city, but only winning the immediate demands of the workers. The unity of the workers, however, raised before the employers the spectre of working-class power, with the potentiality of revolution.

On the side of the workers, their experience was leading them step by step to more serious challenge of the capitalist class, teaching them the necessity of extending the struggle for power, bringing them face to face with the state power as the guardian of capitalist profits and the force driving down the workers' standards; at the same time it was giving the workers a new understanding of their own power and ability to shake the very foundation of capitalist rule. In this sense, the strike was truly the greatest revolutionary event in American labor history.

LAUNCHING THE TERROR AGAINST THE REDS

After four days, the San Francisco general strike came to an end. the working class had earned a brilliant victory through its heroic struggle, but it was cheated by a miserable compromise. Not yet fully swung into action, with its fighting spirit high and mounting higher every day, the working class of San Francisco was defeated not so much by the superior strength of the open capitalist forces, but primarily because these worked in close co-operation with the capitalist agents inside the working class, the A. F. of L. leaders who occupied the post of formal leaders of the general strike. The local A. F. of L. officialdom, headed by Vandeleur & Co., had placed themselves at the head of the general strike precisely in order to smash it from within, to prevent it from going over their heads, and further hoping to use its betrayal as an instrument to smash simultaneously the prolonged heroic marine workers' battle.

While the strike was betrayed from within by the A. F. of L. leaders, from outside it was attacked by terror unexampled in American history. San Francisco and the Bay area waterfront were military camps. Armed vigilante fascist bands were turned loose against all Left-wing organizations—the Marine Workers' Industrial Union, the *Western Worker*, official organ of the strike as well as of the Communist Party, the offices of the Communist Party, International Labor Defense, Workers' Ex-Servicemen's League, Workers' School, various workers' clubs, etc. The offices were wrecked and their contents destroyed. Homes were invaded, and treated in the same manner. Hundreds of militant workers were arrested. These fascist gangs, organized and directed by the police, were followed up by police detachments to finish the job and to arrest the attacked workers. All this was the necessary prelude to forcing through a vote to end the strike by the A. F. of L. leaders.

Precisely in the midst of this terror came William Green with his infamous contribution where he disowned the strike, declaring it was unauthorized and inadvisable. Even under this tremendous assault the strike remained firm and the pressure upon the officialdom by the rank-and-file was so great that even in the General Strike Committee, composed of officials of all the unions, the decision to end the strike was declared to be carried only by a vote of 191 to 174. Even this slim majority was declared by Harry Bridges, the longshoreman leader, to have been achieved by the last minute rushing in of dozens of new and unaccounted-for "members" of the committee. Further, even in this body of officials, in order to obtain this narrow majority, it had been necessary to combine with the campaign of violent suppression and the anti-Red hysteria a series of concessions of a very important character. The original capitalist program of open-shop smashing of the mass trade unions had to be publicly renounced. A few days later, in order to conclude the marine strike, which they had thought to smash through this betrayal, the employers were forced to make further concessions, to agree publicly to treat with all the striking marine unions on all questions in dispute and to acknowledge the Solidarity Pact between the marine unions, whereby they had pledged to stand or fall together, by providing for similar and simultaneous settlement of all demands of all marine unions. Tremendous power, generated by the general strike movement, was thus effective even in the hour of its betrayal to register some fragments of the victory which had been won by the workers and snatched away from them by their leaders.

The terror campaign against the San Francisco general strike, which quickly extended throughout the State of California and since has broadened through the entire nation, requires special study because of the far-reaching character which it has taken on. Who initiated, organized and led this campaign? Who was participating in it? It must be registered, first of all, that the signal for the terror was given by General Hugh Johnson, who the night before the raids delivered a speech in the University of California in which he declared that the Communists had gained control of the trade unions and were planning a revolution as a result of the strike. He called upon all patriotic citizens to join together to "exterminate them like rats." General Johnson was declared in the newspapers to be speaking as the personal representative of President Roosevelt. It is clear that the Roosevelt regime placed itself at the head of, and accepted full responsibility for, all the fascist outrages that followed. General Johnson was ably seconded by the liberal Secretary of Labor, Madam Perkins, who simultaneously announced a campaign of deportation of all foreign-born workers handed over to her by the local vigilantes and police. The Republican Party, locally, in the State, and nationally, organized a serious competition with the Democratic Party as to which should have the most "credit" for the fascist terror. Upton Sinclair seized the opportunity not to protest against the fascist terror, but to denounce the Communist Party, to disclaim the slightest connection with the hunted "Reds," and to place upon the Communist Party responsibility for the terror. The *New Leader,* organ of the S.P., Right wing, denounced the Communists as being responsible for the breaking of the strike and provoking the fascist terror. Even the "militant" Socialist leader, Norman Thomas, while mildly disapproving of the terror, gave his blessings to the betrayal of the strike with the declaration that "the general strike was soon called off by labor itself."

General Johnson's command to the A. F. of L. officials that they should "exterminate the Communists like rats" found a quick response from William Green of the A. F. of L. Executive Council, who publicly proclaimed a campaign of expulsion of all militant elements in the trade unions. This campaign has already resulted in the expulsion of whole local organizations, notably Local No. 499 of the Painters' Union in New York. The campaign has been taken up by the American Legion, the fraternal societies of the Elks, Eagles, etc., as well as by all the professional Red-baiting societies throughout the country.

The capitalist press, with Hearst at its head, is carrying on the most vicious incitation to fascist violence against all Reds, which means all militant workers' leaders. The growing list of criminal-syndicalist cases reflect the terror as applied by the courts, while dozens of reports come in every day showing a mounting wave of fascist criminal assaults against militant workers. In Oregon the campaign takes such form as the publication of lists of all signers of the Communist election petitions and the inciting of fascist violence against the signers unless they publicly repudiate their signatures. The leaders of the American Legion Convention in California climaxed this hysteria by proposing a concentration camp in the wilds of Alaska for all Reds, a proposal which was widely publicized throughout the country. The terror used to break the San Francisco general strike has thus been spread over the whole country and serves as an enormous stimulus to the whole tendency toward fascism inaugurated by Roosevelt's New Deal.

It is becoming clear that the growing strike movement and especially the San Francisco general strike has brought about a certain crisis in the evolution of the New Deal policies. Already in the early spring of 1934 decisive circles of finance capital had placed a serious check upon the Roosevelt demagogy around Section 7a which was first expressed in the automobile and steel settlements negotiated by Roosevelt with the assistance of William Green. In connection with the automobile settlement Roosevelt declared: "We have charted a new course." The nature of the new course was explained by the auto manufacturers who "were particularly pleased that the clarification of Section 7a seems to uphold their contention in behalf of the company union." But even this new course of the New Deal which was a sharp rebuff to the trade unions in the basic industries, together with all the ensuing maneuvers of National Industrial and Regional Labor Boards, of Arbitration Committees, with the wholehearted collaboration of the

A. F. of L. officialdom, has not been able to keep down the rising anger of the masses or halt the mounting strike wave. Capitalists generally were willing to accept the Roosevelt demagogy as useful in 1933, after the bank crash when, as General Johnson said: "Both industrial and banking leadership had fallen in the public mind to complete and utter disrepute." But now that their profits are mounting again, while the working class is breaking from control of all their elaborate machinery, they are beginning to ask whether this demagogy has not outlived its usefulness.

This is the spirit behind the fascist terror, behind the newly formed American Liberty League, behind the announcement of the steel industry that it will withdraw from the code in order to evade the application of Section 7a; it is behind the proposals for new legislation against general and sympathetic strikes and for government control of the trade unions, etc.

It is a foregone conclusion that the decision of the leading circles of finance capital on these issues will immediately be carried through by the Roosevelt administration, with each step carefully camouflaged by Roosevelt's sweet smile and soft speech about the necessity to protect human rights and property, etc. While the precise forms of such new features as will be introduced into the New Deal cannot yet be accurately forecast, their general direction is clearly along the lines of further legal limitation upon the trade unions, their effectual exclusion from basic industries of mass production, and further progress of fascization.

SPECIAL FACTORS IN THE SAN FRANCISCO STRIKE

In addition to those general influences producing general strike sentiment throughout the country, there were special factors at work in San Francisco, which, combined with the general factors, brought the general strike into being there in 'Frisco and not elsewhere. It is false to seek to explain the higher stage of the strike movement there through any supposed higher level of the radicalization of the workers.

The special factors at work were concrete and measurable things. Chief among them were: First, the San Francisco general strike arose out of a broad industrial general strike of the whole Pacific Coast marine industry. It was thus given a broader base and a sharper appeal than the general strike movement in any other locality. At the same time San Francisco was the *concentration point* of the Pacific Coast marine strike. Second, the strike-breaking A. F. of L. officialdom had no strongholds inside the organizations of the longshoremen, who were the determining driving force in the whole strike movement, while the militant Left-wing elements dominated this strategic center. This factor was due to the extent to which the treachery of the International Longshoremen's Association officials had resulted in wiping out the

San Francisco locals for over ten years and with them the entrenched local bureaucracy, substituting for them the company unions. When the I.L.A. locals arose again in 1933, militant elements who built these unions kept them in the control of the rank-and-file. Third, the extreme open-shop, union-smashing program of the Pacific Coast employers and the government, centering in San Francisco, who had refused to adopt the Roosevelt demagogy of the New Deal, with its tactic of combining corruption of trade union officialdom, arbitration boards, etc., and double-meaning promises to the workers, and had by its open threats roused all existing trade unions to the realization of immediate life-and-death danger. The Left-wing and Communist groupings, small and of comparatively recent origin, were thus enabled to exercise a mass influence out of the ordinary proportion to their number and maturity. This favorable relation of forces placed the revolutionary elements, with Communists in the center, at the head of this great elementary upheaval.

What were the decisive features of the Pacific Coast marine strike? The marine workers on the Pacific Coast were able to develop a general strike movement while on the Atlantic Coast and in the Gulf ports, although suffering even worse conditions, they could not do so. This is due to the relatively weaker position of the American Federation of Labor officialdom, in the first place the officials of the International Longshoremen's Association, headed by Joseph Ryan of New York. This weak position was not confined to San Francisco, but arose out of the betrayal of the longshoremen's and seamen's strike in 1920-22. In those struggles the marine workers had learned two main lessons, namely: (1) that divided action and leadership among the marine unions, faced with a united enemy, brought defeat, and (2) that this division was deepened and accentuated by the national officials of their own unions. In some of the local unions that survived the period since 1922, militant rank-and-file elements thus came to leadership. To this Left-wing nucleus was added in 1933 the decisive influence of the rank-and-file militants who revived the longshoremen's union in San Francisco, Seattle, Portland, San Diego, San Pedro, and which in San Francisco played the decisive role from the beginning.

Thus it was that the regular routine N.R.A. strike settlements broke down in the Pacific Coast marine strike. Through rank-and-file initiative the Pacific Coast Conference was held in February, formulated demands and decided upon strike action to enforce them. The I.L.A. officials, unable to head off the movement, in March appealed to Roosevelt for direct intervention. Roosevelt's promise to adjust the demands succeeded in postponing the strike, but after two months of the usual N.R.A. procedure, producing nothing for the workers, the local union took matters into their own hands and called the strike on May 9.

It is interesting to note that on May 9 when the decision for strike was taken by the San Francisco longshoremen, this decision came as a surprise to the officials of the A. F. of L. and the International Longshoremen's Association, and *at the same moment came as a surprise to the revolutionary group, the leader of which spoke against the decision to call the strike at that moment.*

HOW THE M.W I.U. SPREAD THE STRIKE

Up to the point of the beginning of the strike, the Marine Workers' Industrial Union had played a minor role. In the organization of the longshoremen it had thrown its full support to those militants who had revived and reorganized the International Longshoremen's Association's locals, and had refrained from all competitive organization among them, concentrating its independent organizational activities upon the seamen, who were almost entirely unorganized. The International Seamen's Union had relatively few members. Its activities were confined to that of a group of hard-boiled trade union bureaucrats, typified by Paul Scharrenberg, maintained not by the workers, but pursuing independent careers as labor politicians. The I.S.U. officials allowed no membership meetings. They even refused to recruit new members. They set themselves solidly against the seamen being involved in the strike. But with the docks tied up, the seamen on every ship that came to port, burning with their own grievances, fired by the dockers' example, were eager for strike action. The only organizing center they could find was the Marine Workers' Industrial Union, which openly entered the situation, calling the seamen to strike, opened recruiting halls, recruited over 800 seamen in a brief time, tying up every ship which came into port. This intervention of the M.W.I.U. was decisive in breaking the official A. F. of L. embargo on general action in the industry. In order to maintain even a pretense of representing the seamen, the I.S.U. was forced, finally, to declare itself on May 19 for the strike and begin recruiting and call meetings. As a result of this the small unions of harbor workers of various crafts were also soon drawn into a complete industrial general strike. It was thus that the energetic action of an independent industrial union was the essential factor that brought into the battle the other A. F. of L. unions, made the strike general, and laid the basis for the next forward step, the setting up of the Joint Strike Committee of all unions, and the signing of a Solidarity Pact between all the striking organizations.

It was the conscious and growing spirit of industrial solidarity among all the marine crafts, eventually crystallized during the course of the strike in the Joint Strike Committee and the Solidarity Pact, which again and again defeated all efforts of Joseph Ryan, International Longshoremen's Association head, and Edward McGrady, Roosevelt's representative, to bring about a separate settlement for longshoremen along the lines of the notorious auto and steel industry settlements. It was this which after the defeat of Ryan's second attempt to sell out the strike enabled the militants to carry through the slogan "All Power to the Rank and File Strike Committee" and publicly declare that Ryan had no right to speak for the strikers, repudiating him in a great public mass meeting. These events demonstrated the enormous importance and power of elected strike committees responsible and reporting back to the members and taking complete control of strike negotiations and settlements.

THE PROBLEMS OF THE ORGANIZED RETREAT

The San Francisco general strike in the ninth week of the marine workers' struggle, brought the whole marine movement to a climax. The betrayal of the general strike discouraged and choked off similar solidarity movements on the verge of explosion in Portland and Seattle. The expressed intention of the Vandeleur gang of betrayers was to smash not only the general strike movement, but also the whole Pacific Coast marine strike and take the marine unions out of the hands of the militant rank-and-file. It was the firm determination of the trade union bureaucrats and the employers that the ending of the San Francisco general strike would be followed by a demoralized rout of the marine workers. But they reckoned without the steadying influence of the organized rank-and-file strike committees, and the firm guidance given by the Communist Party in this critical moment. It was, however, the judgment of the strike committees that under these conditions, the strike could not hold out much longer. They decided that a retreat was necessary, but this retreat was an organized one, salvaging all possible gains, however small, out of the betrayal by the officialdom, and guarding to the last moment, as a matter of proletarian honor, the sacredness of the Solidarity Pact between the marine unions.

The strikers and their committees stood firm, with the result that after a few days the capitalists announced new concessions to the workers. This appeared in the newspapers in the extraordinary form of a joint statement issued by a meeting of the Industrial Association, the Shipowners' Union, all independent shipping companies, and the six daily newspapers in the San Francisco Bay area. This statement in substance recognized the Solidarity Pact of the marine unions by, for the first time, agreeing to settle with all the unions simultaneously and by the same procedure. Previously they had stood fast for arbitrating only the demands of the longshoremen and refusing any consideration to the demands of the other unions. They further agreed to the hiring of workers without discrimination at the docks, thus in effect abolishing the company-union hiring system, although not accepting the demand for union-controlled hiring halls.

On the basis of these concessions, they proposed all demands relating to wages and working conditions be submitted to the arbitration of the President's Board. The Strike Committee agreed to submit these questions to a referendum of the membership, at the same time passing a special motion reaffirming the Solidarity Pact which required that an affirmative vote by the longshoremen would only take effect when and if the proposal was ratified by the other unions involved. The marine strike continued solid for another week, while the votes were being taken on the entire coast and organizational guarantees established for the simultaneous return of all marine unions in all ports. The ending of the marine strike is an outstanding example of orderly retreat in a defeated strike.

THE ROLE OF THE COMMUNIST PARTY
IN THE STRIKES

That the open shop offensive of the California employers was beaten back and the trade union movement on the Coast generally is stronger than ever, is in the first place to the credit of the Communist Party which placed itself at the head of the militant rank-and-file, helping them to find organizational forms for their struggle, to establish rank-and-file leadership, to defeat the intrigues of the A. F. of L. bureaucracy in many critical moments of the strike, and when the strike was finally betrayed, leading them in orderly retreat which salvaged some basic gains from the struggle.

It was the concentration work of the Communist Party on the waterfront, especially in San Francisco and Seattle, which consolidated the nucleus of militant leadership in 1932 and 1933, which in February, 1934, crystallized in a Coast-wide rank-and-file delegates' conference that organized the marine strike, making it general along the whole Coast. It was the stubborn struggle of this leadership which kept the strike out of the hands of Joseph Ryan of the I.L.A., and defeated his repeated attempts to sell out the strike, break up the solidarity of the marine unions, and send them back to work demoralized and disrupted. It was this solid leadership in the heart of the marine strike, that made it possible to develop the general strike movement against the will of the A. F. of L. leaders in San Francisco, Vandeleur & Co. The work of the Communist Party brought this elemental upheaval to a higher level of consciousness and organization than any previous great labor struggle in America.

With the rise of the anti-Communist terror, at the ending of the strike, the Party went through a testing by fire, all along the Coast. It was driven underground, all known premises destroyed, printing plant burned down in San Francisco, hundreds assaulted by fascist vigilantes, more hundreds thrown into prison, private homes were violated and smashed, vigilante and police dragnets hunted down all known Communists and sympathizers, even the homes of suspected middle- and upper-class sympathizers were attacked.

The Party stood up very well under these attacks, especially in San Francisco and Seattle. The Party committees never ceased to function, nor lost their connections with the main body of the lower organizations. Connections with the masses was maintained by a constant stream of leaflets, both from the District Committees and from the units on their own initiative. We must verify all of these things because as yet we have only very fragmentary reports and we should have further reports of the functioning of the Party organizations, especially the lower organs of the Party during the strike. However, we can say that there was sustained connection with the masses through the issuance of literature, initiative by the lower organs in getting out leaflets, etc. We also have what is usually a very important indicator for the Center—the continued growth of the dues payments throughout this period down to today.

Already on August 1 in San Francisco the Party broke through the terror, holding an open public meeting under the auspices of the American League Against War and Fascism; within two weeks the *Western Worker* appeared again, as well as the *Voice of Action* in Seattle. In both of these main cities where the terror was sharpest, the Party came through this most severe test in a manner which must obtain our approval. The Party never ceased to function. We can be proud of the fact that these two important districts, in this most difficult situation, showed their ability in this respect. Similar conditions have existed in Alabama, District 17, in connection with the strike movement there, with arrests, confiscation of the *Southern Worker*, etc. Here also a young district, with relatively few members, stood up excellently and strengthened the Party during the struggle. The same sort of experience can be reported from Southern Illinois, which has gone through an exactly similar period of fascist terror, and in which the Party has been strengthened in the course of the fight.

WEAKNESSES AND MISTAKES IN THE STRIKES

However, we must not spend too much time congratulating ourselves upon our achievements. More important for us is to give some detailed attention to the mistakes and weaknesses of our Party, in the first place of the Party leadership, in the most important struggle in San Francisco. There are such weaknesses, mistakes, we must say, notwithstanding the excellent work of the Party, a series of weaknesses and mistakes showed themselves in the course of the strike. In conducting a self-critical examination, we by no means want to set up a standard of perfection. We do not demand that our comrades shall be all-conquering heroes—that is too much to demand of our comrades. We cannot demand that they shall always be victorious, or that they always defeat the enemy the moment he comes on the scene. It is not in this sense we make our criticism. But we must do our best always to see that no mistakes of political orientation shall serve to weaken the struggle.

Our comrades in California made such mistakes of orientation— serious ones. In the struggle against the A. F. of L. official strike-breakers, our leading cadres saw the main danger to be guarded against as coming from the "Left," in the form of stupid or clumsy or un-timely exposure, which the masses would not be prepared to accept. They saw no danger or very little, from the Right; from lagging behind in the exposure, or entirely failing in this central task. Against "Left" deviations the comrades were very, very sensitive. But Right deviations they could not see at all. As a result, they made Right deviations of the most serious kind.

When Ryan went to the Coast to make his first sell-out effort, our comrades were of the opinion that his past record of strike-breaking activities, which should have been popularized among the broadest masses before he arrived, was not of particular advantage to the masses in California. The comrades seemed to think that anything happening outside of California was not a legitimate subject for criticism inside of California; they had no warning lesson to the strikers to whom Ryan was coming as their international president. When Ryan was defeated in his first sell-out, and retreated, in order to gain a second chance to sell out, the opinion was expressed, and not fought against, that this maneuver of Ryan's should be greeted as a conversion of Ryan to the point of view of the Strike Committee, under the illusion that if this was not true, it was at least clever tactics for us to make it seem that way!

This completely wrong conception of what is clever tactics was not criticized by our comrades, except in the form of making the expression of it more vague when it got into the *Strike Bulletin*. When the Central Committee and the *Daily Worker* criticized this vague formulation and pointed out what was behind it, the comrades were quite indignant against us. They thought we were hunting for small things to be hyper-critical about. They even protested against us in the columns of the *Western Worker*. They did not understand the serious danger behind this seemingly small matter. There was even rising (as in the case of Comrade Morris, editor of the *Western Worker*, who expressed this tendency in a sharp form) something like a theory that precisely what the Central Committee was pointing out as weaknesses and mistakes were really the greatest virtues of the leadership in California. Comrade Morris seemed to think that these mistakes out there were destined to become the dominating line of the Party nationally in its trade union work, and were correcting the whole Party's trade union line.

Comrade Jackson, a very militant, courageous comrade, whom we all value very much, under the influence of this tendency in the California leadership, wrote a letter to the Central Committee after we

had raised a few points of criticism, in which he invited us to leave
the direction of the strike in the hands of those on the scene, and for
the Central Committee to busy itself with the more fruitful tasks of
organizing strike relief on a national scale!

Comrade Darcy's article in *The Communist* of July, while very
valuable for the information it contained, and treating many separate
questions correctly, took its main orientation from this mistaken point
of view, which even brought an approving thesis from the Lovestone
group, who saw in this some concession to their trade union line.

It was precisely at the moment when we raised these questions with
the California comrades that the general strike movement began to
rise in San Francisco. And here we received the conclusive proof that
our misgivings were well-founded. Before that, our comrades thought
they had a complete answer to all criticism; they said: "You say we
don't criticize Ryan sufficiently. But look, we kicked him out, we
drove him out of San Francisco." And the comrades thought that
closed the question. But came the general strike, and there we per-
ceived the proofs of our position. The comrades carried on practically
no preparations to expose in any decisive manner the role of the
bureaucrats of the Central Labor Council. Some agitational material
directed against them beforehand, was directed exclusively to attacking
their opposition to the general strike, but not one word of the greater
danger of these fakers at the head of the general strike movement.
When these fakers suddenly made a maneuver to head the movement;
even while they were still openly opposed, by appointing this so-called
Committee on Strategy, our marine workers were so unprepared for
this maneuver that the mere announcement of it was sufficient for them
to practically disband the rank-and-file conference that had been called
under our leadership to organize the general strike, to take no decisions
in that conference in spite of the demands from the rank-and-file. Precisely at the moment when the general strike movement was coming
to a head, when the moral leadership of the masses was absolutely in
the hands of the leaders of the marine strike committee, when the
Vandeleur family of fakers was isolated from the masses and stood
exposed before them as opponents of the general strike movement for
which the whole masses had declared themselves—*at that moment* our
leaders declared that inasmuch as Vandeleur and Co. had set up a
committee on strategy, we handed the general strike movement over
into their hands.

When the Committee on Strategy, seeing that the movement was
going over their heads, came out a few days later for the general strike,
our comrades had laid absolutely no basis for any struggle to elect a
General Strike Committee from below. It is true appeals were made
for the election of such committees, but the rank-and-file certainly
didn't feel—had not been prepared to feel—that this was such a burning

issue it should have to be the subject of struggle inside the unions. And no such struggles took place.

It was impossible afterward to remedy the fatal weakness of those 24 hours, when we handed over the leadership of the masses, that was in our hands, into the hands of these discredited fakers.

We have no guarantee, of course, that even the best policy would have succeeded in pulling this leadership from the head of the general strike. But we know that we could have been much stronger, and that by this wrong policy we certainly were guaranteed defeat. Most surely a serious effort to lead the general strike, to take it out of the hands, from the beginning, of Vandeleur & Co., would have strengthened our position many times, have increased the vitality of the general strike so that it would have lasted more than four days—five, six, eight days, stimulated the general strike movement in Portland and Seattle into activity instead of serving to choke them off by giving them an example of a broken general strike. Certainly our whole position would have been improved, the power of the trade unions would have increased, the concessions which were forced out of the employers made more far-reaching, and generally the interests of the workers would have been advanced, the leadership of the workers would have been strengthened.

The comrades in Seattle came out with a more bold policy—at the same time our positions in Seattle were not so strong. Most of the work had to be done from the outside, that is to say, by Party leaflets rather than through inside official positions in the strike apparatus. Comrade Darcy wrongly concludes that our stronger position in the San Francisco strike was a result of our more timid (or, as he would say, more skillful) criticism—that our weakness in Seattle was because of our more bold criticism. But we must reject any such theory. Precisely because of their superior position in San Francisco they could more boldly and effectively carry out this criticism.

When we demand a policy of bold criticism no one can accuse us of asking for stupid, clumsy, untimely criticism. We demand that the criticism be as intelligent, as skillful as possible, that we choose the right moment. But we must insist that in choosing the right moment we do not wait so long for that right moment that we find, as in the San Francisco general strike, for example, that our criticism and warning against the Vandeleurs come after the damage has been done. Here we could quote the old saying that when thieves are around, it is better to lock the barn door before the horse has been stolen.

We must say that in the last days of the strike, our California comrades responded to the pressure of the Central Committee, they improved their work in many respects. Also they made some steps in overcoming the weakness in which the Party appeared before the workers in its own name. . . .

PROBLEMS OF THE UNITED FRONT

I want to review briefly some of the problems of the movement for united action—building the united front. The comrades are familiar with the various proposals that we have made to the Socialist Party National Executive Committee. We are also familiar with the correspondence that developed on these proposals with Norman Thomas, and the action taken just a few days ago by the National Executive Committee in its Milwaukee meeting.

Perhaps we should give a brief characterization of the N.E.C.'s decision as it was reported in the New York *Times*. We have not yet received an official letter that they are reported to have sent to us. Briefly, the action as reported is a rejection of the united front on the grounds that the united front with the Communists would endanger their united front with the A. F. of L. bureaucrats. They cover this up with a platonic endorsement of the idea of a united front, what a good thing it would be if it were possible, and bring out some of the stock tricks to avoid squarely meeting the issue—united action on specific questions. Nowhere do they mention their attitude towards the measures for which we propose united action.

We have already discussed this question in the Political Bureau. In this morning's *Daily Worker* you have an editorial which gives the main lines of our answer to the Socialist Party decision. I must mention in passing, however, that in this editorial there is one mistake, when in speaking of the concrete proposals which we make to the Socialist Party, the editorial speaks of these as "conditions" of the united front. This is wrong. We never made "conditions." We made proposals, which we are ready to discuss, to consider any modifications or limitations that the S.P. wanted to make with regard to them, and to deal with all, or a part, or a single one of these issues. In addition to this editorial, we expect to have within the next few days a formal answer to the Socialist Party, as soon as possible, after we receive their official letter.

In the formal answer we propose to take up precisely as the center of our letter, that question they expressed in the words: "No united action on specific issues is possible between Socialist and Communists except on a basis which also gives hope of ending fratricidal strife within the trade union movement."

We propose that we will quote this from their letter, and raise very sharply a demand for a further explanation of what they mean by this. We will say that there are two possible interpretations of this. It may mean elimination of the fratricidal strife between workers who follow the two parties—the Socialist Party and the Communist Party— in which case we are for the ending of this fratricidal strife and are ready to take all measures necessary to end it and bring all workers together against their common enemy.

On the other hand, this formulation may mean, and to many people it does mean, the ending of the struggle by the Communists against the policy of William Green, Matthew Woll, John L. Lewis, McMahon and Co.—the official leadership of the A. F. of L. Perhaps it means, and for some it certainly means, the demand for the extension of the united front to include those who are part of the Roosevelt governmental machine. And we declare that if this is what they mean by the united front, or conditions for the united front, this condition the Communists will never accept, because this condition is a united front against the working class, making permanent the split in the working class. The fight for the unity of the working class is precisely against this.

We can make use of our letter to the Socialist Party in a broader leaflet which we propose to issue, including this letter, and giving further elaboration of the answers to all of the arguments of the enemies of the united front. This letter is to be addressed to the membership and followers of the Socialist Party and distributed in many hundreds of thousands of copies. We further propose that we will have a special pamphlet dealing with the history of our fight for the united front, especially since March, 1933, reprinting all of our documents and correspondence with the Socialist Party, etc., down to these last letters. A sort of a handbook on the history of this struggle in the United States, a cheap pamphlet, perhaps two or three cents, especially for sale among the S.P. followers, as well as for the better education of our whole Party on this question.

We further propose that in every locality the comrades shall engage in an intensified campaign to approach the lower organizations of the Socialist Party. We must absolutely eliminate any tendency to react to this question by saying, now that the N.E.C. has spoken, we are through with the chapter to win the Socialist Party. Quite to the contrary is our program. This merely opens new efforts to win every branch and member of the Socialist Party from below to the united front.

Any hope of swinging the Socialist Party as a whole and any kind of united action depends entirely upon this basic activity from below. If we do this basic work from below, we do not have to worry as to whether the Socialist Party leadership ever agrees to the united front or not. Because if we do this work from below, we will get the membership, and if we get the membership for united action, we should not worry as to what the leaders are doing. We will worry about them to the extent that they keep their followers away from united struggle.

In addition, we propose that a series of meetings, at least one big meeting in each important district be held at which leading comrades shall report to the workers on this question, inviting leaders of the Socialist Party to come and state their case to the assembled workers, with special attention to get members and followers of the Socialist Party to these meetings.

We must say that in these past months our Party is beginning to understand that for us the united front is a very serious matter. It is a question of fundamental strategy. It is a matter of a long time struggle, a long time perspective, a long time policy. It is not a mere trick in the struggle against the misleaders. It is a basic policy of struggle for the class unity of the workers against the bourgeoisie. Because we more thoroughly understand it in this sense, we are making progress. We have serious developments in the lower ranks of the Socialist Party in practically setting up united front actions—in New Orleans the united front of our Party and the Socialist Party in the magnificent mass demonstration right in between the lines of the rival armed factions of the Democratic Party of Louisiana, demanding that the State and city finances which are being spent in this factional battle over the spoils of corruption should be given to the unemployed, for the relief which had been cut off. This action is being followed up by systematic collaboration by the two parties in New Orleans on current issues, on the calling of a local congress of the American League Against War and Fascism to prepare for the Chicago Congress, etc. In Camden, N. J., the united front August 1 anti-war demonstration was carried out successfully with the participation of the Socialist Party and the Communist Party. A growing number of individual Socialist workers are entering into our struggles; dozens of organizations have demanded of the N.E.C. that it act favorably on our proposals.

The greatest progress has been made among the youth. Without any formal negotiations the Young People's Socialist League and the Young Communist League already find themselves standing upon an agreed platform. This achievement came out of the struggle against the fascist Central Bureau which called the American Youth Congress in which the anti-fascist united front won a complete victory in winning over almost the entire body of delegates to a program entirely opposed to the one proposed by the leaders, with government support, adopting instead a program of struggle against war and fascism, and for the immediate needs of the youth, including unemployment insurance, etc. This victory, the basis of which had already been laid by the Youth Section of the American League Against War and Fascism which. was already a growing united front from below, reaching all strata of youth, now comprises 1,700,000, ranging from Y.M.C.A.'s, Y.W.C.A.'s, church youth organizations, trade union youth sections, settlement houses, etc., clear down to the Y.P.S.L. and Y.C.L. In this, the political center of gravity is the work of our Y.C.L. Practically all the basic proposals and policy came from us or from those circles influenced by us through the unanimous support of this broad youth movement.

The growing movement for united action in the trade union movement is a characteristic feature of the day. In the steel industry, united front conferences included the Steel and Metal Workers' Industrial Union and the Amalgamated Association of Iron, Steel and Tin Workers, in the period of preparations for the strike later choked off by the officials. In the auto industry, serious work in this direction is beginning in Cleveland. In the fur industry, a group of shops are carrying out a united strike of both the A. F. of L. and T.U.U.L. unions, in spite of the bitter opposition of the A. F. of L. officials. In the shoe industry, the struggle for a single industrial union is making progress in spite of the obstacles placed by the reactionary section of the officialdom and their Lovestoneite allies. In the preparations for the great textile strike and in the heat of its first days, we have succeeded in making some decisive moves for unity in Paterson, with possibilities in other places, which had been impossible hitherto when the masses were not in motion. In Paterson our small Textile Workers' Union has amalgamated with the United Textile Workers' locals, with two of our outstanding leaders placed on the executive board, membership secured by exchange of cards, with full rights.

The key point in the whole united front struggle at the moment is the Second U. S. Congress Against War and Fascism to be held in Chicago, September 28-30. In connection with this is a special Youth Congress called by the Youth Section. In the American League Against War and Fascism and in this Congress, we have a broad united front which met and defeated the attempts made to disrupt it last spring. We must say that the Communists have not given the League the help and attention that it deserves and there has been too much of a tendency to place the daily functioning of the League into the laps of the middle class elements.

These elements are valuable; their contribution to the League has been considerable, but they will themselves be the first to admit that the most important work of the League—rooting it among the workers in the basic and war industries, cannot be done by them, but only the trade unions and workers' organizations, and first of all by the Communists. The final work of the Congress in the next three weeks must mark a decisive improvement in the work in this field—engaging of the workers' organizations in this Congress and into active affiliation in the American League.

The biggest political struggle now going on in the United States is the fight for unemployment insurance. The great movement for the Workers' Bill is now taking on a broader form with the preparations for the Social Security Congress in Washington at the time the U. S. Congress opens. It is clear that the time is ripe for broadening the organizational base of the movement such as is proposed in this Congress for Social Security. The sweep of support for the Bill in the A. F. of L. unions which has carried unanimous endorsement in five national union conventions—Molders' Union, Amalgamated Association, United Textile Workers', Mine, Mill and Smelter Workers' Union, Full Fashioned Hosiery Workers'; the endorsement by the City Councils of 48 cities and towns, including Milwaukee, Minneapolis, Buffalo, Canton, Toledo, St. Louis, Bridgeport, Portland, Des Moines, Allentown, Rockford—in 15 States, endorsement by over 5,000 outstanding professionals; the American Newspaper Guild, innumerable locals of the S.P. and lately Norman Thomas; the Farmer-Labor Party of Minnesota; practically all important independent unions, including Progressive Miners'; by practically all mass unemployed organizations, even those under the control of the enemies of the Bill, who have been forced by mass pressure to endorse it. All these things—and we must mention the American Youth Congress which unanimously endorsed the Bill— all this disclosed a mass support for our Bill which if it can be concentrated and centralized will be a mighty power to force the adoption of this Bill at the coming session of Congress next January.

We have many questions coming up out of this movement for united front which we have to clarify continually to our Party. We find obstacles being placed in the way, questions being raised as to whether we are not making serious opportunistic deviations when we reach out and get these masses into these movements. For example: we have questions raised around the participation of Father Devine, the "Negro God," in the anti-war movement. Father Devine brought his followers into the August 4 demonstration of the American League Against War and Fascism; previous to that in the demonstration of National Youth Day, and the participation of this section with its fantastic slogans aroused very grave doubts in the minds of many comrades whether it wasn't a serious mistake to allow these religious fanatics to march in our parade with their slogans: "Father Devine is God"; "Father Devine Will Stop War," etc.

We have answered this question in editorials in the *Daily Worker*. We must emphasize the correctness of this answer which we have given to point out that this is not a special, isolated problem. This problem is perhaps an exaggerated example of the whole problem of reaching the backward masses and bringing them into participation with the most advanced section of the working class in revolutionary struggles. This is our task—not only to bring in the already politically developed vanguard of the workers, but to bring in the millions of masses who will bring with them all their religious superstition, all of their reactionary ideology and to clarify them and to give them political consciousness in the course of the fight. This is the basic task of the united front; and don't think that this merely applies in the aspect of the fight against superstition among the Negroes. You will find exactly the same religious ideology in broad sections of the white working class, and especially you will find it among the broad masses in the Middle West and West of the United States. I grew up right in the midst of just such religious fanaticism, and when I was a boy it was taken for granted that if you were a Socialist, you must at the same time explain which one of the religious sects you belonged to. That went along with socialism in Kansas in the period of 1906-10. This condition is not over. Many workers moving into the struggle are very often carrying with them some extreme religious prejudices. We have to learn to bring them into the struggle and in the process of the struggle to educate them; not first to educate them and make good Leninists of them and then bring them into the Party.

The mass demand for united action is clearly growing into a mighty movement. This is even moving such "advocates of unity" as the Muste group. These estimable gentlemen only a year ago, on two occasions, met with us in formal open conferences of delegates from many organizations, and pledged themselves to united action for the Workers' Unemployment Insurance Bill, for unification of the mass organizations of the unemployed, and for the fight against war and fascism in the American League, whose program was produced by a committee of which Muste was chairman; but they didn't seem to take these public pledges very seriously, never did anything to carry them out, and after months of sabotage they broke away from these united front agreements without any explanation. Now, we received a letter from Mr. Muste and Mr. Budenz. They propose to start a long proceeding of negotiations with us and the S.P., together with their Trotzkyite and Lovestoneite friends, at what they call a "round table" on how to get unity. These gentlemen should understand that the best way to get unity is to carry out agreements when they are made. However, if mass pressure from below is again moving them from their position of open sabotage, we will not give them a negative answer. They deserve serious attention as long as they still exercise some mass influence among the unemployed in three states. We shall propose that those issues closest to the masses whom they influence, namely, the Workers' Bill, the unity of unemployed organizations— these should be made the beginning of some real actions toward unity without wasting too much time in again talking over the state of the whole world. Let them take one single move toward united action among the masses and our faith in their serious support of a more general unity will be raised above zero. Our attitude toward all minor groupings, or leaders, such as the Musteites, is determined by the question whether they have any mass following and where, and on the issues that relate to the daily life of the masses that follow them we will negotiate united actions with them. But by no means do we accept the idea which is being carefully cultivated by enemies of united action, that the united front means to bring the S.P. and C.P. together with the small groups of renegade leaders like the Trotzkyites, the Lovestoneites, the Musteites, the Gitlowites, the Weisbordites, etc., etc. We consider that such united front has absolutely nothing in common with the needs of the masses. In this respect we have an illuminating example of the mistake made by the youth in Belgium. Over there, the Y.C.L., the Belgian Y.C.L., met with the Socialist Youth organization and the Socialist Youth brought forward a proposal as the basis for the united front that they come out for the defense of Trotzky, for the protection of Trotzky against the "persecution" that the capitalists were inflicting upon him. And our Young Communists in their desire for unity at any cost signed their names to the pledge for the defense of Trotzky. That is, to defend the unity of the working class, they would defend the leader of the forces of counter-revolution among the working class. What masses of workers they expect to reach with such a slogan as this is hard to see, because all the Trotzky organizations in all the world combined certainly do not run into even a few thousand. In the face of the burning issues of the class struggle and the fight for bread and civil rights, and against war, against fascism, these people have the nerve to bring forward slogans for the defense of Trotzky, and we have comrades who are even ready to fall for such things! We have to use this example from Belgium as a very severe warning to us against such dangers which will arise here also.

Now, a few words on the textile strike. I refer you to the basic policy which has been outlined in the editorials of the *Daily Worker* to emphasize also that these editorials are political directives of the Political Bureau and Central Committee. Evidently our Party does not understand this fully. We find district leaderships of the Party coming to political conclusions and acting upon them in exactly the opposite sense to the editorials of the *Daily Worker*. We had this in the preparation for the textile strike. The line which we put forward in the *Daily Worker* and also by many special directives to the districts, was the line of preparing for strike struggle. The comrades, however, talked it over among themselves, decided that these A. F. of L. bureaucrats will never lead a real fight, there won't be any real strike; why then should we prepare for it?—it is a waste of time and energy, and nothing was done. Exactly nothing. The comrades were convinced there would be no strike, no matter what we said from the Center, and so they acted upon their conviction. This is really a serious problem for us, comrades, and it represents one of those serious political weaknesses that in different forms we have hammered at time and time again, this idea that the bureaucrats won't lead any struggles. Of course, there will be no struggles if it depends upon the bureaucrats; but it does not depend upon the bureaucrats.

It depends upon the masses. And when the masses are going into the struggle anyway, the bureaucrats go along and head the struggle, and even call the struggle, in order to bring it to an end more quickly. If we believe only that they will never lead the struggle, we disarm ourselves in the fight against the misleaders, as the comrades did in San Francisco in regard to Vandeleur and the general strike. They only shouted that Vandeleur is against the general strike; they did not point out how Vandeleur can mislead the general strike. The comrades make exactly the same mistake in the textile situation. This is no way to fight against the misleaders, this strengthens the bureaucracy whenever the fight really gets under way and prevents us from mobilizing the opposition to block the betrayal of the struggle. . . .

A few words on the question of the drought and our struggle for the Farmers' Emergency Relief Bill. We must say that this problem has not received any attention from the districts, and has not received the serious attention even of the Center. The districts have absolutely neglected it. Every district can do some work among the farmers, every district can reach farmers with the Emergency Relief Bill. We must make this part of the Party's work, not merely of the special apparatus of the Agrarian Commission. In connection with this bill we must point out that many corrections will be made in the form of this bill and will be published in a week or ten days. The amendments that we are making are primarily in the way of eliminating all of those elaborate provisions for farmers' committees to administer the bill, much simplified, and more directly guarding against the creeping in of class-collaboration tendencies and the setting up of confusion among the farmers.

It is necessary to say a few words about the elections. The election campaign is the bearer of all phases of our struggles, that is, it should be. We are making some progress in that direction but there is still too much of a tendency to keep the election campaign separated from the general activity of the class struggle as a departmentalized, specialized form of activity. There is a special weakness in bringing the election campaign into the mass organizations and especially into the trade unions.

In the elections we must give special attention to such issues as the development of the Sinclair movement. The fight against the Sinclair illusions is an essential feature of our whole struggle against social-fascism. Sinclair's type of social-fascism is going to grow in this country. He is going to have a lot of imitators. I am sure that every good "practical politician" in the Socialist Party is searching his heart today to find out how it is that "we practical politicians are sitting around with a few votes; Sinclair goes out and gets half a million." In California the latest was Packard, member of the previous N.E.C. of the Socialist Party, who now announces himself a convert to the

Sinclair program. This will increasingly become a feature of the whole political life of America.

Now, I must say a few words on the *Daily Worker*. First, the circulation. Do you comrades realize the significance of the fact that on the day of the opening of the strike of 600,000 textile workers, the biggest strike the United States has ever seen, the Party extended the circulation of the *Daily Worker* by the "enormous" sum of 7,000 copies? Monday's paper circulated 43,000 and Tuesday's strike special was 50,000. That's our estimate of the value of the *Daily Worker* among half a million striking textile workers. Most of them were not even ordered; we just printed them in the hopes that they would be distributed. And a special textile edition is not just a concession on our part to the needs of the particular industry; a special textile edition is directed to the working class of America. It is just as much of interest to the workers of California and Chicago as it is to the workers of the South and New England.

What can we do to wake up the Party to the question of the *Daily Worker?* We must pose this question as one of the most serious practical matters for the Central Committee and for the Party as a whole. When we will not have the *Daily Worker*, when all our papers will be suppressed, which is quite possible and even probable in the not distant future, when that time comes, when we will have to substitute the *Daily Worker* by the most sacrificing work of printing and spreading small illegal organs at the cost of the sacrifice of lives, then we will wonder what were we doing in the days when we had freedom of action and circulation of a splendid six- and eight-page *Daily Worker*. When we had all this we made no serious attempt to give it a mass circulation. How are we going to answer it? Something must be done to make the Party conscious of the *Daily Worker*. I want to ask everyone to say a word on the matter, to say one word of explanation why we don't go forward seriously in the circulation of our paper. . . .

We must say one or two words about certain features of the Negro work. Especially we must mention some considerable victories that have been achieved in this period. In the first place, the victory of winning the release of Angelo Herndon on bail, of getting the Scottsboro appeal before the Supreme Court again. We can register certain small advances, as yet very small, in raising Negro questions in the work of the trade unions. It is extremely interesting, for example, to hear from the comrades in San Francisco that the Longshoremen's Union is systematically setting itself to break down the Jim-Crow regulations, the exclusion of Negroes from the docks, and as a matter of policy taking in Negro workers into the docks and getting work for them, working side by side with the white longshoremen. Every small sign of work of this kind is "pure gold" for our movement. We must popularize it in order to put much more pressure behind the drive in all the unions to begin to win the basic Negro masses into our trade unions, both the T.U.U.L and the A. F. of L. unions. . . .

I will close with a final word about the problem of cadres. With the rise of the present big mass movement, everywhere there rises the cry for forces. Everywhere you hear the old slogan: we are short of forces; we have no cadres. Again the cry goes up from every district to the National Office: send us more forces. But from where to get these new forces, nobody says. Do we lack forces? I think that we are involved in a serious contradiction if we say that because the working class is rising in great activity, therefore the Communist Party has a greater lack of forces. It is precisely with the rise of the masses to activity that we have released to us tremendous new forces. Why do we cry about a shortage? Because we have not learned to take these forces from the masses and make use of them; because we have too many bureaucratic tendencies reflected in the feeling that nobody can take responsible, leading positions in this mass movement unless he has first gone through our various training schools.

I am a friend of our training schools. I think they have contributed much, but they have also contributed some bad things to the movement. Sometimes our training schools, especially in the districts where not enough attention is paid to them, take a group of good, fresh forces out of the masses and, in from three to six weeks, turn out finished bureaucrats, completely divorced from the masses they just came out of. We have plenty of forces, but we must develop initiative in bringing forward these forces fearlessly, giving them organizational responsibility, helping them and giving them a training and education in the course of the development of their work as leading factors in the movement. In addition, we must have serious development of the school work, which is an essential phase of training of cadres, more serious attention to the type of teaching, more serious check-up in getting a concrete answer to the question—are your teachers teaching Bolshevism or a thousand varieties of Menshevism and Trotzkyism, especially on organizational questions? On these organizational questions there is the widest field for the most fantastic deviations with very little check-up by the districts and sections of the Party.

We have plenty of forces if we learn how to use them. The American working class is ready to give us all the forces we need if we work correctly, go out and get them and bring them into action and show the capacity of bringing these forces into our Party; making them ours. This is the answer to the problem of forces and the answer to the problem of building the revolutionary movement and winning victories in every field of the struggle. This is also the answer to the problem of building a mass Communist Party.

XV

The Situation in the Socialist Party *

WE HAVE a double reason for being interested in and discussing the events that are taking place inside the Socialist Party. The first is the necessity for the Communists to keep up with all the currents of thought, moods and action among all workers including those in the Socialist Party; and the second is the duty which we owe to the Socialist workers who not only ask our opinion on these developments, but who even approach us for information of what is going on in their own party.

A great many developments in the Socialist Party are hidden behind a veil of censorship. There is a sort of martial law in the Socialist Party rising out of the civil war in their ranks. It is very difficult for Socialist workers to learn what is going on inside their own party.

It is hardly necessary for us tonight to review the whole development of the past year in the Socialist Party. We can assume that everyone is generally familiar with the background of the most recent events.

The high-spots of the struggle that is now rending the ranks of the Socialist Party, are of course, the Detroit Convention and the Declaration of Principles and especially the development of the struggle for the united front which is now making deep inroads among the Socialist workers in spite of the fight against the united front by all main leaders.

We can describe the general process taking place as a distinct leftward movement of the rank-and-file members of the Socialist Party and their working-class followers—a movement which is a part of the general radicalization of large masses of the working population in the United States. The response to this radicalization of the workers on the part of the leading elements in the Socialist Party is not uniform. It is quite varied. Out of this variation and difference of opinion as to how to deal with the radicalization of the masses and how to meet the issues as they arise, there has come a series of divisions within the leadership of the Socialist Party.

One of the basic features of the division has been the constant exposure of the bankruptcy of the positions that have been taken up from time to time by the leadership of the Party on various issues of the day, above all on the question of the attitude towards the New Deal, the N.R.A. and the Roosevelt administration generally. The

* Extracts from a speech, February 23, 1935.—*Ed.*

overwhelming majority of the Socialist leaders, you will recall, in the beginning of the New Deal hailed it as a step towards socialism. Norman Thomas, proud of being a non-Marxist, said the New Deal represented about as much as the workers could get under capitalism and that it represented a distinct step in the direction of socialism, although he also admitted that there were certain fascist possibilities within it.

Already, now, this policy of support for the New Deal, the N.R.A., is so thoroughly and completely discredited that the whole position has had to be completely abandoned. This is true not only of the Socialist Party, even the leaders of the American Federation of Labor, firm and loyal servants of Roosevelt as they are, have been forced to break with Roosevelt on the auto code, the N.R.A. Boards, the $50 per month wage on public works, the 30-hour week issue, etc.

In this abandonment of support of the New Deal, the Socialist leaders have not led the way even in relation to the A. F. of L. leadership. They have been driven to abandon their old position by the force of events just as the leaders of the A. F. of L. were driven. We can recall that there was no serious effort even to critically approach the New Deal on the part of the Socialist Party leadership until even the Republican Party finally launched its national attack against the New Deal last year. In this development of the political life of the country as a whole and the part that the Socialist Party leaders played in it, we can clearly see pictured the general process that is taking place, that is, a movement to the Left of the masses of the workers and even considerable sections of the middle class, while the Socialist Party leaders, instead of leading and organizing this Leftward movement, resisted, struggled against it, tried to hold it back. It was only the rise of mass strike movements directed against the N.R.A., its Labor Boards and codes, which finally forced these official leaders to break from open alliance with Roosevelt.

The methods of resisting this development by the leaders have not been uniform. There have been sharp differences of opinion on how to hold back this movement, that explain the break-up of the leadership into various groupings.

There is a growing element of active workers and local leaders in the Socialist Party who are sincerely responding to the Leftward movement of the masses to the best of their ability. These elements, to some degree represented in the Revolutionary Policy Committee and its adherents and also represented in those committees that have been set up in various places in the country for the support of the united front with the Communists (especially in the trade unions and unemployed associations), represent an earnest striving to go along with the Leftward movement of the masses. It has very serious weaknesses and shortcomings, but in general represent a tendency which can only be welcomed, especially insofar as it rallies itself around the united front in immediate class struggles of the day.

Before approaching more concretely the current events within the Socialist Party, we should also say a few words about the position of the Socialist Party leadership towards one of the most burning issues before the country, namely, unemployment and social insurance. As illustrating these general facts that I have just reviewed, we read in the newspapers just a few days ago the announcement on the behalf of the National Executive Committee of the Socialist Party that it had endorsed the Workers' Unemployment, Old Age and Social Insurance Bill (HR 2827) now before Congress. This is the first official word that the Socialist Party as a whole has spoken on this question—this in spite of the fact that the Workers' Bill has been in Congress for considerably more than a year and has been before the country for several years past. This in spite of the fact that the Communist Party and the National Unemployment Councils have made repeated approaches to the Socialist Party proposing united action in support of this Bill and offering to discuss with the Socialist Party any questions they wished to raise with regard to the Bill. This was, further, in spite of the fact that the Labor Committee of Congress itself had officially invited leaders of the Socialist Party to appear before it at its hearing on the Bill.

The Socialist Party was not able to make up its mind. The leadership was not able to speak on this question, to declare itself, until after the Congressional hearings had concluded; and even then, declaring their support of the Bill a conditional support. They appointed, too late, a committee which was supposed to speak for them at the Congressional hearings. To make this seem plausible they named Socialist Party members who had previously appeared at the Congressional hearings as individuals or as representatives of non-party organizations in support of the Bill before they were authorized to speak for the Socialist Party. They were named too late to get to committee hearings.

Previous to this public announcement of support for the Workers' Bill, the Socialist Party leaders and organizations and members have been in a very confused position on the unemployment insurance question. Some have openly supported the Wagner-Lewis Bill, the Administration Bill. Some have supported the Workers' Bill. Others have vacillated between the two unable to make up their minds without guidance from the Party; and even today when the National Executive Committee weakly declares its support of HR 2827, in the same issue of the *New Leader* which announces this, there is also printed an appeal to support the Byrnes Bill in New York, which is an emasculated copy of the Wagner-Lewis Bill.

This very weak and indecisive position on the most burning question before the American masses typifies the paralysis of the Socialist Party leadership today. There is no leader of the Socialist Party today who dares to come before the masses and boldly declare a position in the name of his Party, without fearing he will immediately be repudiated by the other leaders of his Party. This condition in the Socialist Party comes after a period of over ten months of the most intense discussion following a convention, a discussion which culminated in the referendum vote on the Declaration of Principles, in which "democratic procedure" was carried out in a most prolonged and exhaustive fashion such as is rarely seen in political life. But the more the Socialist Party applies these so-called democratic methods, the less it seems to be able to bring about any decisive conclusion to its inner discussion, the less able it is to unite on any well defined program of action, not to speak of a Declaration of Principles.

The referendum vote on the Detroit Declaration of Principles registered a majority for that declaration, a majority which was a victory for the center group, usually identified with Thomas, the Militants, although this is not a unified, homogeneous group, but a block of several groups. This victory for Thomas and his group in the referendum did not result, however, in clearing up the situation in the Socialist Party.

Thomas and his group were frightened by this victory. They did not seem to know what to do with the victory after they got it. They had not fought for the victory while the discussion was going on. They let the Right wing do the fighting, and "let nature take its course." But "nature" produced a victory for Thomas that frightened him and his group.

The result of this fright was that afterwards the National Executive Committee, fresh from its victory, went into the meeting in Boston in December and used its victory in order to surrender to the Right wing. The Right wing brought its forces to the December N.E.C. meeting in a big demonstration. Thomas and the N.E.C. majority backed down completely on their former proposals with regard to the united front, further accepted measures directed against the Revolutionary Policy Committee and its followers, and generally adopted decisions which were dictated by the "defeated" Right wing.

The Thomas group had hoped to work out a compromise with the Right wing on the basis of this capitulation, a compromise which would give the Right wing its political demands, while saving the face of the Thomas group and preserving its position as ostensible leaders of the radicalizing trend among Socialist Party members.

This hoped-for compromise with the Right wing as a result of the concessions made in the December N.E.C. meeting did not materialize. Thomas sacrificed the united front, which was demanded by his followers, but despite this could not buy peace with the Old Guard. In spite of all of the concessions, in spite of all of the practical surrender of the majority of the N.E.C., they could not make peace with the Right wing.

All efforts at a compromise failed. They failed so completely that to-day we see a new outbreak of factional warfare throughout the Socialist Party on a national scale with a sharpness that has never been seen before since 1919 when the Communists were expelled from the Socialist Party.

Thomas' resignation from the staff of the *New Leader* a couple of weeks ago is merely a symptom of that sharp factional warfare that is tearing the Socialist Party to pieces.

What was the cause of the failure to achieve a compromise settlement? We can point out two main causes. The first one was that the Right wing elements, who had been on the offensive from the beginning of the fight, although in a minority, had been taught to have nothing but contempt for the N.E.C. decisions. They had seen time after time majority decisions registered against the Right wing to be followed immediately by surrender to the Right wing. The Right wing therefore was not encouraged to compromise by the surrender of the Thomas group. They therefore sharpened up their demands and increased factional struggle in the Socialist Party instead of slackening it down and creating the conditions for a compromise.

The second factor which brought about this failure is that at the same time the Thomas majority was losing its authority by its incapacity to follow any one line, the Right wing itself was being seriously compromised by the development taking place in the main leadership, *i.e.*, the New York City leadership in the Socialist Party. This Right wing itself is more and more being divided into two tendencies. One of them was entering into official relations with the La-Guardia Fusion Party. This was openly expressed in LaGuardia's appointment of Panken to a judgeship, with the endorsement of the New York Socialist Party leadership, a political alliance which was publicly celebrated at a banquet to induct Panken into his new position, a banquet at which Socialist Party leaders sat side by side with LaGuardia and at which Abe Cahan made a speech in which he welcomed LaGuardia as "one of us."

On the other hand, another part of the New York leadership represented by Waldman was entering into very practical relationships with Tammany Hall.

These two diverse political alliances within the same Right-wing group at the head of the New York Socialist Party not only created the threat of a split among them, but served to seriously discredit the leadership as a whole and make it dangerous for Thomas and his group to conclude the compromise they had in mind.

The extreme belligerency with which the Right wing was conducting its warfare against the Thomas leadership had created a whole series of difficulties for the N.E.C. of the Socialist Party. I will not take time to go into details of this factional fight, but it is necessary to point out a few outstanding developments. First, in the New York City and State organizations there was the developed offensive of expulsions against Left-wingers, against adherents of the Revolutionary Policy Committee, which, while carefully excluding any public declaration that it was directed against Thomas and his group, was actually designed in the first place to undermine the position of Thomas. The New York leaders further reorganized the whole New York Party in such a way as to effectively exclude the militant group from any real participation in the leadership of New York. They organized a whole series of new branches with a careful distribution of their trusted forces in such a way as to secure an iron-clad majority in the City Committee.

At the same time in many Western States, controlled and directed by the Old Guard, they sharpened up the fight against Thomas, the N.E.C. Thus in California a State Convention has been called on the agenda of which is placed the question that the Socialist Party of California will withdraw from the Socialist Party of the U.S.A. pending the repeal of the Declaration of Principles for the declared purpose to safeguard its members from persecutions under the California Syndicalism Law, thus practically declaring Thomas as "illegal."

The Oregon State organization carried through its decision to withdraw from the Socialist Party of the U.S.A. The Oklahoma organization carried through its withdrawal. The Indiana organization was conducting a referendum on withdrawal when Thomas and the N.E.C. finally stepped into the situation, revoked the charter of the Indiana section of the Socialist Party, and seized the records and property of the Indiana organization, proceeding to reorganize the Party and excluding the leadership who had fought against the Declaration of Principles. It was this fight that finally led to the open break between the Old Guard and the Thomas N.E.C., which resulted in Thomas' resignation from the *New Leader* after the *New Leader* refused to publish the statement of the N.E.C.

The New York City and State organization is now in the position of open rebellion against the national leadership of the Party. At the same time rumors are current that they have prepared a list of 50 more expulsions of leading Left-wing elements from the New York Party. Norman Thomas is represented as saying in private conversations that these events have proved that the period of attempted compromise is over and that the attempt was a mistake in the first place. Just in the last few days the Militant faction has had a regional caucus—a caucus of their leading elements throughout the East generally. For some time Thomas had formally kept independent of caucus groups and had publicly criticized the Militants. But this recent caucus meeting received a message from Norman Thomas, I understand, a message of encouragement and support which is generally taken to be a formal, political unification of the faction as an organized group, an endorsement of the general course that was mapped out at this caucus.

The Militants are talking quite bravely now—speaking about demands to be placed before the N.E.C. to reorganize New York—reorganization and reconstituting the membership excluding the Old Guard and restoring the Revolutionary Policy Committee members. There is talk of expelling Waldman from the Socialist Party. With regard to this question of Waldman's position in the Socialist Party, there are even rumors that a section of the Old Guard itself is willing to throw Waldman to the wolves because they find his connection with Tammany is "worse" than their connections with LaGuardia.

It is interesting to note that the renegade from Communism, Gitlow, took a prominent part in the militant caucus. Gitlow was a sort of ideological leader in the caucus. In nothing else is their poverty of leadership so demonstrated as in this pathetic seizing upon the rubbish cleaned out of the Communist Party.

While all this war-like atmosphere prevails in which the Militants come forward as brave fighters against the Right wing, against the Old Guard, it is very instructive to take note that precisely at the same moment, the Thomas majority of the N.E.C. is actually carrying through the pledges that they gave to the Old Guard at the Boston meeting of the N.E.C. in December. That pledge was for an uncompromising struggle against the united front and postponing any consideration of this question until 1936. No matter what the changed relations may be with the Old Guard, this fundamental agreement with the Old Guard they are carrying through 100 per cent. Thus, just a few weeks ago, Clarence Senior, the Secretary of the N.E.C., sent out in the name of the Thomas majority of the N.E.C. a letter of instructions to States and localities from the N.E.C. not to consider any sort of a united front with the Communists. This action was even more drastic than that embodied in the resolution officially adopted in December. In fact, the Old Guard had complained that the December resolution was too lenient in allowing State and local united fronts, so they carried out a referendum vote by mail after the N.E.C. meeting, changing the decision so as to prohibit State and local united fronts.

It is clear therefore that the fight which the Thomas group has been forced to take up against the Old Guard does not mean that they are modifying their course toward the Left. The course of the Thomas majority is distinctly to the Right of what it was during last summer and early fall when they were still playing with the slogan of the united front.

What we see taking place within the Old Guard in New York of orientation towards two different camps in bourgeois politics, is to a certain degree taking form on a national scale as between the Thomas group and the Old Guard group. All of the different leading groupings in the Socialist Party are looking forward and speculating upon the shifts that are expected to take place in national politics between now and 1936. That group that is typified by the partnership between Thomas and Hoan, mayor of Milwaukee, has a general orientation of flirting and negotiating for more formal connections with the La-Follette progressive and the Olson group in Minnesota. Their tendency is towards this open middle-class section of the third party movements. The Old Guard is banking upon connections with the more solid elements such as LaGuardia in the New York Fusion movement, even with Tammany itself, and Tammany will probably emerge in the next elections as a fusion movement also. It might even be with Louis Waldman as candidate for mayor. It has orientated more towards the official A. F. of L. leadership, hoping to have a combination of a third party movement with at least a section of the A. F. of L. bureaucracy.

The chances for these two currents to be united in 1936 largely depends upon their finding a common leader from the camp of the bourgeoisie. Possibly they may be united in the new third bourgeois party under the leadership of Huey Long by that time. This is not idle speculation. Although only a few weeks ago it was very fashionable to speak of Huey Long as a clown, in the last few weeks wonderful changes have been taking place. Huey Long is taken into the sacred "progressive" caucus of the LaFollettes, the Shipsteads, the Wheelers.

Another example of the orientation of the Old Guard leadership is to be found in Connecticut. Connecticut is one of the prize show pieces of the Socialist Party leaders. There they have the mayor of Bridgeport, and the city administration. Jasper McLevy, formerly a member of the N.E.C. of the Socialist Party, and one of the leading figures of the Old Guard nationally, is unchallenged boss, unchallenged effectively so far in the Socialist Party of Connecticut. His election victories have been hailed as one of the outstanding achievements of the Socialist Party. This morning's *Daily Worker* reports a very typical example of what is going on among the Connecticut leaders, in the McLevy group. One of McLevy's associates, Mr. Harry Bender, Socialist representative from Bridgeport in the state legislature, introduced a bill calling for the establishment of the oath of loyalty by teachers and all employes of the State educational institutions, a law which is a direct response to the campaign of Hearst and which is along the lines of the notorious Ives Law in New York. This is such an open reactionary measure that no Republican in the State of Connecticut could be found to introduce it, and a section of the Republicans are criticizing this proposal as too reactionary for them.

At the same time there are even more serious things going on in Connecticut. McLevy's group in the State legislature has formed an

alliance with the Republican party for the control of the State. Local
newspapers are openly speaking about the fact that McLevy, as they
say, "is becoming too big for his Party." McLevy is now a very serious factor in State politics, more serious than his Party. They do not
take his Party so seriously, McLevy they take very seriously. They
have excellent reasons to take him seriously, because he is going along
with all the measures of the Republicans in his State. At such a time
as this, in face of the fact that the Socialist Party organization went
on record against the sales tax in Connecticut, McLevy has openly been
working for the sales tax and includes the revenues from it in his proposed budget for the city of Bridgeport.

It is generally known and discussed in Connecticut that McLevy is
negotiating a form whereby his alliance with the Republicans will be
made more organic and open with a view towards electing McLevy as
the next governor of Connecticut with the support of the Republicans.
The form of this fusion with the Republican Party may perhaps be
covered by the name of "Labor Party." The Labor Party fig-leaf will
be provided by a group of Republican A. F. of L. leaders in the State
of Connecticut. It is quite within the realms of possibility that we
may see this fusion with the Republican party in Connecticut with
such a fake label of Labor Party and possibly we may see the fusion
even without that fake label. We have in the figure of McLevy in
Connecticut a perfect American imitation of Ramsay MacDonald.

Meanwhile what is going on with the Revolutionary Policy Committee? The R.P.C. has played a role which does not measure up in
practice to the possibilities that it has within the Socialist Party. It
has not been able to rally around itself the Left-wing trends, the revolutionary trends among the Socialist Party members. This weakness
has been due to the lack of homogeneity in the R.P.C. leading group.
It is not uniform either in ideas, or in social position, subject to vacillations and retreats, which hamper its effectiveness as a revolutionary
force. It tries to maneuver in this very complicated situation within
the Socialist Party. Maneuvers are of course necessary in practical
political life, but the trouble with the maneuvers of the R.P.C. is that
most of them turn out to be retreats. They are maneuvers which are
undertaken without having established any base to maneuver from,
and without having established some advanced objective that they are
maneuvering towards. The result is that most of their maneuvers degenerate into futility. For example, to illustrate this general criticism
of the work of the R.P.C., we have their recent announcement that
they had requested their former chairman and secretary, J. B. Matthews
and Ruth Shallcross, to resign. Why did they request these leading
figures to resign? Because the association embarrassed them in the
inner-Party struggle since Matthews and Shallcross had published a
book in which they came out very sharply and categorically against

the Old Guard in New York and characterized them as counter-revolutionaries, and at the same moment Matthews had declared openly for serious united front activities. Surely any fighting Left wing within the Socialist Party should welcome the development of two of its leaders taking a strong and bold position in spite of previous vacillations. But the R.P.C. seems to consider boldness as the most dangerous thing in the inner-Party struggle and when two of its leaders become bold, they are asked to resign.

These criticisms are made in the most friendly spirit. We are quite friendly disposed to the efforts of the R.P.C. to find the path of revolutionary struggle in the United States.

Because we have a friendly attitude towards every revolutionary effort, no matter how confused, we consider that the best help is friendly criticism. This kind of politics in the fight within the Socialist Party is merely dragging along at the tail of Norman Thomas and Centrism. It has the same relation towards the Thomas Centrist Militant group that Thomas has towards the Old Guard—the same formal opposition while surrendering the essential political positions.

Why do we criticise the Thomas group so sharply? Because in practice it carries out the line of the Old Guard. That is something every Socialist worker must understand if he expects to travel along the revolutionary path. It is not possible to find the class struggle line while carrying out a policy which is daily surrender to those who are in secret alliance with the old political machines. What is true of Thomas and his group in relation to the Old Guard is true, in spite of all the best intentions, of the Revolutionary Policy Committee in relation to Thomas. Every time they attempt to be "clever tacticians," they repeat on a small scale what Thomas carries through in relation to the Old Guard. This is not serious politics. This is the politics of surrender, of Ramsay MacDonald—typical Social-Democratic opportunism—and is not improved because it is dressed in nice revolutionary-sounding phrases.

We have to speak so clearly, even when we are talking to the Revolutionary Policy Committee, whose intentions we have the greatest regard for. If our advice is worth anything to them, it has to be along these lines: take a bold and principled position and fight for it; establish thereby a center around which can rally the large majority of workers who are really for united front of struggle, who are against the capitalists and the capitalist political machine.

We think we know the members and followers of the Socialist Party even better than many leaders of the Socialist Party. We have had quite a bit of experience coming in contact with Socialist Party workers. When some Socialist leaders say to us: "Yes, we are for the united front personally, but the members are against it; and we believe in democracy," we answer: "We know your members better than you do.

You cannot place the responsibility on the Socialist workers." No, that responsibility has to be placed on the leaders who are blocking the workers in achieving their desire which is to fight shoulder to shoulder with the Communists.

If there is to be any stop put to the growing demoralization among the Socialist Party members and supporters; if we are to prevent a large mass of these workers from being disgusted and dropping out of activity; if we are to bring these members into the class struggle without allowing them to fall by the wayside—it is necessary that we Communists not only do everything to help these workers and establish working relations with them—(we are doing our best to overcome all our past weaknesses in this respect, we are learning how to work with all these workers)—while we do this, we have a perfect right to call on those who aspire to revolutionary leadership among the Socialist Party workers, to ask them to adopt effective tactics of the united front, to come out boldly and courageously, raising high the banner of working-class unity, and to join their efforts with ours in this fight for the uniting of all the revolutionary forces of the working class.

It is in the light of our most earnest and sincere desire to achieve this unification as quickly and effectively as possible that we criticize the past and to some extent the present tactic of the Revolutionary Policy Committee elements and many who are associated with them in the struggles now going on in the Socialist Party.

There is a burning necessity for unity on the every-day issues of the class struggle. There is a necessity that that unity be fought for everywhere where workers are organized. The issue of the Workers' Bill (HR 2827) is merely an outstanding example of a dozen issues upon which working-class unity can and must be built, such as unification of the unemployed organizations, the strike struggles and building the trade unions, the program of the American League Against War and Fascism. The Communists are prepared to cooperate with everyone who is ready to fight for that unity. We are sure that the final solution of all problems of class struggle will only be achieved when one party—the Communist Party—has won the leadership of the overwhelming mass. But we recognize that this process of organic unity goes through a period more or less protracted. We must at once establish a unity which begins with and is forged around immediate issues that can unite groups and organizations of different ideologies and political opinions. It is this *immediate united front* we are fighting for now because it represents not only the life needs of the masses today, but it also represents the highway towards revolutionary achievements and struggles, toward the defeat of our class enemies, towards revolution and the reconstruction of society.

This is why we fight for unity. It is from this point of view we evaluate current events in the Socialist Party.

XVI

The Communist Position on the Labor Party Question *

THE Communist Party is now discussing the change in tactics proposed by its Central Committee on the question of a Labor Party. After five years in which we opposed all proposals to make the Labor Party a practical issue, we have now changed this negative attitude, we now come forward as the advocates of a Labor Party to be built upon the basis of federating the trade unions and other workers' mass organizations, on a platform of the immediate issues of the class struggle.

We make no change in principle in the Party line. Our approach remains the same as that formulated in the Sixth World Congress, in 1928, which, on the proposal of Stalin, resolved unanimously:

> On the question of the organizing of a Labor Party, the Congress resolves: That the Party concentrate its attention on the work in the trade unions, on organizing the unorganized, etc., and in this way lay the basis for the practical realization of the slogan of a broad Labor Party organized from below.

This decision registered the fact that the issue of a Labor Party, as a practical mass question, had passed into the background. Since 1929, any attempt at a Labor Party could only have resulted in either a new appendage to the old parties of the bourgeoisie, or else a mere substitute for the Communist Party with all its weaknesses and none of its strength.

The events of 1934 begin to place this question in a new light. Mass disintegration of the old two-party system has begun. A new mass party, to the left of and in opposition to Roosevelt, will in all probability occupy the foreground by the time of the 1936 presidential elections.

For the opportunists and renegades this is the end of the question, but for us this is only the beginning. For them this development is welcomed because it contains within itself the opportunity to find substitutes for the Communist Party, find means to lead the masses away from class struggle into class collaboration, find the channel to lead those who break away from one bourgeois party immediately into another essentially the same. We Communists look for precisely the opposite elements of the situation, we seek to make the break with the old parties mean a break with the bourgeoisie, we seek to lead these

* Speech at St. Nicholas Palace, New York, February 10, 1935.—*Ed.*

masses onto the path of class struggle, to break the power of the class-collaboration leadership, to bring the working class face to face with the problem of state power, the problem of which class shall wield this power.

Thus in no way do we bring forward the Labor Party as a substitute for the Communist Party. For us, it is merely a part of our struggle to build and strengthen the Communist Party itself among the masses, to extend its authority, to root its principles, tactics and organization deeper among the masses. We stress this even more today, precisely because life itself places the Labor Party as a practical question of the moment; precisely because we are now pledging our readiness to actively participate in the establishment of a Labor Party, all the more must we insist that the Communist Party is the indispensable weapon of the working class, without which it can neither fight successfully for its immediate needs nor find the way out of capitalist oppression into the new socialist society.

To successfully bring those millions now being disillusioned about the New Deal, over fully to the revolutionary path, is, however, a process that can only be completed over a period in which their own experience teaches them, and in which the persistent, unwavering, growing work of the Communist Party completes their education.

Every day brings new evidence of the extremely rapid breaking of the old political bonds. Events of the past two weeks are of historic importance in this respect. Roosevelt's decision on the Jennings Case, in which he threw the Government on to the side of the newspaper publishers and against the Newspaper Men's Guild (incidentally forgetting in most cynical fashion, his direct demagogic promises to the officers of the Guild) was the first open repudiation of the demagogy which has become famous as the National Run Around. Heywood Broun, president of the Guild, coined a clever *bon-mot* when, commenting on this decision, he said: "The newspaper owners cracked down on the President, and the President cracked-up." But this wise-crack could not hide the fact that what really cracked-up was Broun's illusions about Roosevelt and the New Deal. It had become impossible any longer to maintain the fiction that Roosevelt's administration does, or wishes to, aid the labor movement; the fact has emerged before the eyes of millions that Roosevelt heads the offensive of monopoly capital in its determination to save profits at the cost of the degradation of the life of the masses. Broun, who used to write laudations of Roosevelt in his column in the Scripps-Howard newspapers, who regularly reproved the Communists for their "short-sighted" opposition to and exposure of Roosevelt and the New Deal, is silenced on these questions in his column, since his new "revelation." His boasted "freedom of the press" was freedom only to praise Roosevelt and damn the Communists. As a trade union executive whose organization has felt the heel of Roosevelt's boot on its face, he must find other channels for his protests. Broun's education is important only because it typifies a similar process going on in the minds of millions.

Roosevelt's renewal of the automobile code and the Wolman Board, which even Wm. Green and the A. F. of L. Council did not dare go along with any longer, even though they were jointly responsible with Roosevelt for its establishment last March, has brought the whole question to a head. Green himself is forced to repeat the words of the Communist Party, that the New Deal is introducing fascism. Just a month after the C. P. announced its present Labor Party policy, Green finds it necessary to "threaten" Roosevelt with the prospect of a Labor Party led by the A. F. of L. Executive Council. Such a threat by Green cannot frighten Roosevelt very much, knowing as he does by practical experience, the narrow limits of the "fighting" ability of these "leaders," but behind that is the more real threat of a Labor Party over the heads of Green & Co., just as the real strike threat is never that voiced by the A. F. of L. leaders, but that which threatens to go over their heads.

At the 53rd Convention of the A. F. of L., the Communists called for the withdrawal of all trade union representation in the New Deal committees and Labor Boards; we were denounced as impossibilists and disrupters by Green, by Thomas, by Lovestone. Today Green & Co. are forced to take the path we pointed out then, or stand forever discredited before their membership.

The open bankruptcy of the A. F. of L.—Socialist Party leadership's policy towards the New Deal, creates at once the most serious danger of destruction of the trade union movement by the sharpened capitalist attack, and at the same time the opportunity to revive the trade unions with a new policy and a new leadership. Equally important, it opens wide the doors of the labor movement for the development of a real mass Labor Party. The change for a deep-going regeneration of the trade unions is exemplified, above all, by the most promising and healthy rank-and-file movement that has arisen among the steel workers in the Amalgamated Association of Iron, Steel and Tin Workers, which the officials are combating with terrorism and mass expulsions.

Not a single argument of the slightest plausibility can longer be raised, in the light of these events, against the decision on Labor Party policy adopted by the Central Committee of the Communist Party. Already it has been endorsed by the overwhelming majority of our membership, without a single vote against it, and with only a few scattering abstentions. What remains, however, is the mastering of the thousands of detailed problems involved in carrying this policy out in life. It depends upon our practical work to decide what this policy will look like in life.

The major problem connected with the Labor Party is the fight to prevent the mass movement of millions, breaking away from the old parties, to be drawn into the channels of a third capitalist party, a "progressive" party of the LaFollette type.

There does not yet exist a clearly-defined Labor Party movement. There is only the beginning of a mass break-away, within which a struggle is going on between two main class forces. These two forces are those who, on the one hand, will move heaven and earth to prevent this movement going beyond the limits of the fundamental interests of monopoly capital, of profits and private property in the means of production; and, on the other hand, those who would throw this movement into struggle against capital, for the preservation and improvement of living standards at the cost of profits and private property of the rich.

Our main political task among the million-masses is to bring out clearly these two antagonistic class forces, to differentiate the general movement into these two main camps, to raise the issues of this struggle so sharply and clearly that the millions can see and understand, and to secure thereby the defeat and isolation of the leaders who are the agents of capital in this movement, trying to direct it into channels harmless to Wall Street.

The leaders and groups which typify the pro-capitalist tendency, are the LaFollettes, the Upton Sinclairs, the Olsons, the Huey Longs; they are being joined by that part of the Socialist Party leadership typified by Louis Waldman and the right-wing New York Committee; William Green threatens to join them, and may even be forced to do so before long. But it is clear that a party dominated by such a leadership, even if it called itself a Labor Party, would only be another edition of the LaFollette movement of 1924, which in a previous period of upheaval, led the movement off into a blind alley, betrayed it, and dispersed it.

Against such a party, organized from above by such leaders and controlled by them, the Communists must fight, allying ourselves with all loyal fighters for a Labor Party of struggle against capital.

In this struggle, we must guard against two deviations, two errors, which will appear again and again, in all sorts of disguises. First, is the error of narrowing down the broad class-struggle section of the movement only to its revolutionary wing, to those who accept the class struggle clear up to and including the revolutionary overthrow of capitalism and the dictatorship of the proletariat. Against such a narrowing tendency we must fight, demanding the fullest united front of all who are ready for the militant fight for the immediate demands of the workers, for support to the trade union struggles, strikes, etc.; for the Workers' Unemployment, Old Age and Social Insurance Bill (HR 2827); for Negro rights, for civil rights generally, against developing fascism and war, and for a Labor Party democratically controlled from below. Beyond these basic items, there should be no further test of loyalty to a real Labor Party, except the actual carrying out of a disciplined and organized fight for these things.

The second error, or deviation, which must be guarded against, is that of compromising with, or failing to struggle against, the enemy camp within the general mass movement, with the top trade union bureaucracy, with the LaFollettes, the Olsons, the Sinclairs, the Longs, the Waldmans. The Labor Party is not, for us Communists, a means of making peace with these gentlemen, but on the contrary a means to make more effective war, to defeat them and isolate them from the masses. Unless this dominates all our thought and activity, we will be certain to make damaging opportunist mistakes which objectively betray the interests of the masses.

To what extent do we propose that the Communists shall take initiative in bringing about the *formation* of such a Party as we endorse? We propose the fullest immediate initiative by all Communists, everywhere, in raising this question, discussing it among the masses, and bringing the organizations to adopt resolutions of support for such a movement, thus creating the solid foundation to bring such a party into existence.

We do not propose to initiate at once a movement to organize such a Labor Party on a national scale. Before that is done, we want all the political-class issues involved in the party and its program to be raised clearly before the masses; we want to give the masses the opportunity of an intelligent choice between the class-struggle line we propose, and the class-collaboration line of the enemy camp. It is the opportunists, the reformists, the conscious social-fascists, who want to rush quickly into the organizational crystallization of the Labor Party from the top, on a national scale, before the masses below have had a chance to prepare themselves for an effective participation in deciding the character and form of the Party. We, on the contrary, base ourselves upon the masses in the lower organizations, in the localities. And in the localities we find many places where the issues are more clear, the movement more matured than is true on a national scale. In all such localities, the moment the time seems to be ripe, we urge all who follow us to join in taking the initiative for the formation of a local Labor Party of the sort we have described. A measure of ripeness for such a move is to be seen in whether or not the majority, or a considerable section, of the local trade unions and other workers' organizations, are ready for participation in the movement.

The question is being asked, would the formation of a local or State Labor Party mean that the Communist Party would disappear from the ballot, would cease to conduct its own independent campaign? The answer to this is: No, by no means. The Communist Party, participating in such a Labor Party, would register its own ticket on the ballot, placing in nomination the same candidates who are named by the Labor Party as a whole. It would conduct its independent campaign, urging all workers to vote the Labor ticket, and urging all who agree with the necessity to strengthen the revolutionary section to vote Labor through the Communist list which contains the same names. This technique of elections is a common-place in American election procedure, which time and again has seen the same candidates appear on different tickets. This is done even among the big capitalist parties; thus, in California last November, Hiram Johnson was nominated on Republican, Democratic and Commonwealth tickets. The technique these gentlemen use for their own opportunist, capitalist aims, we can appropriate for our own revolutionary needs.

The key to the break-away of the masses from the Roosevelt New Deal is in the economic struggles, in the trade unions. The present struggles in auto and steel are the center, and give the type, of the process which we must hasten, further develop, and guide into correct channels.

It is therefore clear that all achievements in the fight for a Labor Party will, in the first place, depend upon fearless, energetic, and correct work in the unions of the A. F. of L., upon the leadership of economic struggles, and especially the strike movement. Our Labor Party policy, therefore, depends upon and is an outgrowth of, our general trade union policy and practice. The changes in this field, which we are now completing after a year of cautious experiment and testing of our ground, have proved their correctness up to the hilt, have kept us among and at the head of the most important mass struggles and movements. The Party membership has already mastered most of the lessons of this changed trade union policy. It will more quickly master the Labor Party policy in all its details, when it understands this as only a further extension of the trade union policy, of the whole struggle for the united working-class front against capital.

XVII

For National Liberation of the Negroes! War Against White Chauvinism! *

I HAVE purposely refrained from preparing a formal report, my purpose being to give the views of the Central Committee as informally as possible. I want to speak fully, frankly, and intimately about all the problems, especially the incidents showing the influence of white chauvinism, that have arisen in the school. I hope it will be possible to make this a Party meeting in the fullest sense of the word, that no one comes here with any reservations whatever, that we will liquidate all differences and unify the Party on the basis of the single Bolshevik approach, of one Bolshevik line.

We approach our problems here by speaking first of all of the Party, because we have failed to find a clear understanding among the students that the Party and its Leninist theory is the only possible instrument for solving our problems. On the contrary, we found a tendency toward groupings, toward a division of the Party members, instead of unification. The disintegrative tendency had affected the entire student body. We consider this to be one of our gravest problems, because when the unity of the Party is threatened, when groups of Party members begin to look toward group tendencies and attitudes for solution of their problems rather than toward the Party, then we are in a bad way, for then we are in danger of losing the only instrument whereby our problem can be solved.

Why do we have such problems as these white-chauvinist mistakes by our white comrades? Are these problems in the school of an accidental nature, or have they a connection with the state of our struggle among the masses? I think we will entirely fail to understand these problems in the school, of relation between white and Negro students, unless we take them in direct connection with the problems of the mass struggle arising in the United States.

What have we in the U. S. A. today? We have an unprecedented economic crisis which has shattered the old mass illusions about "permanent prosperity," and the new "Victorian Age" of American imperialism. The crisis has gone so deep that it has plunged large sections

* Extracts from a report to a meeting of American students, on behalf of the Central Committee, Communist Party of U. S. A., on the subject of the struggle for Negro rights in connection with the relation between white and Negro students in the School, in 1932.—*Ed.*

of the working class into starvation, is submerging sections of the lower middle classes and farmers, and is sharpening every antagonism, every contradiction, of American society.

In the past year the C. P. U. S. A. has been able in this situation to mobilize increasing masses of the oppressed for struggle against these conditions. We have proved the effectiveness of the Party line by certain results in the fields of struggle, in strikes against wage-cuts and speed-up, building the revolutionary unions; in mass struggles for unemployment relief and insurance, for building the Unemployed Councils; and the struggle for Negro rights, mobilizing white and black workers for joint battle on concrete issues. We have shown that our program is correct, and that we are beginning to find the forms and methods of work, whereby it can be brought into life among the masses. We must approach our inner problems upon the basis of these mass struggles.

Among the political advances of our Party during 1931, the most decisive was precisely in the struggle for Negro rights. In what did these victories consist? In this, that the Party raised concretely the issues of Negro rights on the basis of the Leninist program on the national question, and aroused masses of Negroes and also of whites, to struggle upon these concrete issues. The masses have responded to our program, and in the struggle there has begun a sharp class differentiation among the Negroes.

Our Party for many years has raised the slogan of struggle for Negro rights. Why have we only now begun to arouse mass struggles? There are objective and subjective reasons for this. First, the results of the crisis, which fall heaviest upon the Negro masses, including the sharpening repression and lynch terror. The second includes primarily the improved work of our Party, based upon clarification of its political line and its concretization in immediate issues and daily struggles.

The reason for our comparative lack of success in the previous years cannot be found in lack of sincerity, determination, energy, in carrying on our work. There were weaknesses in these matters, but the main explanation was the unclarity of our program, the lack of Leninist theoretical approach to the Negro question. Because we failed concretely to apply Bolshevik theory we fell into errors in the nature of bourgeois liberalism, and of a social-democratic approach to the Negro masses. We tended in practice to approach them with the attitude of bourgeois-liberal humanitarianism, unrelated to the consideration of the Negro masses as an oppressed nation. We failed to develop the Bolshevik conception of the Negro question, in sharp contradiction to all the varieties of bourgeois thought. Consequently, we fell into the position of competing with bourgeois liberalism on its own terms, dragging at its tail.

It was the assistance of the Comintern which enabled us to overcome these fatal weaknesses on the Negro question. The Bolshevik program on the Negro question was not simply a generalization of our own experiences in America. It was an application of Lenin's program on the national question which summarized the world experience of generations of revolutionary struggle and especially the experiences of the revolutionary solution of the national question in the Soviet Union. We could not have arrived at our program only upon the basis of our own American experience. It was the existence of the World Party of Communism which made possible for us the elaboration of a correct Leninist program on the Negro question.

Have we used this program? Yes, only a beginning, but still sufficient to prove how tremendously powerful it is. But, comrades, we have not made the entire Party master of this powerful weapon, and therefore our progress lags far, far behind its possibilities—and necessities.

We can mention three or four high points in our work in the past year, which stirred the masses. First, was the war against white chauvinism, which we dramatized in the now famous Yokinen trial. We seized upon an incident of discrimination against a Negro by a member of our Party, held a public mass trial, which proved the guilt of white chauvinism, and expelled the guilty one from the Party.

It is impossible for the Communist Party to lead the struggle for Negro liberation unless it begins by burning out of its own ranks every manifestation and trace of the influence of white chauvinism, of the bourgeois system of ideas of Negro inferiority which stinks of the slave market. The Yokinen trial was mass propaganda for this beginning of the struggle.

The purpose of our work on the Negro question is to establish unity of white and black proletariat in a common struggle to overthrow capitalism, and the leadership of the proletariat over the Negro masses in the struggle for their national liberation. The purpose of the ruling bourgeoisie is to destroy this unification, and to establish the leadership of the bourgeoisie over the Negro masses. The main ideological weapon of the bourgeoisie is that of white chauvinism; secondarily, it makes use of Negro nationalist tendencies. Therefore white chauvinism is the main enemy, against which we must conduct an intolerant war of extermination, against all its forms, open and concealed, a war of political fire and sword. That was the meaning of the Yokinen trial.

At first we expected only our Party and its close sympathizers to be interested and affected by the Yokinen trial. But we received a surprise and a great political lesson. We learned that the Bolshevik idea is so powerful that when we began to apply it seriously even within the confines of our own Party, this becomes sensational news for all America. The trial was reported at length with photographs by every important newspaper in America. Why? In the first place, because all America

·was interested in a public challenge dramatically flung into the face of a basic bourgeois principle of social relationships in America. Secondly, the bourgeoisie thought by this publicity to arouse a storm of white chauvinism against us. They were mistaken. There was mass interest, the entire country was "shocked" to hear of such a bold challenge to the "American institution" of Jim-Crowism. But instead of a storm against our Party, the result was a big wave of sympathy and approval, in the first place among the Negro masses, but also among the white workers. This shows us how the smallest events inside of our Party may have most profound consequences among the masses. This applies both ways, favorably and unfavorably. Our mistakes drive the masses away from us, while a firm Bolshevik line draws them to us. The expulsion of Yokinen, expressing our declaration of war against white chauvinism, exerted a tremendous influence to draw the Negro masses closer to us. At the same time we must say, that whenever we allow to go unchallenged within our Party, any manifestation, even the smallest and most indirect, of white chauvinism, this echoes and re-echoes among the masses and drives them away from us. The Negro masses know everything that goes on in our Party that relates to the Negro question. It is not possible for us to extend our political influence among them except upon the basis of daily, continuous, uncompromising, relentless war against every manifestation of white chauvinism.

Soon after the Yokinen trial, followed the mass struggle to save the nine boys at Scottsboro from legal lynching. If we had not previously had the experience of the Yokinen trial, probably the Scottsboro boys would have become merely another item in the long list of Negro lynchings which disgrace America daily. If our Party had not been awakened, made politically alert on the Negro question, by the Yokinen trial, then in all likelihood the Scottsboro boys would have been executed with little ceremony and less protest as so many hundreds and thousands of others equally innocent have been. But because the Communist Party had been politically armed and prepared, this made it possible to seize upon the Scottsboro case for a national mobilization of protest and struggle which aroused large masses throughout the country, and even throughout the world.

We had many weaknesses in the Scottsboro struggle. But on the whole, we must say the Party conducted it correctly and with great effect among the masses. Already in this struggle we begin to achieve a sharp beginning of the process of class differentiation among the Negroes. At first, the Negro bourgeois and petty-bourgeois leaders and newspapers were thrown into confusion by the Communist raising of the Scottsboro issue so widely and effectively. In the first days some of them came out in our support. But very quickly the deep-going nature of the Communist appeal to the masses frightened them and forced these petty-bourgeois elements to turn sharply against us, and to make common cause with the Southern state power of the lynching white bourgeoisie. Very soon we had the mass movement, on one side, headed by the Communist Party and sympathetic organizations; while on the other side, we had the lynch-law government, the Negro petty-bourgeois leaders, the Socialist Party and the white liberals; and these two sides engaged in the sharpest political struggle. This was a tremendous step forward in the education of the masses. It threw a searchlight upon the machinery of class rule in America, for all to see. Here we begin to see the slogan of unity of white and black workers, taking on its full political significance, while the masses begin to understand that the Communists are quite different from the liberal humanitarians who speak of "human brotherhood" and "class peace," but tolerate and actively support the machinery of legal and extra-legal lynchings and Jim-Crowism.

In the midst of the Scottsboro campaign we made another political step forward, in the struggle of the Negro share-croppers in Camp Hill. This battle was the first struggle directly resulting from our penetration of the Black Belt, of the agrarian population. It brought out the basic question of the Negroes as a nation, the question of the land and land-tenure, the question of the agrarian revolution, the overthrowing of the semi-feudal agrarian relationships. While immediately Camp Hill was only a struggle for certain partial demands, and correctly so, it threw a bright light upon the basic problem of the land, and thereby became a political milestone in the development of our Negro work.

We have other experiences of political importance. For example, in Detroit we were able to hook up together the struggle for Negro rights with the struggle for protection of the foreign-born workers, by a joint movement of the Scottsboro case and against the alien registration law of Michigan. This effectively countered the efforts of the bourgeoisie to develop among the Negroes anti-foreign sentiment on the grounds that "foreigners are taking away the jobs of American Negroes," and anti-Negro sentiment among the foreign-born on the basis of white chauvinism. When two such struggles are united together they take on multiplied political importance and power. Our Communist Party is the only organization that can even conceive the idea of such fusion of the two mass movements for joint effort.

In Chicago and Cleveland, we had a higher development of unity of white and black in mass action, in the protest movements against the police massacre of Negro workers fighting against eviction of unemployed workers from their homes. These movements led by the Party and Unemployed Councils stirred the masses to their depths. In Chicago, more than 60,000 white and Negro workers marched shoulder to shoulder in the streets in defiance of police prohibitions, supported by 50,000 more in the meetings in addition to the marchers.   Before this demonstration the capitalist press was openly agitating and organizing for a repetition of the so-called "race riots" of 1919, when they tried to smash the union of slaughterhouse workers by instigating armed struggle between white and black masses; the demonstration on August 8, effectively smashed these efforts, and instead of "race riots," the bourgeoisie was forced to begin to talk about "the menace of unemployed riots led by the Communists."   In Cleveland the same experience was repeated on the smaller scale called for by the smaller size of the population involved.   These two mass actions greatly stimulated the growth of the Unemployed Councils; previously the white and Negro workers were slow to come into the Councils, but after they experienced the tremendous power of joint actions on the streets when white and black fought shoulder to shoulder, fighting for the demands of the unemployed and for Negro rights in particular, masses began to flock into the Councils.   The greatest success of the Unemployed Councils followed directly from the taking up of the mass struggle for Negro rights.

Comrades, I have spoken at length about our experiences lately in the mass struggle in order to show, first of all, how everything that touches upon the Negro question is for our Party a question of fundamental principle importance, a matter of life and death.   This is equally true of the questions that have arisen among the students in the school. When we saw our students dividing themselves into groups, fighting among themselves, with the main line of division being whites versus Negroes, it was at once clear to us that we are dealing with the influence of bourgeois ideas among our students, the influence of an enemy class, which could take effect because our students have been insufficiently armed with Bolshevik theory.   Just as the tremendous problems of the mass struggle in America require the instrument of Bolshevik theory to solve, so also do the smallest problems in the school.

We have a difficult situation among the students; relations are strained and passions are inflamed.   But it is not impossible of solution, if we can secure the collaboration of every Party member, upon the Party line, to raise these questions to a political level and apply Bolshevik theory.   The Central Committee of our Party is determined that such a scandalous, disgraceful situation of white and Negro Party members quarreling among themselves, unable to unite in daily practical work, shall be immediately liquidated.

Have we the ability within ourselves to overcome these difficulties? I think we have.   Let me recall to your minds the words of Comrade Stalin, when he pointed out that "our difficulties are such that they contain within them the possibility of overcoming them."   This also applies to our present problems.   For you students, members of the

C. P. U. S. A., the meaning is that, by coming together as members of one Bolshevik Party, by applying in practice our Bolshevik theory, we will find everything necessary to solve these problems.

Of course, we will fail to solve our problem if we look outside of ourselves for the solution. There is no magic formula, no vague "higher power," which will come and do the job for us. This meeting here, your collective and individual participation in it, must provide everything necessary to set into motion such forces as weld solidly together, in unbreakable unity, the white and black members of our Party for our common Party purposes, and liquidate every trace of the influence of enemy class ideas, first of all, of white chauvinism.

It is my distinct impression that among the students there has been a process of disintegration, of breaking up into groups and grouplets. Perhaps there are no definitely crystallized groups, but the tendency has affected the entire student body. The main reason for this is, that when faced by certain mistakes by some white comrades in the direction of white chauvinism, the student body as a whole was not sufficiently mature politically to squarely face this situation and liquidate it. Instead, there developed a subjective and personal approach, and then to form groupings to solve the problem. Immediately, this resulted in the rise of a great zeal to find and correct the mistakes, not of one's self and one's little group, but of someone else and another group. I must say that there has been no lack of zeal among the students for the correction of mistakes—but always the mistakes of the other person. There is no eagerness for self-correction. But it is clear that mistakes have been general, both political and practical, and that what is required is a general self-correction and joint effort of the student body as a united fraction of our Party. Unfortunately, our students were insufficiently armed with Bolshevik theory for this task.

If you, students, had sufficiently understood the Leninist theory of the national question, how could the white comrades have left the task to the Negro comrades of correcting the errors of white chauvinism? No one denies that white chauvinist errors were committed; but we do not see white comrades coming forward as the champions for their correction, as is your duty. On the contrary, the white comrades had the tendency to admit such errors only to pass on at once to the detailed examination of errors of the Negro comrades, which they put in the foreground, and to also develop some really grotesque ideas of how to solve the problem.

It is not my purpose in this report to deal with the particular errors and identify them upon certain individuals. That must be done, but I am not the best person to do it, because I have not the closest acquaintance with the details of these errors and their authors. Who is best qualified to really expose each particular error? I think the person who committed the error could do this best. In the name of the Central Committee I invite each one of you to expose and combat your own errors; we will help you, and if it is then insufficiently done, we will supplement your self-criticism. It is necessary to attack individuals only when they defend their mistakes; when they join with us to attack the mistakes, then we are all on one side fighting shoulder to shoulder, the mistakes are on the other side and will thus be driven out of our ranks. Anyone who holds tightly to a mistake, refuses to abandon it, considers it is an essential part of himself which he must protect at all costs, such a person and only such will find himself in conflict with the Central Committee and eventually outside the Party.

What are the mistakes that have been made? They have been concessions to white chauvinism; setting up artificial separation between white and Negro comrades during the journey to the school; a paternalistic attitude toward Negro comrades by white comrades, assuming direction of their daily behavior; failing to correct such mistakes when they occurred, insufficient political sensitivity to the meaning of such mistakes; efforts to counter one mistake of white chauvinism by setting up against it a mistake of Negro nationalist character; allowing the development of bad personal relations, calling of names of "bourgeois nationalist" and "factionalist"; development of ideas of systematic separation of white and Negro, in a proposal of a "Negro Federation" within the Communist Party; and so forth. Further, there was a tendency to minimize the political importance of the whole situation.

These mistakes were contained in what have been described by some comrades as "very little" incidents. But comrades, you must understand that it is precisely such "little" things inside the Party that are the most dangerous because most difficult to combat and eradicate. It is comparatively easy to fight open, unashamed white chauvinism. There is no particular merit in that inside the Party, because there is and can be no such manifestations of white chauvinism tolerated inside. White chauvinists who should happen to find themselves inside our Party are quickly expelled without ceremony. Therefore, all manifestations of the influence of white chauvinism within the Party always and necessarily take on a more or less concealed form, in some "little" incident. We must, as Bolsheviks, have a keen political nose for such hidden chauvinism, drag it out in the open and liquidate it, without vulgarizing the struggle or creating anything where it does not really exist. That is a test of our ability to defend the Bolshevik line, tested in practice by our ability to develop daily solidarity between white and Negro comrades in the common work.

Were these mistakes the results of bad intentions? I am sure they were not. I am sure the comrades involved were shocked to find they had fallen victims to bourgeois ideology. But there is an old saying: The road to hell is paved with good intentions. The comrades, in spite of the best of intentions, fell into the swamp of bourgeois ideology and the whole student body was soon floundering about in contradictions, unable to liquidate the situation.

What was the basic cause of this helplessness? Is this such a bad body of students? No, I think it is on the whole, a very good body of students, of Communists. It represents a selected group of our best. But they *all* made one fundamental mistake, represented in its crassest form in the statement: "We are faced with a practical problem, not a problem of theory."

Whenever we approach a problem from the viewpoint of narrow practicality, we will inevitably fall into rotten liberalism, a form of bourgeois degeneration. You should understand this now, since in our school we are studying at this moment the issues on the theoretical front in the Comintern. This should give you a keener appreciation of the practical implications of theory than before. The greatest weakness of our Party is still its low theoretical level, and the main purpose of your attendance at this school is to equip you with theory, not abstract theory, but Bolshevik theory, which means theory organically connected with daily life and practice.

There have been some complaints that the discussions and struggles on these theoretical questions have interfered with the studies in the school and broken up the regularity of classes. Such a view is a completely formal understanding, and separates theory from practice in such a way as to destroy the revolutionary significance of both. I want to read to you a quotation from Comrade Stalin on theory, which was used in the recent speech of Comrade Kaganovich. It is worth repeating many times. Comrade Stalin said:

Theory is the experience of the movement of all countries, taken in its general aspect. Theory becomes, naturally, objectless, if it is not connected with revolutionary practice, just as practice becomes blind if it fails to illuminate its path with revolutionary theory. But theory may become the greatest power of the workers' movement if it is indissolubly connected with revolutionary practice. Theory, and only theory, can add to the movement certainty, the power of orientation, and understanding of the inner connection of surrounding events; theory, and only theory, may enable practice to understand not only how the classes are moving at present, but also how and where they must turn in the immediate future.

It is precisely from this Bolshevik approach that we must say that the situation among the students is a disgraceful one, because it reveals that weakness, fundamental for a Bolshevik, of separation of our revolutionary theory from the practice of everyday life. We are not bourgeois liberals, humanitarians, ethical culturists. We are Bolsheviks, members of a fighting Party of the working class, who know that the only road to the revolutionary overthrow of capitalism and the establishment of Communism is through welding together the iron unity of our Party, the vanguard, in relentless struggle against all the enemy-class ideology which penetrates into our ranks, as the prerequisite to the effective struggle against the class enemy physically.

To the white comrades it is necessary to say openly: You are primarily responsible for the bad relationship, because through you it was possible for the bourgeois ideology of white chauvinism to be reflected in our school, which was the root of the situation. You were not sufficiently armed theoretically, not enough on your guard, against alien influences. You have not been Bolshevik enough. You must realize your responsibility. You must also make an end of the game of balancing off your mistakes as against those of the Negro comrades, like a little shopkeeper balancing his petty books. You must realize that your mistakes are much more serious for our Party than those of the Negro comrades. If you cannot understand these things, then you are still unable to understand the fundamentals of the Leninist program on the national question.

Does this mean that the Negro comrades have made no mistakes? No, they have also made mistakes, which we will speak of openly. And when we say those of the white comrades are much more serious, this does not mean that we minimize the importance of correcting the Negro comrades. Furthermore, the mistakes of Negro and white comrades are not disconnected. Every sort of deviation from the Bolshevik line is a concession to the ideology of an enemy class. The white chauvinist mistakes were deviations in the direction of the American ruling imperialist bourgeoisie; those of the Negro comrades were deviations towards Negro bourgeois nationalism, in the main. These are two roads toward the same camp.

We thus give the class characterization of these mistakes. At the same time it is necessary to speak sharply against those comrades who speak of the Negro comrades as "Negro nationalists," etc. This is not a Bolshevik method of criticism, it turns the attention away from the political problem toward the person, while our desire is the opposite, to raise the discussion above persons to political issues. Let there be a stop finally to this whole method of political discussion which consists in attaching an enemy label to a Party comrade; when the time comes for such labels, the discussion is over and the issue has become one of putting a non-Communist outside the ranks of our Party.

Both deviations that came to the foreground in this discussion, would have the effect of serving the interests of the bourgeoisie, of American imperialism, by perpetuating the separation of the working class into two parts, white and Negro. It is therefore clear that we have to struggle on two fronts, simultaneously, against both deviations. The main front is that against the white imperialist ruling bourgeoisie, and the main danger is therefore white chauvinism, against which we must make intolerant systematic war of extermination. This struggle must be led by the white comrades, whose special duty it is to react sharply and quickly for struggle against every manifestation of white chauvinist influence.

The front of struggle against Negro nationalism is more complicated and must be handled more carefully. With the beginning of class-differentiation among the Negroes, which we have noted during the Scottsboro campaign, the struggle on this front has become hot. This is our struggle against DuBois, Pickens, Kelly Miller, Walter White and Company of the N.A.A.C.P. (National Association for Advancement of Colored People), and against Garveyism. It is on this front that we especially need the services of our Negro comrades, fully armed with the weapons of Lenin's theories. Your work here in the school should be carried on especially with this in mind. How important this is for our Party can be seen by the highly important place won by our Negro comrade, Harry Haywood, who is one of our leading theoretical workers today, precisely by his contributions on this front.

Comrades, my report was deliberately informal, because I feared that a well-prepared formal report might be taken formally. I have spoken extemporaneously, hoping thereby to come more intimately into your problems, and influence each of you to make an entirely new, fresh approach to the problems of your daily life.

The questions you are dealing with practically today occupy a central place for our Party's development. This very situation must be looked upon as an important moment in the history of our Party, as a crucial test of our Party's ability to face and overcome first of all within itself those problems which must be faced and overcome in a thousand-fold intensified form in the development of the revolution. Thus, today is one of the important moments in our Party development. Each one of you, by the nature of your participation in our discussion, will decide how you are going to influence the future of our Party.

That decision which each of you must make, is not the formal one of whether you hold up your hand for or against a resolution. We might all hold up our hands for the same resolution, but if we then go back into the school, not to remedy the present relationships but to make them worse than before, such a decision would be worse than a waste of time. No, the question each of you must answer is this: "Shall I join with the Central Committee, not only in voting for a resolution, but in transforming the whole life of the school, beginning with a transformation of my own part in it, toward complete unification on the basis of Leninist theory?"

In the discussion that is to take place, it will be important what each one of you will have to say. More important is, what are you thinking? One of the obstacles to achieving the results we wish from this meeting is that some of you are at this moment thinking such thoughts as this: "Yes, I will help the Central Committee; I will help by not saying what I really think." But that is precisely what will not help the Central Committee. It is your very thinking which is at the base of the whole problem, and if we cannot change your thoughts, so that your thinking helps to unify the Party, then your words are worth exactly nothing. With such thoughts you are repeating the mistake of Comrade Mintz, who, discussing the mistakes in the *History of the C. P. S. U.* tried to separate the "politically expedient" from the "objectively true." Such an attitude means one of two things: either one does not understand the fundamentals of dialectical materialism, or one declares that the Communist Party can find "expedient" that which is objectively false, which would mean a belief that the Party line is false. No, with such thoughts you cannot in any way help the Party.

This problem in the school is not accidental, as we have shown. And it cannot be isolated to the school. Its effects will spread far beyond. It is our task to so transform it, that we find within it not only the immediate solution, but also transform this incident into a weapon to raise the whole struggle for Negro liberation to a higher level, and an instrument for the further Bolshevization of our cadres. That means that we must make such a discussion here, and conclude it with such a unanimous resolution, that can be spread far and wide as the best kind of repudiation of all slanders against our Party, and the best proof that our Party not only wants to fight against white chauvinism, and for Negro liberation, but also that it knows how to make the fight, boldly and effectively. By taking part in this discussion now, you will be passing a real test of the Bolshevik qualities of a selected group of the leading cadres of the Communist Party of U. S. A.

CONCLUDING REMARKS AFTER DISCUSSION

Comrades, after some sixty speeches in two days' discussions, I am sure at this late hour no one expects a complete summary. Therefore I will speak only a few concluding words.

In this discussion the line presented for the Central Committee has met a genuine response from the students, which is gratifying. It proves that the Central Committee did not make very big mistakes when it selected this student body; that it has basic Bolshevik qualities in spite of mistakes. We have made a good beginning of real self-criticism. But we cannot be satisfied with this; this must start a process in the daily life of the school, and only then has it permanent significance.

· In our discussion we have spoken about the struggle for Leninism now going on on the theoretical front in the Comintern. In the light of our discussion, which has been a step forward for our Party in concretely applying Bolshevik theory to daily life, in liquidating the gap between theory and practice, we can say that we have begun to carry the line of Comrade Stalin's letter into the life of the Communist Party of the U. S. A.

A few words must be spoken about some general problems raised in the discussion. First as to the extent of white chauvinism among the workers in the United States and in our Party. Two errors must be guarded against on this question. One is, to try to find some mechanical limitation to the influence of white chauvinism among the workers. While it is correct to speak of the labor aristocracy as the special bearers of white chauvinist influence among the workers, because this aristocracy finds a material interest in Negro subjection, it is not correct to limit this influence to the aristocracy of labor. White chauvinist influence penetrates as deeply among the workers as the whole influence of bourgeois ideology; that means, just so far as we have not broken it down by revolutionary education and re-education of the workers. There is a limited spontaneous breaking down of white chauvinism among the workers, but on the whole we can safely say that *only* to the degree that our Party organizes and leads the conscious struggle against white chauvinism, is this influence destroyed among the workers. The opposite kind of mistake is to speak of the whole working class as "white chauvinists." The masses are influenced by white chauvinism but they are not active bearers of this bourgeois poison. Active white chauvinists among the workers are a distinct minority. Similarly, within our Party, we must say that white-chauvinist influences are still widespread, but it is absolutely wrong to speak of white chauvinism as "rampant" within our Party; on the contrary, within the Party it is characterized by its sneaking, slinking character, trying to hide itself, because here it is an outlaw. These facts give us the scope of our inner struggle against white chauvinism, and show its difficulties. It is an essential part of the struggle against the whole system of bourgeois ideology. Each individual white worker finds it necessary to free himself from this influence by conscious inner struggle, as well as participate in the organized Party struggle against it.

Some comrades have tried to develop here the conception of two kinds of "nationalism," one bourgeois and reactionary, the other proletarian and revolutionary. Here is some confusion which must be briefly clarified. We are not dealing with two kinds of "nationalism," but with the national liberation struggle of the masses of the oppressed nation, on the one hand, and with the "nationalist" system of ideas of the bourgeoisie of the oppressed nation, on the other hand, which attempts to control the national liberation movement for its own class interests, and in the era of imperialism almost invariably subordinates it also to the interests of the oppressing imperialist power. These are two different and contradictory factors. The efforts of the subject people to liberate itself from oppression, this is a revolutionary struggle, an integral part of the world struggle to overthrow imperialism as a whole. Our task is to bring this struggle for national liberation under the leadership of the proletariat, defeating the influence of the bourgeoisie which can lead it only to betrayal. This is precisely the central point of Lenin's program on the national question, which is the instrument for unifying these two main forces for common struggle against imperialism. It is precisely a distinguishing feature of the Second International, of reformism, that in the name of a false "internationalism" it denies the right of national self-determination to the oppressed peoples. True internationalism, that is Leninism, places the right of self-determination as a basic programmatic point. The "internationalism" of the reformists is in reality the nationalism of their own respective imperialist rulers; while the national program of Lenin is an essential part of internationalism. Any "internationalism" that denies the right of self-determination to the subject peoples is false, is a mere cover for imperialist chauvinism.

Comrades, these discussions have indeed marked a real mobilization for a political war against white chauvinism, for broader and deeper mobilization of the masses of white and Negro workers in the U. S. A., for the struggle for Negro liberation. This is an essential part of the class struggle, of the struggle for overthrowing the dictatorship of the bourgeoisie. We live and fight within the world fortress of capitalism, of imperialism, which finds one of its main instruments of rule in the division between white and Negro workers. But this division also represents one of the weakest spots of American imperialism, where we can strike quickest and hardest, it represents a pre-capitalist survival, a relic of slavery and feudalism, a crying anachronism, embodying all the contradictions of the decaying imperialist world. In this discussion we have more effectively armed ourselves with the Leninist theory, whereby we can call forth for struggle all the revolutionary forces generated by this national oppression of the Negroes, link them up with the rising forces of the proletarian class struggle under the leadership of the Communist Party, and thus with multiplied capacity for effective battle against the oppressors, the imperialist bourgeoisie, we will "sail into the face of the storm" of the revolutionary mass struggles that are being prepared in America on a gigantic scale.

XVIII

Wipe Out the Stench of the Slave Market *

Now I must speak especially about . . . the work among the Negroes, winning the Negro masses to the revolutionary movement. New York has perhaps the worst showing of any part of our Party on the question of Negro work. Both absolutely and relatively, New York City is the largest center of Negro population in the world, and these hundreds of thousands of Negroes here are at least 95% proletarian, overwhelmingly working class. They suffer from the most extreme exploitation and oppression, the most exploited section of workers in New York. But what do we have among them? What work are we doing among them? How much organization have we got among them? Almost nothing. Is this because the Negroes are especially difficult to approach, because we have not found a political program which will win their support? Not at all. This mass of Negro population has its eyes turned towards the Communist Party. They are distinctly friendly to our Party. Why aren't we able to effectively work among them?

In the first place, the reason for our failure is that the Party as a whole still has not mastered our Party program on the Negro question. How many of our Party members in New York understand that the Negro question is a national question? How many of our comrades understand that when they echo the Socialist Party slogan that the problems of the Negroes are simply class problems of the working class, that this is an opportunistic refusal to recognize the national question among the Negroes? How many of our comrades in this district understand that it is wrong to say that we give equality to the Negroes by treating their problems exactly the same as we would the problems of the workers everywhere? And because our members do not understand these things, it is impossible for us to win the Negroes organizationally and consolidate our influence among them.

The Negroes understand that our Party is something good for them. They understand that something new has come into their life with the coming forward of the Communist Party with its program on the Negro question, and therefore they are friendly to our Party, they listen to us. But when we go among them, our members are not able to consolidate this influence that we have. On the contrary, a very

* Extracts from Report for the Central Committee, at District Convention, District Number Two, June 11-12, 1932.—*Ed.*

large proportion of those Negroes who have come to our Party in the past have not remained, that is, when they were outside of the Party, they saw something good that they want to join but when they got inside they did not find themselves at home.

I know that many very honest workers, members of our Party, get very indignant when we say to them that they are suffering from the influence of white chauvinism. But the fact remains that most every white worker who has grown up under the influence of American institutions, is influenced by the ideology of white chauvinism. The only way in which we can destroy the influence of this ruling class system of ideas about the inferiority of the Negro in the minds of the workers, is by the conscious development of the understanding of the Communist program on the Negro question and the development of a sharp struggle against every manifestation of the influence of white chauvinism.

White workers express white chauvinist ideas without even being conscious of it. We have lived so long in this poisonous atmosphere of the American capitalist system that we no longer smell this stink of the slave market that still hangs around our clothes and we carry this stink around with us without knowing it. But the Negro can smell it. Oh, the Negro can smell it, you can't hide it from the Negro masses, and because he smells this stink of the slave market still around our Party units and our Party committees, he doesn't believe what we say about our program. He has had promises from political parties ever since the Civil War destroyed the system of chattel slavery, and he no longer has any faith in promises. Our program will only mean something for the Negroes when we begin to realize it in daily life, to realize absolute unconditional equality of the Negroes in our movement, in our trade unions, in the unemployed councils and in our Party, and a complete liquidation of unconscious and half-concealed examples of the influence of white chauvinist ideas. That means that we must systematically carry through a program of political education of our Party on the Negro question. Secondly, we must carry on serious mass activities in the Negro neighborhoods to raise the struggle for the immediate needs of the Negro masses, and thirdly, upon the basis of this mass struggle and the development of mass organizations, recruitment of the best workers from among the Negroes into our Party, and the systematic promotion of leading cadres from among the Negroes.

CONCLUDING REMARKS

One final point on the question of Negro work. I think it is necessary that in approaching this question we shall have a very clear understanding of its fundamental importance for our party. The Party cannot become a mass Party, cannot become a Bolshevik Party, unless it wins masses of Negroes, the most active, honest, devoted loyal proletarian Negroes. We have not accomplished this. We cannot rely upon formulas, correct as our formula may be, for the solution of this problem. One thing is clear. Just as long as honest, energetic workers, Negroes, do not feel themselves thoroughly at home in our Party, just so long is something the matter with us and we have got to find it and correct it. Just so long as the Negro workers who come in contact with our Party do not naturally unite with us, and stay inside the Party, the influence of white chauvinism is still at work, and the responsibility for this rests primarily upon the white comrades, and we cannot compromise by one-thousandth part of an inch on this question. That means that the struggle against the influence of white chauvinism must be a permanent feature of our work. The struggle against white chauvinism will not end until after the revolution—and some time after the revolution. What is true of our Party is much more true of the trade unions and still more true of the working class generally. And we have got to make the white comrades, especially those who occupy responsible posts, we have got to make them understand politically the program of the Party, we must make them politically sensitive to every concrete problem of the day that has any relation to the problem of the Negroes. And we must say that our Party is not yet sensitive enough to react to these problems. And very often we drive Negro workers away simply by our lack of sensitiveness, lack of reaction to these problems, by our failing to see them, even the smallest one when it arises.

The very smallest problem may become of the most extreme importance in winning the confidence, not only of one Negro worker, but of thousands of Negro workers. This, the white comrades must understand, especially the leading comrades—that it is they who have to win the Negroes. At the same time it is also necessary to say that the Negro comrades have a very special part to play. Our Party certainly will not be able to win over the Negro masses without the assistance of the Negro comrades, members of the Party. We must struggle to break down the distrust of the Negro masses, the distrust which they have of all organizations in which the white workers predominate in numbers; a distrust which is absolutely justified by their historical experience. We must and can break it down by our work and primarily by the work of the white comrades. At the same time, the Negro comrades have to furnish that absolutely essential part of the work by giving to the Negro masses the concrete example, the live example of Negro workers who have put their absolute confidence in this Party. The Negro comrades have to consciously understand and carry through this task of dissolving the distrust towards our Party. They can do this not by putting forward the Party as a perfect and complete organization from which the influence of white chauvinism is completely absent. Such an attempt to defend the Party would defeat itself because every Negro worker who comes into the Party will inevitably have experiences that prove to him that white chauvinist influences do exist.   But our Negro comrades have to point out to the non-Party Negro masses, not that the Party is perfect, but that the Party is conducting an organized struggle against this, and that the Party is not only the organization that will conduct this struggle against white chauvinism, but it will ultimately destroy white chauvinism.

XIX

"Theory Is Our Guide To Action!" *

I THINK we had a most excellent contribution from Comrade Olgin. After listening to Comrade Olgin's speech, I wondered what one could add, except to emphasize the thought which he brought forward, that our revolutionary theory develops right out of and is a part of our revolutionary practice in the class struggle.

Bourgeois society has not only separated the people into owners and workers. It has also separated the human faculties and placed them in opposition to one another. Knowing and doing are two entirely different categories in bourgeois society. Those who know—they do not do anything. And those who do anything—they are not supposed to know anything. Bourgeois society has placed a deep gulf between theory and practice—so much so, that in the ordinary popular sense one who is particularly ineffectual in action is spoken of as a "theorist."

Of course we cannot accept these traditions and conditions of bourgeois society. Just as it is our task not only to understand present-day society, but to change it, so also it is our task to smash this seeming contradiction between idea and action, between theory and practice. Theory is our guide to action. Theory grows out of action. Theory for us is the instrument of revolutionary action, and it can be the instrument of revolutionary action only insofar as it is theory which is drawn from international experience of the class struggle and the development of human society.

We do not create theory out of our heads. Our theory grows organically out of the development and maturing of the revolutionary class, the working class. It is a historic product. It has the same objective character as all scientific principle. And in just the same way as it is necessary to be very intolerant with all those who wish to revise the fundamental knowledge of mankind in order to insert in its place the arbitrary creations, the phantasies of the individual mind, so also, it is necessary to be intolerant in the struggle against all tendencies to replace our scientific knowledge and our scientific practice with individual, small-group revisions of our revolutionary body of theory. For it is only the proletariat, the only revolutionary class in capitalist society, which is capable of understanding and developing the scientific principles of social development.

* Speech at the Tenth Anniversary Celebration of the Workers School, New York, December 9, 1932.—*Ed.*

Our Workers School of the Communist Party is often accused of being narrow, dogmatic and intolerant, lacking in broad-mindedness, because we struggle against all individuals and groups who try to revise, change and water down the essential features of Marxism-Leninism.

In our approach to the masses whom we are striving to win, to organize, to mobilize for the revolutionary struggle, we always must be tolerant and patient, as well as stubborn and persistent.

But in the field of revolutionary theory, to accomplish our main task of winning the broad masses, the majority of the working class for the proletarian revolution, we must be resolutely intolerant with every deviation in theory, with every effort to revise Marxism and Leninism.

This theoretical intransigence, this unyielding adherence of the Communist movement to the revolutionary theory of Marxism-Leninism is not sectarianism. It is not dogmatism. It is the necessary precondition for the smashing of sectarianism, of all opportunist tendencies in the working class.

Our theory is developed not in schools. Our theory is developed in life, in mass struggle. Only through mass struggle can this theory grow and develop further. Our schools are auxiliaries to the mass struggles. Our schools are those places where we make available the knowledge that has been accumulated from the experience of the past struggles in order to solve the problems of present and coming struggles. Only in these struggles, by arming ourselves with the lessons of the past struggles, do we develop the theory, the knowledge and the practice that makes up Marxism-Leninism.

It is in this sense that we understand the Workers School and its place in the revolutionary movement. This phase is becoming more and more important. And more and more keenly do we feel the necessity of our school, of the service that it renders.

Under the conditions of the class struggle today, it is impossible to imagine that we could tolerate for one moment such influences as in the past have exerted themselves quite strongly on our institution, the Workers School, during the ten years of its existence.

The Workers School itself is the product of struggle. The Workers School was built and grew strong in the course of our struggle against Trotskyism, and the driving out of the influence of the representatives of Trotskyism in America. Perhaps you at present in the Workers School may not know that an influence in shaping the early years of the Workers School was Mr. Cannon, the outstanding representative of Trotsky in America. And for the development of the Workers School it was necessary to fight against deviations and drive out of the movement these Trotskyites and Trotsky theories.

Perhaps some of you can still remember the days when the destinies of the Workers School were in the hands of Bertram D. Wolfe, representative of the right-wing revision of Marxism-Leninism in America.

Another big struggle was necessary to defeat this open opportunism in the Party, in the movement and in the Workers School and to purify the Workers School from the opportunism of Mr. Bertram Wolfe and company, representing the Lovestone group.

The building and the development of the Workers School is a constant struggle, just as the building and development of a revolutionary workers' party is a constant struggle, against all of the influences of the ideas of the class enemy. The Workers School is that institution where we arm our leading cadres with weapons which give them the ability to resist the influence of class enemy ideas, to combat them, to overcome them. The school is where they master the ideological weapons of Marxism-Leninism and put them into effect in the mass struggles. Let us grasp the full meaning of that slogan of our great leader, Marx, that *an idea becomes power when it is seized upon by the masses.* Our ideas are not forces in themselves. They are instruments of the masses for the carrying through of the class struggle.

As our class struggle develops, we more and more need the Workers School. We more and more need to sharpen these weapons, because we are rapidly approaching the time when the struggles in which we are engaged are taking on a more and more decisive aspect, becoming more and more serious, more widespread, involving greater masses. We are coming closer to the days of decisive struggle, when through these instruments that we are forging in the Workers School and in the class struggles led by our Party, we will begin the transformation of society to Communism which is inaugurated with the seizure of power, by the establishment of the proletarian dictatorship. This historical moment is coming in the United States just as inevitably as it came in the Soviet Union.

We celebrate the Tenth Anniversary of the Workers School because it has become one of the essential instruments for the preparation and the carrying through of the proletarian revolution in the United States.

XX

Communism and Literature *

THE CONGRESS which we are opening tonight is unique in the history of our country. Strange as it may seem at first glance, there has never before been a large gathering of writers, the creators of our fine literature, to consider the problems of their work and its relation to the masses of the population, its relation to the problems of the country. Its significance is attested not only by the notable array of participants, but by this meeting, a mass welcome which expresses a much broader mass interest in the Congress. Like most of the many new things we are experiencing, it is one of the products of the crisis—a crisis which is not confined to our industries, but which is threatening the destruction of the whole cultural heritage of mankind.

How does it come about that the secretary of the Communist Party, who has neither the ability nor the time to be able to count himself among the literary creators, is invited to address this Congress, which is overwhelmingly unaffiliated with our Party, at its opening meeting? The answer to this question not only indicates the function of my talk, but throws a bright light on the basic problems of the Congress.

The answer is clear. The overwhelming number of writers who are producing living literature have become conscious, in one degree or another, that the class struggle between capitalists and workers—the two basic forces in modern society—is forcing novelist, dramatist, poet, critic, to choose on which side he shall stand. This Congress consists of those who, having faced the issue, have definitely taken their position on the working class side against the return to barbarism involved in the fascism and war of the decaying capitalist system.

Writers, moving more and more into contact with and participation in the class struggle, have one and all found this current rejuvenating and enriching their artistic work. They have escaped from the corruption that is debasing bourgeois intellectual life. They have found that basic contact with life, for want of which the cultural sphere of capitalist society is rotting and withering away. They have found their place as indispensable forces in the struggle for a better life. In this current they have learned that they are not embarking upon uncharted seas, in some wild adventure for which they must throw away all the treasures of culture accumulated through the centuries; they learn that it

---

* Address delivered at the opening session of the American Writers' Congress, held at Mecca Temple Auditorium, New York, April 26, 1935.—*Ed.*

has a long history, proletarian culture dating from Karl Marx and Frederich Engels—the two most cultured men of history who brought the fruits of ages of culture to the working class. They learn that the school of Marx is not a sect enclosed in the four walls of study or political committee rooms; they learn that it is a growing flood of men and women, struggling for progress on every front of human endeavor, from the struggle for wages, for unemployment relief and insurance, up to and including the struggle for a literature capable of satisfying the cultural needs of humanity in the period of break-up of the old social-economic system, the period of chaos and readjustment, the period of searching for the values of the new society. This new society is not yet in existence in America, although we are powerfully affected by its glorious rise in the Soviet Union. The new literature must help to create a new society in America—that is its main function—giving it firm roots in our own traditional cultural life, holding fast to all that is of value in the old, saving it from the destruction threatened by the modern vandals brought forth by a rotting capitalism, the fascists, combining the new with the best of the old world heritage.

Writers who are coming into this cultural stream are traditionally not interested in political life and problems. In their vast majority they are sceptical of all political parties, if not contemptuous. They find, however, in the new life in which they participate, there is a political party which plays an increasingly influential role, the Communist Party. They find it necessary to define their attitude towards this Party which actively participates in their chosen world. They see that this Party is a force in fine literature, as well as in strikes, in unemployment struggles, in battling for Negro rights, even in a reactionary Congress where it rallied through mass pressure 52 votes for the Workers' Insurance Bill without having a single Communist congressman—as yet. Yes, the Communist Party is a force, in every phase of life of the masses, even that of poets, dramatists, novelists and critics.

In these circumstances, the writers who organized this Congress saw fit to put an official spokesman of the Communist Party on your program. We understand quite well that this does not constitute a commitment of the participants to the Communist Party; we also understand that if you could have found any other political party which had anything significant to say about cultural problems, you would also have invited it to be represented. It is one of the signs of the times that there is no such other party in the United States.

The great majority of this Congress, being unaffiliated to the Communist Party, are interested in what it has to say because all recognize the necessity of establishing cooperative working relations, a united front, of all enemies of reaction in the cultural field. Such a united front against reaction is unthinkable without the participation of that group of cultural workers directly affiliated with the Communist Party and working under its general direction. This group, though a minority, is rapidly growing in influence, an influence that arises directly from the electric current of Marxist-Leninist thought which it transmits to the whole body of progressive fighters on the cultural front.

While recognizing the dynamic role of the avowed Communists, there are many writers in this Congress who have certain misgivings about the possibility of fruitful work in this united front. Most of these doubts are based upon lack of information about the policy of our Party in this field; some of them arise from the fact that Party policy is sometimes distorted by overzealous Communists, particularly the most recent recruits without proletarian background. In my few minutes it will be my task to make clear the Party policy, and to dispel some of these misunderstandings.

First, is the question: Does the Party claim a leading role in the field of fine literature? If so, upon what basis?

Our Party claims to give political guidance directly to its members, in all fields of work, including the arts. How strong such leadership can be exerted upon non-Party people depends entirely upon the quality of the work of our members. If this quality is high, the Party influence will grow—if the quality falls down, nothing in the world besides this can give the Party any leading role. We demand nothing more than to be judged by the quality of our work.

That means that the first demand of the Party upon its writer-members is that they shall be good writers, constantly better writers, for only so can they really serve the Party. We do not want to take good writers and make bad strike leaders of them.

The Party has such a leading role as its members can win for it by the quality of their work. From this flows the conclusion, that the method of our work in this field cannot be one of Party resolutions giving judgment upon artistic, aesthetic questions. There is no fixed "Party line" by which works of art can be automatically separated into sheep and goats. Within the camp of the working class, in struggle against the camp of capitalism, we find our best atmosphere in the free give and take of a writers' and critics' democracy, which is controlled only by its audience, the masses of its readers, who constitute the final authority.

We can therefore reassure all those who fear there is some truth in the stories about the Communists that we want to "control" you, to put you "in uniform," and so on, ad nauseam. I think that Communist collaboration in the gathering of this Congress, and further in its work, will forever lay this venerable ghost.

Second, is the question: Does the Communist Party want to "politicalize" the writers of fine literature, by imposing upon them its preconceived ideas of subject matter, treatment and form?

We would desire, so far as we are able, to arouse consciousness among all writers of the political problems of the day, and trace out the relationship of these political problems to the problems of literature. We believe that the overwhelming bulk of fine writing also has political significance. We would like to see all writers conscious of this, therefore able to control and direct the political results of their work.

By no means do we think this can be achieved by imposing any preconceived patterns upon the writer. On the contrary, we believe that fine literature must arise directly out of life, expressing not only its problems, but, at the same time, all the richness and complexity of detail of life itself. The Party wants to help, as we believe that it already has to a considerable degree, to bring to writers a great new wealth of material, to open up new worlds to them. Our Party interests are not narrow; they are broad enough to encompass the interests of all toiling humanity. We want literature to be as broad.

One of the means whereby the Party hopes to assist in linking up literature with life, lies in participating with you in organizing this field; organizing the writers, organizing a growing audience, and furnishing the connecting links between these two basic factors in cultural life.

We think organization of writers should be concerned, first of all, with the establishment of certain standards, certain beacons marking the main channel of our stream of literary thought. Next, it should be concerned with winning new collaborators, broadening and deepening the movement by drawing in more established writers and training new ones. Third, it should tackle the economic problems of the writer, on the basis of organizing his market and setting up certain standards to work toward.

The Communist Party has given its help to the weekly *New Masses*, precisely because we saw the possibility of this paper, in its new role, as serving some of these needs. The *New Masses*, since it was changed from a monthly sixteen months ago, is no longer primarily a cultural organ. It is a *political* weekly with strong cultural interests; it is one of the links between the cultural field and the broader life of the masses; addressed primarily to the middle classes, its task is to link them up with the working class, the bearer of the new socialist society. While not a party organ, the *New Masses* represents the Communist line, in linking up these related but different phases of life. Its new role has not served to discourage cultural publications as such; on the contrary, it is precisely in the last sixteen months that we have witnessed the greatest growth of purely literary publications on the "left."

We are all of us bound together, forced to work out our common problems collectively, by the menace of a common enemy which threatens to destroy everything that we hold dear. The fight against reaction, against fascism in the inner life of nations and against imperialist war internationally, is our common bond. We cannot fail in our efforts to unite all progressive forces without being guilty of treason to ourselves and to toiling humanity. We are not alone. We have brothers in every land. We have a mighty stronghold in this battle, in the land where socialism is being built, where a new culture is blossoming—the Soviet Union. This fortress against reaction is at this time our greatest protection against the wave of reaction sweeping the world. We must protect it as it protects us. Even in the vast territories of Asia, in China, Japan, India, the Philippines, we have brothers and allies, fighting the same battles against reaction, struggling to build up a new life, a new culture. We must, while organizing our forces nationally, digging deep into the treasures of our national traditions and cultural inheritance, link up our work organically with the forces of progress all over the world. National chauvinism, national limitedness, is the characteristic of reaction, of fascism; those who will build the new world, who will help humanity find the way out of chaos and destruction, will be internationalists.

It is with these thoughts that the Communist Party greets this historic Congress of American Writers. We are all soldiers, each in our own place, in a common cause. Let our efforts be united in fraternal solidarity.

XXI

The Revisionism of Sidney Hook

In *The Communist* for January, Comrade V. J. Jerome opened up a very interesting and valuable discussion of the fundamentals of Marxian theory in the form of a critical examination of the writings of Sidney Hook. Comrade Jerome traced in great detail some of the essential departures of Hook from the principles of Marxism, and came to the conclusion that Hook's interpretation of Marx represents a systematic revision in the direction of the philosophical doctrines of the American bourgeoisie, notably the instrumentalist philosophy of John Dewey.

For American Marxist-Leninists, the question of relationship to the specific American forms of bourgeois philosophy is a crucial one. Marxism-Leninism is the ideological armory of the rising proletariat in mortal combat with bourgeois society. It is the weapon for the destruction of the principal instrument of the bourgeoisie for the enslavement of the toiling masses; namely, the control over the minds of the toilers, the control over their very methods of thinking, exercised through the press, church, radio, schools and in the last analysis by the various philosophical systems which they seek to impose upon all thinking minds. The fundamental struggle between Marxism-Leninism and all systems of bourgeois philosophy has the same sharp, deep-going character as the struggle between the capitalist class and the working class for the control of society. It *is* the class struggle on the philosophical field.

It is essential, therefore, that the issues, which have been so sharply raised in Comrade Jerome's valuable article, shall be followed up with all thoroughness in all their ramifications and details. It is further necessary that out of the detailed examination we shall bring forward in the clearest possible manner the large central issues involved in this ideological battle. Our interest lies in establishing these issues with the greatest objectivity and clarity. We want to deal with real issues and not with imaginary or manufactured ones. We want to conduct the struggle on the plane of precision and clarity and not upon that of an exercise in opprobrious epithets. In this respect the writer wishes to disassociate himself from the tone and method used by Comrade H. M. Wicks in reviewing *The Communist* in the *Daily Worker* of January 10. There we had an example of a certain harmful misconception as to what constitutes "strength" in ideological struggle.

Comrade Jerome's article, on the other hand, is a serious, well-documented preliminary examination of the battlefield wherein must be fought out the struggle against Hook's revisionism. In the main this article establishes its point quite firmly. Certain secondary questions may require further examination and restatement, with some small corrections (which we will deal with later) as a necessary accompaniment to the further development of the polemic.

Sidney Hook has submitted to the editors of *The Communist* a reply to Jerome's article.* This reply is divided into two sections: First, an indictment of Jerome's method of interpretation of Hook's philosophical thought, and, second, a brief positive exposition of his own understanding of Marxism. It must be said that in the second part of Hook's reply, he effectively proves the thesis of Jerome's article which in the first part he disputes; namely, the thesis that Hook's philosophical thought represents a fundamental revision of Marxism.

What is the main characteristic of this reply by Hook? It is that Hook, in the most agile fashion, dodges or slurs over the main points of controversy. Instead of meeting the issues squarely, he takes refuge in the role of a misunderstood and abused person, the role of a martyr to stupidity. He complains of the "epithets of fascist and social-fascist" seemingly under the belief that here we have possible application of that "principle" of instrumentalist philosophy which Hook stated in the following quotation:

> Marxism therefore appears in the main as a huge judgment of practice, in Dewey's sense of the phrase, and its truth or falsity (instrumental adequacy) is an experimental matter. Believing it and acting upon it helps make it true or false. ("Marxism and Metaphysics," *The Modern Quarterly*, Vol. IV, No. 4, p. 391.)

We are not in agreement with this pragmatic idea that we can make a fascist or social-fascist of Sidney Hook merely by "believing it and acting upon it." It is our opinion that Hook's anxiety upon this score is groundless. In whatever direction he moves and in whatever camp he finally makes his home, he must look for the explanation within himself, and in the connection between his own thinking and acting and the social struggles of the day. And if it should chance that Hook some day becomes a consistent Marxist, it will be found that the "epithets" of which he complains have broken no bones. If they should play a role in the future development of Hook, it will be in the opposite sense to that embodied in the above quotation, *i.e.*, if Hook should move toward Marxism and not away from it, they may help him to discard some of the ideological baggage which now weighs upon him and prevents such progress.

Now to the examination of some of the specific complaints by Hook

---

* Sidney Hook's complete reply was published in *The Communist*, February and March, 1933.—*Ed.*

of misquotation. Out of a long series of quotations he picks five which
he claims are either distorted or show his own correctness as against
Jerome. Let us examine the last one first as being the most important
because most directly political. "The last shall be the first, and the
first shall be the last."

Hook contends that Jerome, in denying Hook's assertion that the
labor theory of value is not contained in the *Communist Manifesto,*
merely exposes Jerome's "ignorance" of the fact that the theory of
surplus value was formulated by Marx sometime after writing the *Communist Manifesto.* In this argument of Hook we are presented with
some very interesting phenomena. Hook, the stickler for exactness,
freely interchanges as synonymous the terms "labor theory of value"
and the "theory of surplus value"! Without for the moment raising
the question of the "fundamental intellectual integrity" of this juggling
with two terms, it is certainly necessary to challenge Hook's "true
scholarship" on this question.

What is the true history of the labor theory of value in relation to
Marx's system? Perhaps we can prevail upon Hook to accept Lenin
as an authority on this question. Lenin pointed out in his article,
"Three Sources and Three Constituent Parts of Marxism" that:

His (Marx's) teachings came as a direct and immediate *continuation* of
the teachings of the greatest representatives of philosophy, political economy
and socialism. . . .

It is the lawful successor of the best that has been created by humanity
in the nineteenth century—German philosophy, English political economy
and French socialism. . . .

Adam Smith and David Ricardo, in their investigations of the economic
order, laid the foundations of the *labor theory of value.* Marx . . . showed
that the value of every commodity is determined by the quantity of socially-
necessary labor time spent in its production. (V. I. Lenin, *Marx, Engels,
Marxism,* p. 52.)

Why, therefore, is Hook so indignant that Jerome should be so "un-
scholarly" as to quote from the *Communist Manifesto* that terribly
"Ricardian" paragraph expressing the labor theory of value? Marx
never claimed to be the originator of this theory. He took it over from
the classical economists and developed it further. It is true that the
full development came only with the distinction between *labor* and
labor-power, and the theory of surplus value, in Marx's *Critique of
Political Economy* which appeared in 1859. On the basis of this, however, Hook denies that the *Communist Manifesto* contains the labor
theory of value. But of course it contained the labor theory of value,
even though not in its final Marxian form, and of course this labor
theory of value was an essential element in the *Communist Manifesto.*
According to Hook, the labor theory of value only appears in Marx's

system in 1859. But what then is the significance of Marx's pamphlet, *Wage-Labor and Capital*, which appeared in 1849? Does Hook insist that even *Wage-Labor and Capital* does not contain the labor theory of value? But of course it contained the labor theory of value, already so far developed that Engels in preparing this pamphlet for reprinting in 1891, was able to make it fully consonant with Marx's *completed* economic system by a few changes in the text. As Engels himself explained:

> My alterations center about one point. According to the original reading, the worker sells his *labor* for wages, which he receives from the capitalist; according to the present text, he sells his *labor-power*. (Karl Marx, *Wage-Labor and Capital*, International Publishers' edition, p. 6.)

But of course Hook knew these things when he wrote his reply to Jerome. He knew that the labor theory of value was a constituent part of Marxism as expressed in the *Communist Manifesto*. Of course he knew that the development of Marxism after the *Communist Manifesto* was not by the *introduction* of the labor theory of value, but by its *further elaboration* in the theory of surplus value and the distinction between labor and labor-power. Of course he knew that Marx and Engels never "repudiated" the labor theory of value as expressed in the *Communist Manifesto*, but developed it further and completed it as the keystone of their economic system.

We have for this the most authoritative statement—Marx's and Engels' preface of 1872 to the *Communist Manifesto*. Hook is aware of this statement, since he makes reference to the preface in his reply. The statement reads:

> Though conditions may have changed in the course of the twenty-five years since the *Manifesto* was written, yet the general principles expounded in the document are on the whole as correct today as ever. A detail here and there might be improved.

It is in connection with possible improvement in a detail here and there that the authors state further in the preface that:

> Meanwhile, the *Manifesto* itself has become a historic document which we do not feel we have any right to alter.

Certainly the principle of the labor theory of value is not "a detail here and there." When, therefore, Hook seeks to make the authors' hesitancy to introduce any change refer to the labor theory of value, we have the right to question the frankness of his argument.

Hook further tries to obscure the question by saying, with regard to the disputed quotation from his article "Towards the Understanding of Karl Marx," that "all it asserts is that the Marxian theory of value in the form in which it is found in *Capital* is not contained in the *Communist Manifesto*." But that is not what he said in the disputed paragraph, the argument of which was directed to proving that the theory of surplus value is not a necessary part of the Marxian system because it did not spring forth fully-grown like Minerva from the brow of Jove.

So much for the "distortion," in the examination of which we receive additional light on the "scholarship," not to speak of the "intellectual integrity," of Hook in conducting theoretical polemics. We will deal more fully with this point in dealing with the second section of Hook's reply, where he restates his revisionist theory.

On this point all that can be conceded to Hook's criticism is that Jerome did not bring forth the historical aspects of the development of the labor theory of value in Marx's system. But Jerome was absolutely correct in attacking this point in Hook's writing, and in interpreting it as an attempt to separate Marx's method from Marx's conclusions. This is even more clearly brought out when we examine the more extended quotation offered by Hook. There we see clearly reflected Hook's fundamental idea of a contradiction between "objective and scientific" knowledge, on the one hand, and "revolutionary philosophy," on the other hand. This is only another expression of the idealist trend of Hook's thought. In the above it shows itself in placing the *Communist Manifesto* against *Capital*. In another place it shows itself in his placing Lenin's *What Is To Be Done?* in contradiction with his *Materialism and Empirio-Criticism*. In each case it is a way of placing theory in opposition to action. In each case it is a denial of the objective scientific validity of the revolutionary program of the Communist Party.

Now let us consider "distortion" number two, *i.e.*, the quotation of Hook's characterization of Lenin's polemics against the idealists in *Materialism and Empirio-Criticism*. Jerome clearly and correctly exposed Hook's acknowledged and unacknowledged "genuine disagreement" with Lenin and Marx on the theory of cognition. Here it might be said by the over-fastidious that Jerome proved too much when he interpreted this as expressing Hook's personal "disgust" with Lenin's polemics, because this is not a *necessary* but only a *possible* conclusion. And the *necessary* conclusion from the full paragraph as quoted by Hook, is that it is an example of an apologetic attitude towards the characteristically Marxist-Leninist nature of the book under examination, its character as an energetic assault upon bourgeois philosophical systems. To apologize for the polemical nature of Marx's and Lenin's writings means to attack the essence of Marxism. Precisely the absence from Hook's writing of any attack against the bourgeois philosophies, precisely its replacement by a conciliatory attitude at best and in the worst case of the open indentification with these bourgeois philosophies, serves as one of the best indications that Hook's Marxism is in reality a fundamental revisionism. Jerome would have made a stronger case against Hook on this point if he had ignored the irrelevant question of Hook's "stomach" and given more attention to Hook's mind where the disorder was more serious.

Now to "distortion" number three. Can it be said that Hook has improved the situation by giving the largest paragraph from which Jerome took the sentence about the dangerousness of the God idea? Hardly. It is quite true that in evaluating philosophical trends, Marxists have always gone behind the verbal form to find the true nature of the thought; and that they have found essential elements of materialist philosophy, and even the rudiment of a materialist system, embodied in the thought of idealist and deist philosophers. But can one jump, as does Hook, from this fact to the position that "God is dangerous to the social revolution only if he is an active God—only if he creates worlds"? By no means. One cannot do this, unless he abandons the ground of Marxism. It is not only a fully developed theology that is "dangerous to the social revolution," but also every fragment of religious ideology, even it its most attenuated form. Hook's refutation of Jerome, therefore, only serves to emphasize and round out the judgment, that on this question Hook departs from Marxism in a serious manner. That is, indeed, at the very least, opening the doors for "smuggling in religionism."

"Distortion" number four. Here Hook complains of a particular paragraph from which he is interpreted as ascribing to Marx himself the responsibility for the varying interpretations of Marx. Against this he quotes a different paragraph which, in a vague way, indicates another possible interpretation. Perhaps if these two paragraphs stood alone, it would be possible to concede a "Scotch verdict" to Hook on this question: "Not proved"! But unfortunately for Hook's rebuttal, this question has to be considered in connection with other things he has written. It would have been more to the point that Hook should explain the meaning in this connection of the quotation from his article reproduced in the January issue of *The Communist*, p. 66. There he said that "in Russia it (Marxism) is a symbol of revolutionary theology; in Germany, of a vague social religion; in France, of social reform; and in England and America, of wrong-headed political tactics." If in the light of this paragraph Hook wishes to refute Jerome's specific charge, it can only be by confirming the general charge that Hook had (and by implication still has until he publicly corrects himself), an understanding of Marxism in conflict with that of the Communist Party and the Communist International. But he cannot eat his cake and have it too. He cannot cry out against "distortions" and proclaim that our differences have been willfully created by us, for some mysterious reason, and at the same time maintain his own freedom to light-heartedly dismiss the Marxism of Lenin and Stalin as "theology."

And now the final "distortion"; namely, the quotation from the paragraph regarding the German Social-Democrats' vote for the war budgets in 1914. Here, if we were confined to the evidence given, formal justice would require a verdict for Hook against Jerome. Jerome's crime in this respect is serious, because he thereby detracted slightly from the full force of his attack against Hook's revisionism. The connection between Hook and Bernstein is more deep and fundamental (and at the same time more subtle) than can be disclosed by any interpretation of a crude endorsement of, or apology for, the voting of the war budgets. But this must not allow us to forget the *substantial* point under examination, that Hook insists that Bernstein's economic views "could all be retained with certain modification within the framework of the Marxian position." In other places Hook goes out of his way to praise Bernstein.

Jerome was fully justified in relating Hook to Bernstein. The true depths of this must be traced, however, in their common denial of objective scientific validity to Marxism, their common rejection of the goal of the proletarian movement as something that can be a matter of knowledge before it is reached, the exaltation of method over the product of the method, etc. It is not in the complicity in a particular historical action, or judgment of that action, that the unity of thought between Hook and Bernstein is expressed, but rather in the fundamental direction of their thought on basic questions of philosophy, resulting in each case in efforts to revise the Marxian system.

So much for the first section of Hook's reply to Jerome. It is clear that Jerome's indictment stands. When Hook thought he was delivering a smashing "left hook" that would score an ideological knockout, he was swinging wide of the mark, and left himself more open for counter-attack than before. This may serve as an additional object-lesson in the futility of logical agility in conflict with the objective truth of the monolithic Marxian system. From the light exercise of countering these puny blows, we may pass on to more serious business.

II

In the first part of this article, we refuted complaints of Sidney Hook that his views had been distorted and misrepresented. In the course of answering these questions, we already indicated the most essential features of a critical examination of Hook's system as a whole. Facilitating the further development of the argument, we have Hook's own formulation of what he considers the most essential features of his understanding of Marx, written as the second section of his reply to Comrade Jerome's article.

What is the outstanding feature of the self-characterization of Hook's Marxism? In my opinion it is, on the one hand, the critical attitude towards and attempts to correct Marx, Engels and Lenin, accompanied by, on the other hand, the uncritical acceptance of the theories of John Dewey as the basis for a revised Marxism.

Already I indicated the significance of the absence from Hook's writings of any consistent or sustained polemics against the various schools of bourgeois philosophy. This in itself constitutes sufficient proof that Hook is a revisionist of Marxism. There still remains the question of who is correct. Is it Marx, Engels, Lenin and Stalin? Or has Hook, with the assistance of John Dewey, really discovered some profound truths which escaped the minds of the greatest revolutionary thinkers? It is this question that we will attempt to briefly answer in the present article.

What is the great contribution of John Dewey which Hook thinks has "improved" on Marx and Lenin? It is Dewey's theory of cognition or "theory of perception." Just what this theory signifies may be seen from a few quotations directly from Dewey himself:

It may well be admitted that there is a real sense in which knowledge (as distinct from thinking or inquiring with a guess attached) does not come into existence until thinking has permeated in the experimental act which fulfills the specifications set forth in thinking. (*Philosophy of John Dewey*, selected and edited by Joseph Ratner, George Allen & Unwin, p. 159.)

And further:

The object has to be "reached" eventually, in order to get clarification or invalidation, and when so reached, it is immediately present. . . . Short of verificatory objects directly present, we have not knowledge, but inference whose content is *hypothetical*. The subject matter of inference is a candidate or claim to knowledge requiring to have its value tested. (*Ibid.*, p. 210.)

This is the theory which, according to Hook, "is part of the science of our day and no thinking dialectical materialist can reject it."

A classical application of the theory is contained in the hypothetical case of the man lost in the forest and seeking a way out. (I think this originated with James and was taken over by Dewey. I am sorry not to have had time to hunt up reference to text on this and am forced to quote from memory.) According to this example, the lost man beginning to think about his plight, projects various inferential ways out of the forest and then proceeds to act upon one or other of these inferences. When one of these has been acted upon successfully and has led him out of the forest, then and only then, in the process of realizing the truth of an inference, has the man gained knowledge. The knowledge gained in one experience is of value for other experiences only in enriching his stock of inferences from which to choose. The process of accumulation of knowledge is one of broadening the possible choice of various inferences. According to this, only the ignorant man can feel sure of anything before it happens and the more knowledge he acquires, the more he has to hesitate in face of his growing stock of inferences from which he must choose. The truth cannot be a matter of fore-knowledge because it is a product of the action of the subject, who has *created* the truth by successfully acting upon an inference.

It is in order to make room for this pragmatic theory that Hook rejects the basic postulate of dialectical materialism that an idea is "an image corresponding to the perception of the external phenomena," and that "sensation is nothing but a direct connection of the mind with the external world; it is the transformation of energy, of external excitation into a mental state." (V. I. Lenin, *Collected Works*, Vol. XIII, p. 31.)

In order to more effectively attack this Marxian understanding (which is an essential feature of the thought of Marx, Engels, Lenin and Stalin), Hook proceeds to make "images" into "carbon copies"; *i.e.*, he makes the dialectical materialism of Marx synonymous with the mechanical materialism of the Encyclopedists. He tries to prove that correspondence between objective reality and mental processes results in fatalism and reliance upon the automatic processes; he declares that only ·when this is "corrected" according to Dewey, does Marxism really become an effective theory and practice of social revolution. He sums up this thought in his formulation that if "Marxism is not fatalism," then "communism is not inevitable."

In support of his contention that communism is not inevitable, Hook, in true revisionist manner, aims to bring forward Marx as his supporter. He cites the passage in the *Communist Manifesto* which, in referring to class struggles in past societies, says of the classes:

They carried on perpetual warfare, sometimes masked, sometimes open and acknowledged; a warfare that invariably ended, either in a revolutionary change in the whole structure of society, or else in the common ruin of the contending classes.

Basing himself on this passage, Hook contends that he has Marx's sanction for the theory that communism is not inevitable, that the struggle of proletariat against bourgeoisie may likewise end "in the common ruin of the contending classes."

In advancing this argument, Hook merely betrays his utter inability to apply dialectic materialism to history, shows his metaphysical concept of historic parallelism for all ages and all class societies, and incidentally, his ignorance of Marxism. For, in *Die Deutsche Ideologie* (Adoratsky Edition, *Volksausgabe*, pp. 43-44), Marx and Engels expressly state:

It depends entirely on the extensiveness of commercial relations whether or not the attained productive forces, namely inventions, of a locality are lost for later progress. As long as there is no market extending beyond the immediate vicinity, each invention must be specially made in each locality, and mere accidents such as the invasions of barbarian peoples, even ordinary wars, are sufficient to bring a country with developed productive forces and wants to such a pass that it must start again from the beginning. In early history every invention had to be renewed practically daily and in each locality independently. How little assured developed productive forces are against complete decline, even those with a relatively very extensive trade, is shown by the Phoenicians, whose inventions and discoveries were for the most part lost for a long time through the exclusion of this nation from trade, through the conquest by Alexander, resulting in its complete decay. Likewise the art of staining glass in the middle ages, for example. *Only when commercial intercourse has become world trade and has as its base large-scale industry, and all nations have been drawn into competitive struggle, only then is the duration of the attained productive forces assured.*" (*Die Deutsche Ideologie*, pp. 43-44. Italics mine.—*E.B.*)

It is clear from these words of Marx and Engels that it was to past societies and not to capitalist society that the reference to "the common ruin of the contending classes" was made in the *Manifesto*. Let the authors of the *Manifesto* attest to this. The following passage from the *Communist Manifesto* certainly leaves no doubt as to the views of Marx and Engels on the inevitability of the fall of capitalism—not together with the proletariat, but attended by the rise of the proletariat as the ruling class:

What the bourgeoisie therefore produces above all, is its own grave-diggers. *Its fall and the victory of the proletariat are equally inevitable.* (Italics mine.—*E. B.*)

We offer this instance of Hook's attempt to rest on Marx as typical of the manner in which the revisionists seek to hallow their revisionism with "quotations" from Marx.

What Hook is accomplishing by this revision, is to surrender dialectical materialism to idealism—to that specific brand of idealism which calls itself pragmatism, or instrumentalism. He promises us that through this exchange we will emerge from a condition of helpless puppets of blind forces, into a condition of masters of social processes —that we will emerge from the kingdom of necessity to that of freedom. But his advertisements for his wares are highly exaggerated. It is one of the contradictions of all idealist philosophy that the more it promises, the less it delivers. This is excellently illustrated in the case of Hook.

In the course of a debate with Mr. George Soule, I have already had occasion to evaluate briefly the relation of pragmatism to the problems of the revolutionary working class. I repeat what I said then, because it applies fully at this point:

. This pragmatism that recognizes the truth only *a posteriori* (as the learned gentlemen say), only as something that has already arrived, cannot distinguish the face of the truth amidst falsehoods and illusions. It has an inherent inability to recognize the face of the truth, it proclaims that the only possible way to recognize the truth is when you see it from the rear, when you see its backside, when it has already passed into history. This is a convenient philosophy for that bourgeoisie which is "sitting on the top of the world," the bourgeoisie in ascendancy. But when bourgeois society falls into a crisis, this philosophy of pragmatism falls into crisis also along with the whole capitalist system. Where in the period of "Coolidge prosperity" it gave all the answers required to all of the problems of the bourgeoisie, today it begins to give the wrong answers to the bourgeoisie. Even if we judge the capitalist system today by that final criterion of the pragmatists, *Does it work?*, we have the answer, "No, it does not work." So capitalism stands condemned by the standards of the philosophy of the bourgeoisie itself. By the same standard if we ask about the dictatorship of the proletariat in the Soviet Union, the new Socialist planned economy, and ask, *Does it work?* the answer is, "Yes, it does work. In the midst of a world that is going to pieces it works!" So pragmatism has failed its class creators in the crucial moment. It is unable to give capitalism any answer to the question, What way out? Because all the thinkers for capitalism are bound within the philosophical framework of pragmatism, they are unable to even formulate any proposals for a way out and are in the same position as the one who says, "Maybe the revolutionists are right, maybe the reformists are right, who knows? Let us wait and see."

But if pragmatism is of no use to the capitalist class to find a way out of the crisis, we must say it is of no use to the working class, either. The only effect of the influence of this ideological system upon the working class is a very poisonous one, to create hesitation, indecision, hesitation again, more indecision, wait and see, wait and see.

The working class must have a different kind of philosophy, because the working class faces the future—not only faces the future, is already beginning to control the future. That is the essence of planning, *to control the future*. And you cannot control the future if your approach to the future is that it is impossible to know what is the truth until after the future has become the past. Those who are going to control the future must know what is the truth before the event, before it happens, and by knowing it, determine what is going to happen and see that it does happen. That is the revolutionary working class, the only power that is able to put into effect a planned economy, and the only class that is capable of developing the whole philosophy and the understanding of society, which is necessary to put a plan into effect.

III

Before passing over to an examination of the consequences of Hook's revisionism, we will briefly examine the other three points of his statement.

Hook is quite delighted with the fact that Morgan's anthropology, which was accepted by Engels has been basically corrected on a certain point by modern research. He cites this, however, not from any interest in the questions involved, but because behind this he thinks he can smuggle in his whole system of separating Engels from Marx, both of them from Lenin, and their system of thought from the working class and its revolutionary Party. The significance of this point in his reply above, is to be found not in the text, but in what he has written elsewhere. Just a few quotations will suffice to indicate this system.

Certainly there is no justification for the easy assumption made by the self-styled orthodox, that there is a complete identity in the doctrines and standpoints of Marx and Engels.

It was Rosa Luxemburg, however, and not Lenin who delivered the classic attack against revisionism from the standpoint of dialectical Marxism.

There must have been aspects at least of Marx's doctrines which lent themselves to these different interpretations.

In these efforts at the disintegration of the Marxian system into an eclectic combination of more or less contradictory tendencies, we have at once both the rejection of Marxism as a science and also, an expression of the theory of inferences, of numberless possible ways out.

Behind these statements is the concerted effort of international revisionism to break the unity and continuity of Marxism in Marx, Engels, Lenin and Stalin. The effort expresses itself in various ways, but the central purpose of the revisionists is to show that Marxism was variously interpreted by its very founders, and at the same time to make Engels appear to sanction the opportunism and open treachery of the Second International. In this effort the revisionists stop at nothing, not even at forgery, as in the case of Bernstein's proved forgery of Engels' preface to Marx's *Class Struggle in France,* wherein Bernstein sought to make Engels appear a supporter of opportunist parliamentarism. The attacks upon Engels by social-fascism today are particularly directed against his development of the Marxian theory of the state and the seizure of power by the proletariat, in his *Anti-Dühring* * and *The Origin of the Family.*

Following upon his distortion of the role of Engels in the development of Marxism, Hook turns his attention to Lenin. We repeat in this regard, the above mentioned quotation:

It was Rosa Luxemburg, and not Lenin, who delivered the classic attack against revisionism from the standpoint of dialectic materialism. (*Towards the Understanding of Karl Marx,* p. 350.)

We dwell on this statement because in it is contained the essence of the semi-Trotskyist article by Slutzki, "The Bolsheviks and German Social-Democracy in the Period of its Pre-War Crisis," which appeared in the *Proletarskaya Revolutzia* (No. 6, 1931), and against which Comrade Stalin launched his famous attack.

* Frederick Engels, *Herr Eugen Dühring's Revolution in Science* (International Publishers).—*Ed.*

The position that Slutzki took in that article was that, in the period before the war, Lenin and the Russian Bolsheviks failed to carry on a relentless struggle for a breach with the opportunists and the Centrist conciliators of the German Social-Democracy and the Second International, that Lenin and the Bolsheviks failed to give full support to the Left-wingers in the German Social-Democracy (Parvus and Rosa Luxemburg), thus retarding the struggle against revisionism and opportunism.

Comrade Stalin lays bare the falsity of this contention by recalling the revolutionary, anti-opportunist role of the Russian Bolsheviks who, as far back as 1903-04, worked for a breach with the opportunists, not only in the Social-Democratic Labor Party of Russia, but in the Second International as a whole, and especially in the German Party. Comrade Stalin brings Bolshevik critical judgement to bear on the role of the German Left-wingers at that time—a role that was far from being Bolshevist, and which prevented the influence of Lenin and the Russian Bolsheviks from being exerted in the German Party against the opportunists and the Centrists.

Comrade Stalin declares:

And what point of view was adopted by the Left Social-Democrats in Western Europe? They developed a semi-Menshevist theory of imperialism, rejecting the principle of the right of self-determination of the nations according to the Marxist conception (including separation and the formation of independent states), repelled the thesis of the serious revolutionary significance of the liberation movement in the colonies and oppressed countries, the thesis of the possibility of the united front between the proletarian revolution and the national emancipation movement, and counterposed the whole of this semi-Menshevist hodge-podge, representing an entire underestimation of the national and colonial question, to the Marxist idea represented by the Bolsheviks. It will be remembered that later on Trotsky seized upon this semi-Menshevist mixture and employed it as a weapon in the fight against Leninism.

These are the errors, known to all, of the Left Social-Democrats in Germany.

Admittedly, the Left-wingers in Germany did more than commit grave errors. Their record contains great and truly revolutionary deeds. ·

It was against Lenin's criticism of the semi-Menshevism of the German Left-wing that Slutzki brings the charge of failure to support *without serious reservations* the Left Social-Democracy.

Comrade Stalin shows up this anti-Leninist "historianship" as the work of "a calumniator and falsifier."

Sidney Hook advances the same charge against Lenin, when he states the Slutzkist thesis: "It was Rosa Luxemburg, however, and not Lenin, who delivered the classic attack against revisionism from the standpoint of dialectical materialism."

And what more correct characterization can be given to Sidney Hook's version of history than Comrade Stalin's characterization of Slutzki—"calumniator and falsifier"?

Of the same nature is Hook's placing one part of Marxian theory against another, of which we spoke in the previous article. He also invades the field of economics to declare that the fetishism of commodities is "the central doctrine of Marx's sociological economics" and considers "the theory of surplus value as an abstract and derivative expression." (*Modern Quarterly*, Vol. V, No. 4, p. 435.) This simply means he understands neither, and that he is substituting both. It is an old revisionist trick to try to fight Marx with Marx, but it has failed for some generations as it will for many more. The exposure of the fetishism of commodities is a part of the theory of surplus value, and the two can no more be placed in opposition than can the kidneys be cited against the lungs. Only a revisionist, one who denies Marxism as a system, can play at such a game. In insisting that the theory of surplus value is an "abstract and derivative expression" Hook robs Marxism of its very foundation in understanding the exploitation of labor and the class struggle. Not a metaphysical abstraction, not a secondary expression, but "The doctrine of surplus value is the essence of the economic theory of Marx." (Lenin.)

This basic tendency of Hook's thought is also expressed in his excluding of dialectics from the field of nature and confining it exclusively to the consciousness of man. Because consciousness is involved in the dialectical movement of society, Hook concludes that where there is no consciousness there can be no dialectics. Hook poses the question thus: either "social life is merely a chapter of physical life and explicable in physical terms," or, if this is not so, Marxism must be "freed from its coquetry with Hegelian terminology and disassociated from the illegitimate attempts to extend it to natural phenomena in which human consciousness does not enter." (*Towards the Understanding of Karl Marx*, p. 63.)

In the face of this very clear denial by Hook of dialectics in nature, one marvels at the sudden lapse of memory, to put the matter mildly, that causes him to protest in the statement he has just submitted—"and I have never denied it." The fact is that Hook's denial of the universality of dialectics is typical pragmatism, with its denial of the possibility of a unified body of knowledge, corresponding to a material universe, of which man and society is an expression and product.

Hook's final point in his reply above is also masked and not open and frank. Under cover of the platitude that no man "has said the final word on anything," he is really affirming his own license to change at will the Marxian system and to reassemble its fragments under the hegemony of the pragmatist philosophy. The fact that he calls this disintegration of Marxism by the euphonious name of "creative Marxism" does not need to confuse us. This is only another example of what Lenin described in the following words:

But after Marxism had dislodged all the diverse teachings hostile to it, the tendencies expressed in these teachings began to search for new outlets. The forms of, and the reasons for, the struggle have changed, but the struggle itself continues. The second half century of the existence of Marxism began with the struggle within Marxism against the tendencies inimical to it. . . . Pre-Marxian socialism is smashed. It continues to struggle not on its own ground any longer, but on the general ground of Marxism, as revisionism.

The struggle against revisionism is a struggle against bourgeois philosophy. But this bourgeois philosophy does not appear openly in its own name, it comes forward as "Marxism," even as "creative Marxism," it proclaims itself as "dialectical materialism" with only the "little correction" of substituting Dewey's for Marx's theory of cognition. The revisionists "agree with the Party's political program in the main, but retain a few philosophical reservations." The example of Hook helps us to understand the feeling with which Lenin exclaimed:

It is a shame to confess, yet it would be a sin to conceal, that this open enmity towards Marxism makes of Chernov a more principled literary opponent than are our comrades in politics and opponents in philosophy. (*Collected Works*, Vol. XIII, p. 73.)

IV

What are the practical consequences of Hook's pragmatism parading as Marxism? Hook's views have been eagerly seized upon by the reformists and renegades. This is not only because he furnishes them with philosophical justification for existence, as alternative inferences which are "candidates for truth." More important is his justification of all schools of revisionism by denying the existence of any body of established Marxian truth. What could be more sweeping in its contemptuous dismissal of the various Communist Parties and of the Communist International, than Hook's article in *Modern Quarterly*, Volume 5, No. 4? In that article it is made clear that Hook believes he alone truly understands Marx, that the Communist Parties are merely repeating with mechanical stupidity the formulae of Marx. Let us recall again Hook's description of Marxism as expressed practically in world mass movements.

In Russia, it is a symbol of revolutionary theology; in Germany, of a vague social religion; in France, of social reform, and in England and America, of wrong-headed political tactics.

Modesty may require us to ignore Hook's cynical characterization of the Communist Party of the U. S. A. as an expression of "wrong-headed political tactics." We merely note in passing that in this judgment, he unites with the renegades and reformists of all brands. But what shall we say of a man, who professing to be a Marxian and a dialectical materialist, was able to dismiss the gigantic achievements of Marxism in the Soviet Union as "a symbol of revolutionary theology"! This is nothing but the sickly egotism of an idealist closet-philosopher, who thinks that the advances in human knowledge are being produced by his own brain, rather than by the mass action of the millions for whom Marxism is not an intellectual exercise, but a guide for transforming the world.

Hook puts forward his ideas in the name of Marxism. Those who are more open and frank bring forward the same ideas to explain their rejection of Marxism. For example, Max Eastman, who conducts a feverish crusade to destroy dialectical materialism, does so because he agrees with Hook that "it is a symbol of revolutionary theology." A close kinship with this thought is also expressed by Mr. Norman Thomas, who wrote in the same issue of the *Modern Quarterly* with Sidney Hook, the following:

I agree that the philosophy of dialectic materialism is "disguised religion." The psychological resemblances between communism and religion are indeed so great as scarcely to be disguised. Which makes me wonder whether its prophet, Lenin's mind was essentially scientific, despite his genius for a ruthless realism and the large element in him of the creative will. These things are not uncommon in great leaders of religious movements.

This agreement between Hook, Eastman and Thomas is not an accidental one. No matter how varied may be the philosophical facade with which each one distinguishes himself from the others, the substantial foundation of each is identical; namely, pragmatism. It is true that in the national elections Hook supported not Thomas, but Foster. It is clear, however, that he was brought to this act not by the logic of his revisionism, which would lead straight to Thomas, but by something else. That other factor was the rise of a considerable mass movement of intellectuals toward the Communist Party, a movement which carried with it precisely that public to which Hook makes his most immediate and direct appeal. After all, a vote for Foster and Ford, even though not entirely logical for a revisionist, is a small price to pay for the privilege of passing unchallenged as "the foremost Marxist in America"! But the Communist Party does not, and cannot participate in such business.

V

We pointed out above that dialectical materialism, free from the pragmatic revisions of Hook, is necessary for the working class because the working class represents the future development of society. In the working class we have that complete correspondence between the objective and subjective factors of society, between the laws of economic and social development and the class needs of the workers, which for the first time makes possible the unity between the class needs and aspirations and the most coldly objective, scientific study and understanding of the society in which that class conducts its struggles. Precisely this is what Hook does not and cannot understand.

It cannot help the working class to perform its revolutionary tasks to teach it, as does Hook, that our program has no objective validity, except that we may by acting on it make it true to some extent. It is quite correct to emphasize the active character of the working class as the maker of the revolution, but to put this in Hook's form, means to demoralize and divide the working class into groups and sections each of which has its own separate program with equal claim to truth (objective validity), and each of which will actually be made true to the extent that workers believe in it and act upon it. This idealistic conception of Hook, while it puts on a brave revolutionary face as emphasizing action, more action, achieves the opposite result in reality by laying the foundation for confusion and disruption. The necessary precondition for effective action of the working class is its unification, not around any or all programs, but around that single program which alone corresponds to the laws of social development and the needs of the masses.

Only this understanding of the objective and scientific character of our program and our philosophy, gives us the capacity for carrying through the proletarian revolution. The revolution is not, as Hook falsely states, *merely* the struggle for power, it is the struggle for power in order to use that power for a definite, specific purpose; namely, the establishment of socialism as the first stage of communism. This is not some general abstract goal in the nature of a "social myth." This is a concrete program of action, directed towards the development of a planned society, all the essential features of which are matters of fore-knowledge and plan.

Of course, while we reject the idealistic inflation of the role of consciousness given by Hook, we simultaneously reject unconditionally that understanding of the historical process as the product of those large impersonal forces, of which men are mere automatic reflexes. Communism is inevitable, but it is only inevitable because the working class will inevitably fight to overthrow capitalism and consciously establish communism. The inevitability of communism by no means belittles the active role of the working class, as Hook would have us believe, but on the contrary.

Hook and all revisionists, by rejecting the scientific character of Marxism, contribute not to the development of the revolution, but to the building of obstacles against the revolution. In order to further intensify the confusion on this question, they assure the workers that to refuse to follow the Hooks, to insist instead upon mastering the science of Marxism, that this means in reality to fall into the swamps of religion. Such an argument may sound preposterous. And it is! But it is seriously made by Sidney Hook.

It is no longer possible for Sidney Hook to explain away our controversies with him on the basis of "distortions and misunderstandings." It is quite clear that we have two sharply opposed conceptions of Marxism, expressed by Hook and by the international Communist movement. Our first task was to prove that these two lines existed in conflict with one another. Our second and larger one, is to prove that all revisionist theories, such as those of Hook, are objectively false and subjectively dangerous to the working class. To fully carry out this second task is a long process of class struggle, political and ideological. We gain mastery of the science of dialectical materialism through the development of the struggle for control of society; and we win control of society only through our growing mastery of dialectical materialism.

XXII

Religion and Communism *

1. *What is the official position of the Communist Party of the United States on the question of religion?*

The Communist Party takes the position that the social function of religion and religious institutions is to act as an opiate to keep the lower classes passive, to make them accept the bad conditions under which they have to live in the hope of a reward after death.   From this estimate of the social role of religion it is quite clear that the Communist Party is the enemy of religion.   We Communists try to do the opposite of what we hold religion does.   We try to awaken the masses to a realization of the miserable conditions under which they live, to arouse them to revolt against these conditions, and to change these conditions of life now; not to wait for any supposed reward in heaven, but to create a heaven on earth; that is, to get those things which they dream about as good things, to realize them in life.   It is clear that any serious movement to rouse and organize the masses to the realization of a better life now, must struggle against anything that tends to create passivity, to create the idea that it is better to submit passively to the powers that be.

On the other hand, the Communist Party is absolutely opposed to any form of coercion on religious matters.   Communists are for religious freedom unconditionally.   The Communists do not consider religion a private matter when it concerns revolutionists.   But they consider that in relation to state power, to governmental policies, religion is a private matter.   The state should not interfere with, or in any way dictate to, the religious institutions and beliefs.   This explains the seeming paradox that fascism, which puts itself forward as essentially a religious movement, discloses itself in practice as a supreme denial of religious liberty, whereas communism, which has a negative attitude towards religion, is the only social movement today that releases religion from all artificial constraints and regulations, from the denial of freedom.

In Germany we have had a very thorough and convincing demonstration of what fascism means for religion and for religious institutions. I do not think that I need to elaborate.   I think everybody is familiar with what is going on in Germany.   We have an equally thorough

---

* Discussion with a group of students of the Union Theological Seminary on the question of Religion and Communism, February 15, 1935.—*Ed.*

example of what communism means in governmental policy towards religion in the development of more than 17 years of workers' and farmers' government in the Soviet Union. In the Soviet Union there is complete religious freedom. At the same time, the Communist Party, which is the government Party, carries on an active anti-religious campaign. This anti-religious campaign is purely educational. The Communists consider it would be the greatest mistake to use coercion in the fight against religion. We consider that this would defeat our own purpose. We consider that the most effective fight against religion, to remove it completely as that social factor which stands in the way of reorganizing society, is precisely the granting and guaranteeing of complete religious freedom. Complete religious freedom, of course, means the complete withdrawal of governmental support of religion and of all special privileges for religious institutions. It also means that the religious education for the young stands on its own feet without any artificial support.

As for the religious workers, the Communist Party does not make the abandonment of their religion a condition of joining the Party, even though it carries on educational work which is anti-religious. You may be interested in knowing that we have preachers, preachers active in churches, who are members of the Communist Party. There are churches in the United States where the preachers preach communism from the pulpits, in a very primitive form, of course. In one particular church service described to me, the substance of the sermon (I do not remember the exact title) was that the Communists were the angels of God that had been sent like Moses to lead the people from the wilderness, while the representatives of the devil were the capitalists and their agents. This, of course, is not an expression of the official Communist attitude on these questions, as you will understand; but we do not expel such people from the Party. The test for us is whether such people represent the social aspirations of the masses, which may take on a religious form, but which are essentially social rebellion. When such is the case, we welcome them into our Party. Even within the Party, where we do not consider religion a private matter, we have no sort of coercion towards such religious remnants, even towards their active religious expressions.

2. *Would you say, Mr. Browder, that religion might serve a revolutionary function?*

I would say that revolutionary social movements may sometimes take on a religious form; this form, however, would not be an accelerating factor, but a retarding one. That does not mean that there could not be—and in fact there are to an increasing extent—common objectives between the Communists and religious organizations, for which joint efforts and struggle would be put forward. We have seen this in the political field recently in the Saar, where some sections and prominent leaders of the Catholic church, realizing the loss of religious freedom which would be involved by incorporation in the Hitler regime, formed a united front with the Socialists and Communists to fight for the status quo in the Saar. Such concrete joint struggles will develop more and more, in which instances it could be said, from a certain point of view, that the religious movement was serving a revolutionary purpose. There it is not religion as such which serves the revolutionary purpose, but the struggle against oppression, the struggle for the right of the masses to express themselves even in their confused fashion. The struggle for this right is revolutionary, and in that sense religious organizations and movements can play a revolutionary role.

3. *What do you mean by saying religion is not a private matter where revolutionaries are concerned? I took it to mean that you would not consider anyone holding a religion to be a revolutionary; yet you said that you accepted religious workers into the Party.*

When workers come into the Party still actively religious, we accept them, not because we accept their religion, but because we know that the process of discarding religious beliefs, which are in the last analysis reactionary, is a more or less protracted one. We expect religion to be eliminated only in the course of a few generations of the new society, the socialist society.

We do not consider this religious belief a private matter among revolutionaries; for those who join the revolutionary movement will have to submit all their beliefs to criticism. As members of the revolutionary movement, everything they think and everything they say affects the development of this movement which they have joined and of which they have become a part. While we do not exact of them that they give up their religion, we will subject their religious beliefs to a careful and systematic criticism, and we expect that the religious beliefs will not be able to stand up under such criticism. We would not, for example, place in the most responsible leading positions of the movement people who had strong religious beliefs. We consider that they would be dangerous because they would be left open to social influences which would endanger the direction of the masses they would have in their charge.

4. *On the other hand, since a large proportion of the American population is either connected with the church in one form or another, or even very sympathetic to the church, won't your tactics, in order to win these people over, have to take that into account pretty thoroughly? That is, are you able to present a front against religion in America comparable to that used in Russia when you are working with the American masses?*

Certainly we will have to take the religious beliefs of the masses into account and respect them—and we do. Certainly, the revolution, which will be an act of the majority of the people, will involve those holding religious beliefs. If religion stands as an absolute barrier to the revolution, that would, postpone the revolution for a considerable period. We do not think that it does. We think religious-minded people will participate in the revolution, will help to carry through the change. This is in no way a concession in principle to religious ideas. Concessions to the desires and prejudices of masses who hold religious views—yes. The utmost respect for their right to hold these views, by all means. Complete absence of any system of coercion on these questions, by all means. In this form, taking these religious beliefs into account and respecting them, do we meet the question, but not with any concessions in principle.

5. *Suppose that the members of this group go out into the various churches that they will serve and that they, together with the people in their congregations, would become revolutionized and would feel that they were being animated by religious motives, would the Communist Party examine that evidence and give it scientific weight, and possibly modify its conviction that religion cannot be a revolutionary force?*

I would not want to hold out any hopes that the Communists will be converted to religion. For us as Communists the question is answered and, while we always examine all evidence that is brought forward scientifically, we have no reason in our experience to believe that any future evidence will modify our conclusions. We would not want to give the slightest indication that there is any prospect of a rapprochement between communism and religion as such.

6. *Are you sure there will never be any evidence?*

While we always examine every bit of evidence that comes forward, we consider the question as settled for us. We do not expect to have to reopen it.

7. *Do you distinguish between the religious spirit and religion as it is institutionalized?*

Yes, we do.

8. *Do you think there are any values in the religious spirit not found in the church or the institution of religion?*

Values, no. But the institutionalized religion is the particular enemy. Institutionalized religion is still used by the present rulers 99-44/100 per cent for strengthening the present regime, whereas the unorganized sentiments act only as a brake upon the development of the individual.

9. *It would appear to me from your definition of policy that the very policy which you define for the Communist Party is coercion in a very subtle form in case the Communist Party should come into power. The Communist Party separates all education from the church and makes it all secular, and at the same time carries on an active anti-religious campaign through the secular means of education, at one time disarming all forms of religious education and at the same time arming yourself with all the power of secular education to destroy any religion that remains. Now, if propaganda is coercion, which I think most Communists say it is, is it not in that case?*

No, not coercion. The whole concept of freedom of religion becomes real only when it includes freedom not to be religious. That is something that most religious institutions do not accept. I think it is one of the accepted maxims of religious institutions that the mind of the child should be molded so that he will not be capable of rejecting religion. How can such a child have religious freedom if in his formative period he is very carefully isolated from any ideas which challenge these religious beliefs? So long as the child in his formative years is controlled by religious institutions, religious liberty is denied him.

10. *Is that not true when Communists separate him from all religious influences and subject him to communism?*

He is free to develop his full powers, and if religion has any basic value and responds to any basic need in the human being, it certainly does not need to be imposed upon the mind of the child, but will come, as the product of a full social life.

11. *But religion is not any more spontaneous than communism is, and both are products of education, pretty much.*

If one takes that view of religion, then he is rejecting its basic claim. That is a Communist view of religion.

12. *Is it true that they stopped Paul Robeson from singing in Moscow as soon as he sang religious songs over the radio station?*

That never happened. About a week after that lie was circulated, Paul Robeson was greeted in Moscow as an honored guest of the Soviet Union. He sang in the biggest state theaters of Moscow and declared to the newspapers his great pleasure at the comradely reception accorded him in the Soviet Union, the like of which he had received nowhere else. Robeson sang every song he wanted to sing.

13. *Does not the Communist Party forbid parents to give religious instruction to their children? Are they allowed to carry on family worship and instruction of the children?*

The socialist state, under the leadership of the Communist Party, permits and guarantees full liberty of religious education and practise.

14. *Most of the things you have said about religion are critical from the standpoint of function, but I wonder what you say from the philosophical point of view. Communism has a certain world view, and particularly a conception of man's relationship to nature and to the world. You believe that man can cooperate with, and fundamentally subdue, the plain forces of nature. It seems to me that you have an irrational belief, certainly not a thoroughly scientific belief, concerning something that is distinctly in the psychological realm of thought.*

It is true, communism differs basically in its philosophy from all religions. That is, essentially all religions presuppose a power outside of the human realm directing human beings. There are religious schools that take on philosophical form, veiling their religious character; but essentially religion is the belief in a higher, supernatural directing power to which man must submit himself. Often, a certain analogy has been drawn between this feature of religion and that feature of the Communist process where the individual merges himself in the great mass movement and finds his completion in a larger whole. This analogy, however, fails to bring out the essence of the difference. For, whereas in religion the individual merging with God and finding his completion in his religious unity with God becomes separated from the tasks of mankind, in the Communist larger unity he realizes the tasks of taking charge of these problems himself together with his fellows, establishing social control of his own life.

15. *What objections would you have to a group of ministers going out and working with the people in their congregations, proclaiming that God is a revolutionary God, that God is definitely working for the establishment here on earth of a Communist cooperative society?*

We would consider such a move a distinct social advance over the ordinary type of preaching. It would represent one step in the emancipation from religion.

16. *How do you fit religion into dialectics—what is the role of religion in dialectical materialism?*

Religion does not fit into a dialectical materialist system of thought. It is the enemy of it. One cannot be a thorough materialist, that is, a dialectical materialist, and have any remnants of religious beliefs. Both the older materialism that preceded the dialectical materialism and the non-materialist dialectics were in the final analysis of a religious character; but not so dialectical materialism. Dialectical materialism is completely materialist and excludes religion, but, of course, it includes the explanation of religion.

17. *Could you not be convinced of dialectical materialism and consider religion of value?*

No. This was already answered in the previous question.

18. *Because when you begin to work out the unity of opposites and contradictions, you would have to have religion in the picture—*
Yes, religion must be in the picture in order to be eliminated.

19. *Would your dialectics move towards some sort of synthesis?*
Well, the dialectical conception of synthesis does not include carrying over obsolete and outlived forms of thought. Some of the functions that are performed by religion will certainly be performed by certain other institutions. There is no question about that. A large part of the functions of organized religion are purely social. All such functions will certainly be taken over by new forms of organization and thinking.

20. *What will be the regenerative center of the Communist movement in about another century when it has gotten a pretty good foothold and achieved its end? What will keep it from degenerating? Enthusiasm, you know, cannot last. Will they go back to Lenin and Marx, do you suppose?*
No, the guarantees against degeneration are in the living forces of the people. They will, of course, make use of the teachings of the best thinkers of the past, but they will have their own lives. The teachings are the instruments representing merely the past growth, which are further developed by the living force of the people themselves.

21. *Does this development come through contradiction? It is a little hard to see how these contradictions could rise in a Communist world; yet according to dialectical materialism we get development through contradictions.*
The contradictions of the future society will not arise from the economic base. Contradictions in the present society arise from the economic base of society, which fundamentally divides society into warring classes. With the rise of socialist society and its passing over into full communism, this, of course, will be absolutely gone. That means that the class struggle will disappear as the motive force of history. In classless society, the dialectic contradictions will not assume the form of class antagonisms.

22. *I just wonder how your philosophical concepts would be able to keep these contradictions in a materialist sense in a materialist realm?*
There will be no fundamental contradictions in the material base of society under communism.

23. *Do you mean by that that man can completely conquer nature, that such things as drought and earthquakes and floods can be completely regulated?*
Man can progressively move in that direction. For example, even in this past year the Soviet Union already demonstrated the power to control droughts. The Soviet Union was hit by droughts, as bad as

those which hit the other countries, but the results were vastly different from those in the other countries. In the Soviet Union, where farming had already been brought into the socialist economic structure, they were able to fight against the drought and reduce its effects so much that the total production of grain dropped only two per cent and the total collections of grain actually increased over the previous year.

Similarly, floods are generally looked upon as a natural phenomenon, but to a great extent they are social phenomena, economic phenomena. The country that suffers the most from floods is China; but anyone who has been in China must recognize that the floods of China are distinctly the product of the militaristic rule of that country and not of anything else, that they are not the product of water, that they are the product of the breaking down of the social control of that water.

24. *Are not the attitudes of devotion and sacrifice which characterize many ardent Communists religious?*

We consider them social. We consider them as rising out of the sense of social solidarity and the understanding that the individual completes himself in the social whole of which he is a product, and that isolated from it he is nothing. We believe that devotion and sacrifice do not come from the outside to mankind, but arise from the natural development of man.

25. *But you do have, that is the Communists have, a transcendent value, which, the attitude of devotion and—one might be tempted to use the word worship—indicates that these attitudes are religious?*

We have values which transcend everyday life, but which do not, however, transcend human life as a whole. Our values arise right out of life. They are not given to us from on high or from God. Our values which transcend daily life are drawn from the whole experience of the human race.

26. *Do you recognize loyalty to this ideal of great importance?*

Yes, but we should say, not loyalty to an ideal, but loyalty to ourselves. Loyalty to our best values.

27. *Would you say communism contains the combination of the dialectic process as far as economic forces are concerned, that is economic forces as the motivating force in the change of history?*

Yes, the economic organization of society, that is, the way in which mankind makes its living, is the basic fact; that is what we mean by economics. That does not eliminate the human factor, for economics is what man does in order to provide food, clothing and shelter. Economic forces are not different from and exclude the actions of man, but on the contrary exert themselves only through human beings.

28. *Do you explain according to the Communistic theory that the whole process of history is due to this economic force? Then, if we*

attain this Communistic society then does that thing end the dialectic process—or would you say there would still be dialectic forces going into higher development?

According to our understanding, dialectical thought is the growing awareness of the human mind of the natural processes that go on outside of it, and human action upon nature guided by this understanding. It is not an invention of the human mind which is imposed upon the world, as Sidney Hook maintains it is. It is not merely an instrument of the mind which happens to be useful for the moment by an accident. Dialectics is this growing understanding in the human mind of the process of change and development that goes on throughout the universe. We do not limit it merely to the social sphere or to the class struggle going on now. Dialectics is universal. There is a dialectics of nature, there will always be a dialectics for every phase of life. Since life changes its forms, dialectics will never be eliminated. The dialectical process will not be eliminated in the future society. It will take new forms; it will no longer assume the form of the basic antagonisms of class society.

29. *Do you not consider that dialectical process a hypothesis at all? You consider it as an established fact?*

We consider it as the most generalized truth.

30. *Many of us are interested in seeing a new society brought about and we feel that in the ideals of Jesus we have presented a goal towards which we are moving and we feel that this gives us something of a motive power. In what way would you say a group of people feeling that way can best work towards a new society, or are they entirely up the wrong tree?*

I think that they could best serve the movement, not by concentrating too much upon the question of religion and its relation to the revolutionary movement, but by concentrating upon the practical questions of the day, as, for instance, to what extent there can be brought about a practical cooperation of all forces, religious and non-religious, for certain practical aims. In this field there is great room for work. I think, for example, that people who are essentially religious today and who see that their religious freedom is threatened by the growing reaction in America, could very well find those points in the social set-up in which they could cooperate with the non-religious forces in the fight against reaction. So that even from the essentially religious interests of such people there could be points of contact with the anti-religious revolutionary movement, such as the fight against fascism, the fight against war. Certainly war, which has become an immediate menace, is something that violates the religious beliefs of the masses; and to mobilize these religious feelings for an effective struggle against war, could be very helpful.

31. *Is it because of this basic argument that the Communist Party is willing to enter into the American League Against War and Fascism and enter into a united front with religious groups to fight a given enemy?*

Yes, in the American League the Communists are only one small section and are in a minority; but perhaps a large majority of the people in the American League are religious people, even though they did not come into the League from the religious organizations. A growing number of religious organizations have affiliated, and of all those who have become affiliated through other organizations, undoubtedly the majority are religious. Communists have no hesitation whatever in such contacts with religious people. We do not shy away from religious people at all.

32. *To what extent does the Communist Party cooperate with such church federations which are for the destruction of capitalist society?*

We have no direct contact with these organizations as such. Some of the leading individuals in these organizations are active in united front organizations where we are active. In the American League Against War and Fascism, Dr. Harry F. Ward, who is connected with the Methodist Social Service Institution—I forget the exact name—is chairman of the League. Also connected with the League is Dr. Wm. Spofford, who I believe is one of the leaders of the Church League for Industrial Democracy. Only in this indirect way have we contact with these church organizations. Indirectly all of these forces which have an anti-capitalist tendency come into a certain broad cooperation through the American League Against War and Fascism.

33. *You said that religion opposes revolutionary activity on two grounds—on the ground of belief and on the ground of its institutional form at the present time. Do you find that in its educational and organizational set-up there are tendencies towards a reactionary or passive attitude in the present belief and the desire to keep the belief reactionary?*

I would say that the outstanding feature of the development of thought in religious organizations today is the growth of revolutionary trends, and not a growth of reactionary trends. A prominent churchman said to me some months ago that the Communists are going to "capture" the church before we do the A. F. of L. Of course, we do not believe that; but it is more than a joke, because it tends to emphasize that there is a surging growth of social thought even within church organizations, which is essentially revolutionary thought. It is a struggle against the reactionary character of present capitalist rule; it is a revolt against all of the reactionary features of capitalism which become more and more pronounced from day to day.

34. *As regards the content of teachings that you discuss. If one were an instructor, one would assume there are forms of teachings which would tend to produce an uncritical attitude to things, an acceptance of the status quo in the way the thing was taught, apart from the content of what was taught. Do the Communists, in the way in which they teach their own doctrine, promote a critical attitude that can be seen in the method of teaching?*

The Communist teaching is essentially critical, and, indeed, it is not directed towards developing uncritical acceptance. Sometimes those who champion the cause of criticism do not understand this, however, because the critical approach of the Communists does not involve the splitting up of the movement into its separate parts, but on the contrary serves to weld it closer together, creating greater unity of thought, so that the very thought process and the very criticism itself become a social and not an individual act, a social act in which the individual participates, but of which the individual himself is not the expression. In the Communist Party this expresses itself in our inner-Party life. We develop our thought through discussions and a very intensive development of literature. We probably circulate more literature per member of our organization by ten times than any other organization in existence. It is very intensive collective thought life in which is involved the whole critical approach to everything. The revolutionist is first of all a critic of the universe and everything that is in it, including himself. But we avoid at all costs the type of criticism which comes from the individualist society where criticism is purely an individual function. For the Communist, criticism is a social function, an organized function. In bourgeois society criticism is essentially a divisive process. With us it is the opposite; it is the process of consolidation of the masses.

35. *You do that by keeping this constant circulation of criticism so that whatever anyone thinks is immediately registered?*

Every view established as the view of our movement has been established as the result of the most thorough criticism. No point is ever established as the view of the Communists until it has met and answered every possible criticism that can be made. After the question has been faced and answered, we do not consider it necessary that it shall forever continue to be an open question. There are many questions which are closed for us. Therefore, those people for whom this is still an open question consider that our approach is uncritical because for us the question has already been answered. That is only because we have met and answered these questions before.

36. *Do you claim that this increase in revolutionary temper which shows itself in the church is a social product and not a product of religious idealism as we do?*

We consider that essentially this comes not out of the religion, but out of the conditions of life of the people who make up these bodies and who, having no better channels through which to express it, express it through their religious channels.

37. *If such religious organizations enter into a united front with the Communist Party, then, in the coming years when the social revolution is successful, will the Communist Party, if it is in power, enter into a campaign against these organizations that have helped in achieving this new society?*

Communists will never carry on any kind of activity which the masses will feel is against their interests. The Communists will never carry on any kind of coercion against religious institutions. Let that be clear. In the Communist fight against religion, the Communists will limit themselves purely to ideological weapons, the weapons of argument and thought, the expression of thought.

38. *If the expression of social thinking that you find in churches is a result of the social situation of the people that are doing the thinking, why do you not find the same amount expressed in other professions? We are not patting ourselves on the back, but I think you will agree that there probably is more social thinking done in the ministry over the country than in any other profession.*

We would not say more. There perhaps is still, for the time being, a little more freedom of expression in the church than in the schools. In the schools we have laws directed against the expression of social thinking. Outside of the Catholic church, it is not yet true of the church institutions. However, I wouldn't if I were a member of these church organizations, congratulate myself too much on this. You do not know how long it will last. You may have your Dickstein Committee in the Methodist church soon and in the Protestant churches generally.

39. *When you mention the fact that the Communist group would not carry on any offensive against church institutions, are you assuming there, that church institutions would be taken over by the masses who do not control these institutions at present?*

We are assuming that there would be no capitalist class organized and controlling these churches. These religious institutions would be controlled by the people who are in them. They would not be enemies of the new society, because the masses who would be in them would be actively cooperating in the new society.

40. *If a church group were definitely counter-revolutionary and acting against the Communist regime, there would be no hesitation in wiping that group out?*

It would be dealt with on political, not religious, grounds.

41. *Would you agree that there is a gambling chance that the people in the religious organizations might make such a powerful force working for social justice in case we have a revolution, that the Communist Party might reopen the question?*

I think the more the masses now in the churches become active in the social struggle, the less need will they find for religion, so that the more they participate in the revolution, the less likelihood is there of the church becoming any essential feature of the new social set-up.

42. *Would you say that the participation in building a new social order would be a substitute for religion?*

Religion itself, even where it does not disappear, will tend to become de-institutionalized.

43. *If we are going forward into a period of fascism, is there not the possibility of religion keeping alive this spirit of revolt, because of certain factors that have always been more or less connected with religion and for that reason it may become a very powerful ally?*

I think the church as an organized institution is much more likely to fall under the control of the fascist forces.

44. *Where do you find the evil—in the capitalist or in capitalism?*

Both, the capitalist system is so essentially evil that it cannot produce good men at the top.

45. *Which is first—man or capitalism?*

Mankind is first, but not man as an individual.

46. *If in the social struggle the church does not line up with the fascist organizations, but proves to be helpful to the social revolution, will there be any recognition of that fact?*

Certainly, I think the Communists would be more happy about that than anybody else. Perhaps we will be surprised.

47. *I do not think religion today, as we understand it, will postpone happiness for the future life. We are working definitely for an abundant life here, rather than in the future. Some of us do not believe in the hereafter, and are striving to establish a good society here. I think we are working towards the same objective.*

It is incorrect to draw an analogy between the vague socio-religious aspirations and Communism. There is, of course, a positive social content accompanying some religious teachings, though not all; but this is not the feature which gives them the character of religion.

48. *I think we are arguing about terms. What we call religion you call something else. It is a matter of definition.*

I think the things that we Communists call religion are, you might put it, the "established truths" about religion. They may take very subtle forms, but they will always reveal that supernatural character that we are speaking about here.

49. *Every idea has its political and social effect. You cannot have an idea without having it have some political connection. Therefore, in the Communist set-up we are open to your definite pattern of thought, ideology. Any variation from that would be counter-revolutionary, even if perhaps some people think it a higher step. In other words, the Communist pattern may become crystallized just as the capitalist system is now, so that there will be no progress, no change.*

The Communists have no fixed system in the sense of a hard and fast strait-jacket. The very essence of Communist thinking is the progressive development and realization of all the creative forces of the human mind. That is the essence of the whole Communist position of life as seen in the Communist program of practical action. Certainly, no one can say that where the Communists are the directing power, as in the Soviet Union, the mind has been put into a strait-jacket. There has never been in human history such a release of all initiative of the individual and the development of capacities as in the Soviet Union. You can go into the Soviet Union and find men occupying the highest positions in every field of life, from the arts and sciences to government, who but five or six years ago were backward people on the land, the most backward illiterate peasants. What society in the world ever showed such an enormous development of the capacity of the individual human mind? Never in history has anything like it been seen. So, if you judge by experience, you cannot draw the conclusion that communism tends to strait-jacket human development.

50. *A little while ago, you said the individual, as such, is not worth any consideration at all.*

I said the individual finds his development and completion only as a part of the group, as a part of society. Isolated, the individual is nothing.

51. *Do the Communists consider it psychologically possible to build up a classless society, a society in which no classes exist?*

Yes, the Communists accept that view.

52. *But in practice there is always a class.*

In the Soviet Union classes still exist, that is true. And the class struggle within the Soviet Union is still sharp. But enormous progress is being made towards the classless society precisely through that struggle. Precisely through the class struggle, do we come to the classless society. Some believe that the way to get a classless society is to stop fighting, to stop the class struggle; on this we disagree. We say that precisely the only way to come to a society without classes is through the development of the class struggle to the point where one particular class—the working class—obtains power. By making this one class predominant, that particular class whose historic revolutionary role is to remove the basis for class division, we can reach the classless society—but only in this way. The interests of this class lie in doing away with that material foundation of society which produces classes. Only when you abolish that which produces classes, can you abolish the class themselves. What produces classes is the division of society into those who own and those who work. When that is abolished and those who work are also those who own, then it is only a matter of time that all classes in society will disappear.

53. *Has the Communist line on religion changed in the last three or four years, particularly in regard to the Negro in America? Now people who still maintain religious beliefs can join the Party. Is this a change in the line of the Party, or has it been a development?*

It may be said to be a change in the growing understanding of Party members on the meaning of Party line, but in the authoritative expressions of this line there is no change. Our standard text-book is the writings of Lenin on these questions—writings that extend over many years, mostly before the revolution in Russia. There certainly is no essential change. There are, of course, certain changes in our application of this line because of the changing situation. There were, for example, a few years ago very few practical questions concerning our relations to social movements within the church because such social movements were largely non-existent. Today their existence takes on an immediate practical political importance that brings out features of the Communist attitude towards religion which were not outstanding before. But it is a change of development of events of the day rather than any change of the development of the Party line.

54. *On that same question, the official tactic perhaps for the immediate situation has been changed in regard to some of these groups, but is it not true that many of the rank-and-file have failed to catch up with the change? I refer to your discussion before of the inner-Party life, the discussion that goes on within the Party, it seemed that that indicated that many of the Party members, whom we consider to be Party members, do not seem to follow the official line on many of these questions. I am thinking in particular of instances in the American League where trouble seems to have come out of the failure of Party members to adopt a united front policy.*

I have an idea that probably most of such difficulties that you speak of come not from Party members, but from non-Party people who may call themselves Communists. It is true that many of our best friends are sometimes our worst enemies because they do not familiarize themselves with the correct position on fundamental questions. Of course, it is also true that not all Party members are fully grounded in all of these questions, for our Party reflects all the shortcomings of the working class. We have 31,000 members where a year and a half ago we had from 17,000 to 18,000 members. That means we have had 14,000 members coming into the Party in a year and a half; some have been in for only a couple of months and are certainly not experts on the policy of the Party.

55. *Is there also Communistic propaganda among the Negroes? Is there a good field there?*

Considerable. It was reported in the newspapers that a Negro religious leader had stated that the churches were in danger of losing their hold over the Negroes because of the tremendous inroads made by the Communists and had therefore called upon the churches to fight the Communists more energetically; this is some evidence of how strong is the political influence of the Communists among the Negro population generally. We have not any great organization among the Negro masses. Our organizational strength among them is growing; but the influence of our ideas, especially those ideas expressed in the practical day-to-day struggle for Negro rights, creates a tremendous effect among the majority of Negroes in America. In this sense many say that the majority of the Negroes are influenced by the Communists.

56. *Do you regard the Hebrew prophets and Jesus as historical figures, and if so, have they social significance?*

They are historical figures at least in the sense that they have played quite a role in the historical development of the human mind. Whether they were the product of the human mind or whether they had some more direct material basis is not important to us. We do not enter the field of higher criticism.

57. *How seriously is the Communist Party taking the present drive to outlaw it? Today's papers give the report of the Dickstein Committee which, if it is embodied in bills and these bills are passed, will eventually put the Communist Party out of business.*

We take them very seriously; not that we think that that will put the Communist Party out of business, because the Communist Party will never be put out of business. We take these proposals very seriously because we see that they are part of a system of development which is represented by Roosevelt's actions in the automobile situation, by the whole company union drive, by the drive to smash the trade unions and to outlaw the Communist Party as an inevitable feature of such a drive against the working class as a whole. Under the legislation proposed by the Dickstein Committee, it would become illegal to quote the Declaration of Independence.

Index

CPSIA information can be obtained
at www.ICGtesting.com
Printed in the USA
BVHW092007191118
533517BV00005B/219/P